INUBAKA

CRAZY FOR DOGS

3

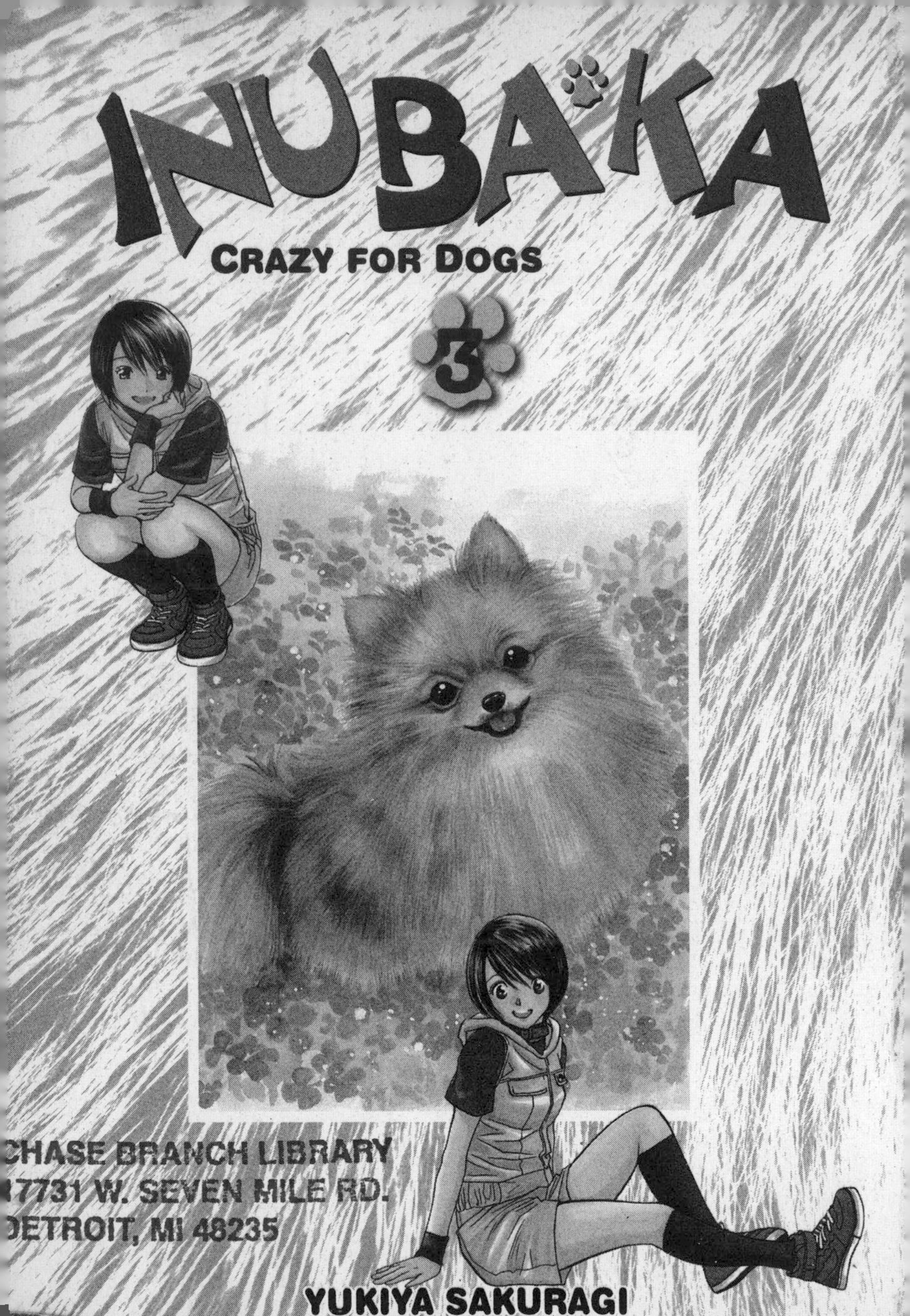

YUKIYA SAKURAGI

Contents

Chapter 20
The day the puppy comes
7

Chapter 21
Chanta's biting habit
25

Chapter 22
An overnighter at Woofles
43

Chapter 23
A bond between hearts
62

Chapter 24
Suguri learns about nightlife!
79

Chapter 25
The whereabouts of the presents
97

Chapter 26
Dogs are not things
115

Chapter 27
Operation: Save the Dogs
133

Chapter 28
Tracing the evidence
151

Chapter 29
Has a high-tech strategy succeeded...?!
169

Chapter 30
Real family
187

Story thus far

Teppei is the manager of the recently opened pet shop Woofles. He intended to breed his black Labrador Noa with a champion dog, but instead Noa was "taken advantage of" by an unknown and unfixed male dog!

The unknown dog's owner was Suguri Miyauchi and her dog was a mutt named Lupin. Suguri is now working at Woofles to make up for her dog's actions.

Suguri's enthusiasm is more than a little unique. She has eaten dog food (and said it was tasty), caught dog poop with her bare hands, and caused dogs to have "happy pee" in her presence. Teppei is starting to realize that Suguri is indeed a very special girl.

Kentaro's bandmate, who is also an employee at Woofles, has taken a liking to Suguri, but his fear of dogs prevents him from becoming close with her. He has been trying hard to get over his fear, and he has just declared that he would take a Shiba dog that lost its owner...!

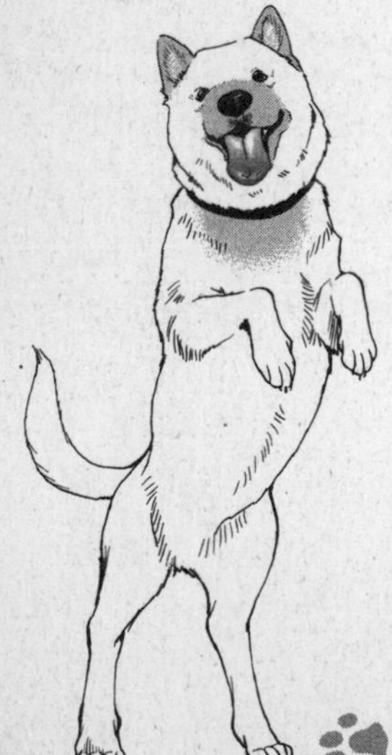

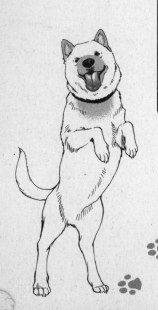

CHARACTERS

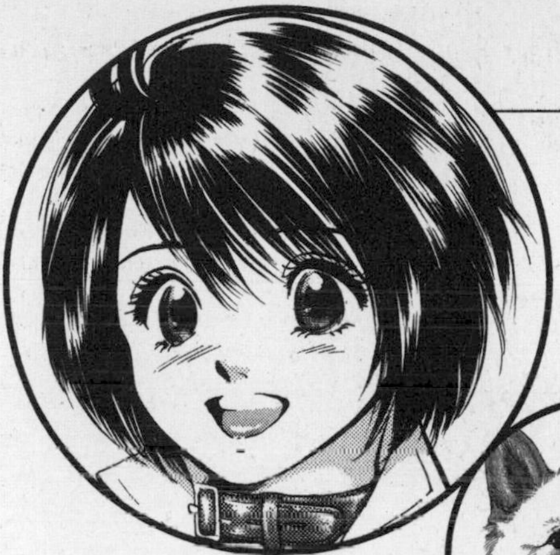

Suguri Miyauchi

She seems to possess an almost supernatural connection with dogs. When she approaches dogs they often urinate with great excitement! She is crazy for dogs and can catch dog droppings with her bare hands. She is currently a trainee at the Woofles Pet Shop.

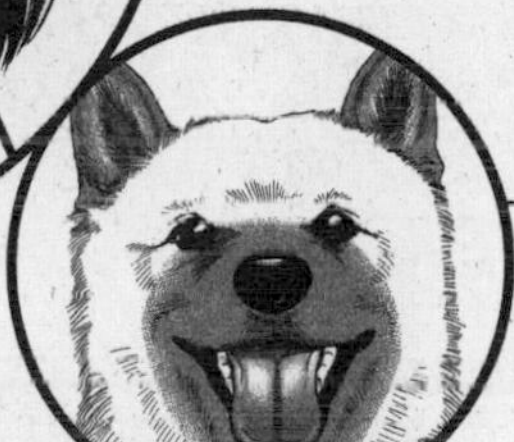

Lupin

♂ Mutt (mongrel)

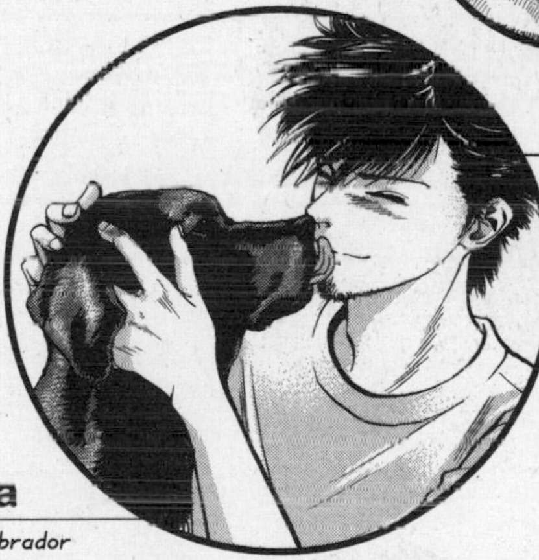

Teppei Iida

He is the manager of the recently opened pet shop Woofles. He is aware of Suguri's special ability and has hired her to work in his shop. He also lets Suguri and Kentaro crash with him.

Noa

♀ Labrador Retriever

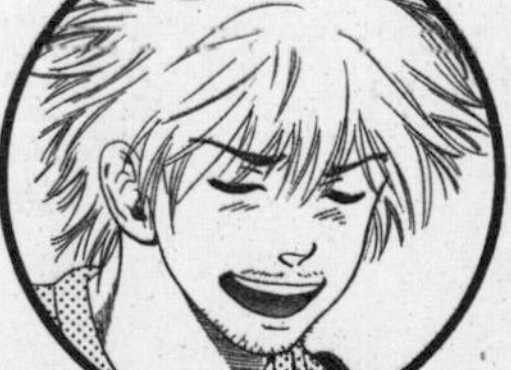

Kentaro Osada

A wanna-be musician and buddy of Teppei's from high school. Teppei saved Kentaro when he was a down-and-out beggar. He has a crush on the piano instructor Kanako, but not her dog...

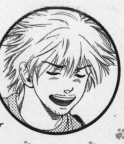

Melon

🐾 *Chihuahua*

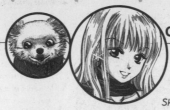

Chizuru Sawamura

She adopted a Chihuahua, Melon, after her long-time pet Golden Retriever Ricky alerted her that he was ill. She works at a hostess bar to repay Melon's medical fees.

Kanako Mori

She teaches piano on the second floor of the same building as Woofles. Her love for her dog, Czerny, is so great that it surprises even Suguri!

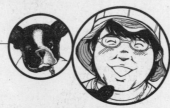

Czerny

🐾 *Pomeranian*

Zidane

🐾 *French bulldog*

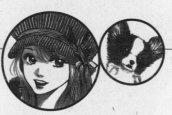

Hiroshi Akiba

Pop idol otaku turned dog otaku. His dream is to publish a photo collection of his dog, Zidane. He is a government employee.

Mari Yamashita

She is a model whose nickname is Yamarin. She decided to keep an unsold Papillon, Lucky, who was her co-star in a bread commercial.

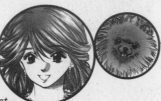

Lucky

🐾 *Papillon*

Chanta

🐾 *Shiba*

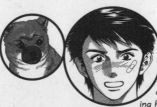

Kim

A Korean international exchange student and friend of Kentaro. He had a phobia of dogs, but he has been working hard to get over it in order to get close to Suguri, whom he has a crush on. He bought a Shiba dog!

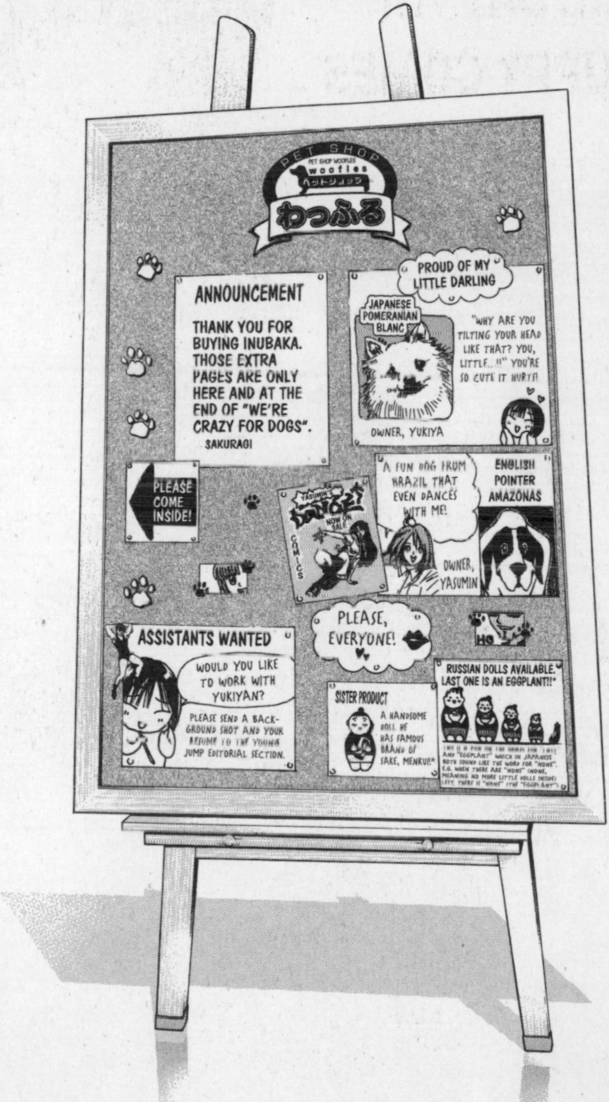
PET SHOP
PET SHOP WOOFLES
woofles
ペットショップ
わつふる
ANNOUNCEMENT
THANK YOU FOR BUYING INUBAKA. THOSE EXTRA PAGES ARE ONLY HERE AND AT THE END OF "WE'RE CRAZY FOR DOGS".
SAKURAGI
PROUD OF MY LITTLE DARLING
JAPANESE POMERANIAN BLANC
"WHY ARE YOU TILTING YOUR HEAD LIKE THAT? YOU, LITTLE...!!" YOU'RE SO CUTE IT HURTS!
OWNER, YUKIYA
PLEASE COME INSIDE!
YASUMIN'S DANCE!
NOW ON SALE
COMICS
A FUN DOG FROM BRAZIL THAT EVEN DANCES WITH ME!
ENGLISH POINTER AMAZONAS
OWNER, YASUMIN
PLEASE, EVERYONE!
ASSISTANTS WANTED
WOULD YOU LIKE TO WORK WITH YUKIYAN?
PLEASE SEND A BACKGROUND SHOT AND YOUR RESUME TO THE YOUNG JUMP EDITORIAL SECTION.
SISTER PRODUCT
A HANDSOME DOLL HE HAS FAMOUS BRAND OF SAKE, MENKUI!*
RUSSIAN DOLLS AVAILABLE. LAST ONE IS AN EGGPLANT!!*
AND "EGGPLANT" WHICH IN JAPANESE BOTH SOUND LIKE THE WORD FOR "NONE". E.G. WHEN THERE ARE "NONE" (NONE, MEANING NO MORE LITTLE DOLLS INSIDE) LEFT, THERE IS "NONE" (THE "EGGPLANT")

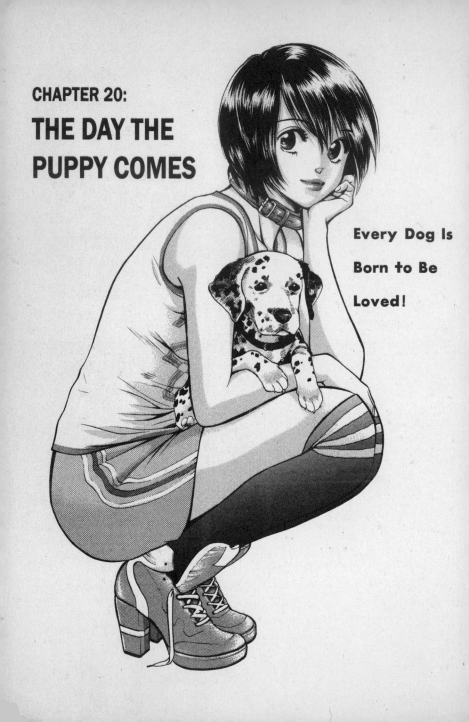

CHAPTER 20:

THE DAY THE PUPPY COMES

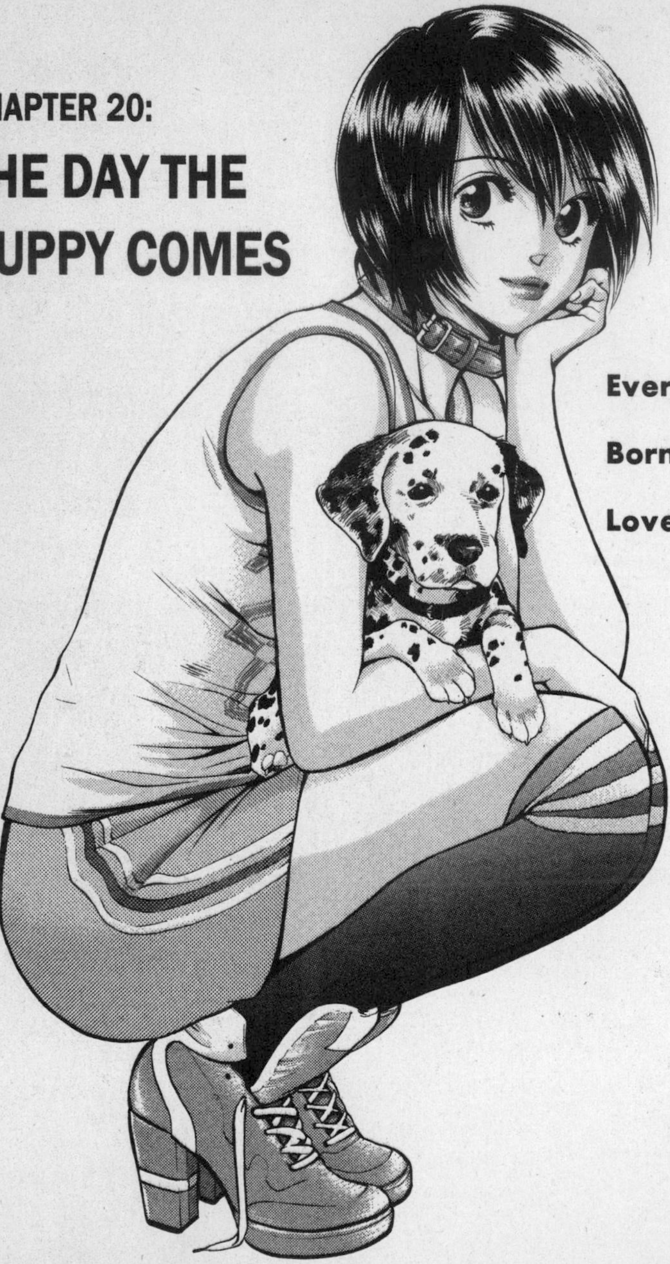

Every Dog Is Born to Be Loved!

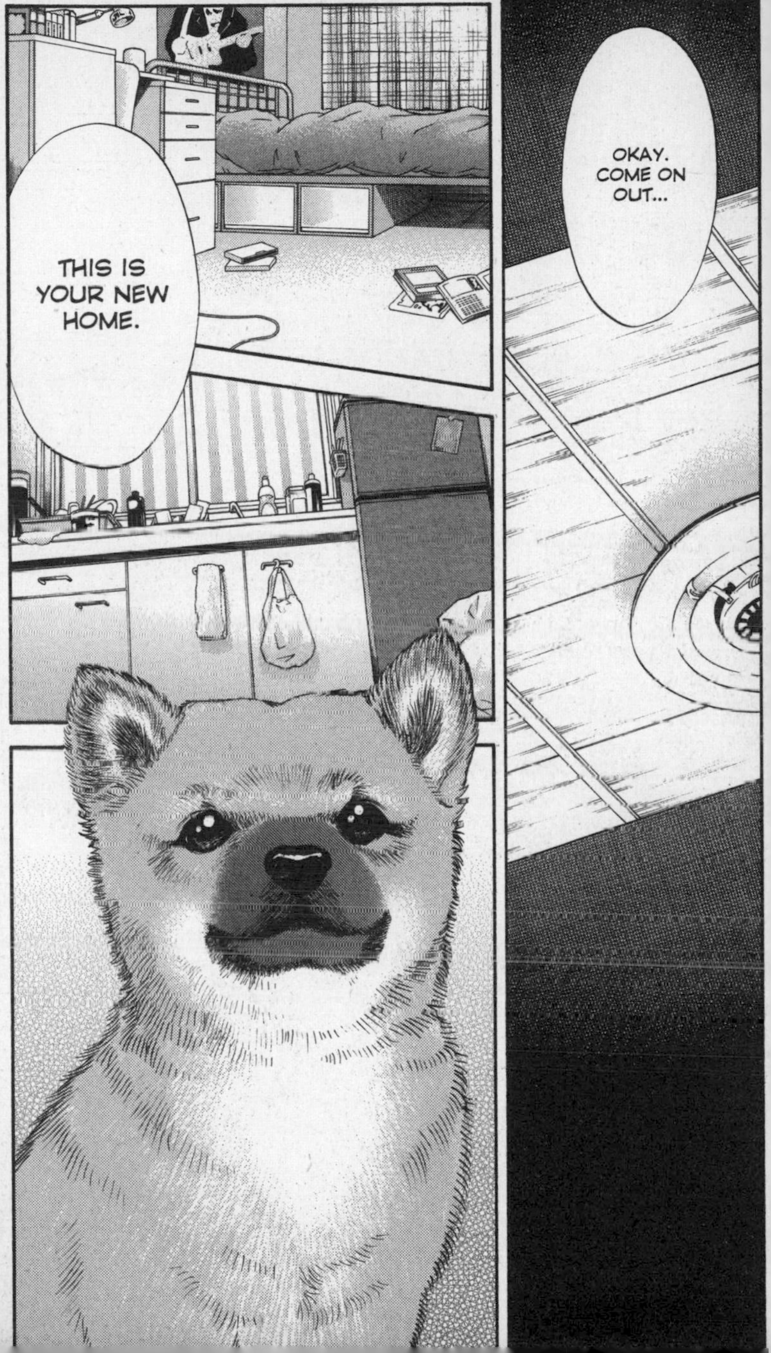
OKAY. COME ON OUT...
THIS IS YOUR NEW HOME.

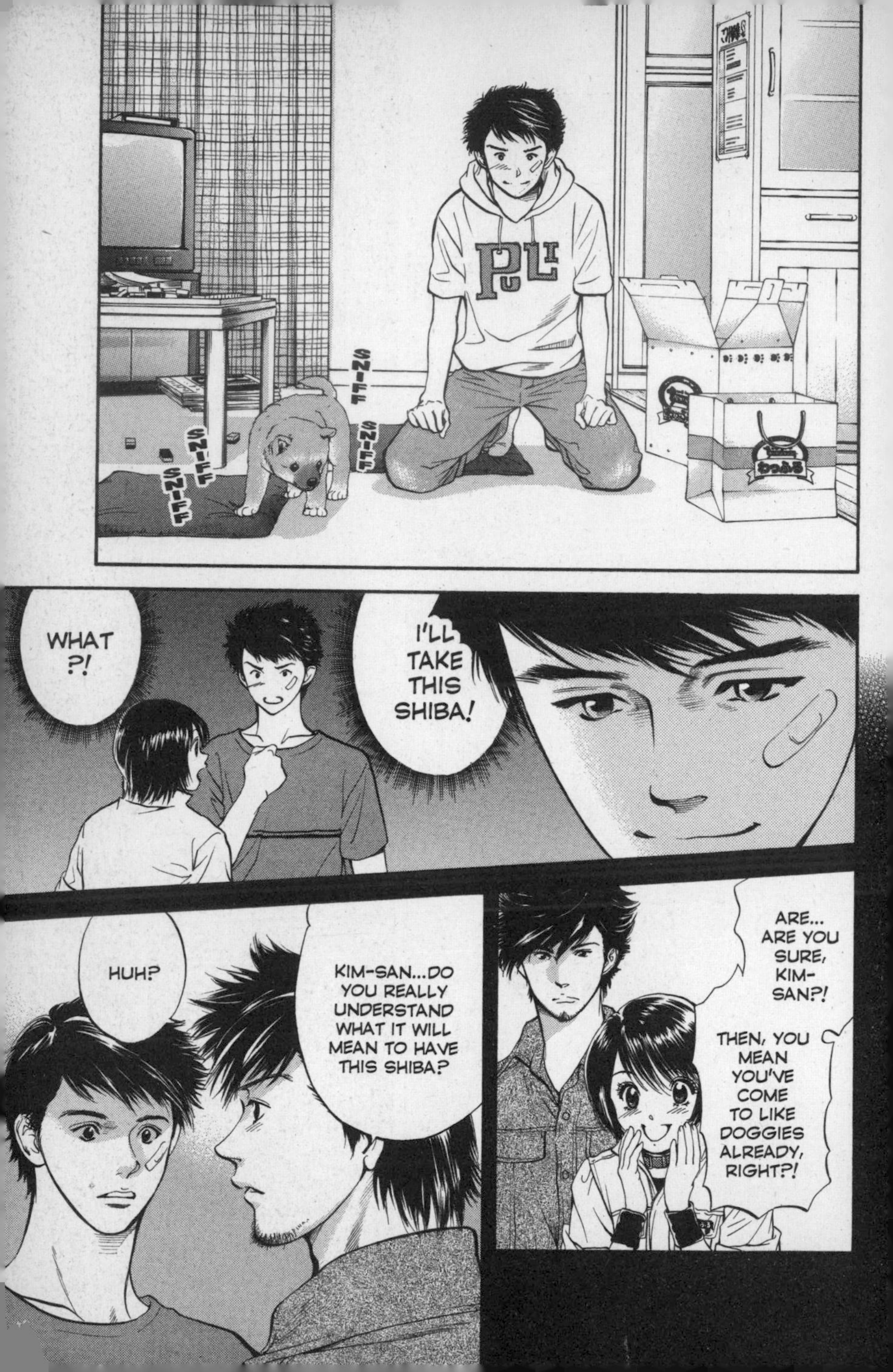
SNIFF
SNIFF
SNIFF
SNIFF
I'LL TAKE THIS SHIBA!
WHAT?!
ARE... ARE YOU SURE, KIM-SAN?!
THEN, YOU MEAN YOU'VE COME TO LIKE DOGGIES ALREADY, RIGHT?!
KIM-SAN...DO YOU REALLY UNDERSTAND WHAT IT WILL MEAN TO HAVE THIS SHIBA?
HUH?

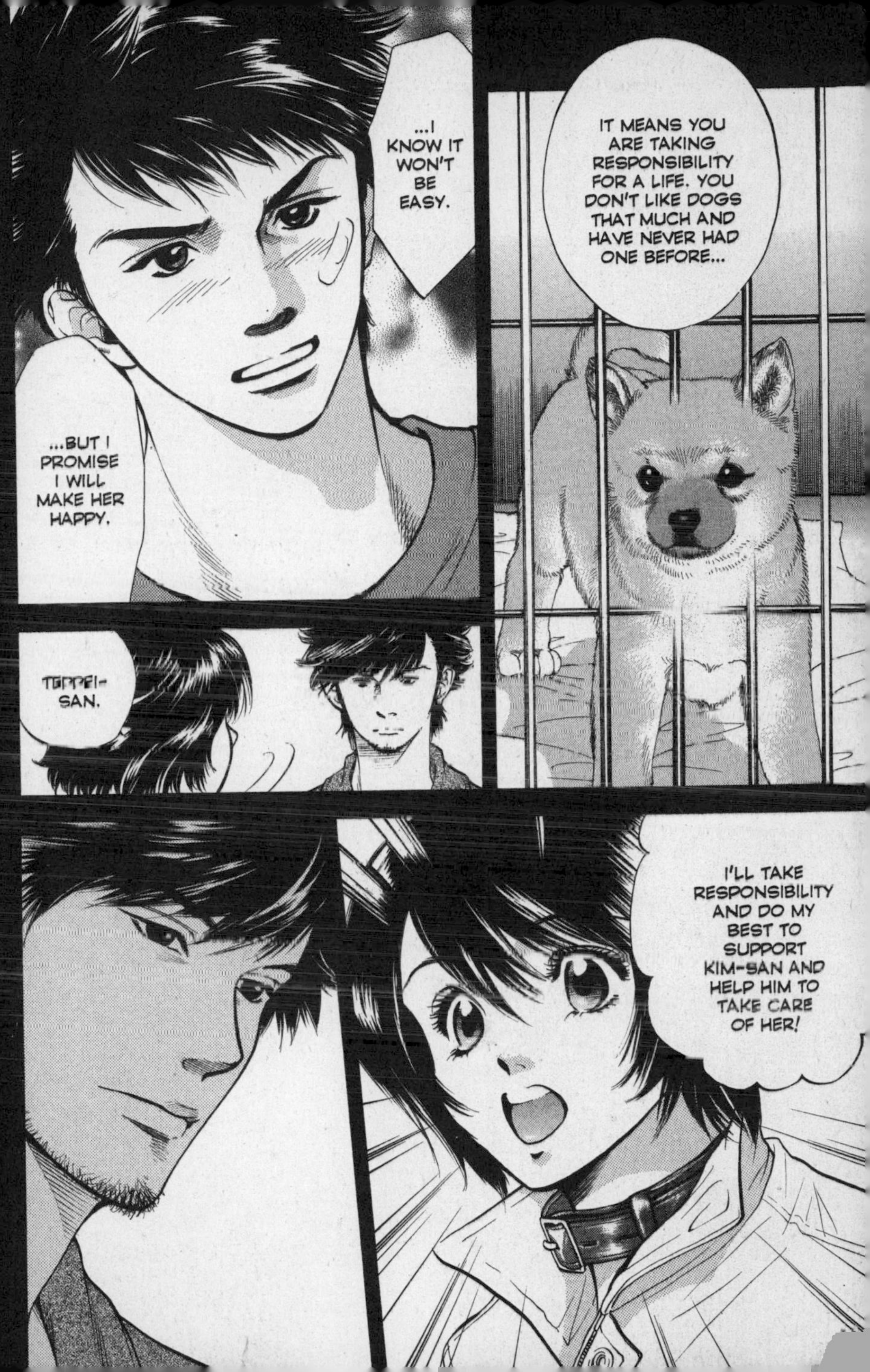
IT MEANS YOU ARE TAKING RESPONSIBILITY FOR A LIFE. YOU DON'T LIKE DOGS THAT MUCH AND HAVE NEVER HAD ONE BEFORE...
...I KNOW IT WON'T BE EASY.
...BUT I PROMISE I WILL MAKE HER HAPPY.
TEPPEI-SAN.
I'LL TAKE RESPONSIBILITY AND DO MY BEST TO SUPPORT KIM-SAN AND HELP HIM TO TAKE CARE OF HER!

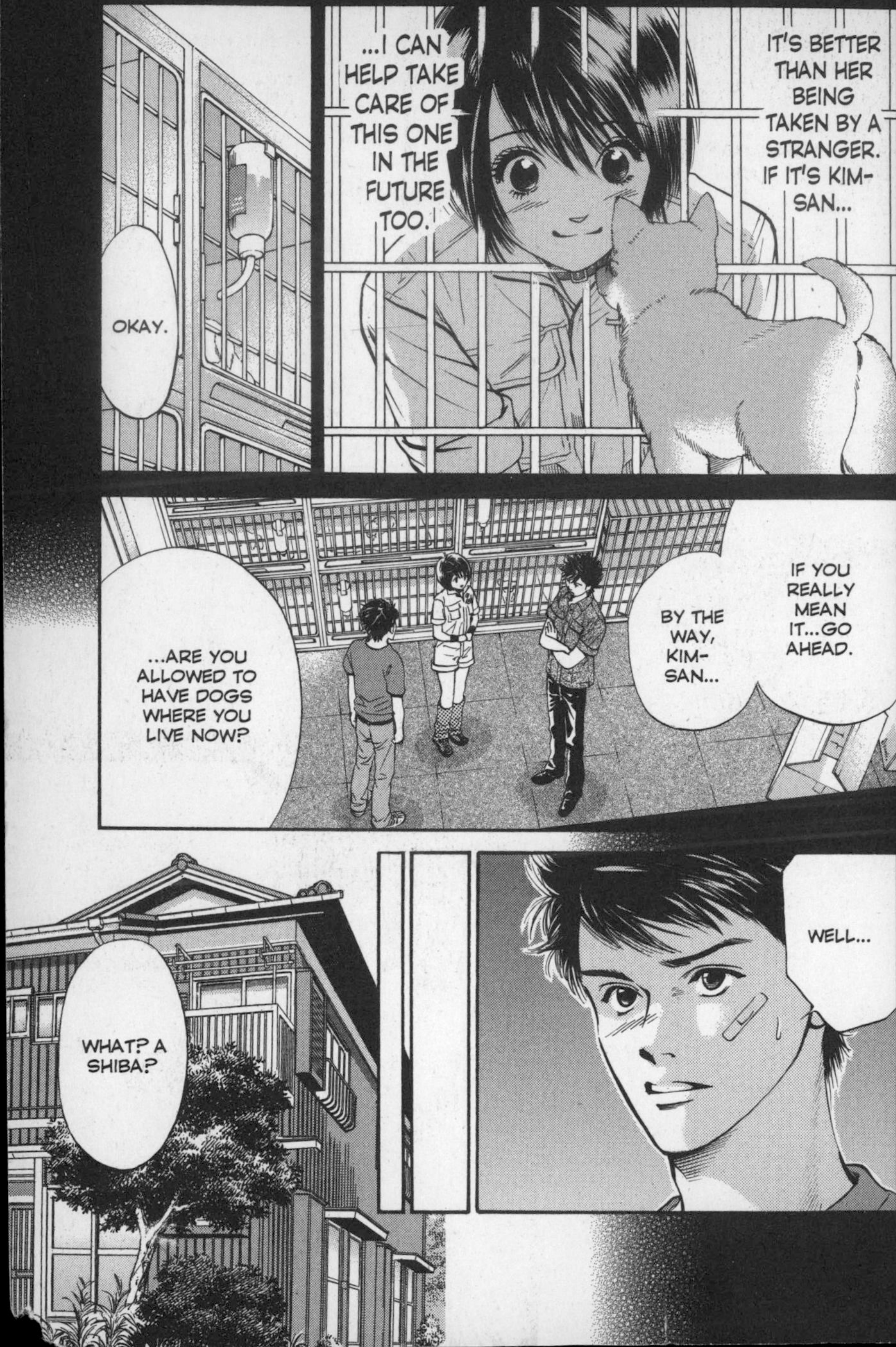
IT'S BETTER THAN HER BEING TAKEN BY A STRANGER. IF IT'S KIM-SAN...
...I CAN HELP TAKE CARE OF THIS ONE IN THE FUTURE TOO.
OKAY.
IF YOU REALLY MEAN IT...GO AHEAD.
BY THE WAY, KIM-SAN...
...ARE YOU ALLOWED TO HAVE DOGS WHERE YOU LIVE NOW?
WELL...
WHAT? A SHIBA?

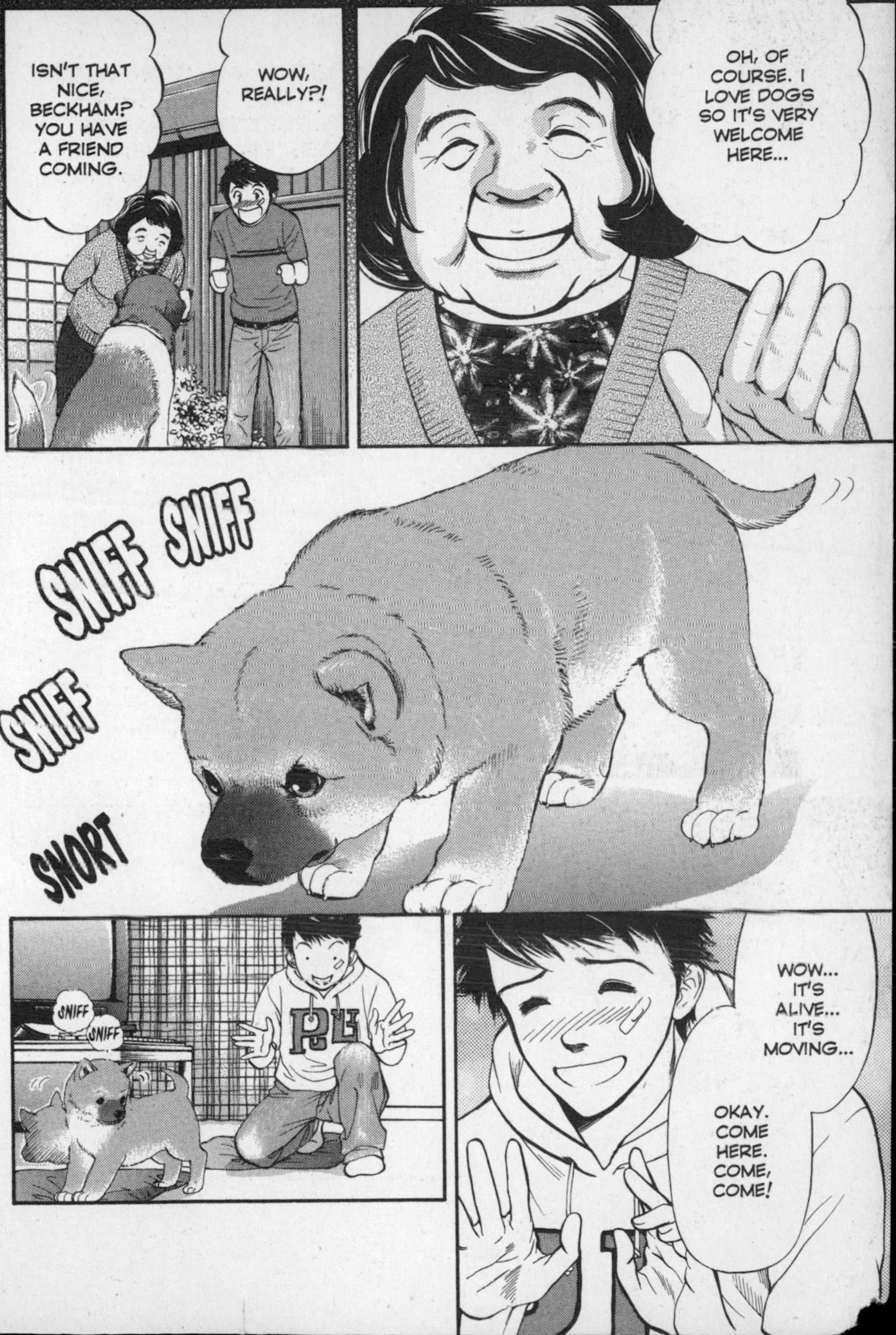
OH, OF COURSE. I LOVE DOGS SO IT'S VERY WELCOME HERE...
WOW, REALLY?!
ISN'T THAT NICE, BECKHAM? YOU HAVE A FRIEND COMING.
SNIFF
SNIFF
SNIFF
SNORT
WOW... IT'S ALIVE... IT'S MOVING...
OKAY. COME HERE. COME, COME!
SNIFF
SNIFF

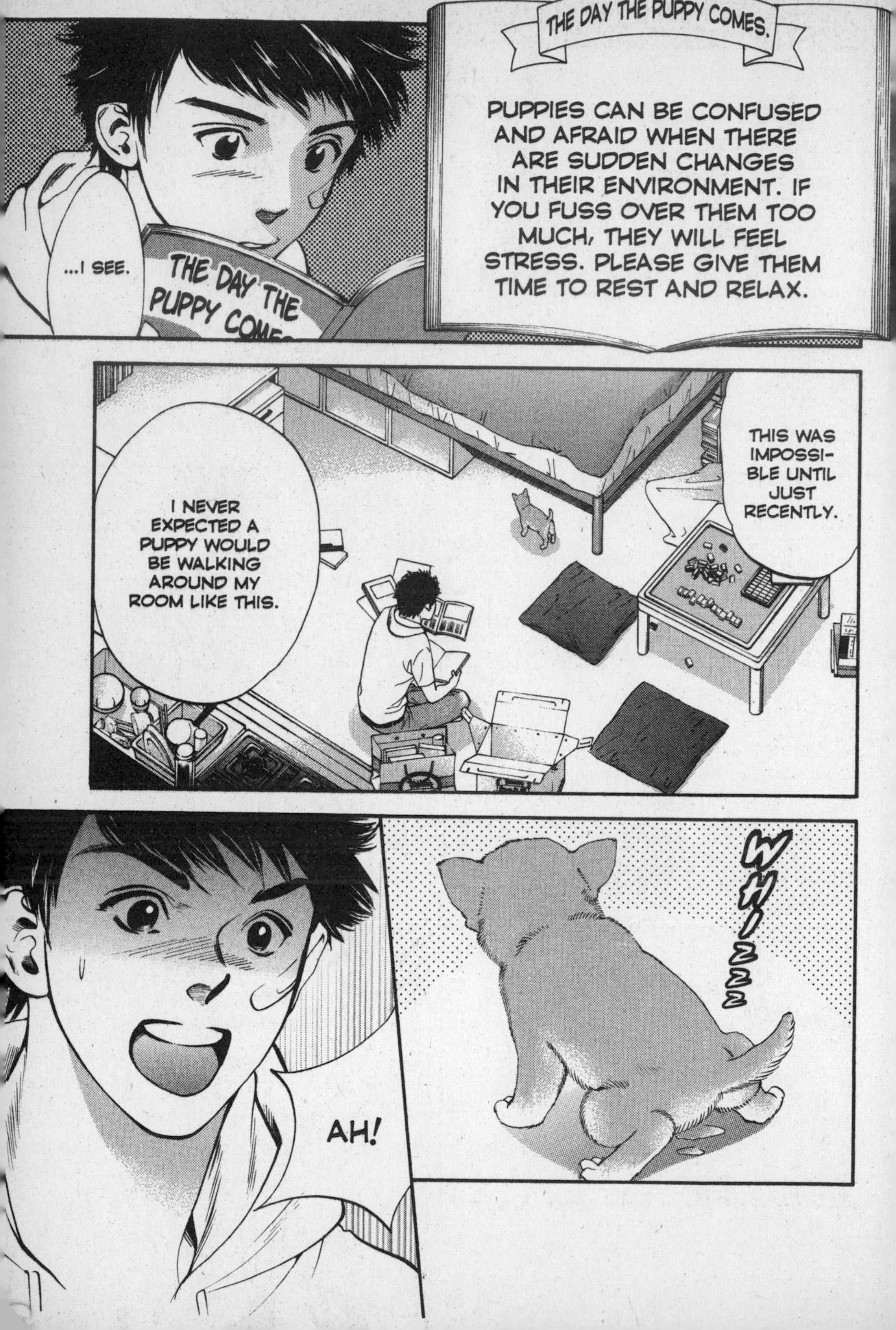
THE DAY THE PUPPY COMES.
PUPPIES CAN BE CONFUSED AND AFRAID WHEN THERE ARE SUDDEN CHANGES IN THEIR ENVIRONMENT. IF YOU FUSS OVER THEM TOO MUCH, THEY WILL FEEL STRESS. PLEASE GIVE THEM TIME TO REST AND RELAX.
...I SEE.
THIS WAS IMPOSSI-BLE UNTIL JUST RECENTLY.
I NEVER EXPECTED A PUPPY WOULD BE WALKING AROUND MY ROOM LIKE THIS.
WHIZZZ
AH!

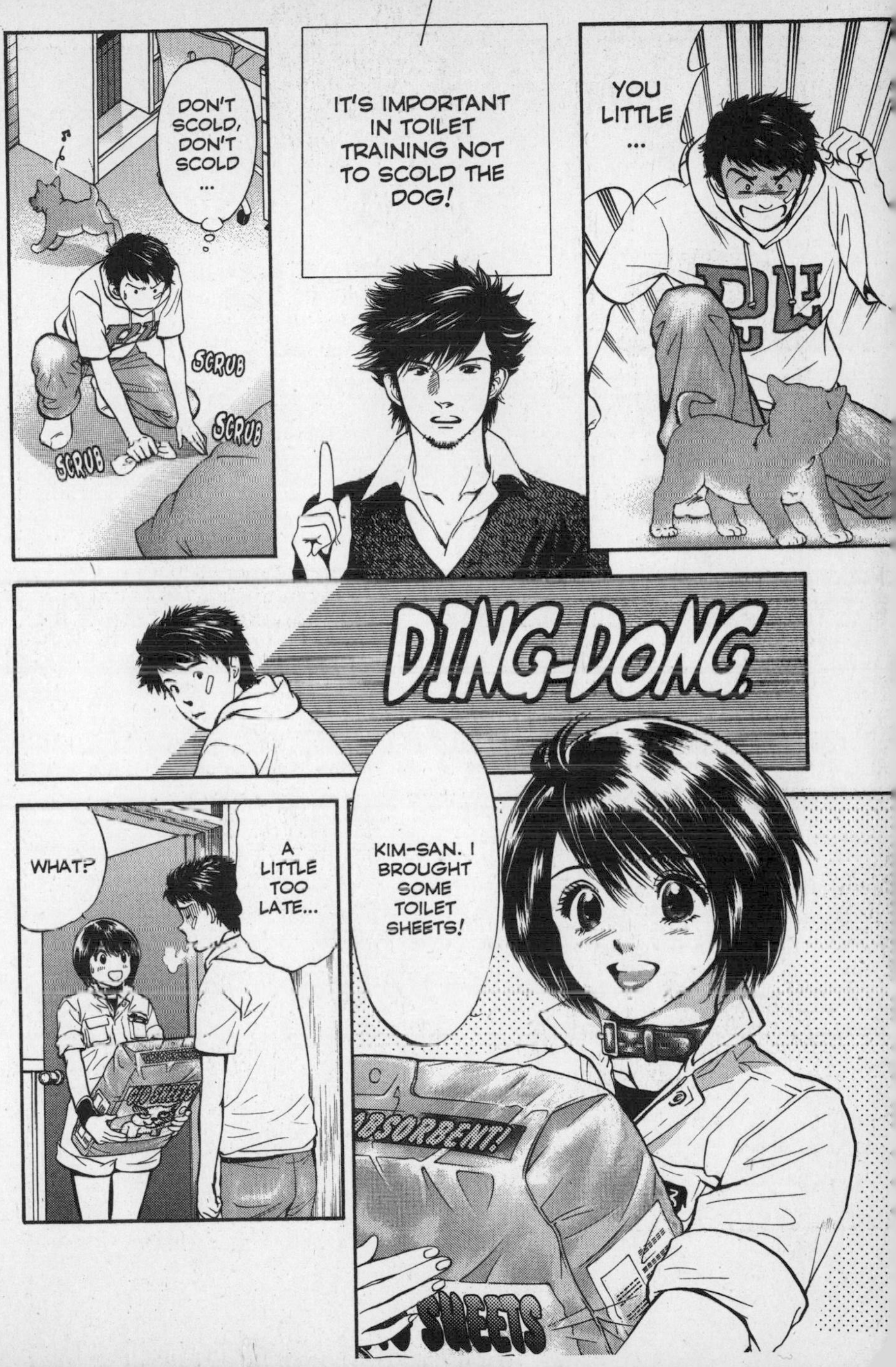
YOU LITTLE ...
IT'S IMPORTANT IN TOILET TRAINING NOT TO SCOLD THE DOG!
DON'T SCOLD, DON'T SCOLD ...
SCRUB
SCRUB
SCRUB
DING-DONG.
KIM-SAN. I BROUGHT SOME TOILET SHEETS!
ABSORBENT!
SHEETS
A LITTLE TOO LATE...
WHAT?

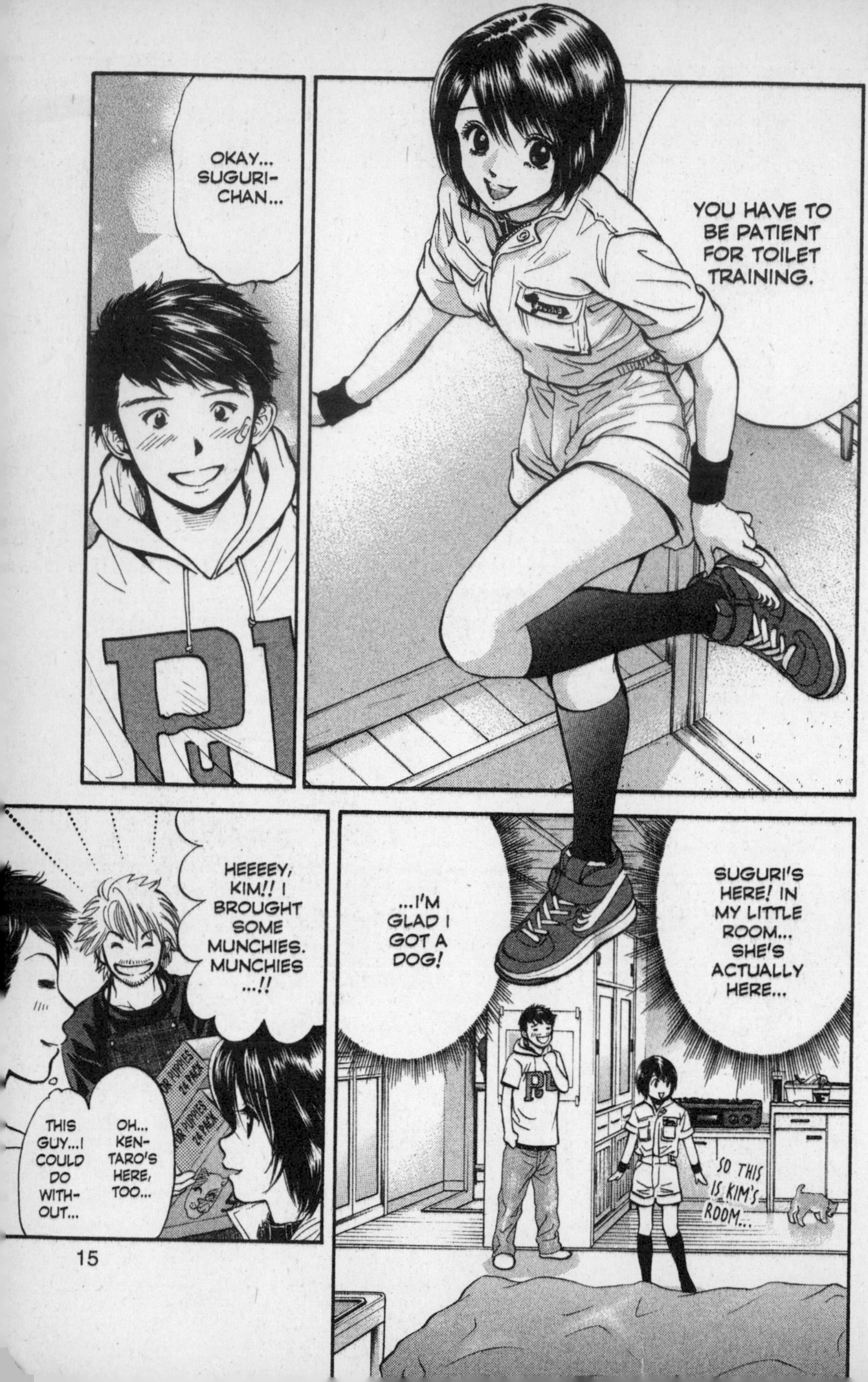
YOU HAVE TO BE PATIENT FOR TOILET TRAINING.
OKAY... SUGURI-CHAN...
SUGURI'S HERE! IN MY LITTLE ROOM... SHE'S ACTUALLY HERE...
...I'M GLAD I GOT A DOG!
SO THIS IS KIM'S ROOM...
HEEEEY, KIM!! I BROUGHT SOME MUNCHIES. MUNCHIES ...!!
OH... KENTARO'S HERE, TOO...
THIS GUY...I COULD DO WITHOUT...

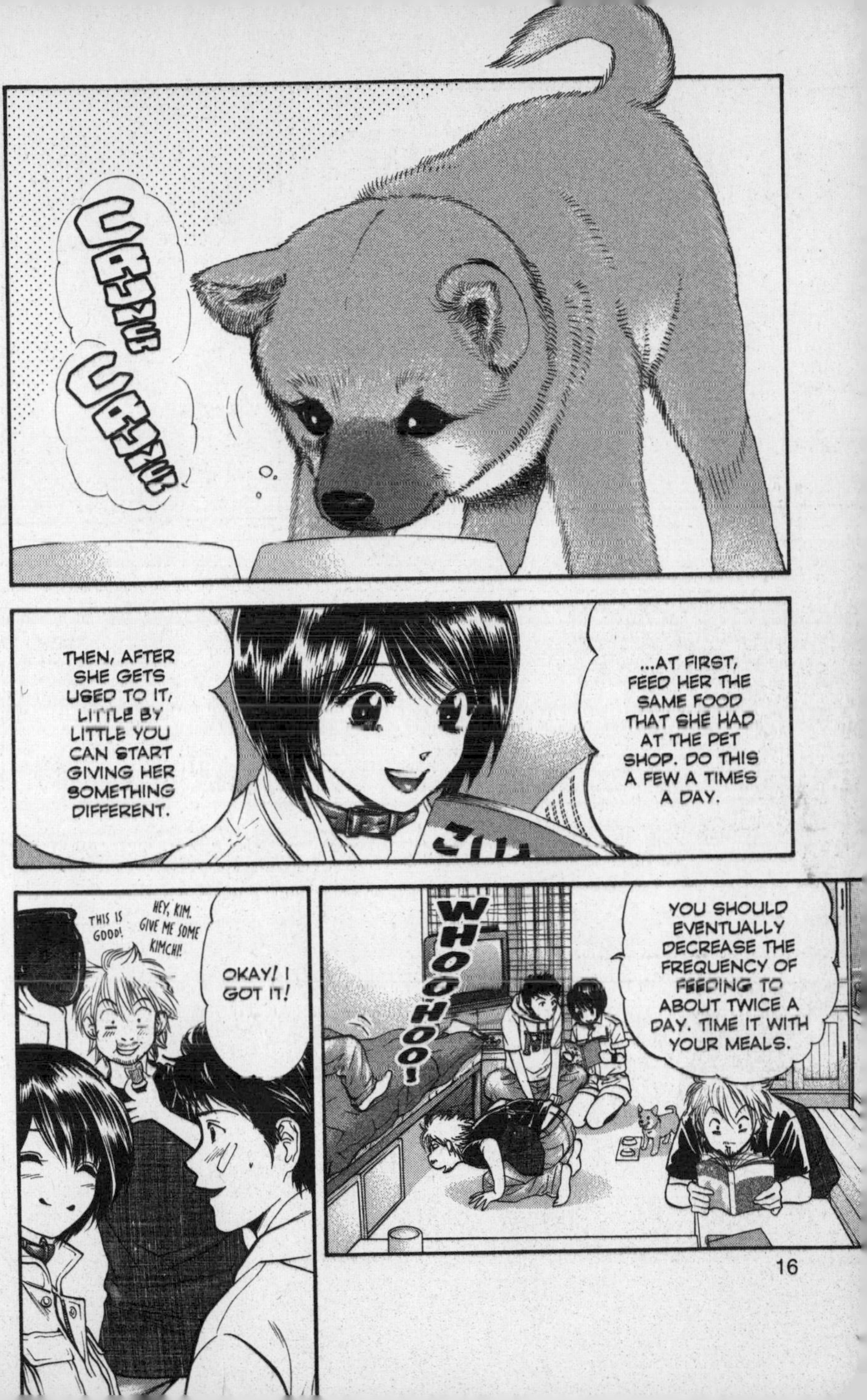
CRUNCH CRUNCH
...AT FIRST, FEED HER THE SAME FOOD THAT SHE HAD AT THE PET SHOP. DO THIS A FEW A TIMES A DAY.
THEN, AFTER SHE GETS USED TO IT, LITTLE BY LITTLE YOU CAN START GIVING HER SOMETHING DIFFERENT.
YOU SHOULD EVENTUALLY DECREASE THE FREQUENCY OF FEEDING TO ABOUT TWICE A DAY. TIME IT WITH YOUR MEALS.
WHOOOHOO!
OKAY! I GOT IT!
HEY, KIM. GIVE ME SOME KIMCHI!
THIS IS GOOD!

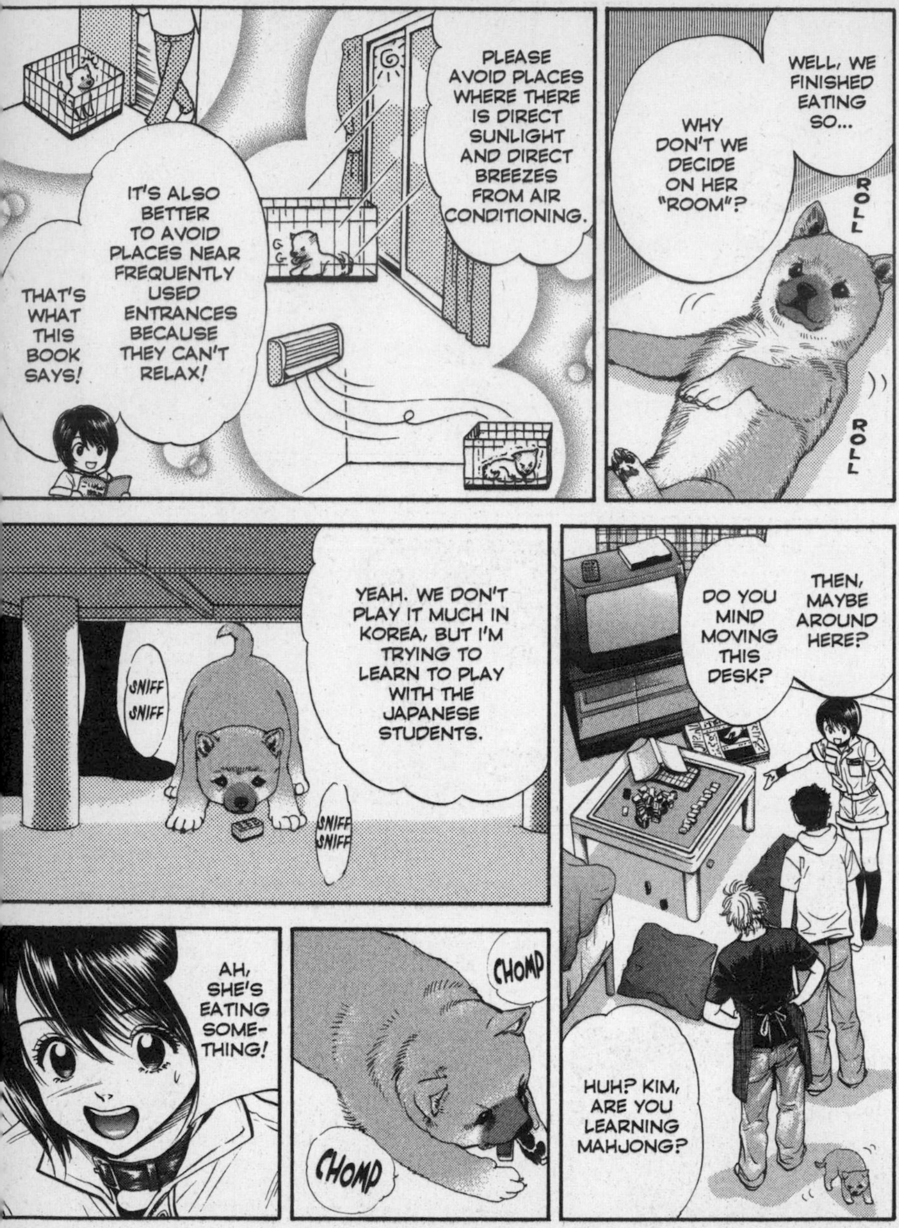
WELL, WE FINISHED EATING SO...
WHY DON'T WE DECIDE ON HER "ROOM"?
ROLL
ROLL
PLEASE AVOID PLACES WHERE THERE IS DIRECT SUNLIGHT AND DIRECT BREEZES FROM AIR CONDITIONING.
IT'S ALSO BETTER TO AVOID PLACES NEAR FREQUENTLY USED ENTRANCES BECAUSE THEY CAN'T RELAX!
THAT'S WHAT THIS BOOK SAYS!
THEN, MAYBE AROUND HERE?
DO YOU MIND MOVING THIS DESK?
HUH? KIM, ARE YOU LEARNING MAHJONG?
YEAH. WE DON'T PLAY IT MUCH IN KOREA, BUT I'M TRYING TO LEARN TO PLAY WITH THE JAPANESE STUDENTS.
SNIFF SNIFF
SNIFF SNIFF
CHOMP
CHOMP
AH, SHE'S EATING SOME-THING!

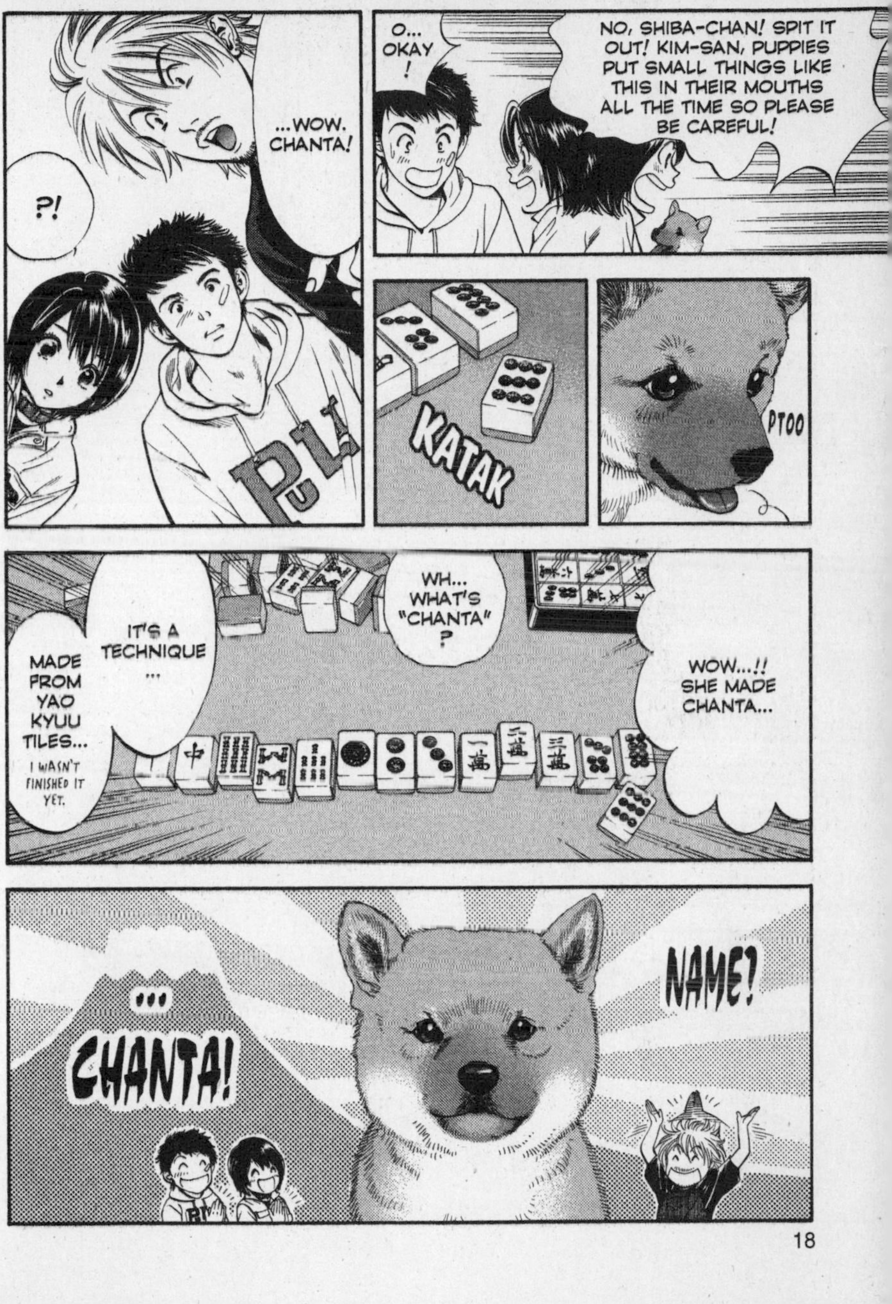

NO, SHIBA-CHAN! SPIT IT OUT! KIM-SAN, PUPPIES PUT SMALL THINGS LIKE THIS IN THEIR MOUTHS ALL THE TIME SO PLEASE BE CAREFUL!
O... OKAY!
PTOO
KATAK
...WOW. CHANTA!
?!
WOW...!! SHE MADE CHANTA...
WH... WHAT'S "CHANTA"?
IT'S A TECHNIQUE...
MADE FROM YAO KYUU TILES...
I WASN'T FINISHED IT YET.
NAME?
...
CHANTA!

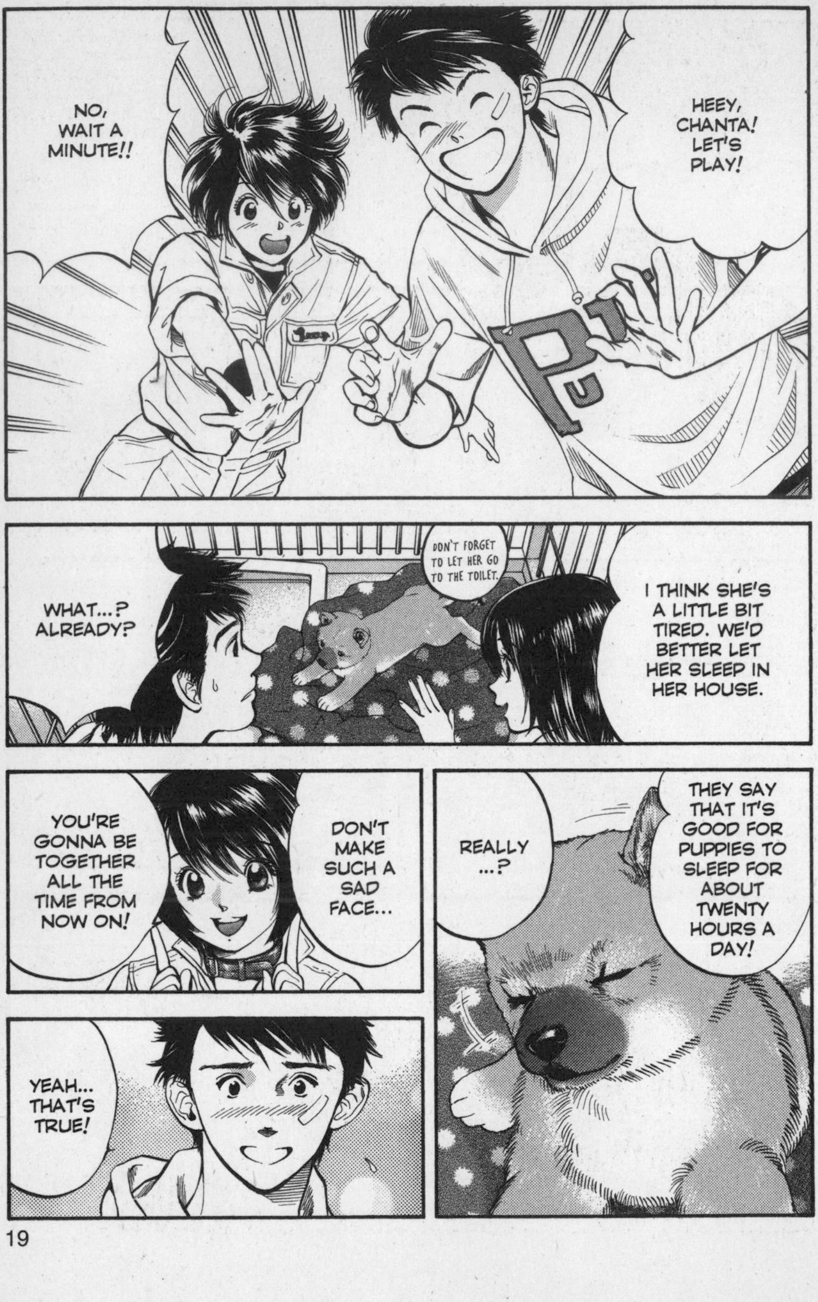
HEEY, CHANTA! LET'S PLAY!
NO, WAIT A MINUTE!!
I THINK SHE'S A LITTLE BIT TIRED. WE'D BETTER LET HER SLEEP IN HER HOUSE.
DON'T FORGET TO LET HER GO TO THE TOILET.
WHAT...? ALREADY?
THEY SAY THAT IT'S GOOD FOR PUPPIES TO SLEEP FOR ABOUT TWENTY HOURS A DAY!
REALLY ...?
DON'T MAKE SUCH A SAD FACE...
YOU'RE GONNA BE TOGETHER ALL THE TIME FROM NOW ON!
YEAH... THAT'S TRUE!

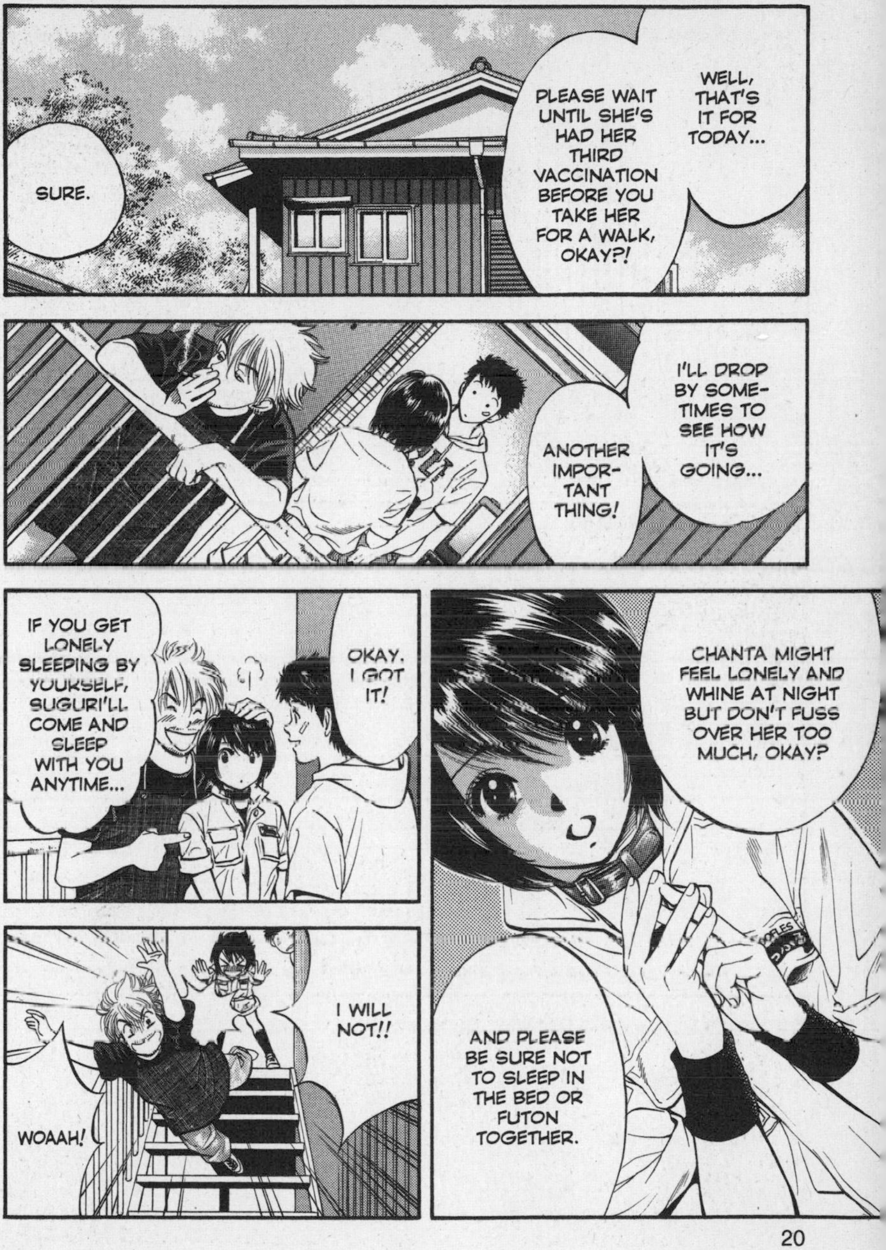
WELL, THAT'S IT FOR TODAY...
PLEASE WAIT UNTIL SHE'S HAD HER THIRD VACCINATION BEFORE YOU TAKE HER FOR A WALK, OKAY?!
SURE.
I'LL DROP BY SOME-TIMES TO SEE HOW IT'S GOING...
ANOTHER IMPOR-TANT THING!
CHANTA MIGHT FEEL LONELY AND WHINE AT NIGHT BUT DON'T FUSS OVER HER TOO MUCH, OKAY?
AND PLEASE BE SURE NOT TO SLEEP IN THE BED OR FUTON TOGETHER.
OKAY. I GOT IT!
IF YOU GET LONELY SLEEPING BY YOURSELF, SUGURI'LL COME AND SLEEP WITH YOU ANYTIME...
I WILL NOT!!
WOAAH!

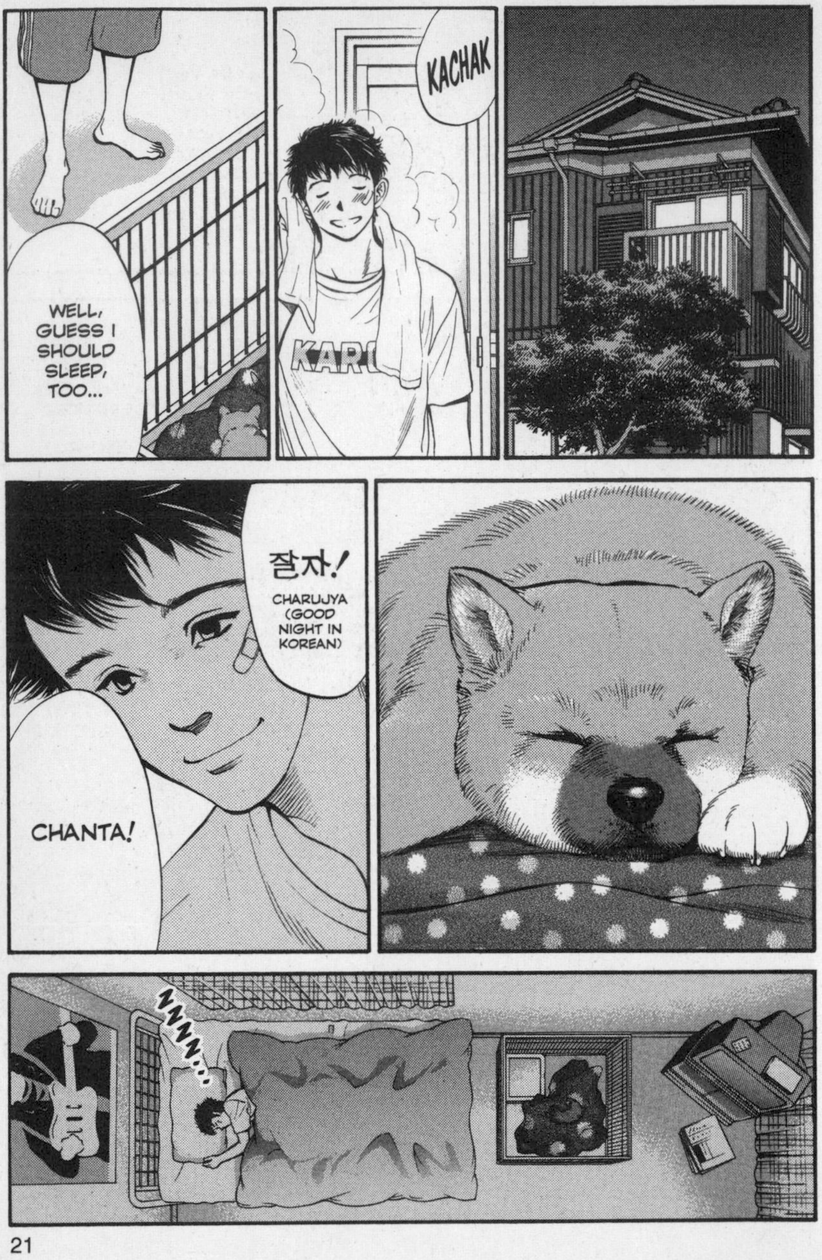
KACHAK
WELL, GUESS I SHOULD SLEEP, TOO...
잘자!
CHARUJYA (GOOD NIGHT IN KOREAN)
CHANTA!
ZZZZ...

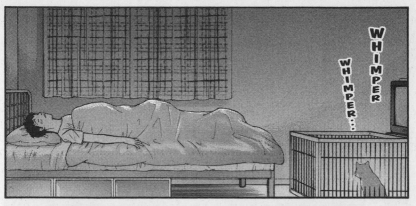

WHIMPER

WHIMPER...

WHIMPER

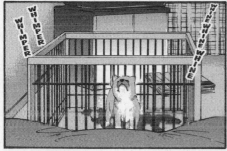

WHIMPER

WHIMPER

WHINE WHINE WHINE

HUH?

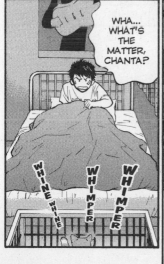

WHA...
WHAT'S
THE
MATTER,
CHANTA?

WHINE WHINE

WHIMPER

WHIMPER

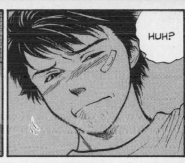

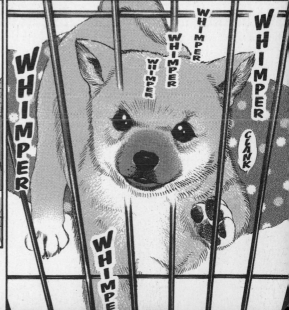

WHIMPER

WHIMPER

WHIMPER

WHIMPER

CLANK

WHIMPER

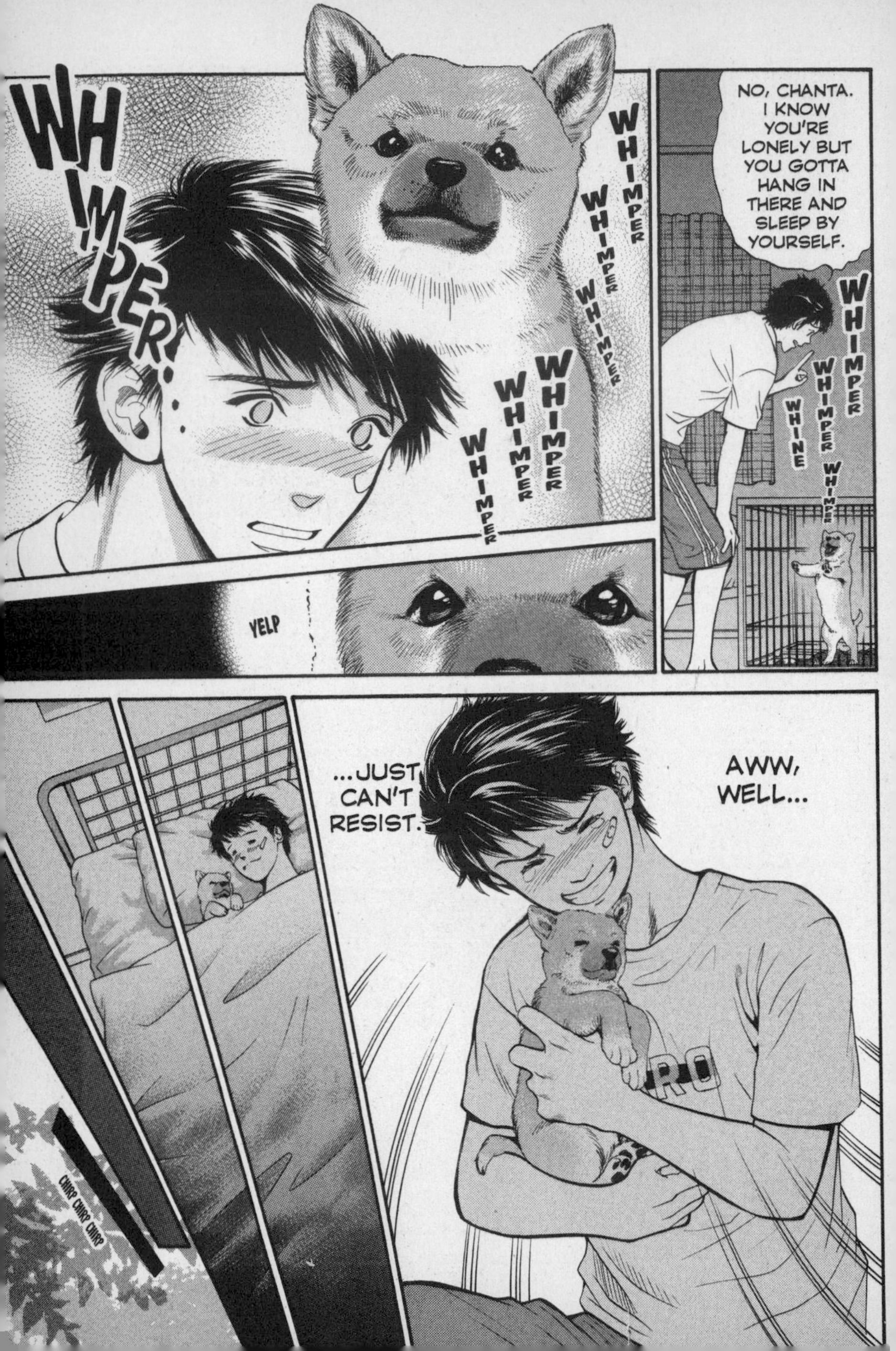

NO, CHANTA. I KNOW YOU'RE LONELY BUT YOU GOTTA HANG IN THERE AND SLEEP BY YOURSELF.
WHIMPER
WHIMPER
WHINE
WHIMPER
WHIMPER
WHIMPER
WHIMPER
WHIMPER
WHIMPER
WHIMPER
WHIMPER
YELP
AWW, WELL...
...JUST CAN'T RESIST.
CHIRP CHIRP CHIRP

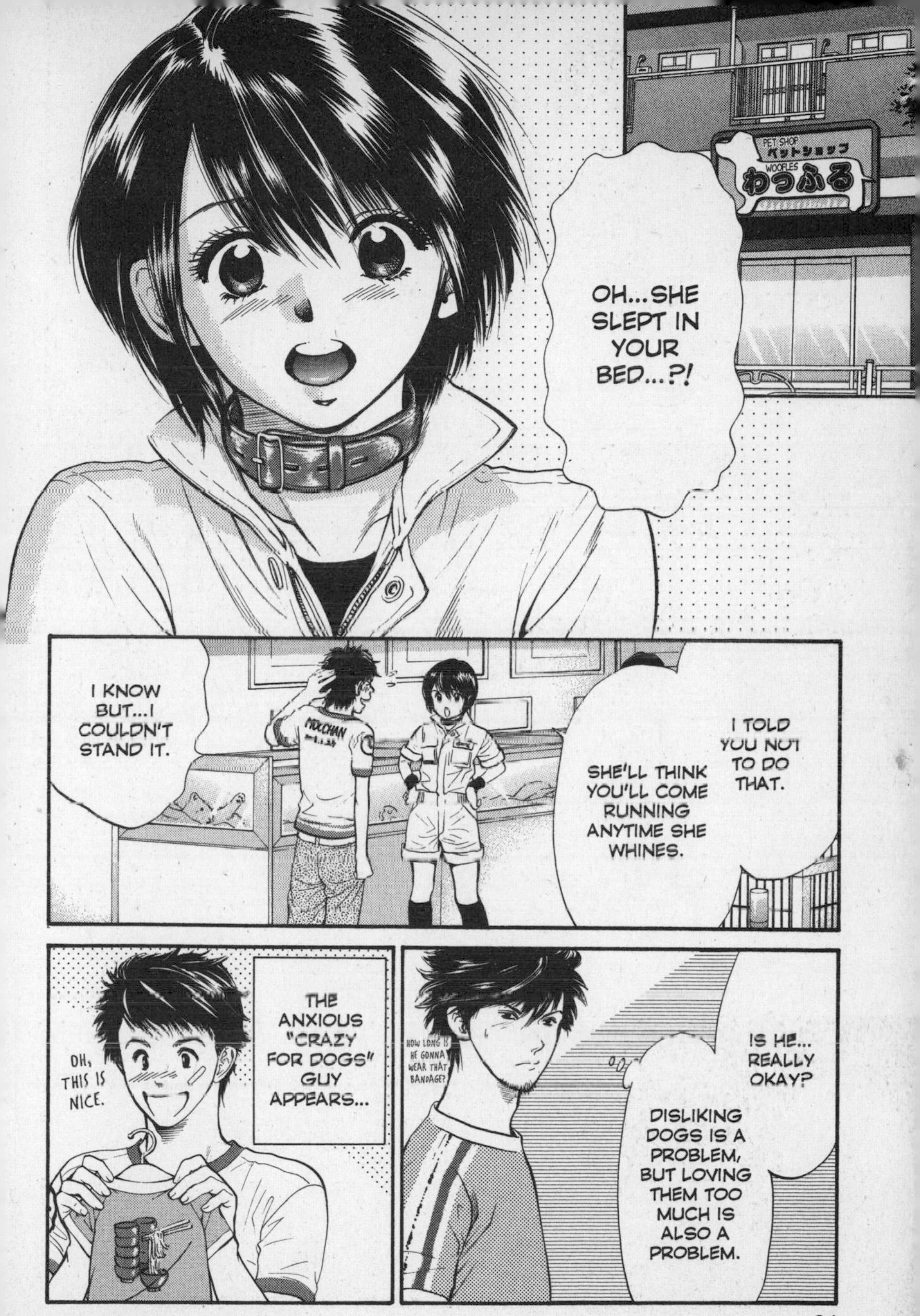
PET SHOP
ペットショップ
WOOFLES
わっふる
OH...SHE SLEPT IN YOUR BED...?!
I TOLD YOU NOT TO DO THAT.
SHE'LL THINK YOU'LL COME RUNNING ANYTIME SHE WHINES.
I KNOW BUT...I COULDN'T STAND IT.
IS HE... REALLY OKAY?
DISLIKING DOGS IS A PROBLEM, BUT LOVING THEM TOO MUCH IS ALSO A PROBLEM.
THE ANXIOUS "CRAZY FOR DOGS" GUY APPEARS...
HOW LONG IS HE GONNA WEAR THAT BANDAGE?
OH, THIS IS NICE.

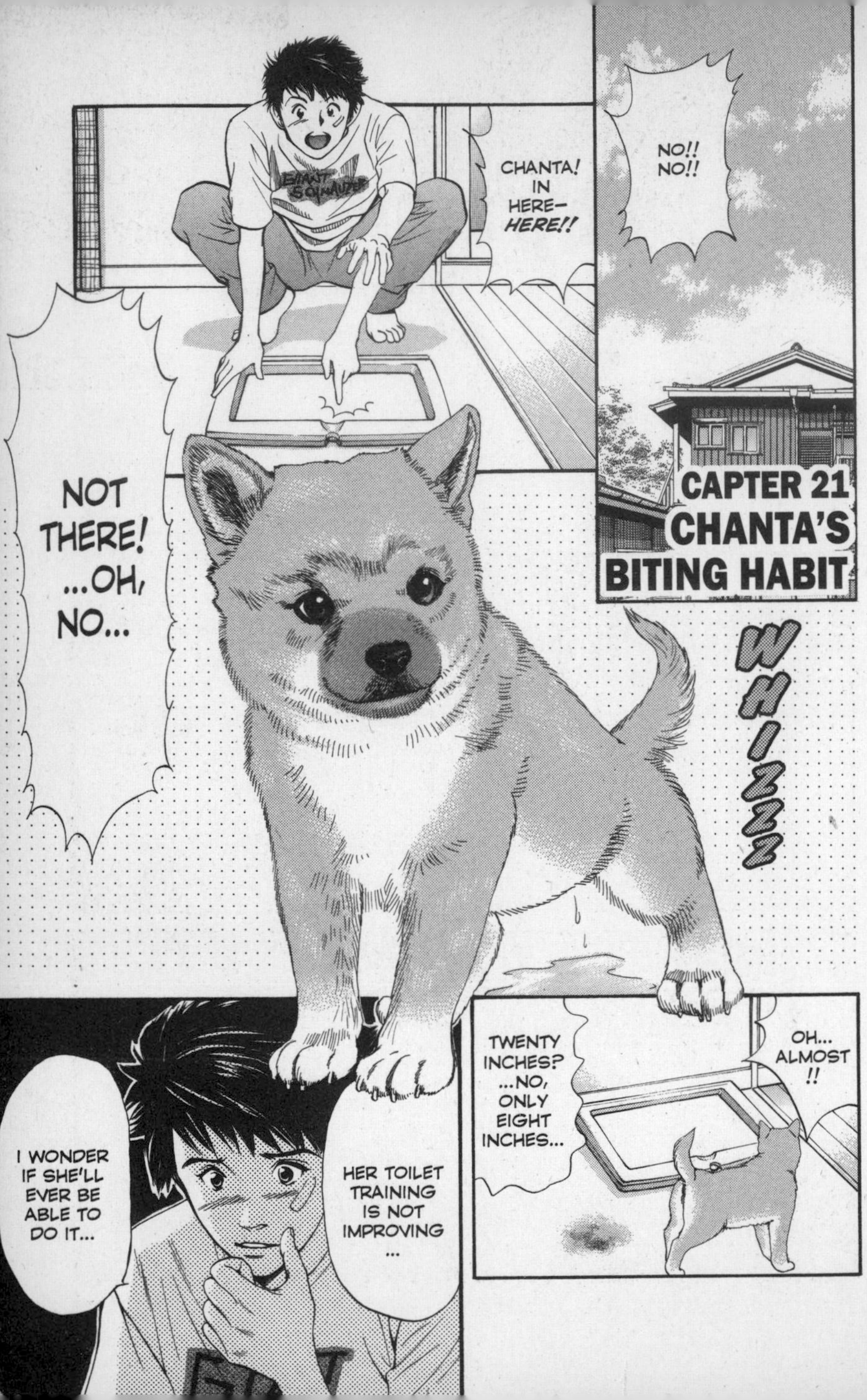
NO!! NO!!
CAPTER 21
CHANTA'S BITING HABIT
CHANTA! IN HERE— *HERE!!*
WHIZZZ
NOT THERE! ...OH, NO...
OH... ALMOST!!
TWENTY INCHES? ...NO, ONLY EIGHT INCHES...
HER TOILET TRAINING IS NOT IMPROVING ...
I WONDER IF SHE'LL EVER BE ABLE TO DO IT...

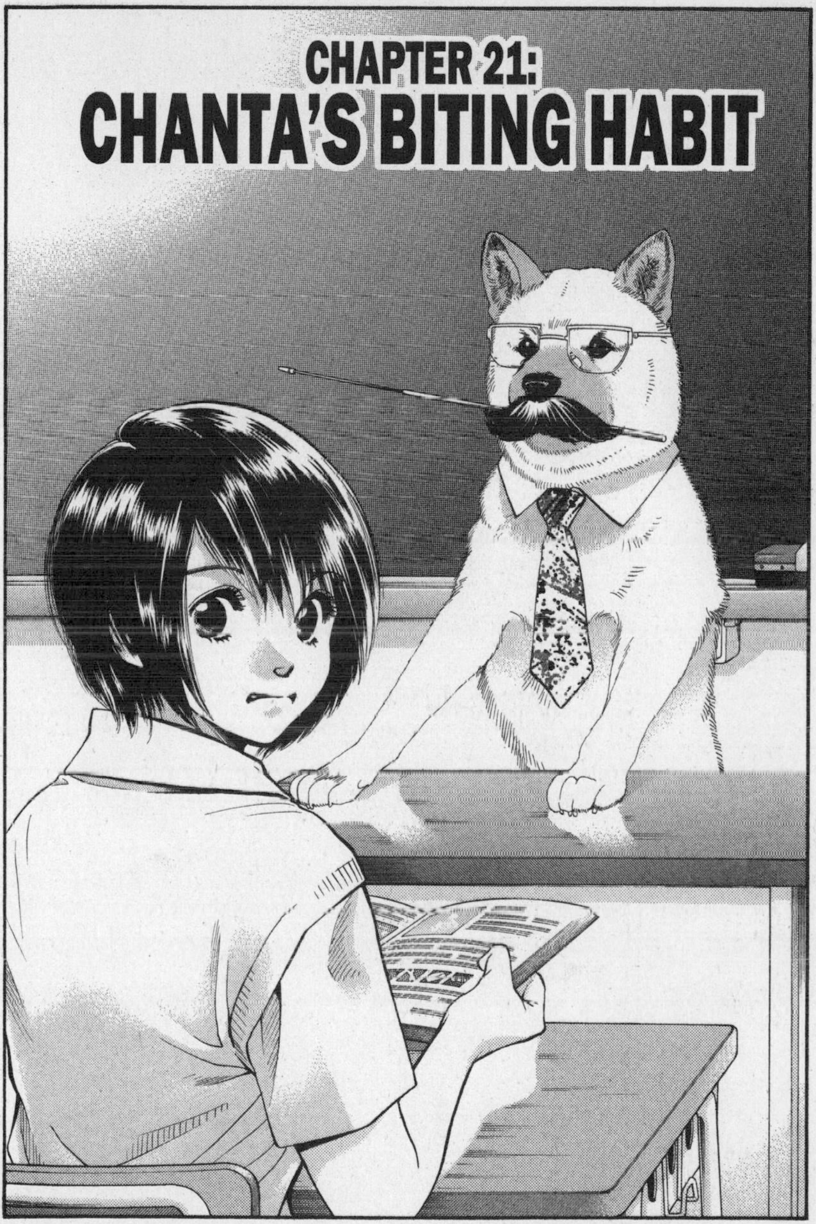
CHAPTER 21:
CHANTA'S BITING HABIT

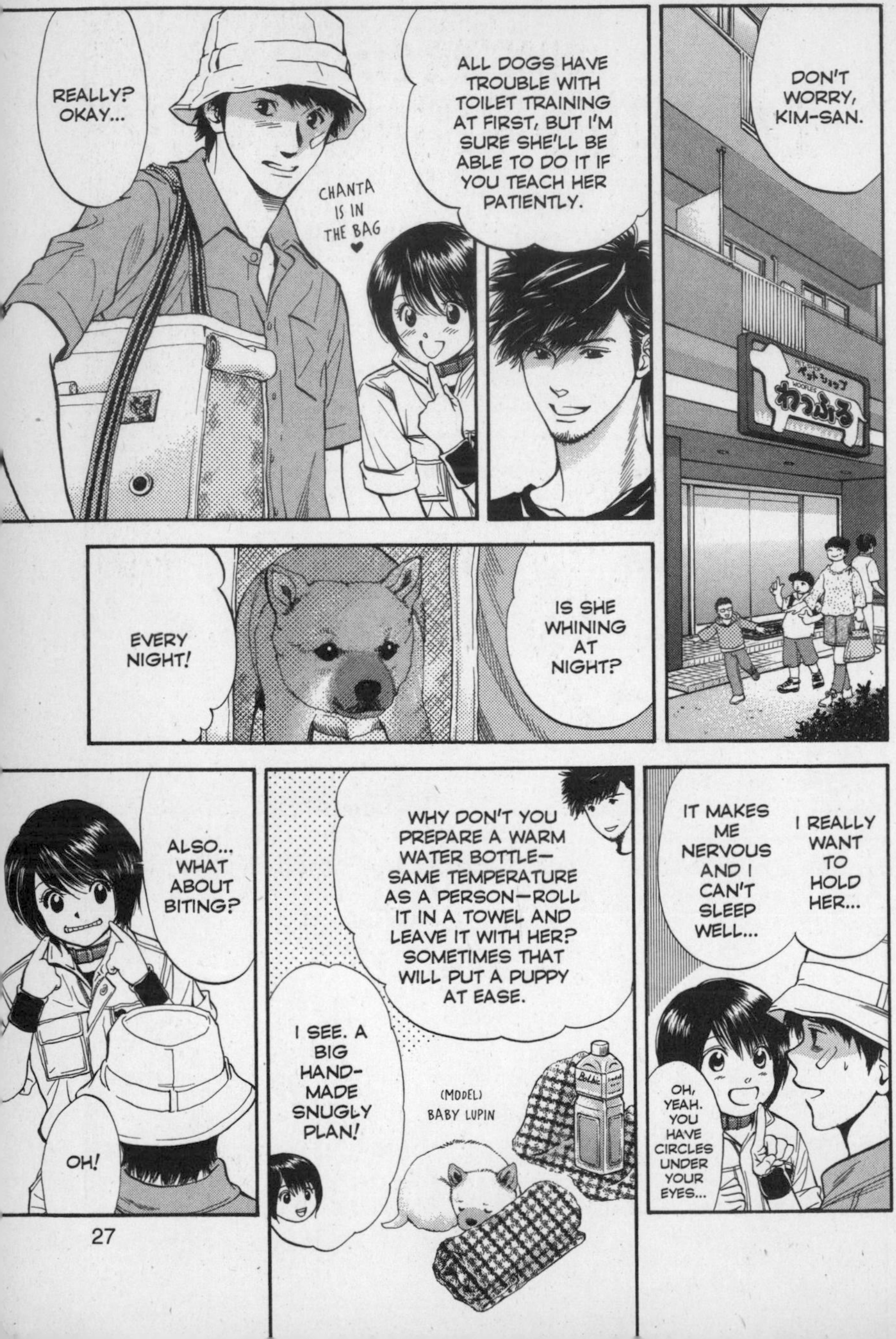
DON'T WORRY, KIM-SAN.
ALL DOGS HAVE TROUBLE WITH TOILET TRAINING AT FIRST, BUT I'M SURE SHE'LL BE ABLE TO DO IT IF YOU TEACH HER PATIENTLY.
CHANTA IS IN THE BAG
REALLY? OKAY...
IS SHE WHINING AT NIGHT?
EVERY NIGHT!
I REALLY WANT TO HOLD HER...
IT MAKES ME NERVOUS AND I CAN'T SLEEP WELL...
OH, YEAH. YOU HAVE CIRCLES UNDER YOUR EYES...
WHY DON'T YOU PREPARE A WARM WATER BOTTLE—SAME TEMPERATURE AS A PERSON—ROLL IT IN A TOWEL AND LEAVE IT WITH HER? SOMETIMES THAT WILL PUT A PUPPY AT EASE.
I SEE. A BIG HAND-MADE SNUGLY PLAN!
(MODEL)
BABY LUPIN
ALSO... WHAT ABOUT BITING?
OH!

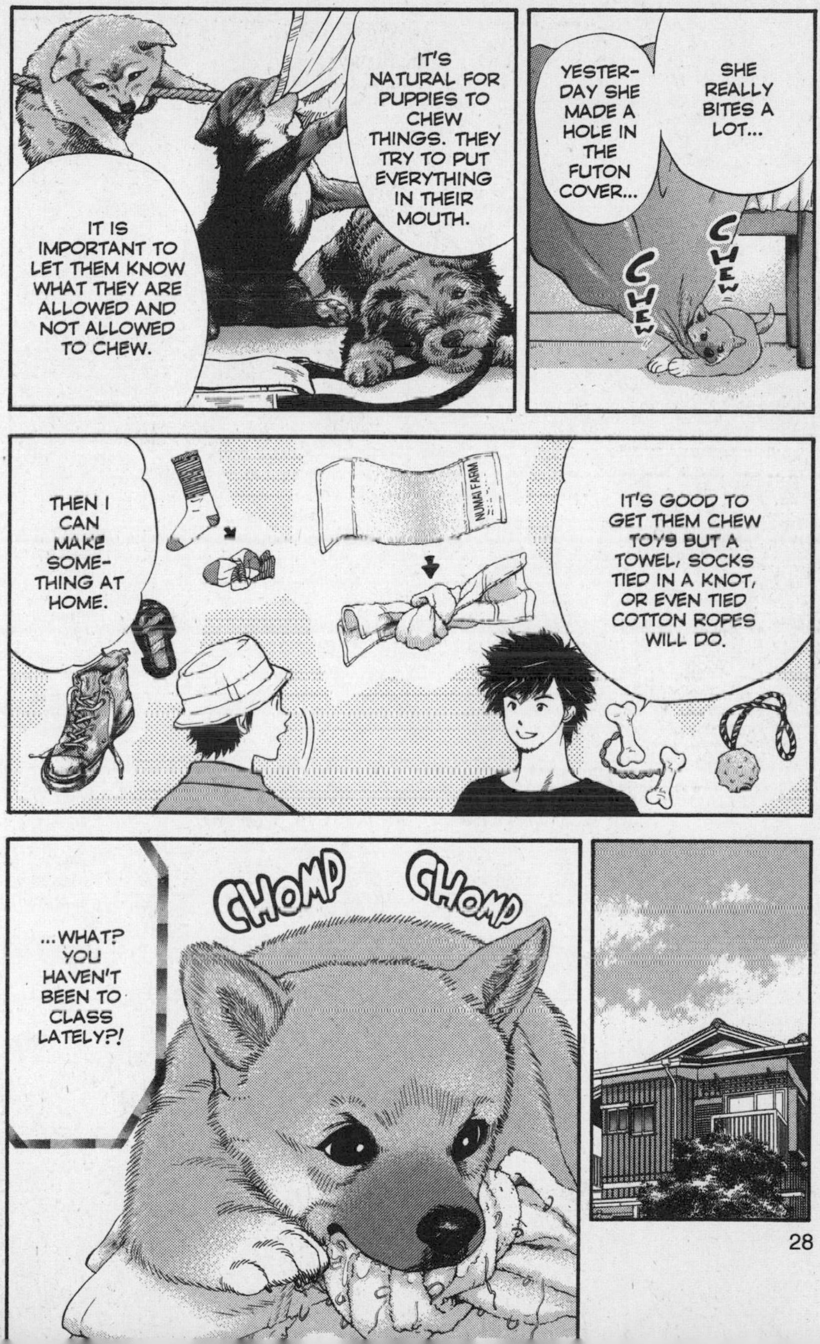
SHE REALLY BITES A LOT...
YESTERDAY SHE MADE A HOLE IN THE FUTON COVER...
CHEW
CHEW
IT'S NATURAL FOR PUPPIES TO CHEW THINGS. THEY TRY TO PUT EVERYTHING IN THEIR MOUTH.
IT IS IMPORTANT TO LET THEM KNOW WHAT THEY ARE ALLOWED AND NOT ALLOWED TO CHEW.
IT'S GOOD TO GET THEM CHEW TOYS BUT A TOWEL, SOCKS TIED IN A KNOT, OR EVEN TIED COTTON ROPES WILL DO.
NUMAI FARM
THEN I CAN MAKE SOMETHING AT HOME.
CHOMP
CHOMP
...WHAT? YOU HAVEN'T BEEN TO CLASS LATELY?!

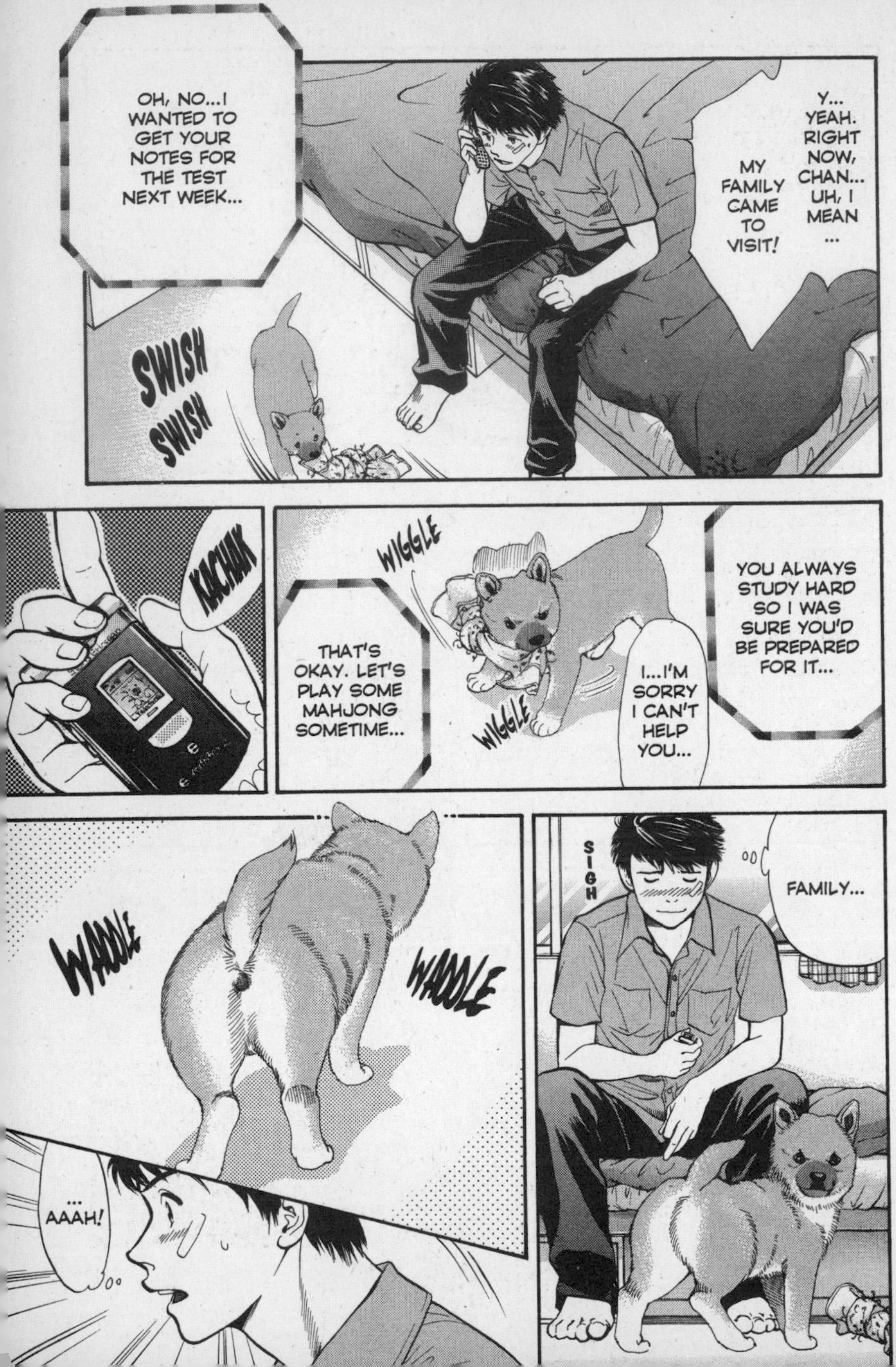
Y... YEAH. RIGHT NOW, CHAN... UH, I MEAN ...
MY FAMILY CAME TO VISIT!
OH, NO...I WANTED TO GET YOUR NOTES FOR THE TEST NEXT WEEK...
SWISH SWISH
YOU ALWAYS STUDY HARD SO I WAS SURE YOU'D BE PREPARED FOR IT...
I...I'M SORRY I CAN'T HELP YOU...
WIGGLE
THAT'S OKAY. LET'S PLAY SOME MAHJONG SOMETIME...
WIGGLE
KACHAK
FAMILY...
SIGH
WADDLE
WADDLE
... AAAH!

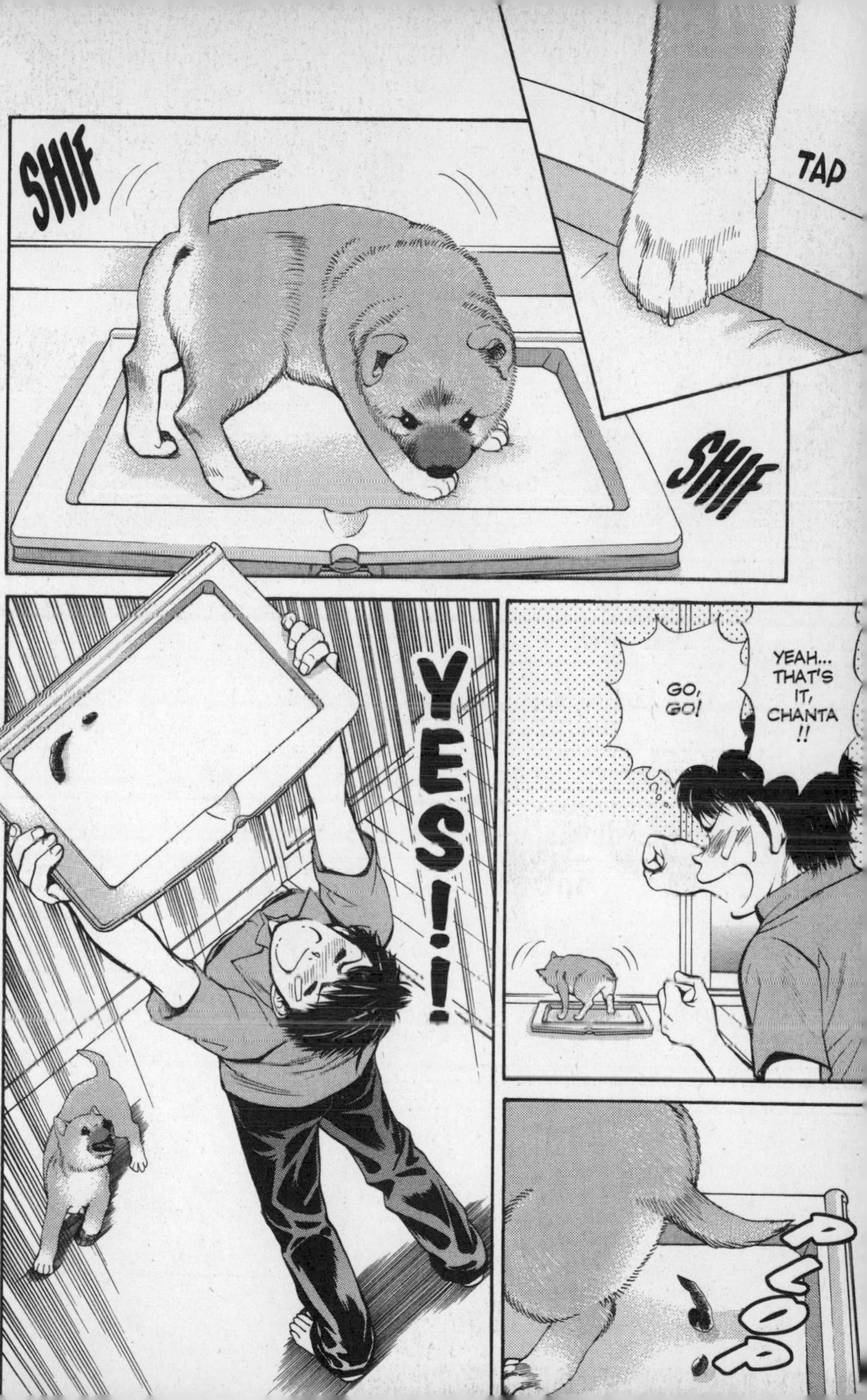
TAP
SHIF
SHIF
YEAH... THAT'S IT, CHANTA!!
GO, GO!
PLOP
YES!!!

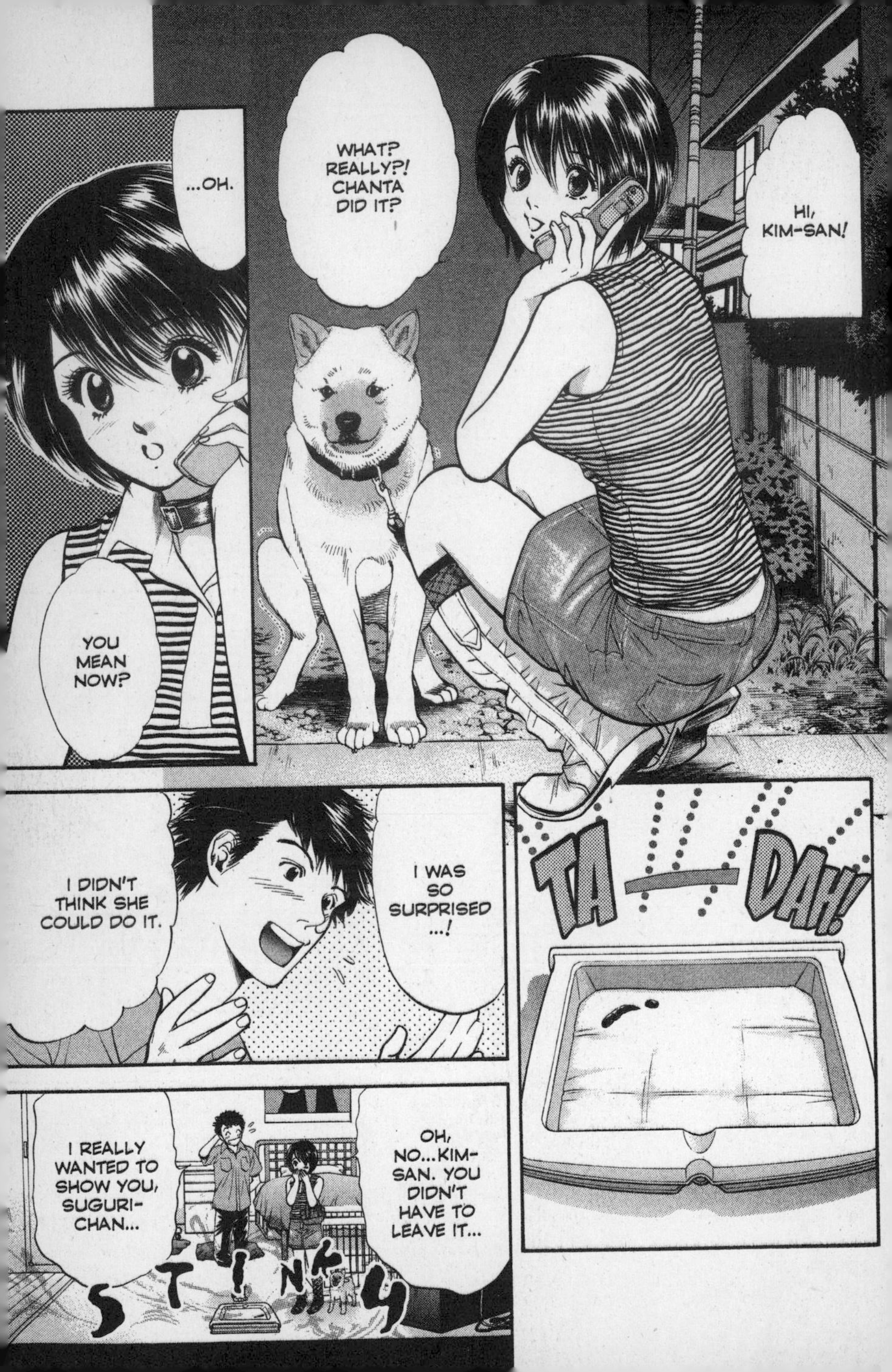
HI, KIM-SAN!
WHAT? REALLY?! CHANTA DID IT?
...OH.
YOU MEAN NOW?
TA—DAH!
I WAS SO SURPRISED...!
I DIDN'T THINK SHE COULD DO IT.
OH, NO...KIM-SAN. YOU DIDN'T HAVE TO LEAVE IT...
I REALLY WANTED TO SHOW YOU, SUGURI-CHAN...
STINKY

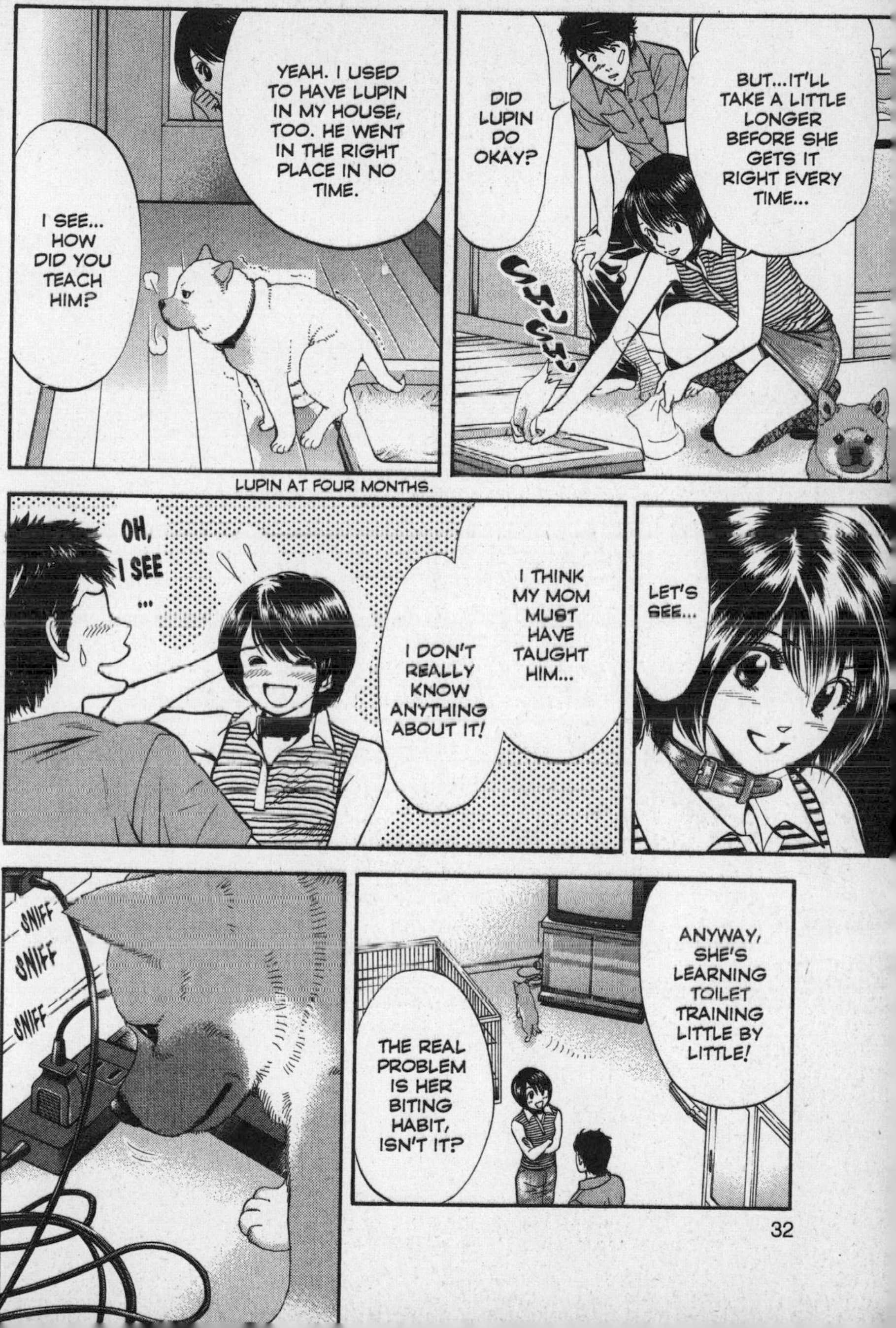

BUT...IT'LL TAKE A LITTLE LONGER BEFORE SHE GETS IT RIGHT EVERY TIME...
DID LUPIN DO OKAY?
SHU SHU
YEAH. I USED TO HAVE LUPIN IN MY HOUSE, TOO. HE WENT IN THE RIGHT PLACE IN NO TIME.
I SEE... HOW DID YOU TEACH HIM?
LUPIN AT FOUR MONTHS.
LET'S SEE...
I THINK MY MOM MUST HAVE TAUGHT HIM...
I DON'T REALLY KNOW ANYTHING ABOUT IT!
OH, I SEE ...
ANYWAY, SHE'S LEARNING TOILET TRAINING LITTLE BY LITTLE!
THE REAL PROBLEM IS HER BITING HABIT, ISN'T IT?
SNIFF
SNIFF
SNIFF

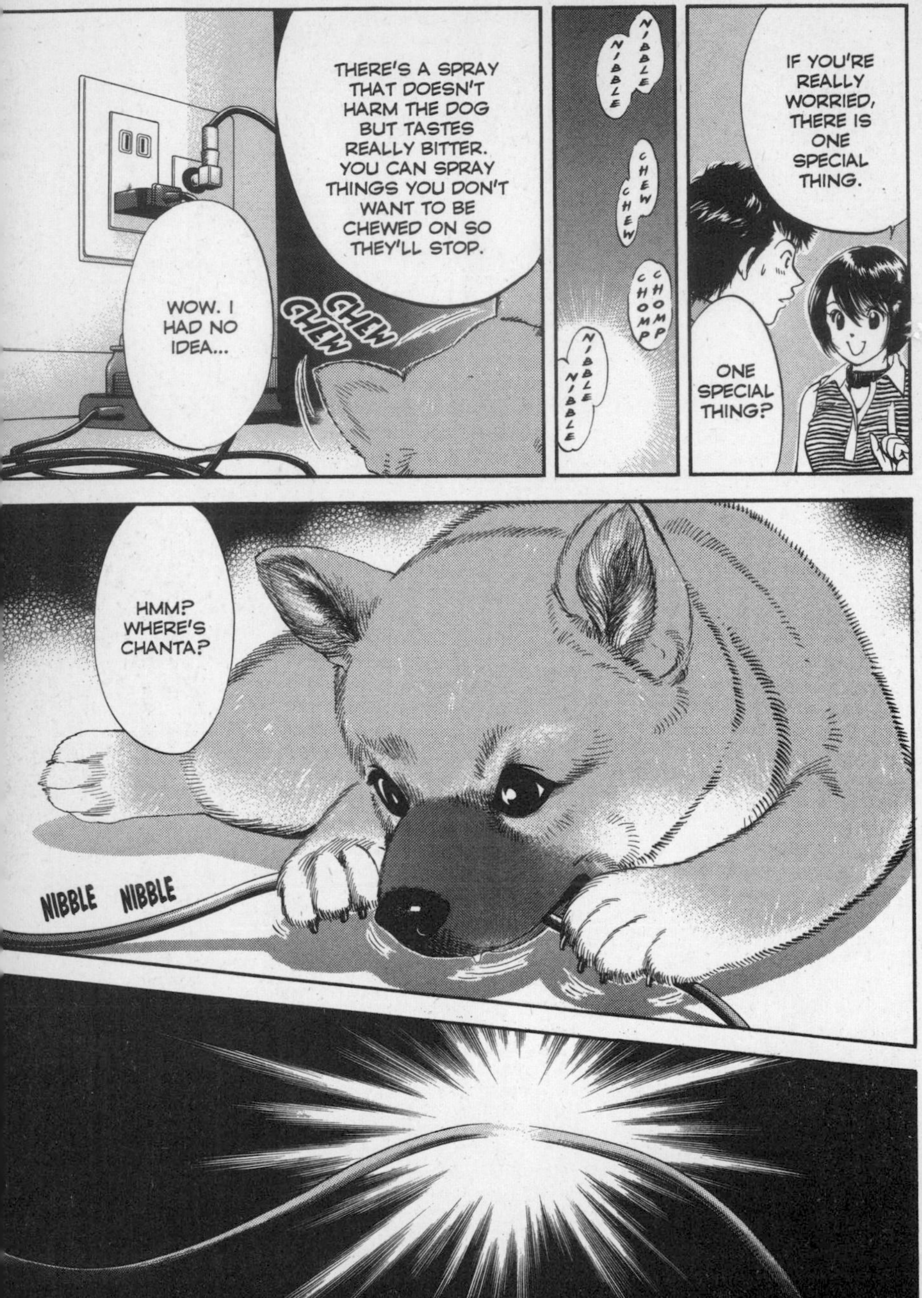
IF YOU'RE REALLY WORRIED, THERE IS ONE SPECIAL THING.
ONE SPECIAL THING?
NIBBLE NIBBLE
CHEW CHEW
CHOMP CHOMP
NIBBLE NIBBLE
THERE'S A SPRAY THAT DOESN'T HARM THE DOG BUT TASTES REALLY BITTER. YOU CAN SPRAY THINGS YOU DON'T WANT TO BE CHEWED ON SO THEY'LL STOP.
WOW. I HAD NO IDEA...
CHEW CHEW
HMM? WHERE'S CHANTA?
NIBBLE NIBBLE

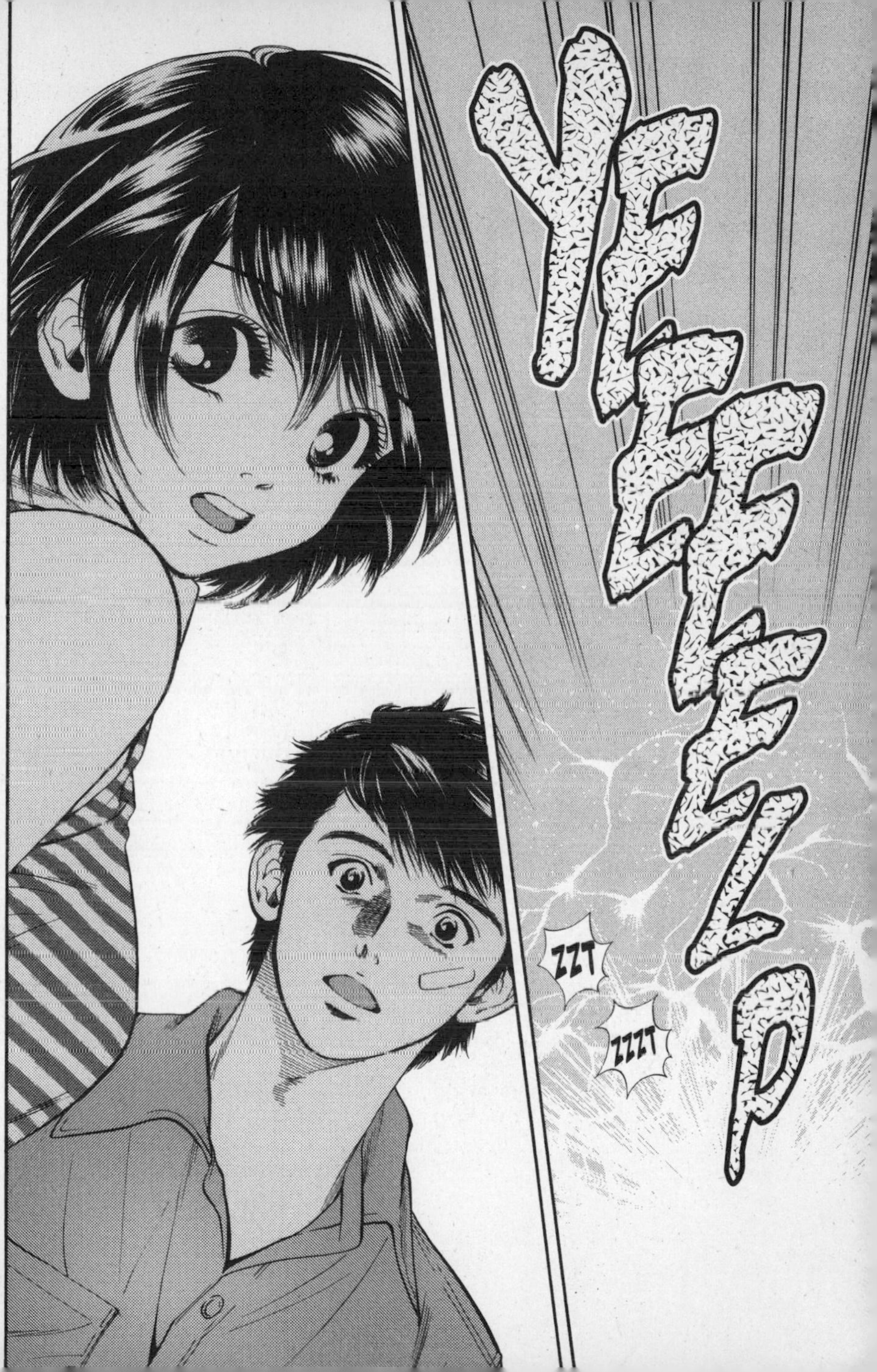
YEEEEEP
ZZT
ZZZT

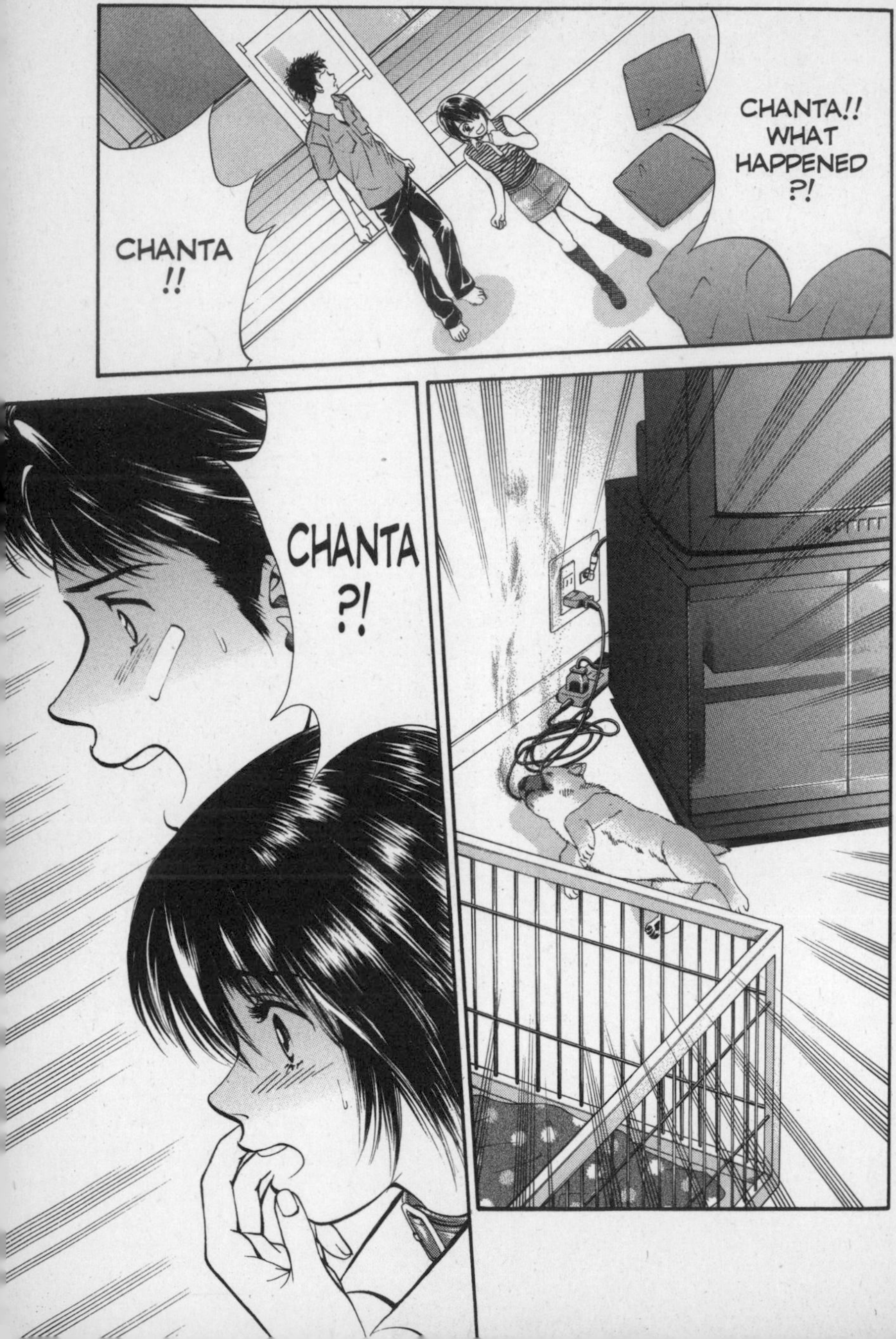
CHANTA!! WHAT HAPPENED ?!
CHANTA !!
CHANTA ?!

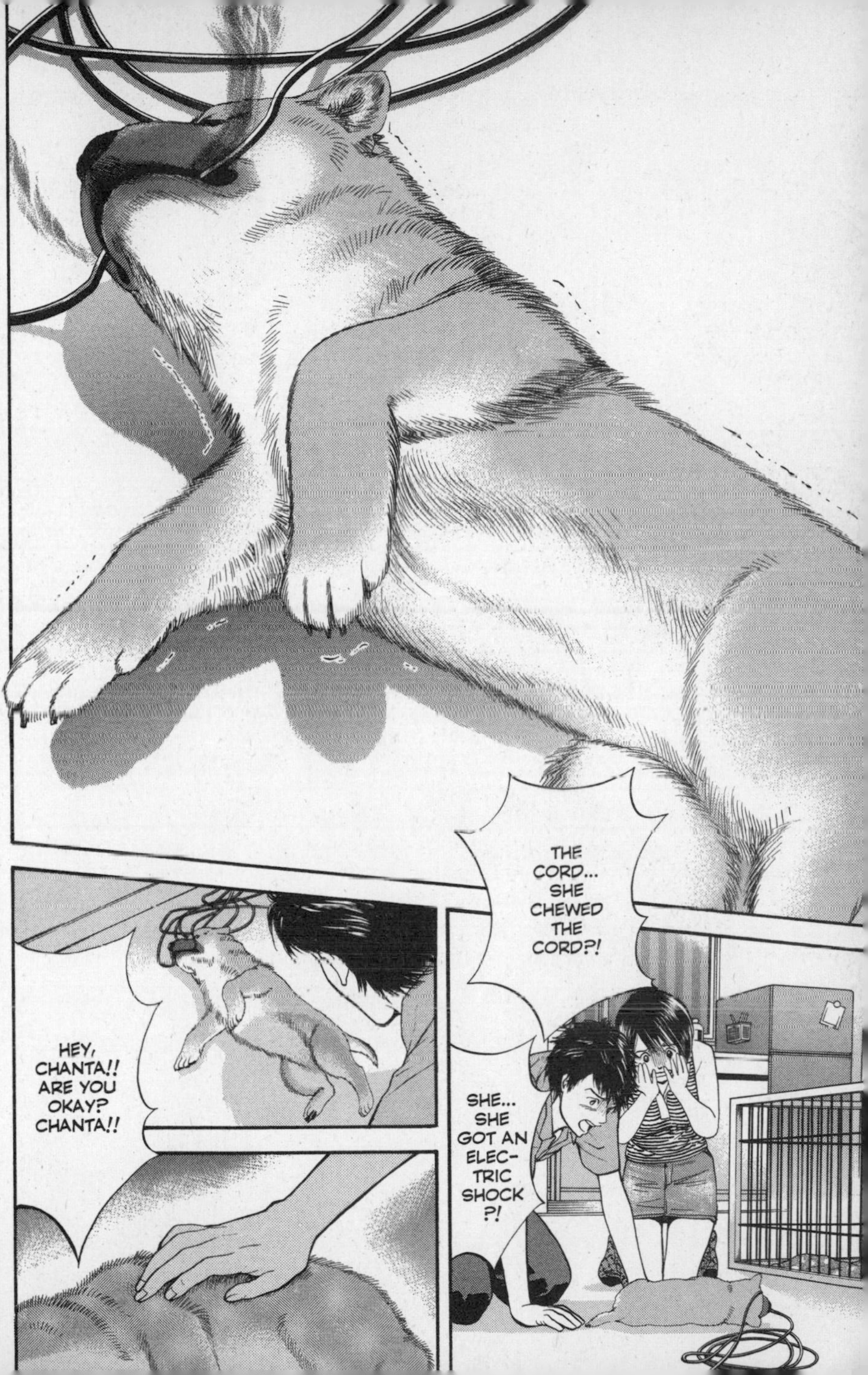
THE CORD... SHE CHEWED THE CORD?!
SHE... SHE GOT AN ELEC-TRIC SHOCK?!
HEY, CHANTA!! ARE YOU OKAY? CHANTA!!

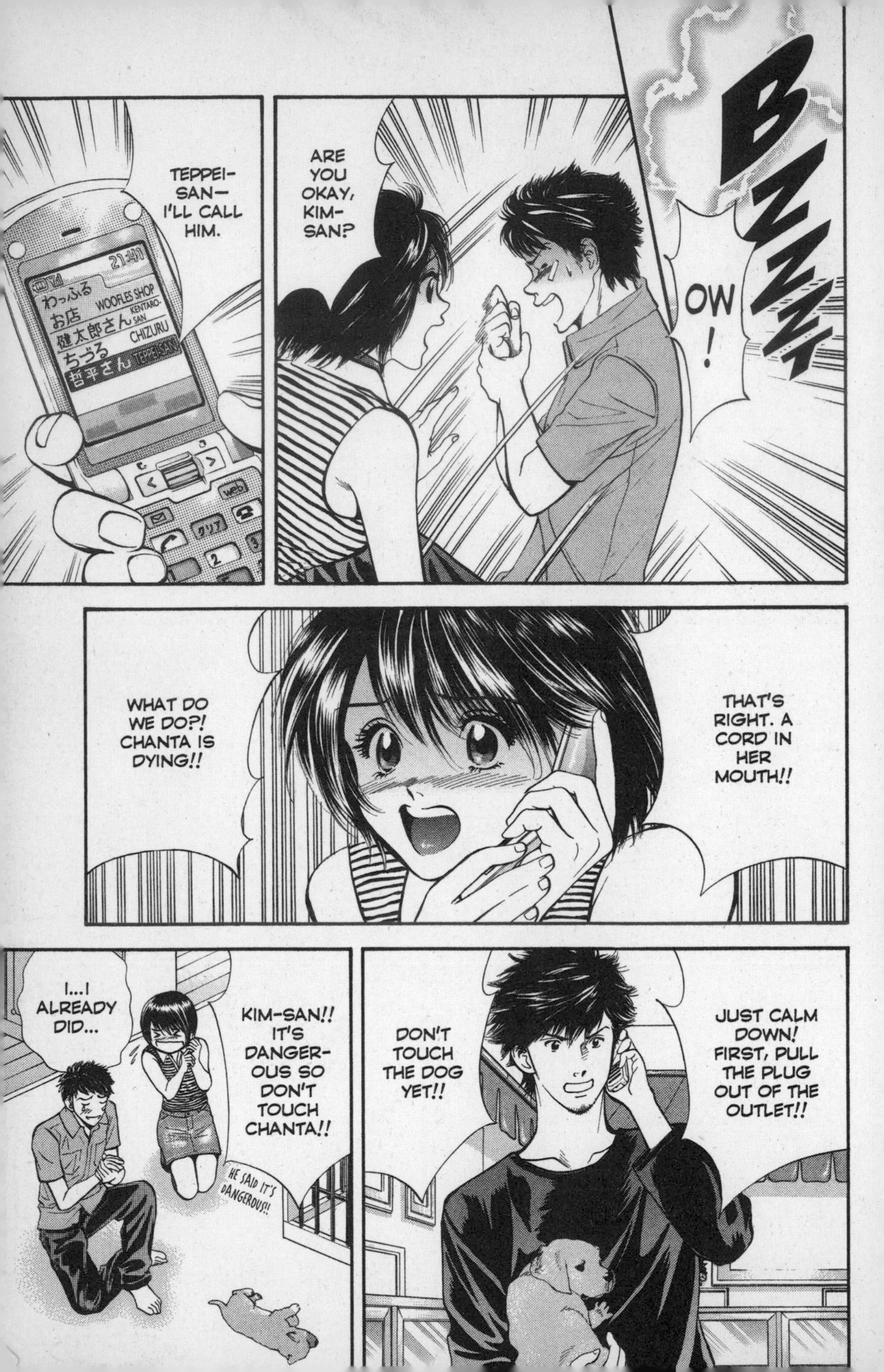
BZZZK
OW!
ARE YOU OKAY, KIM-SAN?
TEPPEI-SAN— I'LL CALL HIM.
わっふる
お店
WOOFLES SHOP
健太郎さん
KENTARO-SAN
ちづる
CHIZURU
哲平さん
TEPPEI-SAN
THAT'S RIGHT. A CORD IN HER MOUTH!!
WHAT DO WE DO?! CHANTA IS DYING!!
JUST CALM DOWN! FIRST, PULL THE PLUG OUT OF THE OUTLET!!
DON'T TOUCH THE DOG YET!!
KIM-SAN!! IT'S DANGER-OUS SO DON'T TOUCH CHANTA!!
I...I ALREADY DID...
HE SAID IT'S DANGEROUS!!

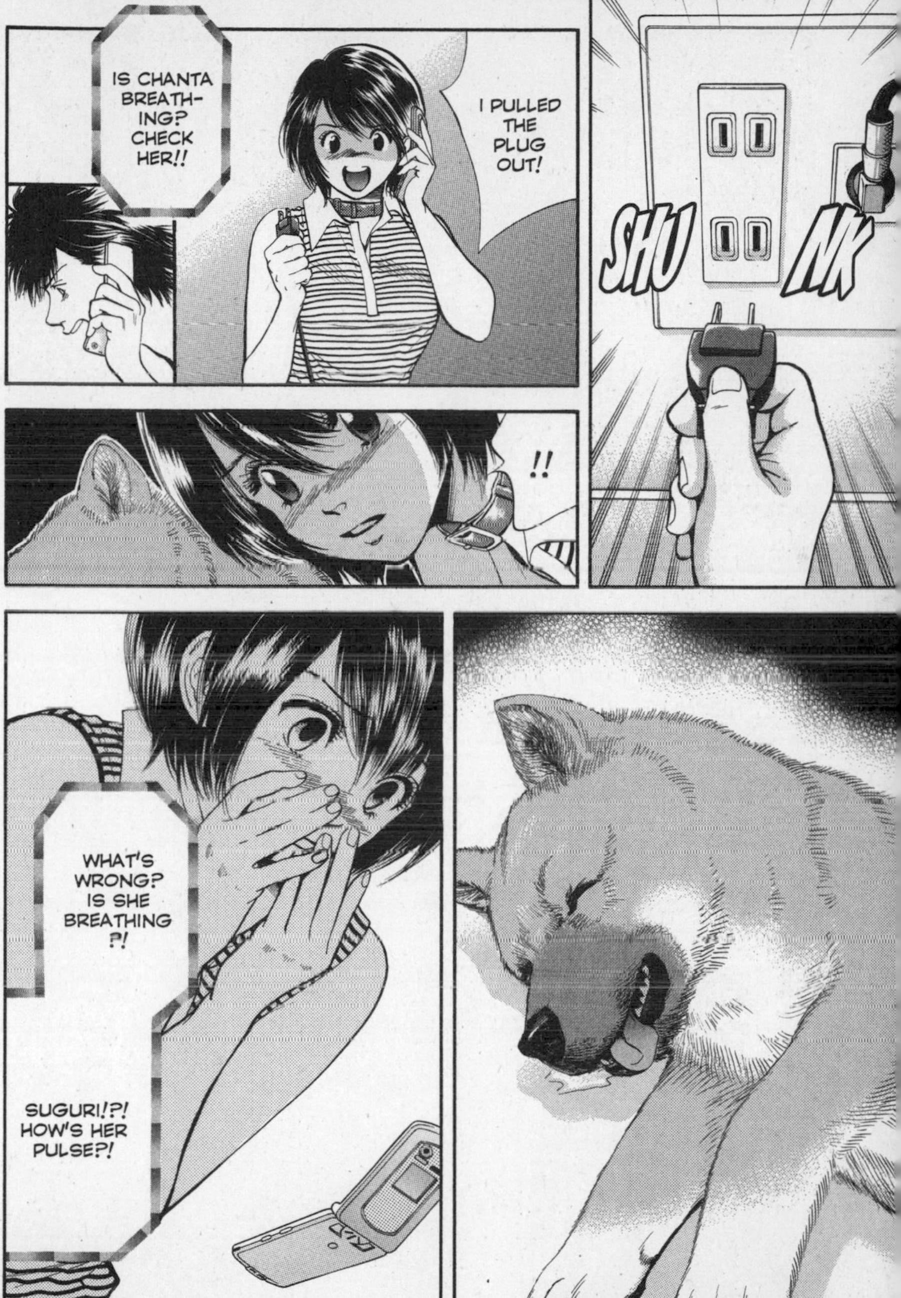
SHU
NK
I PULLED THE PLUG OUT!
IS CHANTA BREATHING? CHECK HER!!
!!
WHAT'S WRONG? IS SHE BREATHING ?!
SUGURI!?! HOW'S HER PULSE?!

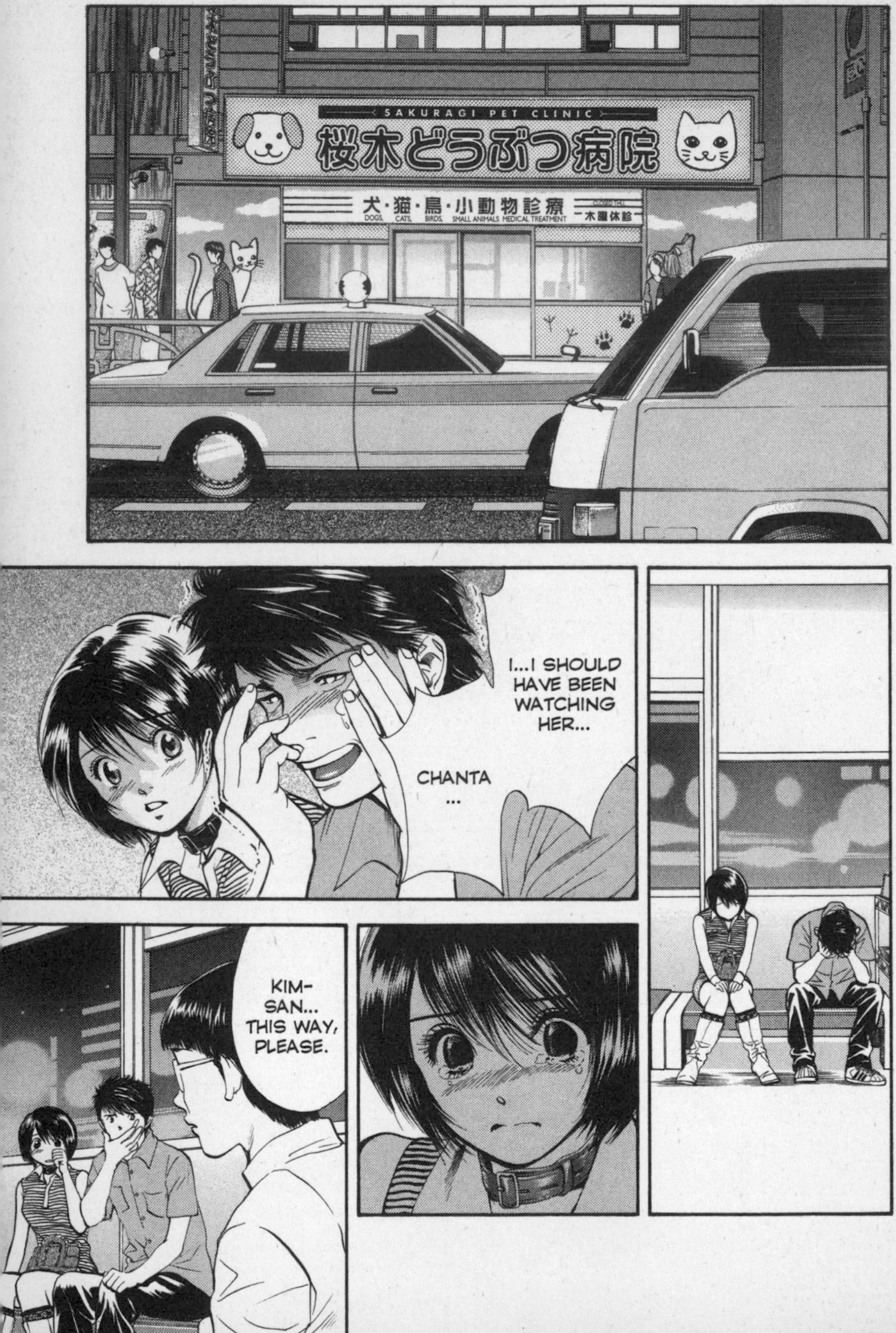
SAKURAGI PET CLINIC
桜木どうぶつ病院
犬・猫・鳥・小動物診療
DOGS, CATS, BIRDS, SMALL ANIMALS MEDICAL TREATMENT
CLOSED THU.
木曜休診
I...I SHOULD HAVE BEEN WATCHING HER...
CHANTA ...
KIM-SAN... THIS WAY, PLEASE.

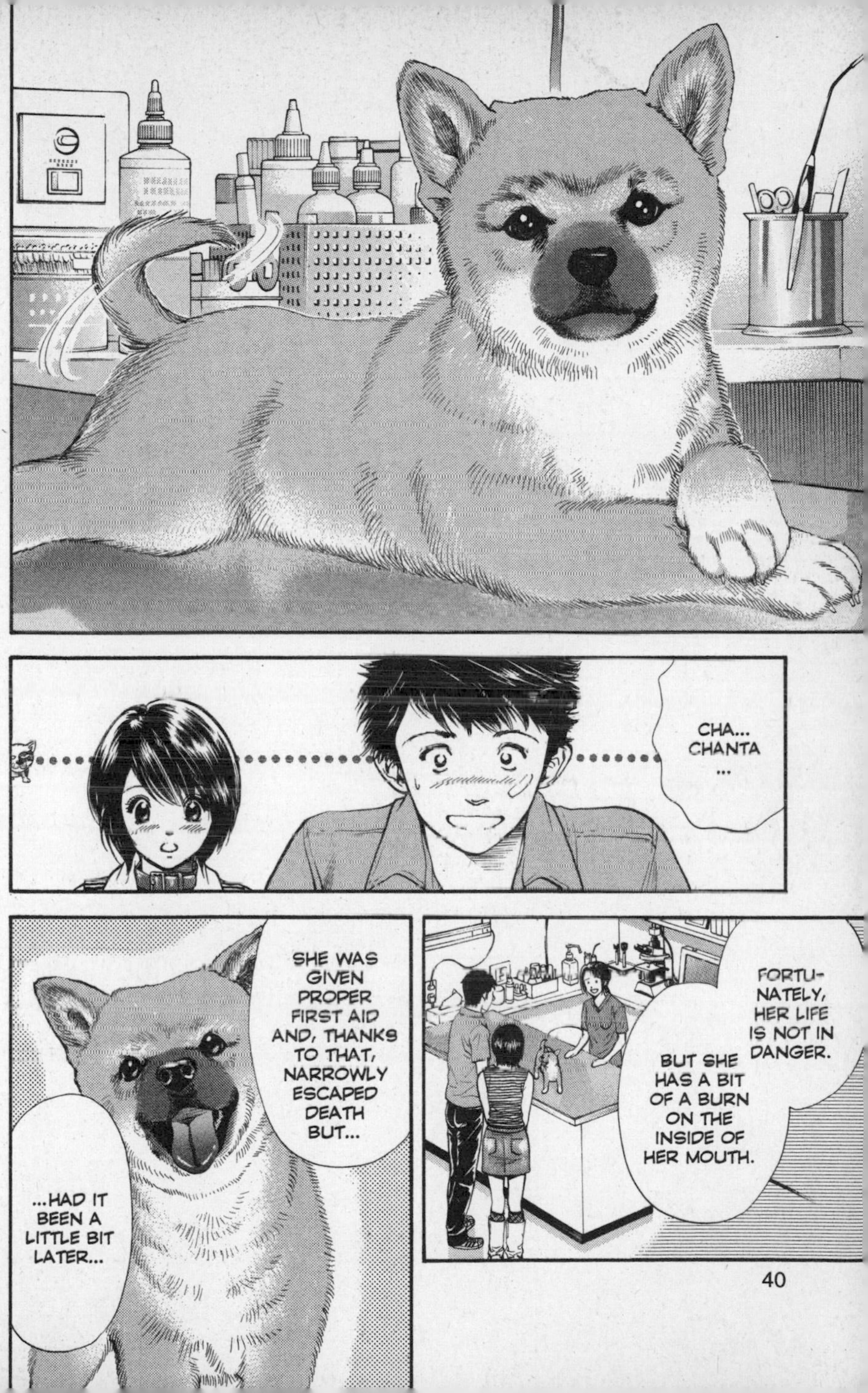
CHA... CHANTA ...
FORTU-NATELY, HER LIFE IS NOT IN DANGER.
BUT SHE HAS A BIT OF A BURN ON THE INSIDE OF HER MOUTH.
SHE WAS GIVEN PROPER FIRST AID AND, THANKS TO THAT, NARROWLY ESCAPED DEATH BUT...
...HAD IT BEEN A LITTLE BIT LATER...

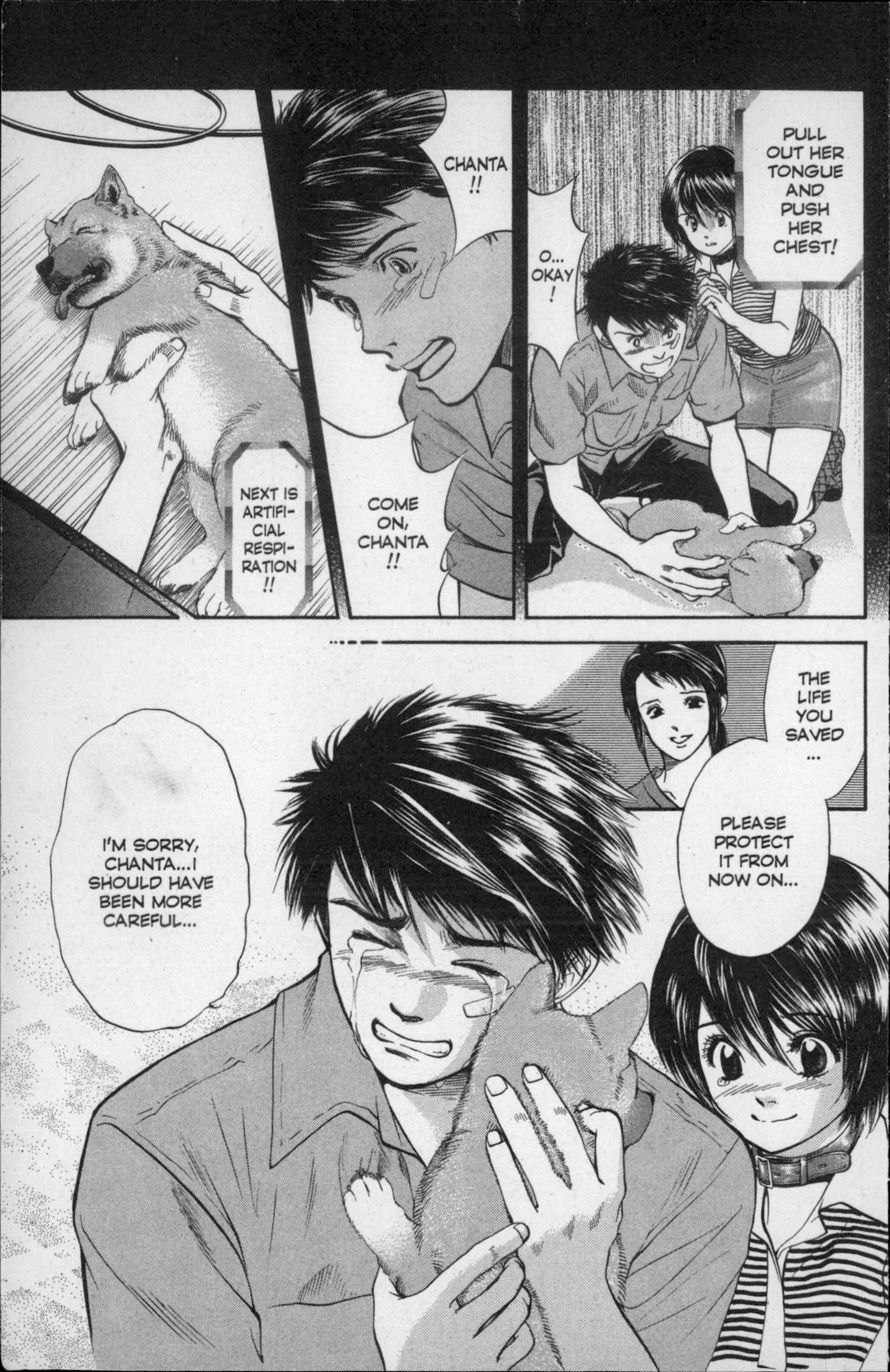
PULL OUT HER TONGUE AND PUSH HER CHEST!
O... OKAY!
CHANTA!!
COME ON, CHANTA!!
NEXT IS ARTIFI-CIAL RESPI-RATION!!
THE LIFE YOU SAVED...
PLEASE PROTECT IT FROM NOW ON...
I'M SORRY, CHANTA...I SHOULD HAVE BEEN MORE CAREFUL...

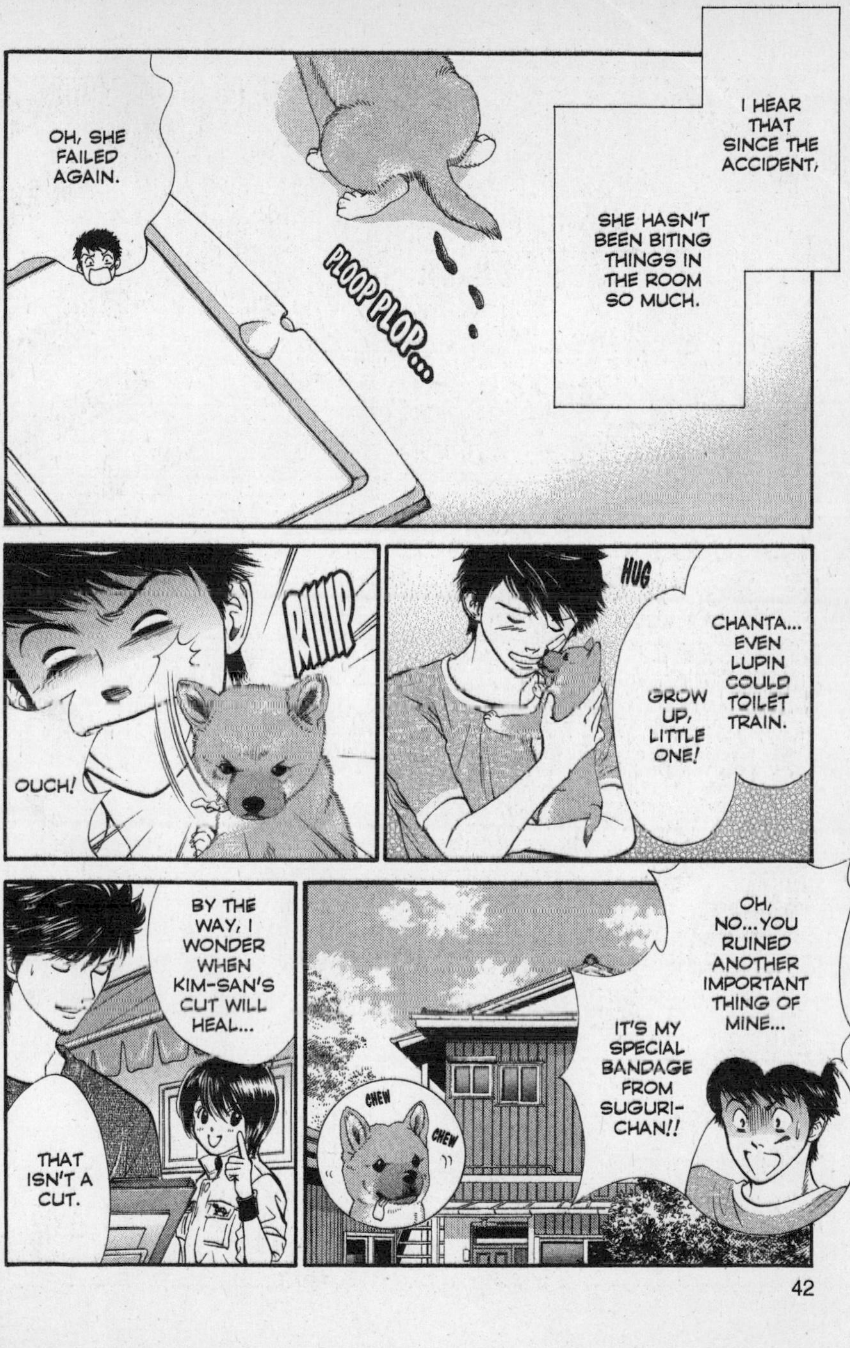
I HEAR THAT SINCE THE ACCIDENT,
SHE HASN'T BEEN BITING THINGS IN THE ROOM SO MUCH.
PLOOP PLOP...
OH, SHE FAILED AGAIN.
HUG
CHANTA... EVEN LUPIN COULD TOILET TRAIN.
GROW UP, LITTLE ONE!
RIIIP
OUCH!
OH, NO...YOU RUINED ANOTHER IMPORTANT THING OF MINE...
IT'S MY SPECIAL BANDAGE FROM SUGURI-CHAN!!
CHEW
CHEW
BY THE WAY, I WONDER WHEN KIM-SAN'S CUT WILL HEAL...
THAT ISN'T A CUT.

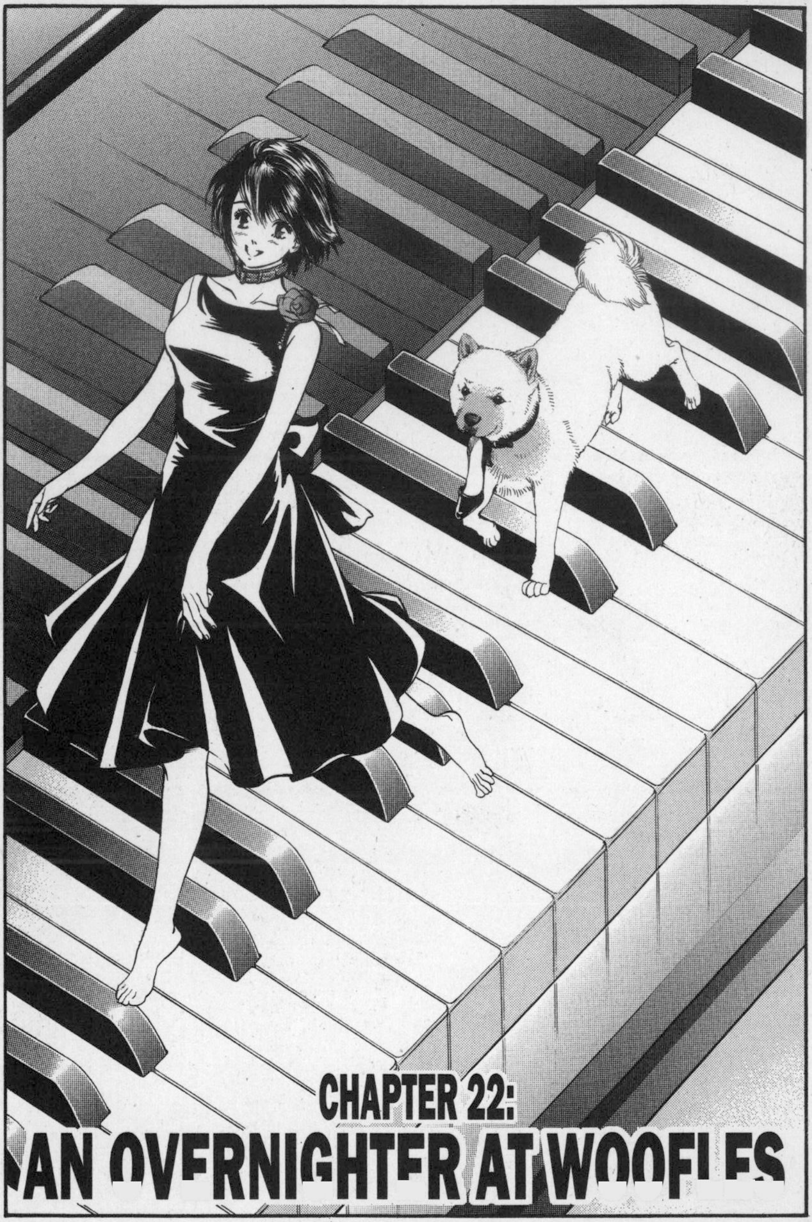
CHAPTER 22:
AN OVERNIGHTER AT WOOFIES

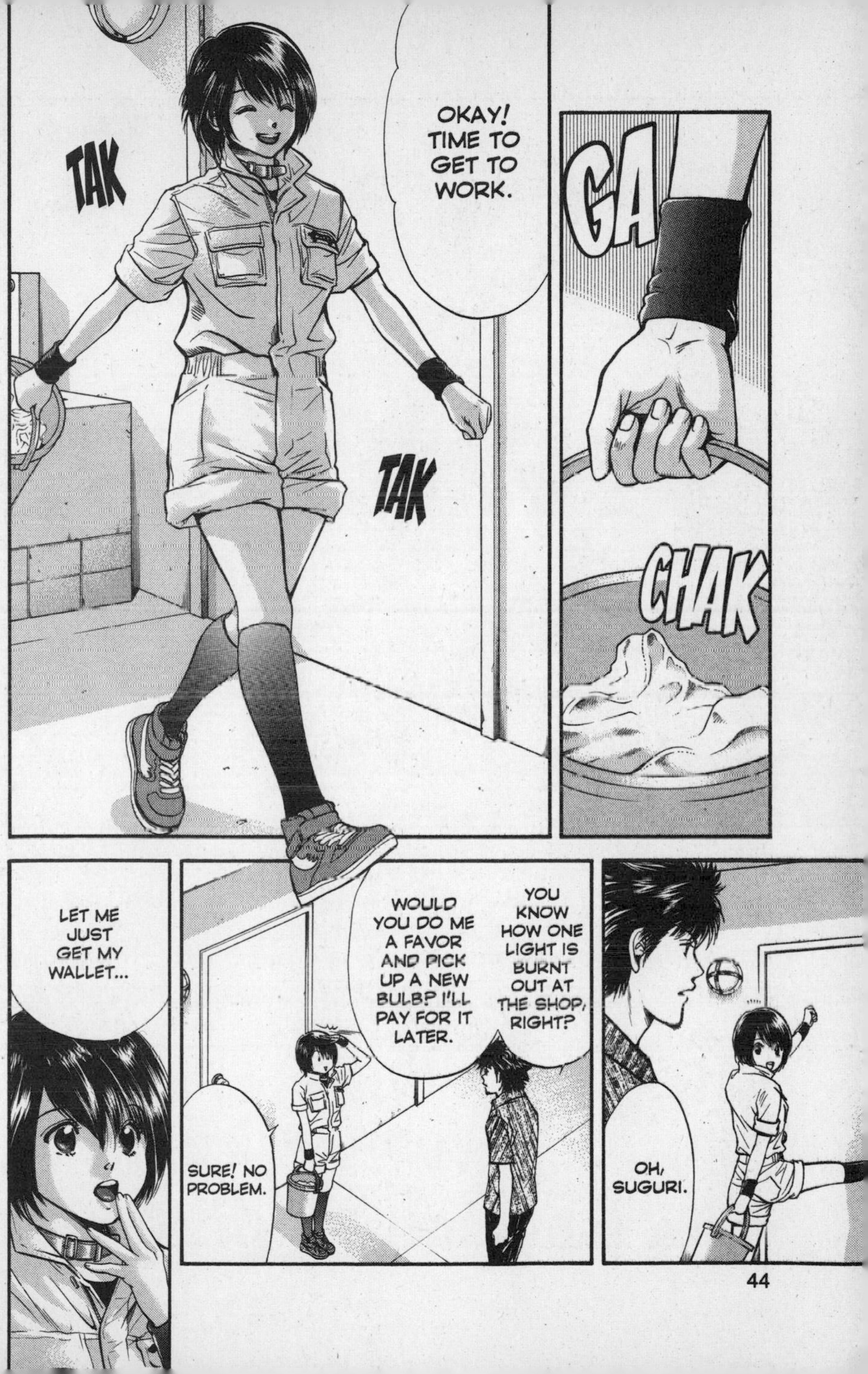
GA
CHAK
TAK
OKAY! TIME TO GET TO WORK.
TAK
OH, SUGURI.
YOU KNOW HOW ONE LIGHT IS BURNT OUT AT THE SHOP, RIGHT?
WOULD YOU DO ME A FAVOR AND PICK UP A NEW BULB? I'LL PAY FOR IT LATER.
SURE! NO PROBLEM.
LET ME JUST GET MY WALLET...

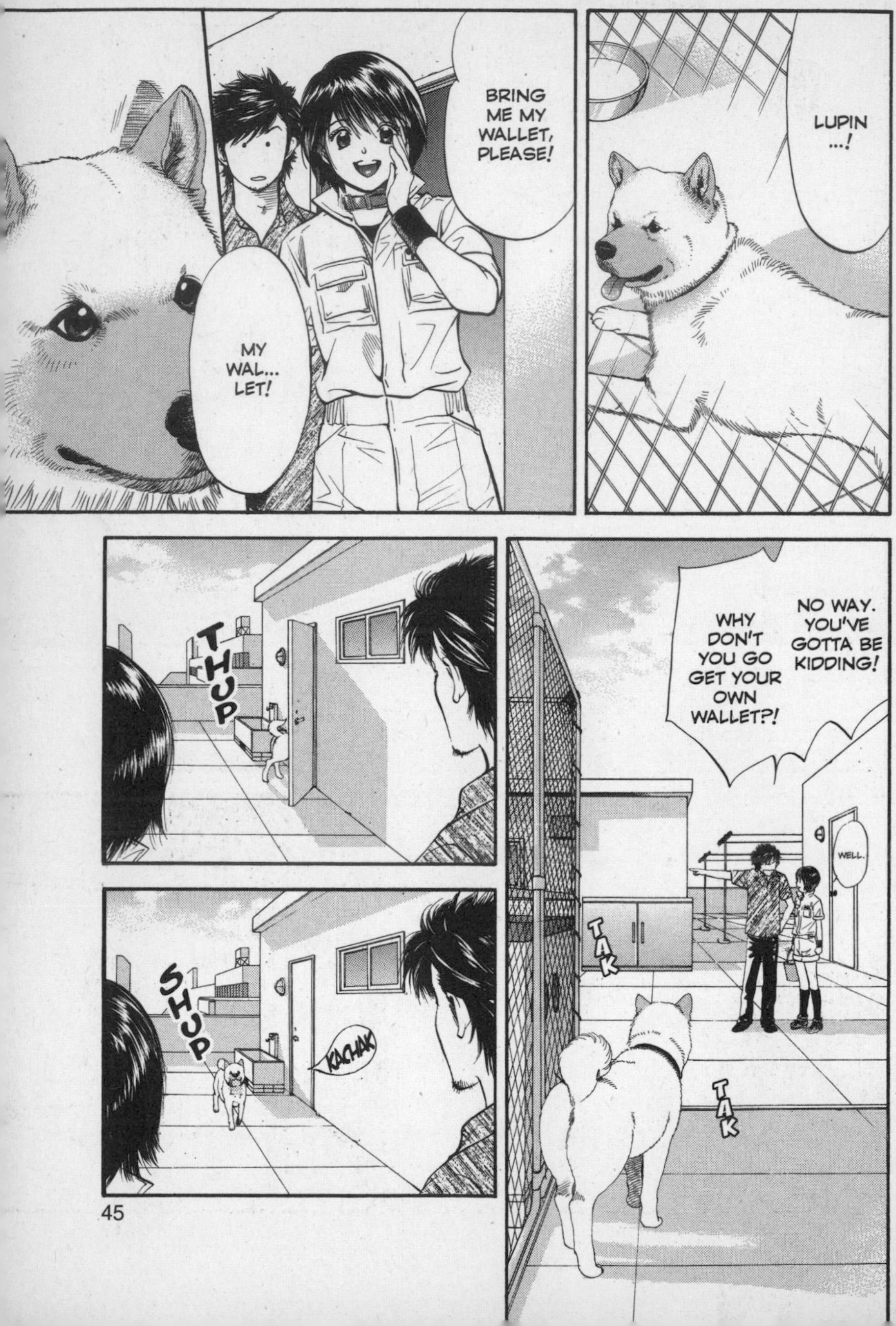
LUPIN ...!
BRING ME MY WALLET, PLEASE!
MY WAL... LET!
NO WAY. YOU'VE GOTTA BE KIDDING!
WHY DON'T YOU GO GET YOUR OWN WALLET?!
WELL.
TAK
TAK
THUP
SHUP
KACHAK

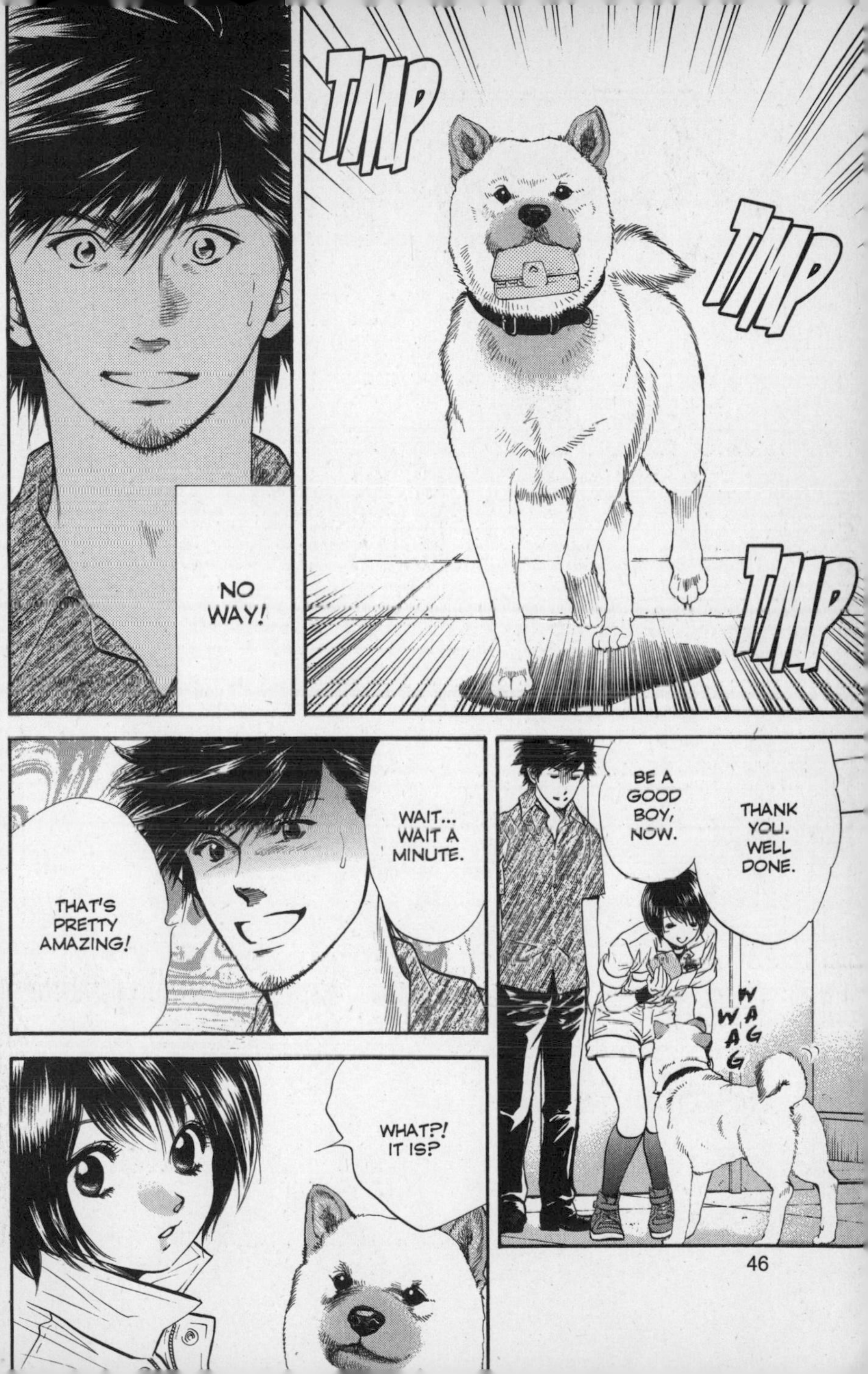
TMP
TMP
TMP
NO WAY!
THANK YOU. WELL DONE.
BE A GOOD BOY, NOW.
WAG WAG
WAIT... WAIT A MINUTE.
THAT'S PRETTY AMAZING!
WHAT?! IT IS?

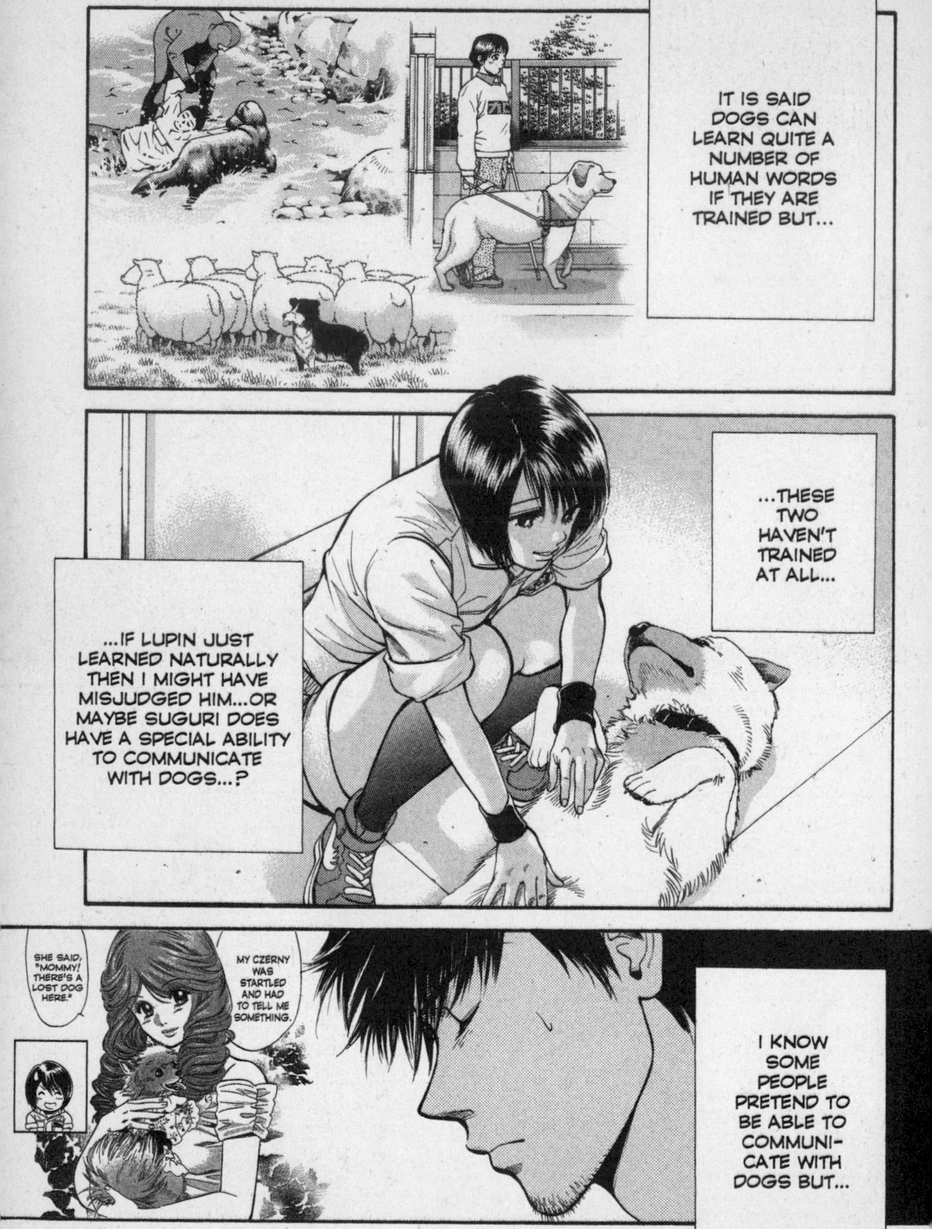
IT IS SAID DOGS CAN LEARN QUITE A NUMBER OF HUMAN WORDS IF THEY ARE TRAINED BUT...
...THESE TWO HAVEN'T TRAINED AT ALL...
...IF LUPIN JUST LEARNED NATURALLY THEN I MIGHT HAVE MISJUDGED HIM...OR MAYBE SUGURI DOES HAVE A SPECIAL ABILITY TO COMMUNICATE WITH DOGS...?
I KNOW SOME PEOPLE PRETEND TO BE ABLE TO COMMUNI-CATE WITH DOGS BUT...
MY CZERNY WAS STARTLED AND HAD TO TELL ME SOMETHING.
SHE SAID, "MOMMY! THERE'S A LOST DOG HERE."

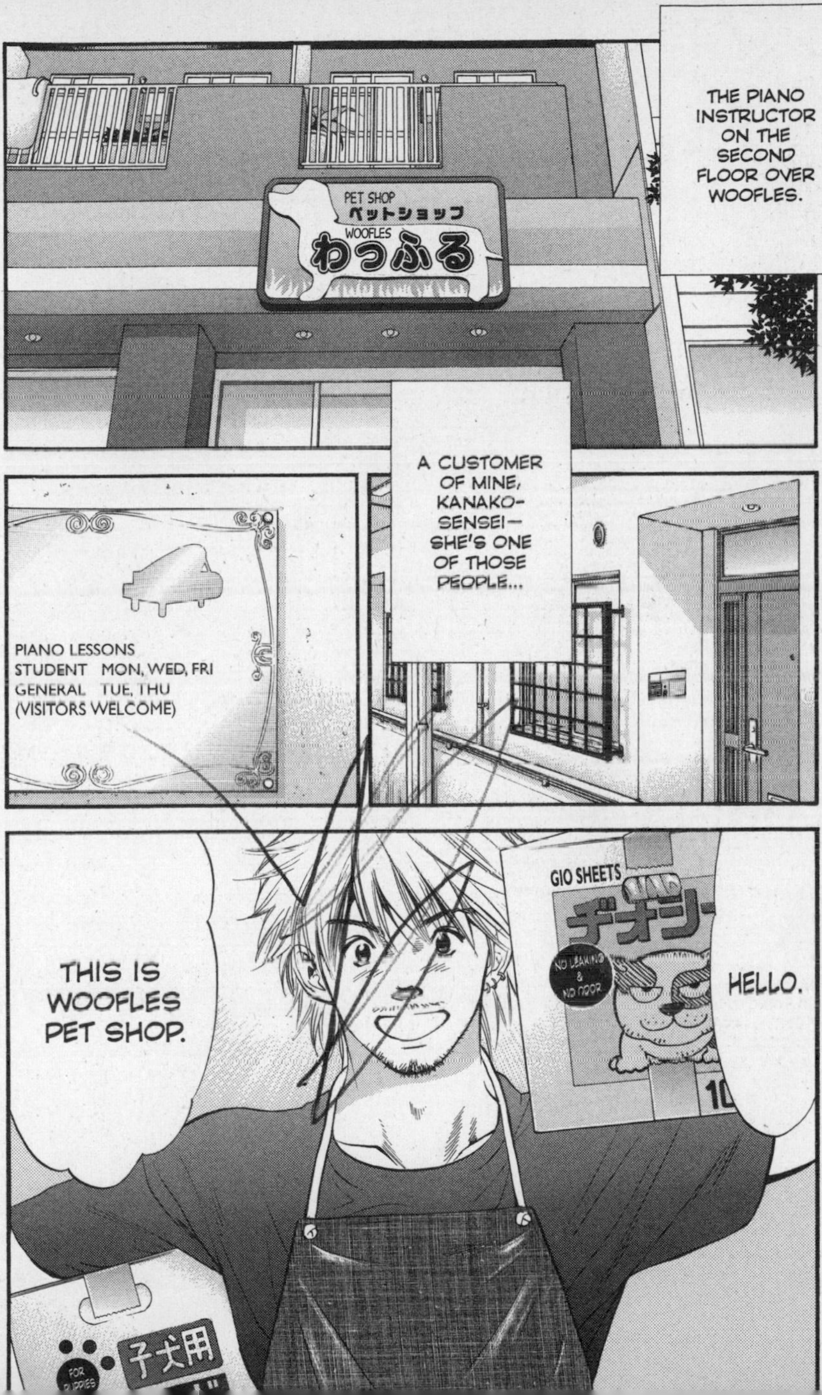
THE PIANO INSTRUCTOR ON THE SECOND FLOOR OVER WOOFLES.
PET SHOP
ペットショップ
WOOFLES
わっふる
A CUSTOMER OF MINE, KANAKO-SENSEI— SHE'S ONE OF THOSE PEOPLE...
PIANO LESSONS
STUDENT MON, WED, FRI
GENERAL TUE, THU
(VISITORS WELCOME)
HELLO.
GIO SHEETS
NO LEAKING & NO ODOR
THIS IS WOOFLES PET SHOP.
FOR PUPPIES
子犬用

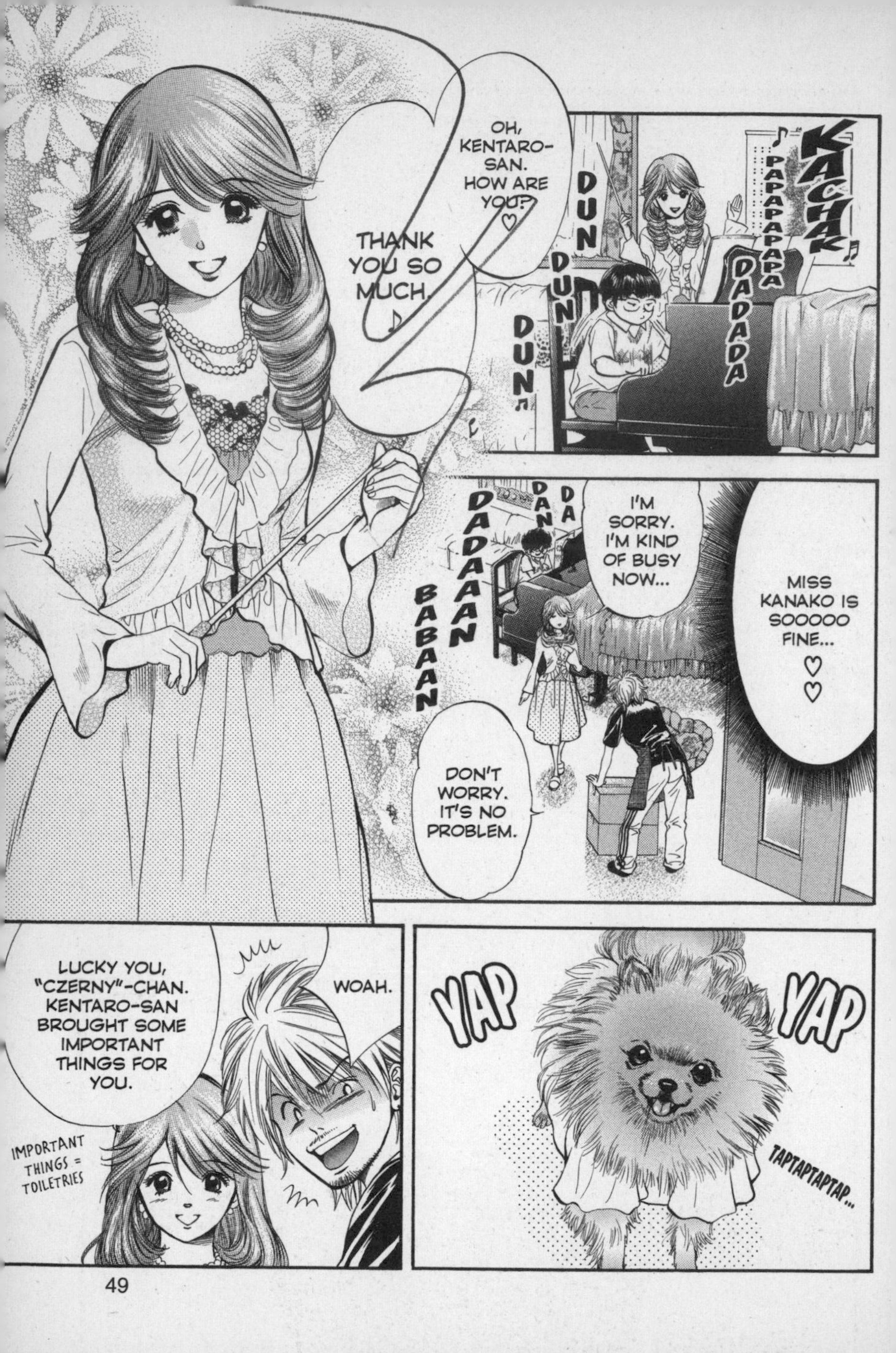
KACHAK
PAPAPAPA
DADADA
DUN DUN DUN DUN
DA DAN DADAAAN BABAAN
MISS KANAKO IS SOOOOO FINE... ♡ ♡
I'M SORRY. I'M KIND OF BUSY NOW...
DON'T WORRY. IT'S NO PROBLEM.
OH, KENTARO-SAN. HOW ARE YOU? ♡
THANK YOU SO MUCH. ♪
YAP YAP
TAPTAPTAPTAP...
WOAH.
LUCKY YOU, "CZERNY"-CHAN. KENTARO-SAN BROUGHT SOME IMPORTANT THINGS FOR YOU.
IMPORTANT THINGS = TOILETRIES

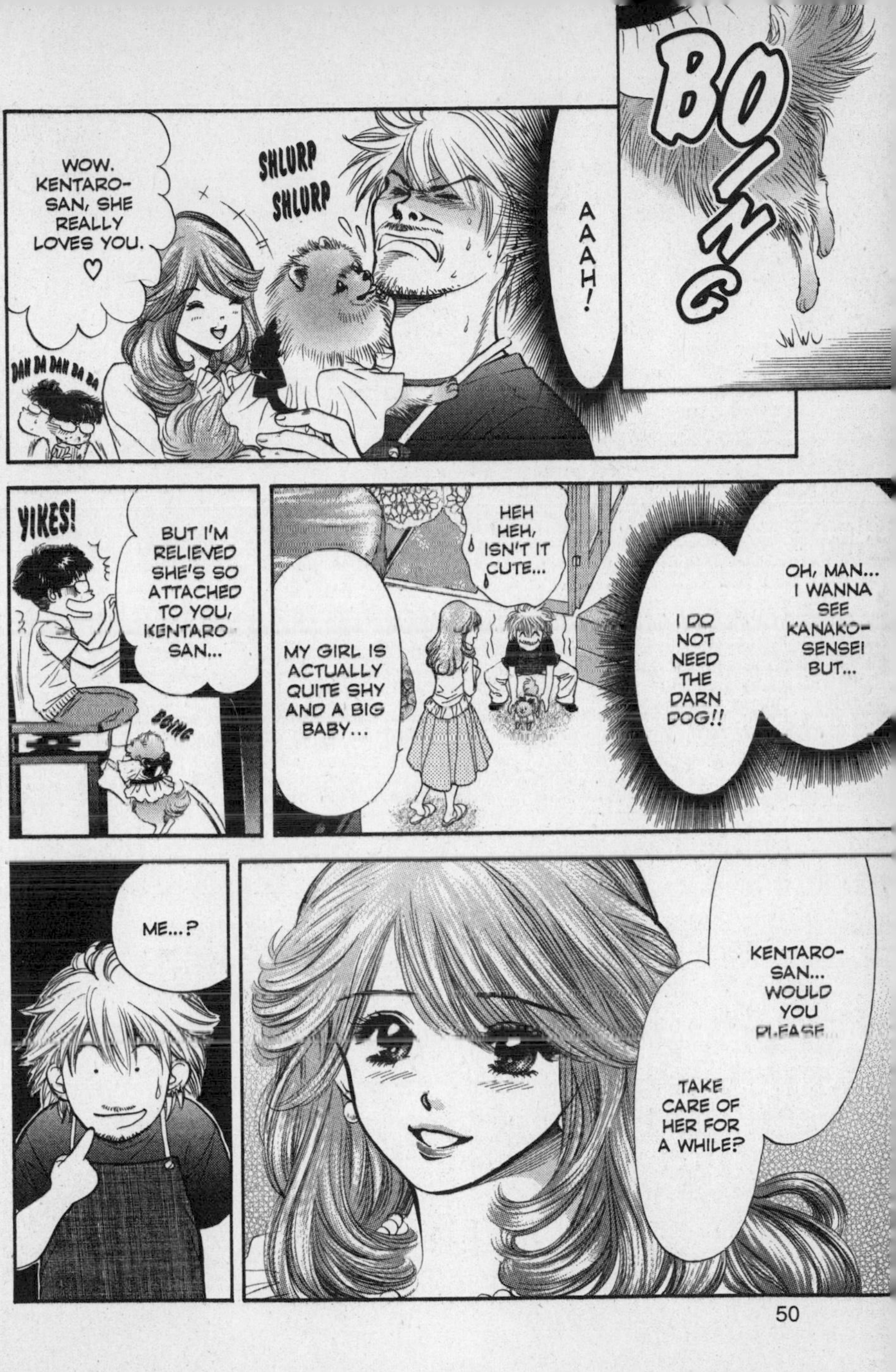
BOING
AAAH!
SHLURP SHLURP
WOW. KENTARO-SAN, SHE REALLY LOVES YOU. ♡
DAH DA DAN DA DA
OH, MAN... I WANNA SEE KANAKO-SENSEI BUT...
I DO NOT NEED THE DARN DOG!!
HEH HEH, ISN'T IT CUTE...
MY GIRL IS ACTUALLY QUITE SHY AND A BIG BABY...
BUT I'M RELIEVED SHE'S SO ATTACHED TO YOU, KENTARO-SAN...
YIKES!
BOING
KENTARO-SAN... WOULD YOU PLEASE...
TAKE CARE OF HER FOR A WHILE?
ME...?

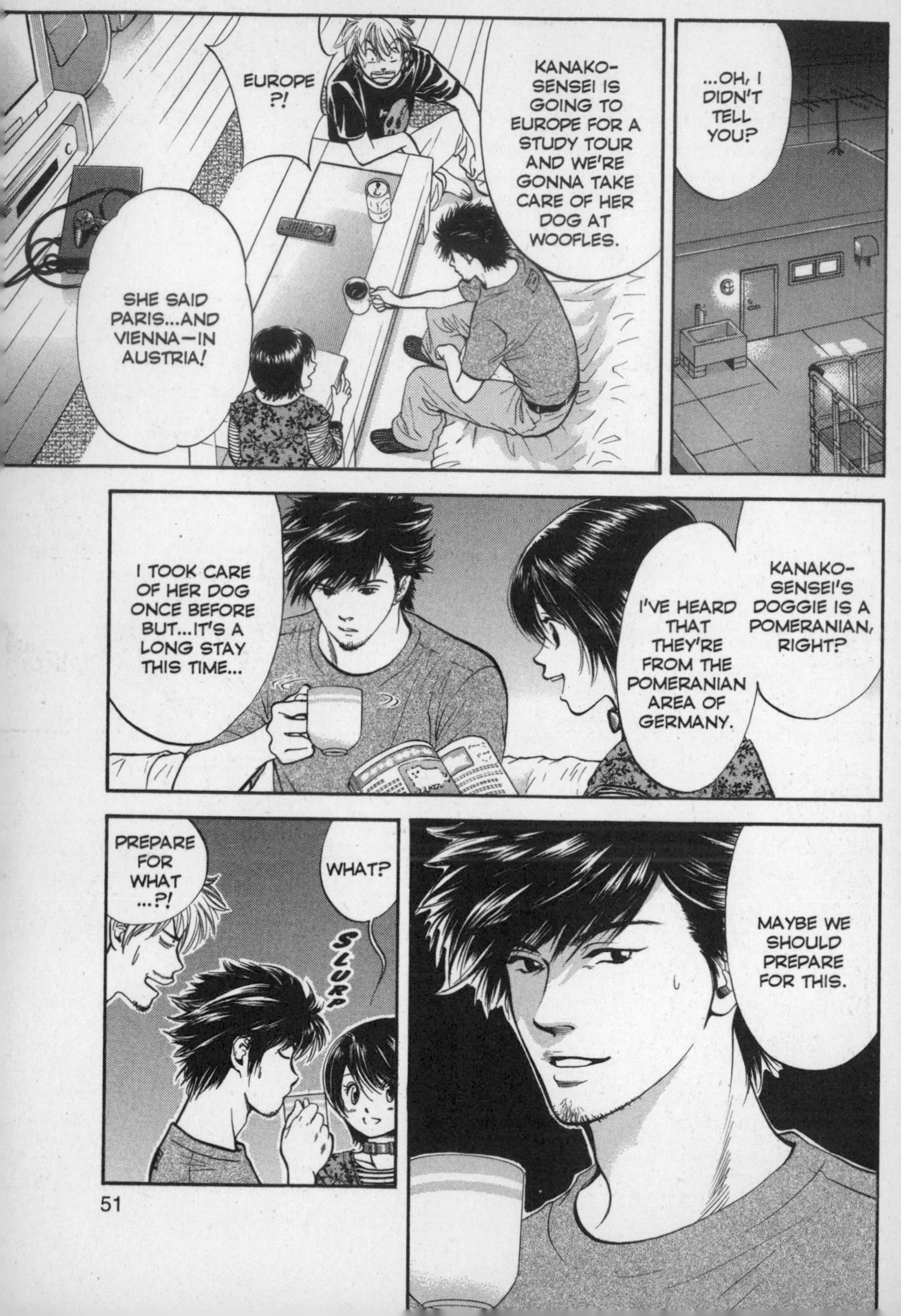
...OH, I DIDN'T TELL YOU?
KANAKO-SENSEI IS GOING TO EUROPE FOR A STUDY TOUR AND WE'RE GONNA TAKE CARE OF HER DOG AT WOOFLES.
EUROPE ?!
SHE SAID PARIS...AND VIENNA—IN AUSTRIA!
KANAKO-SENSEI'S DOGGIE IS A POMERANIAN, RIGHT?
I'VE HEARD THAT THEY'RE FROM THE POMERANIAN AREA OF GERMANY.
I TOOK CARE OF HER DOG ONCE BEFORE BUT...IT'S A LONG STAY THIS TIME...
MAYBE WE SHOULD PREPARE FOR THIS.
WHAT?
SLURP
PREPARE FOR WHAT ...?!

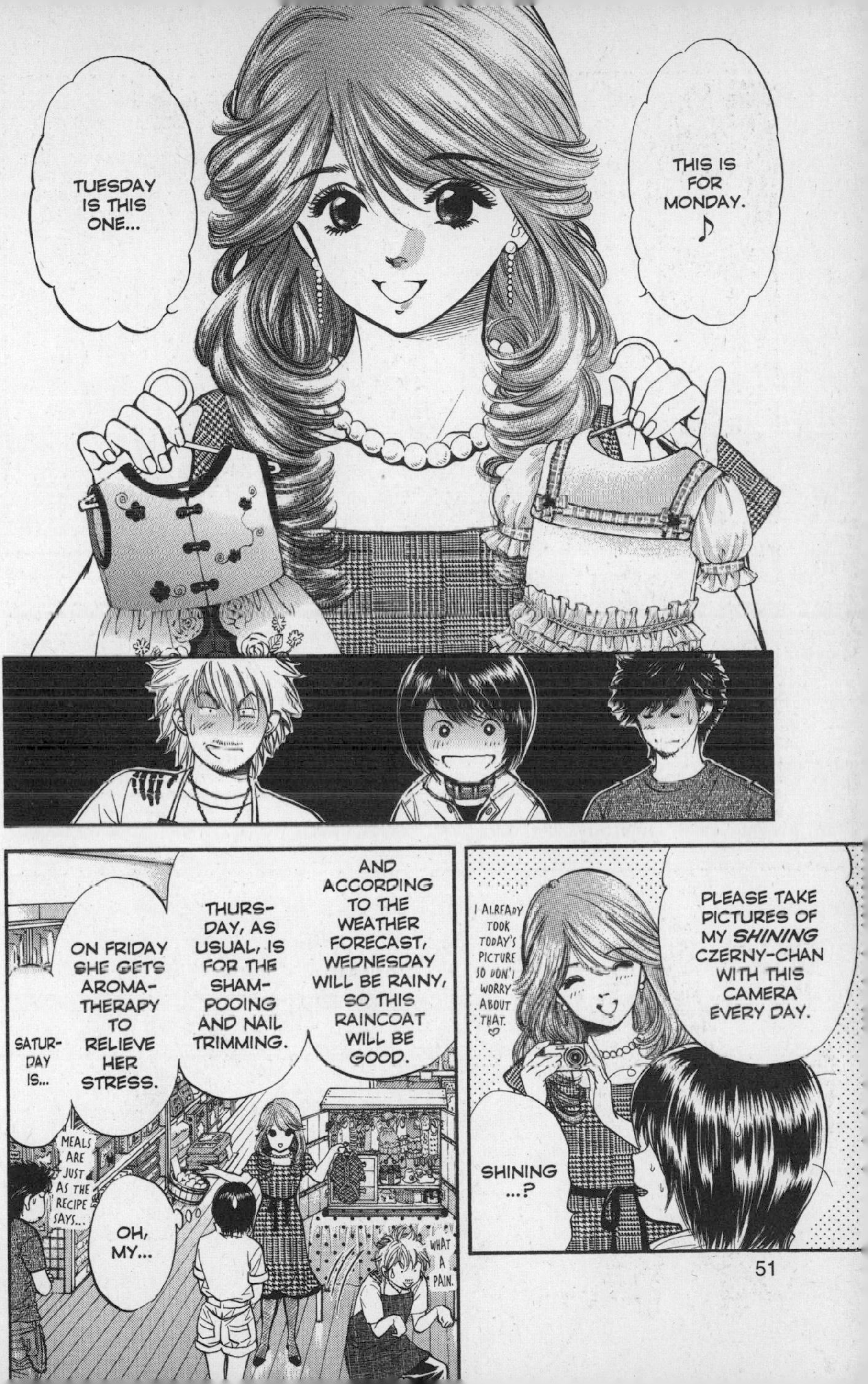

THIS IS FOR MONDAY. ♪
TUESDAY IS THIS ONE...
PLEASE TAKE PICTURES OF MY *SHINING* CZERNY-CHAN WITH THIS CAMERA EVERY DAY.
I ALREADY TOOK TODAY'S PICTURE SO DON'T WORRY ABOUT THAT. ♡
SHINING ...?
AND ACCORDING TO THE WEATHER FORECAST, WEDNESDAY WILL BE RAINY, SO THIS RAINCOAT WILL BE GOOD.
THURS-DAY, AS USUAL, IS FOR THE SHAM-POOING AND NAIL TRIMMING.
ON FRIDAY SHE GETS AROMA-THERAPY TO RELIEVE HER STRESS.
SATUR-DAY IS...
MEALS ARE JUST AS THE RECIPE SAYS...
WHAT A PAIN.
OH, MY...

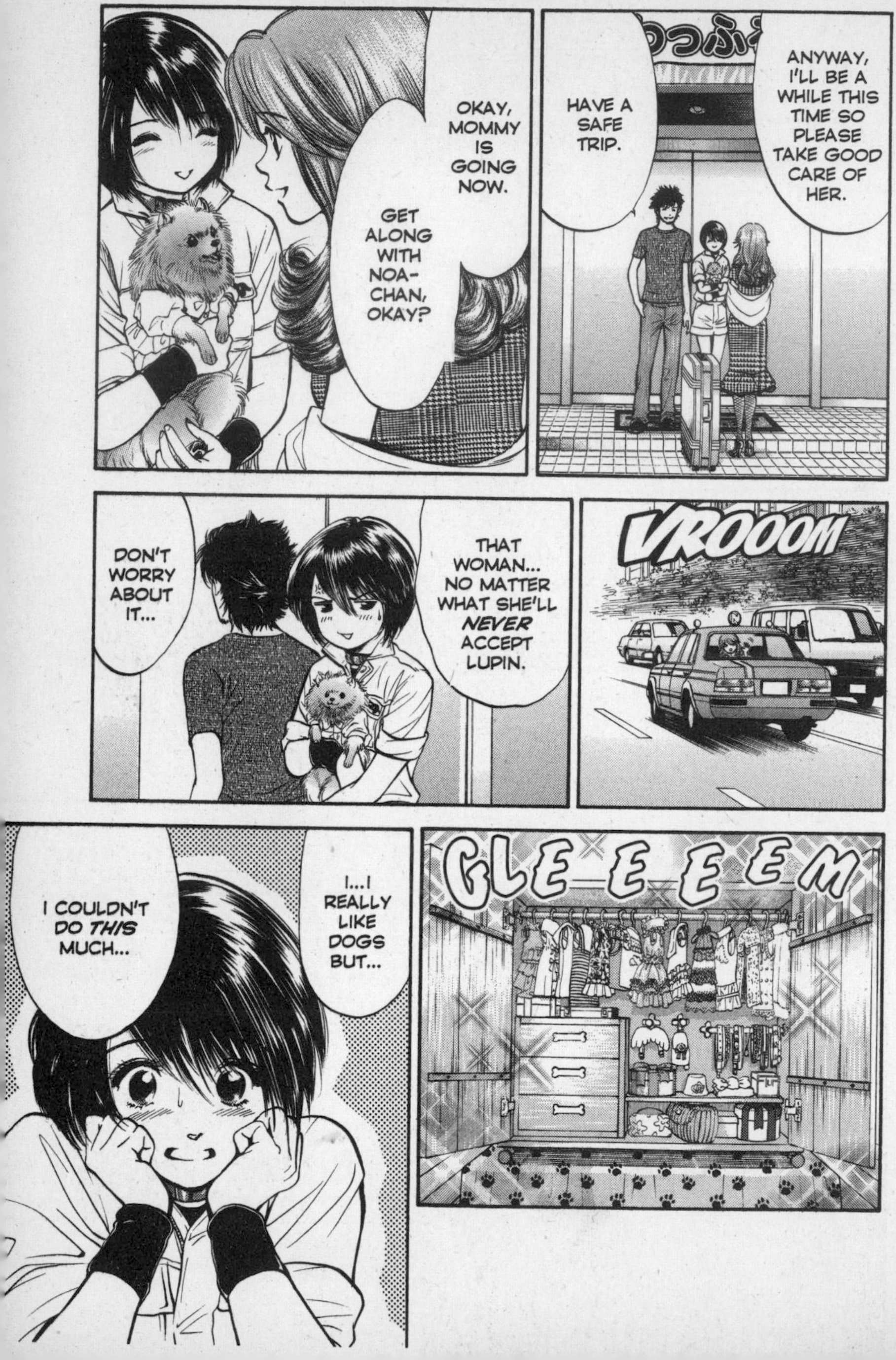
ANYWAY, I'LL BE A WHILE THIS TIME SO PLEASE TAKE GOOD CARE OF HER.
HAVE A SAFE TRIP.
OKAY, MOMMY IS GOING NOW.
GET ALONG WITH NOA-CHAN, OKAY?
VROOOM
THAT WOMAN... NO MATTER WHAT SHE'LL *NEVER* ACCEPT LUPIN.
DON'T WORRY ABOUT IT...
GLE E E EM
I...I REALLY LIKE DOGS BUT...
I COULDN'T DO *THIS* MUCH...

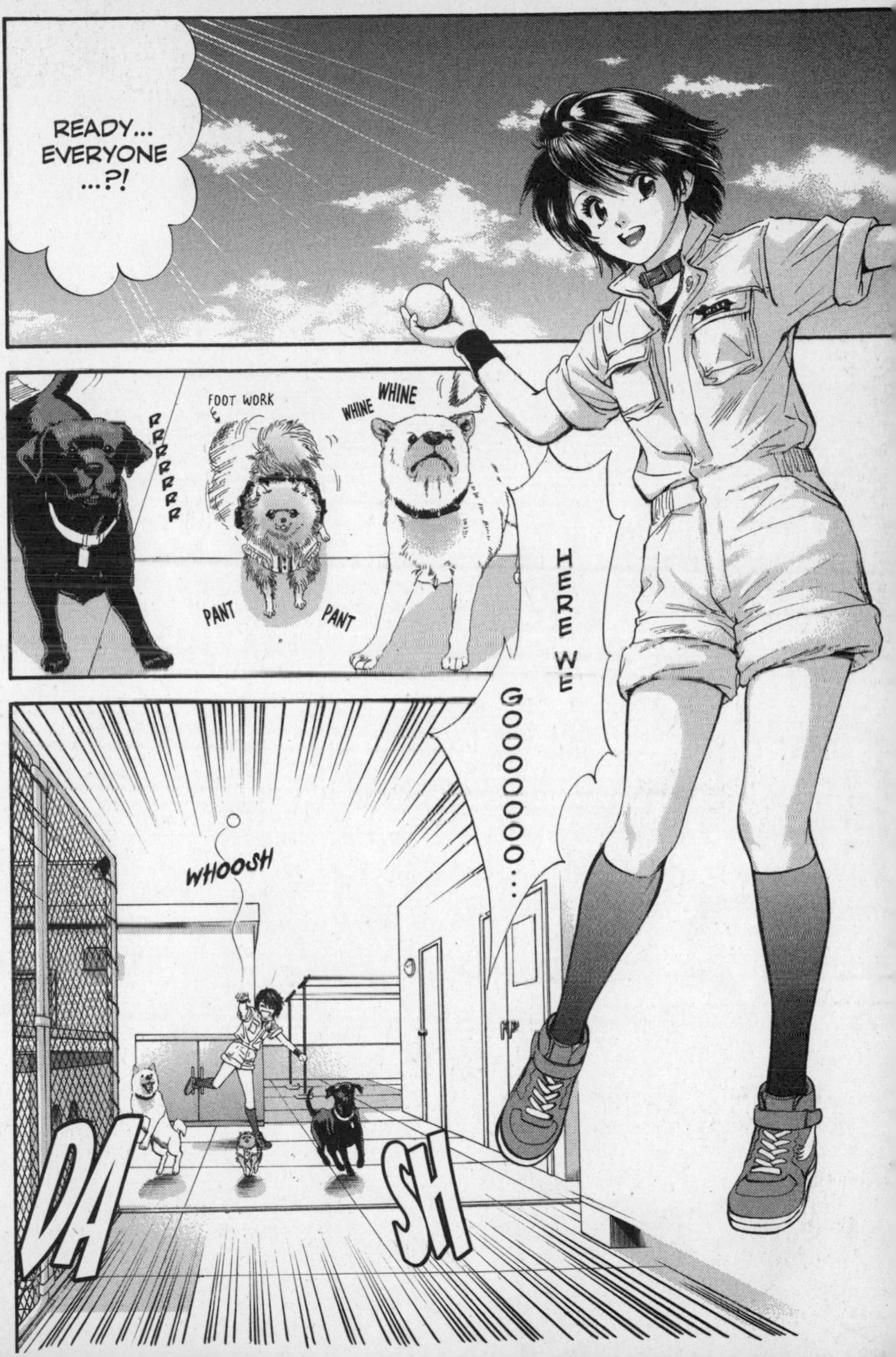
READY... EVERYONE ...?!
WHINE WHINE
FOOT WORK
PANT PANT
RRRRRRR
HERE WE GOOOOOOOO...
WHOOSH
DASH

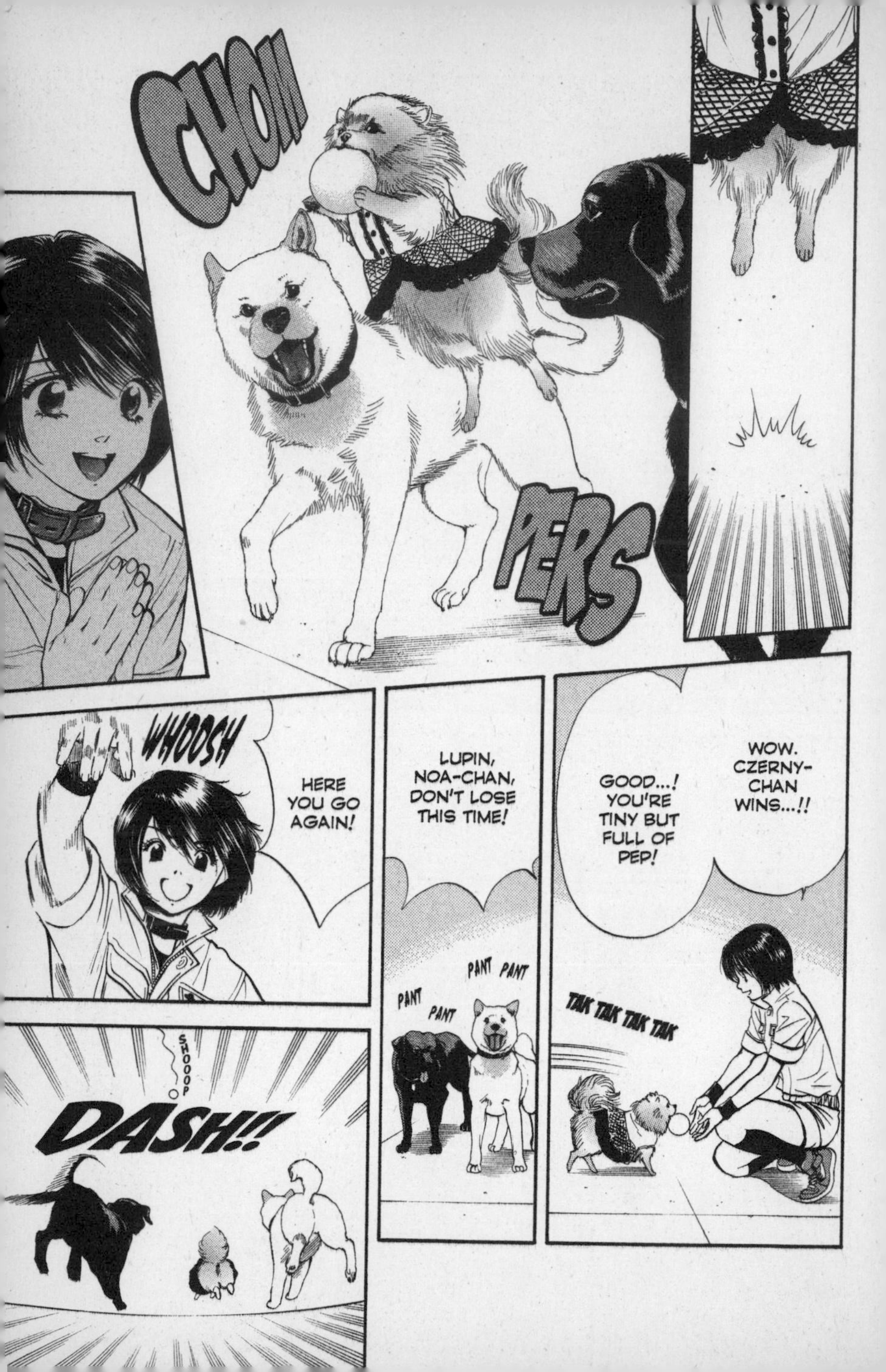
CHOM
PERS
WOW. CZERNY-CHAN WINS...!!
GOOD...! YOU'RE TINY BUT FULL OF PEP!
TAK TAK TAK TAK
LUPIN, NOA-CHAN, DON'T LOSE THIS TIME!
PANT PANT
PANT PANT
WHOOSH
HERE YOU GO AGAIN!
SHOOOOP
DASH!!

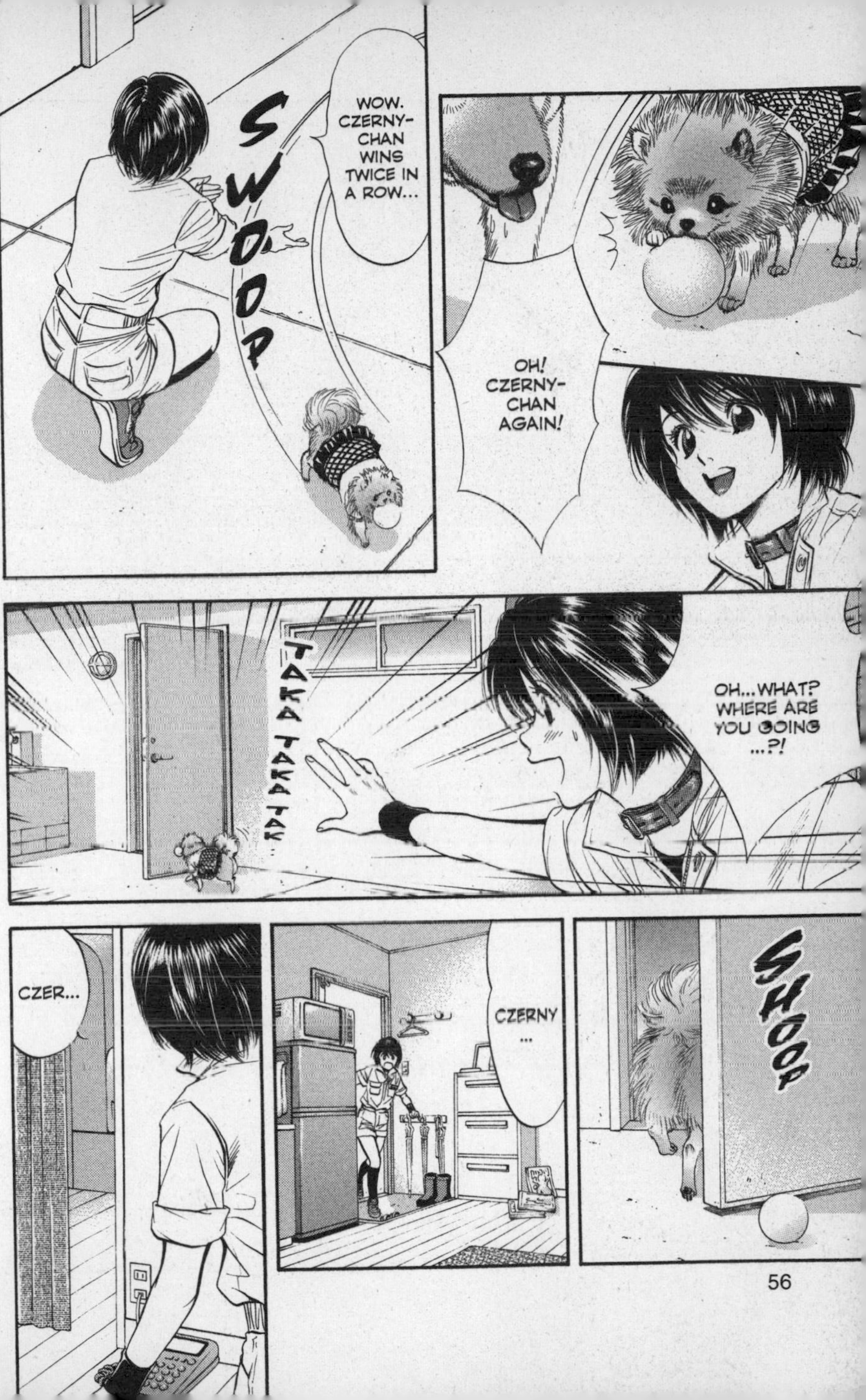
OH! CZERNY-CHAN AGAIN!
WOW. CZERNY-CHAN WINS TWICE IN A ROW...
SWOOP
OH...WHAT? WHERE ARE YOU GOING ...?!
TAKA TAKA TAK...
SHOOP
CZERNY ...
CZER...

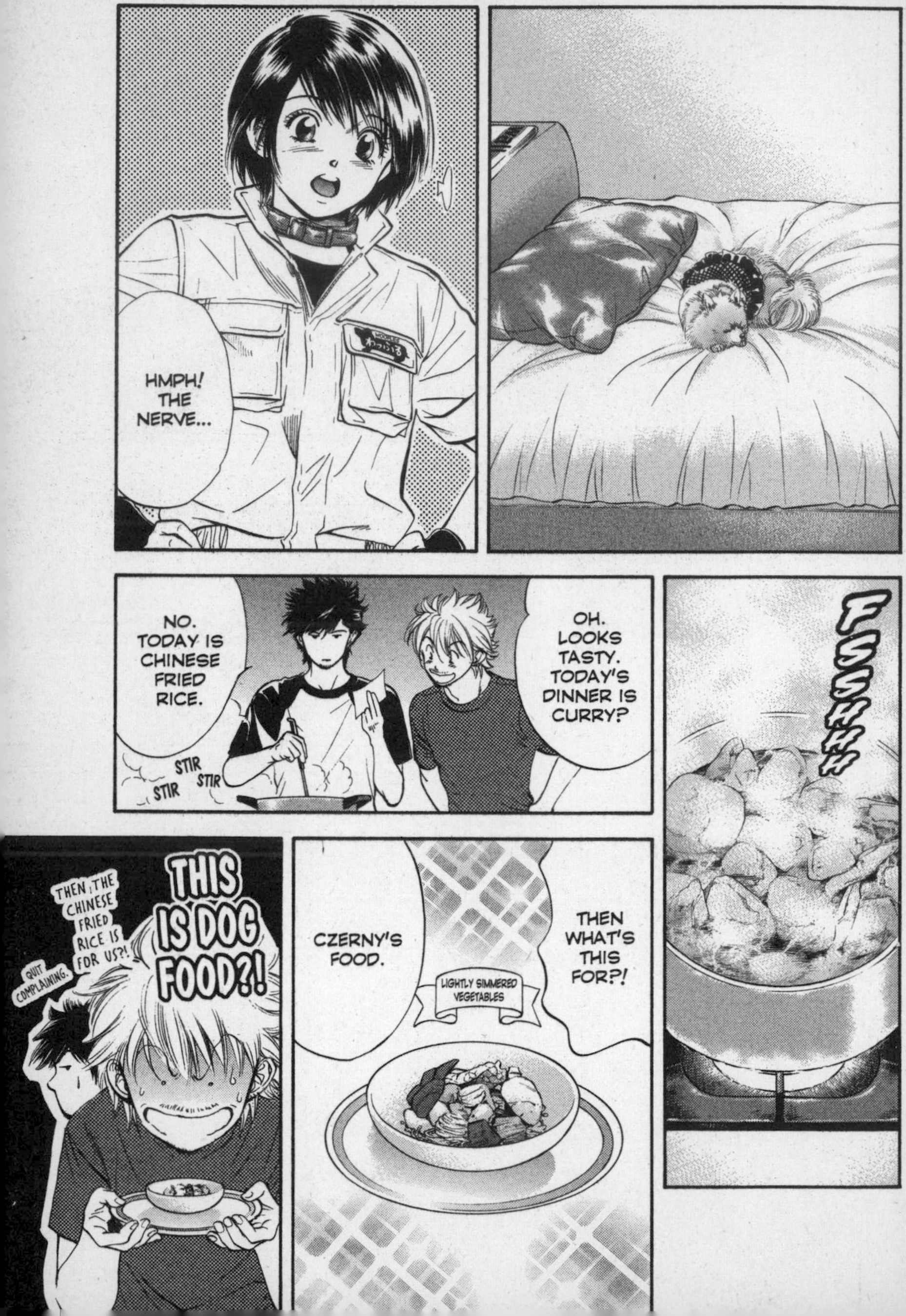
HMPH! THE NERVE...
FSSHHH
OH. LOOKS TASTY. TODAY'S DINNER IS CURRY?
NO. TODAY IS CHINESE FRIED RICE.
STIR STIR STIR
THEN WHAT'S THIS FOR?!
CZERNY'S FOOD.
LIGHTLY SIMMERED VEGETABLES
THIS IS DOG FOOD?!
THEN, THE CHINESE FRIED RICE IS FOR US?!
QUIT COMPLAINING.

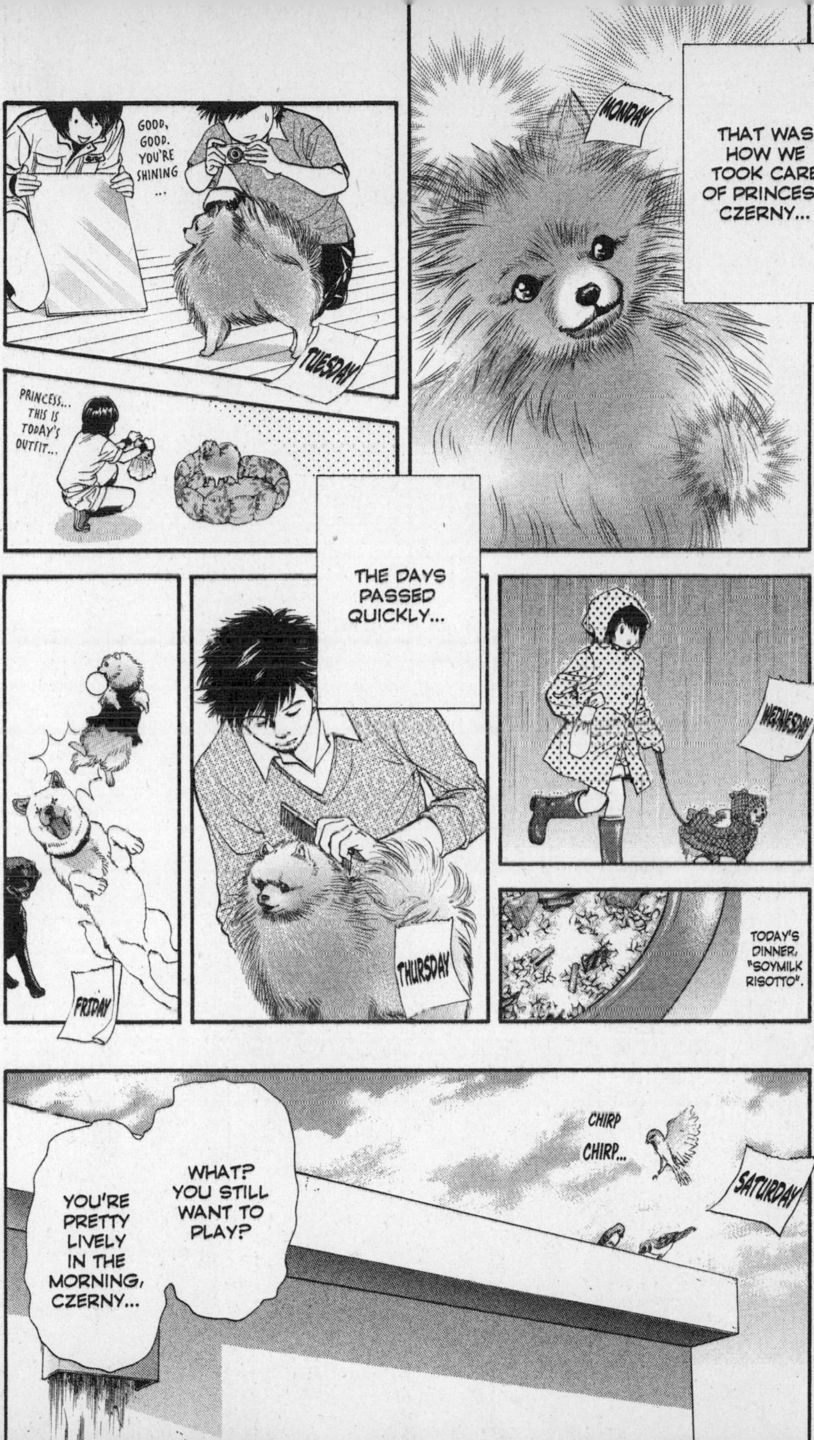
MONDAY
THAT WAS HOW WE TOOK CARE OF PRINCESS CZERNY...
GOOD, GOOD. YOU'RE SHINING ...
TUESDAY
PRINCESS... THIS IS TODAY'S OUTFIT...
THE DAYS PASSED QUICKLY...
WEDNESDAY
TODAY'S DINNER, "SOYMILK RISOTTO".
THURSDAY
FRIDAY
SATURDAY
CHIRP
CHIRP...
WHAT? YOU STILL WANT TO PLAY?
YOU'RE PRETTY LIVELY IN THE MORNING, CZERNY...

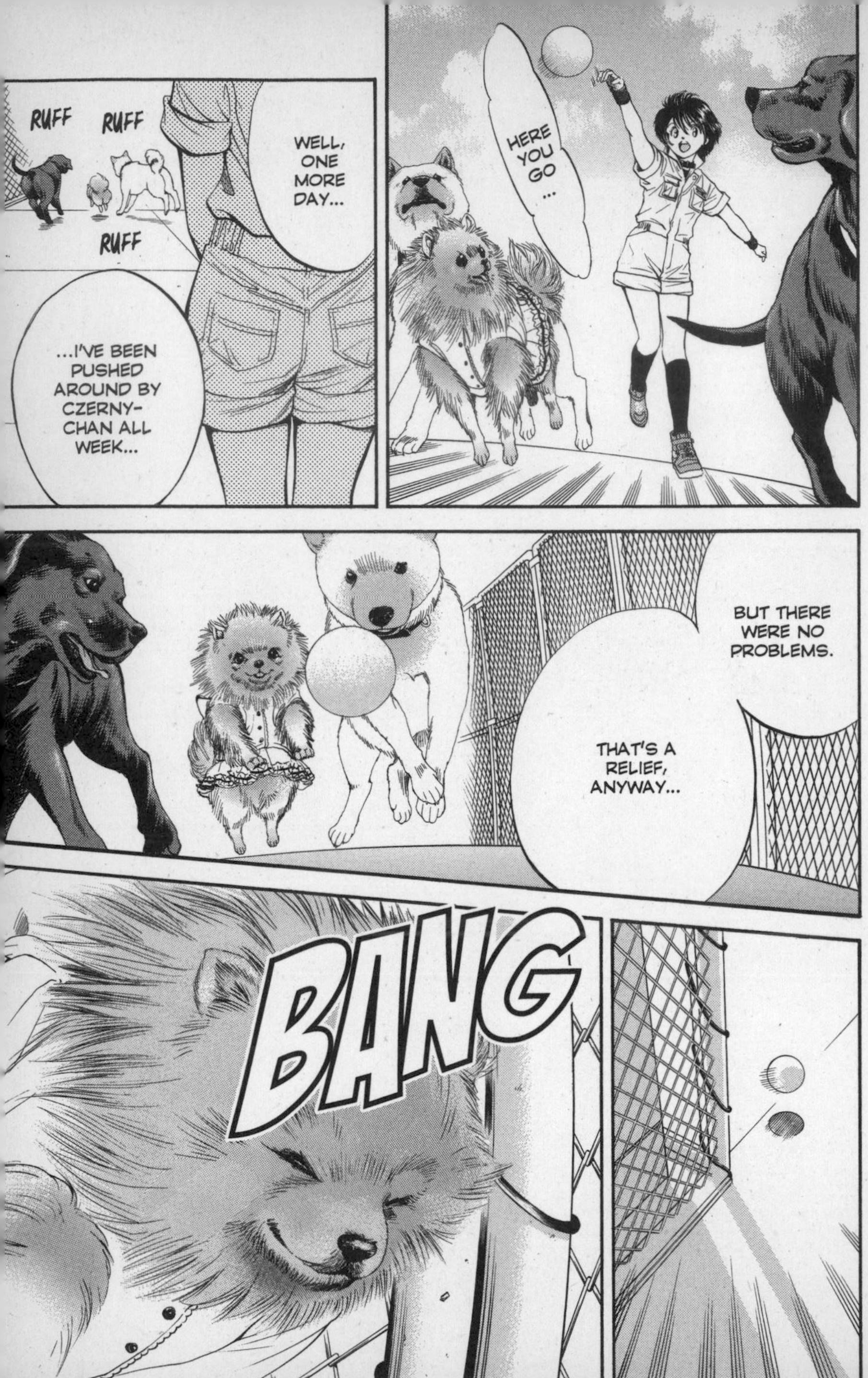
HERE YOU GO ...
WELL, ONE MORE DAY...
RUFF
RUFF
RUFF
...I'VE BEEN PUSHED AROUND BY CZERNY-CHAN ALL WEEK...
BUT THERE WERE NO PROBLEMS.
THAT'S A RELIEF, ANYWAY...
BANG

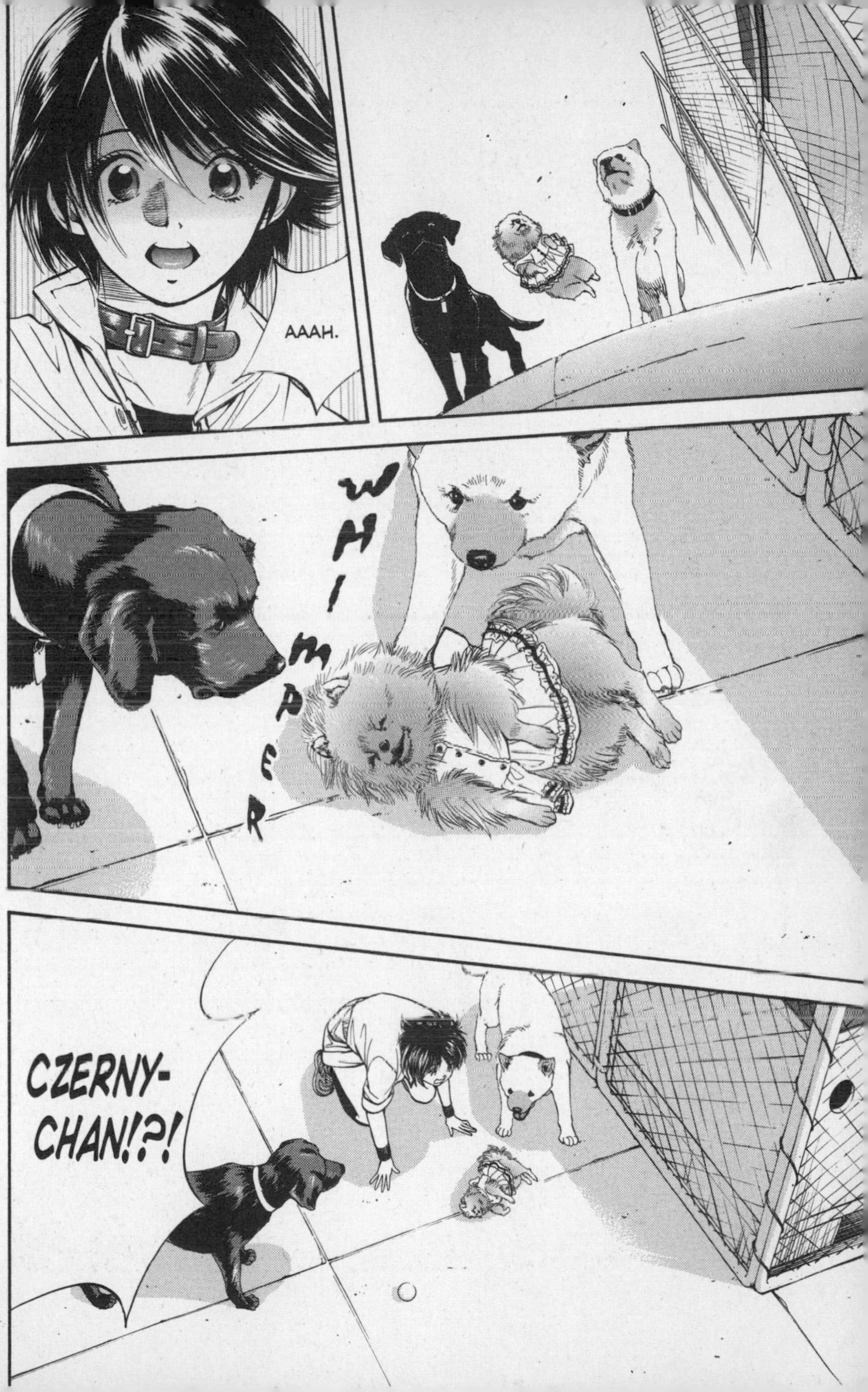
AAAH.
WHIMPER
CZERNY-CHAN!?!

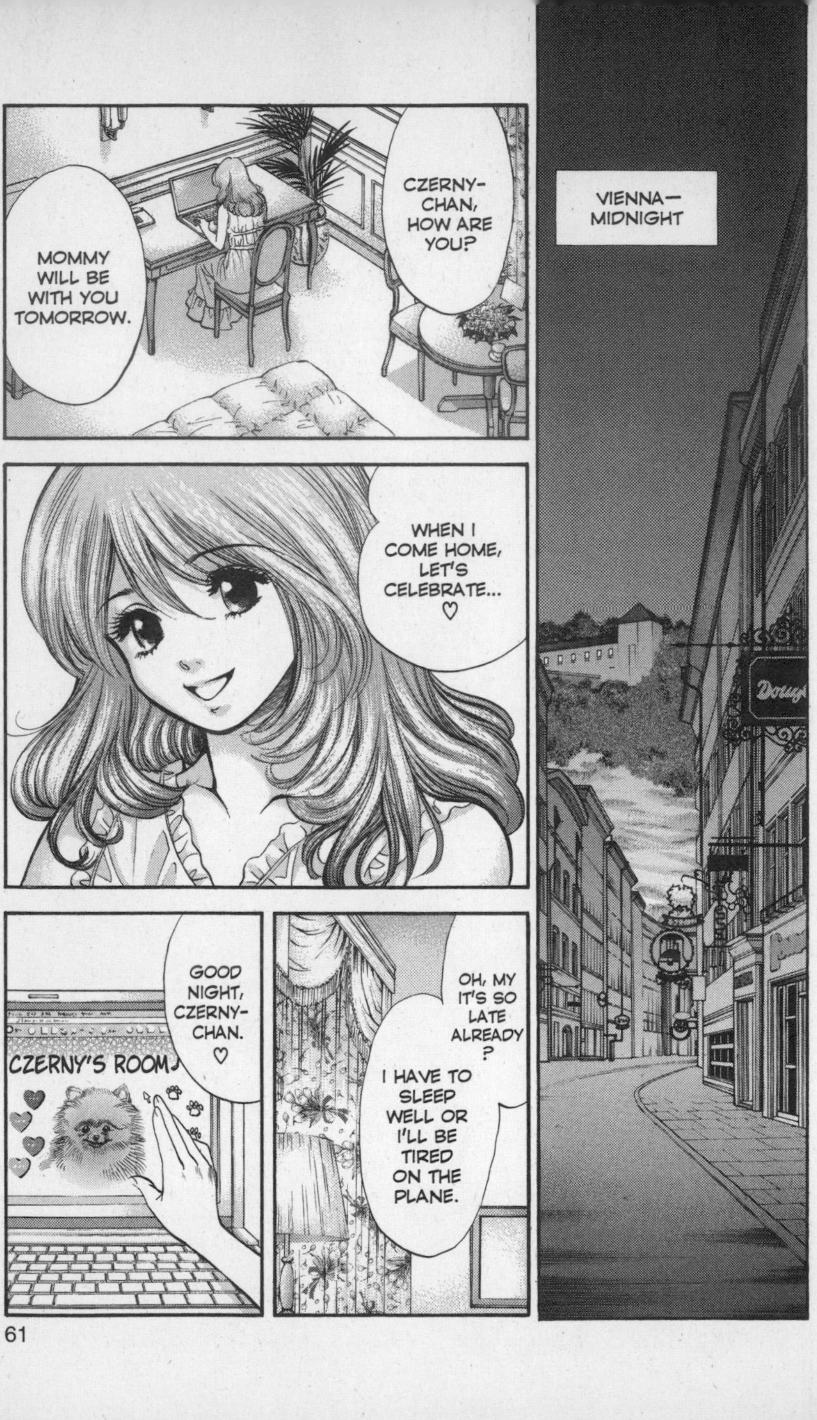
VIENNA—MIDNIGHT
CZERNY-CHAN, HOW ARE YOU?
MOMMY WILL BE WITH YOU TOMORROW.
WHEN I COME HOME, LET'S CELEBRATE... ♡
OH, MY IT'S SO LATE ALREADY?
I HAVE TO SLEEP WELL OR I'LL BE TIRED ON THE PLANE.
GOOD NIGHT, CZERNY-CHAN. ♡
CZERNY'S ROOM

CHAPTER 23: A BOND BETWEEN HEARTS

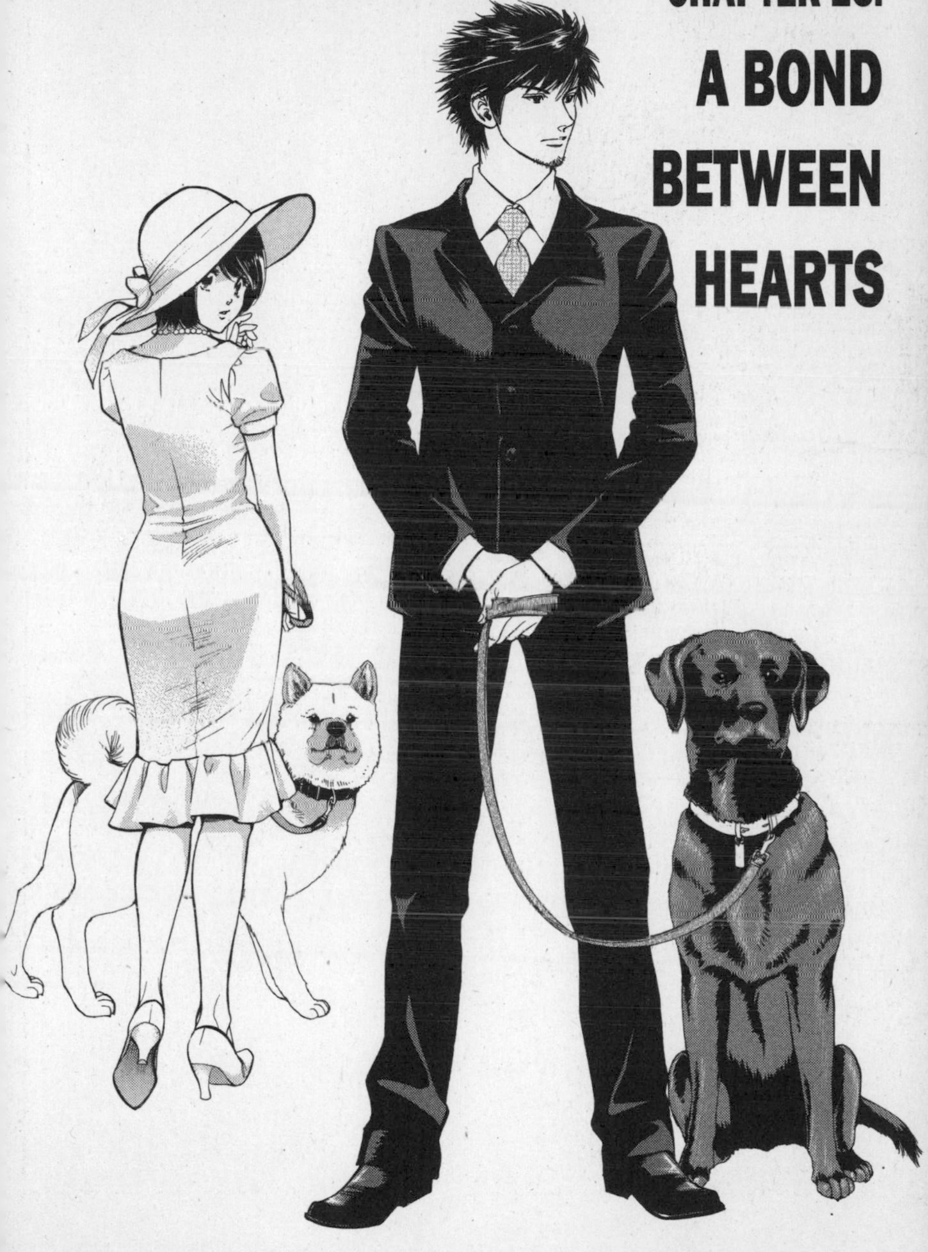

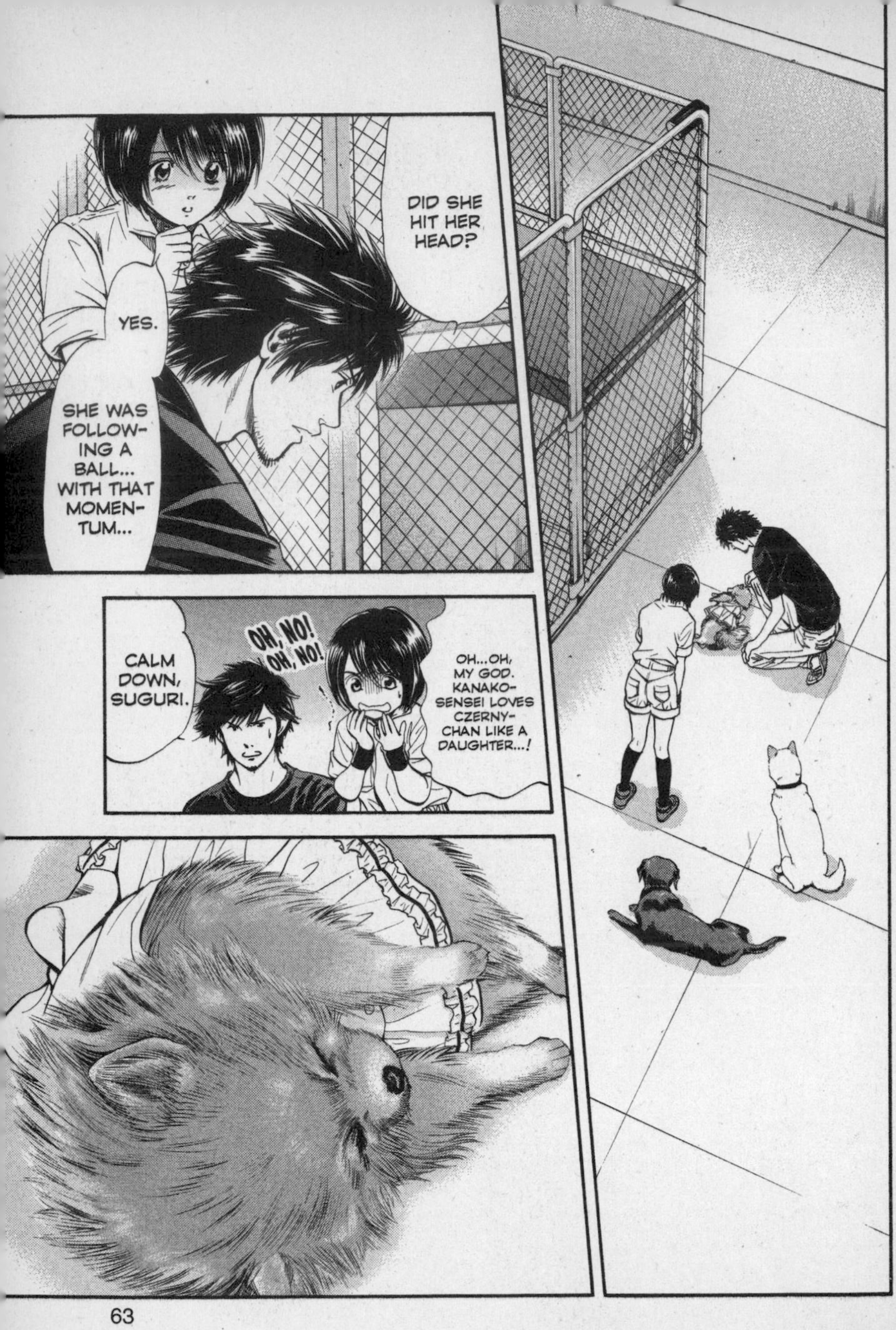
DID SHE HIT HER HEAD?
YES.
SHE WAS FOLLOWING A BALL... WITH THAT MOMENTUM...
OH...OH, MY GOD. KANAKO-SENSEI LOVES CZERNY-CHAN LIKE A DAUGHTER...!
OH, NO! OH, NO!
CALM DOWN, SUGURI.

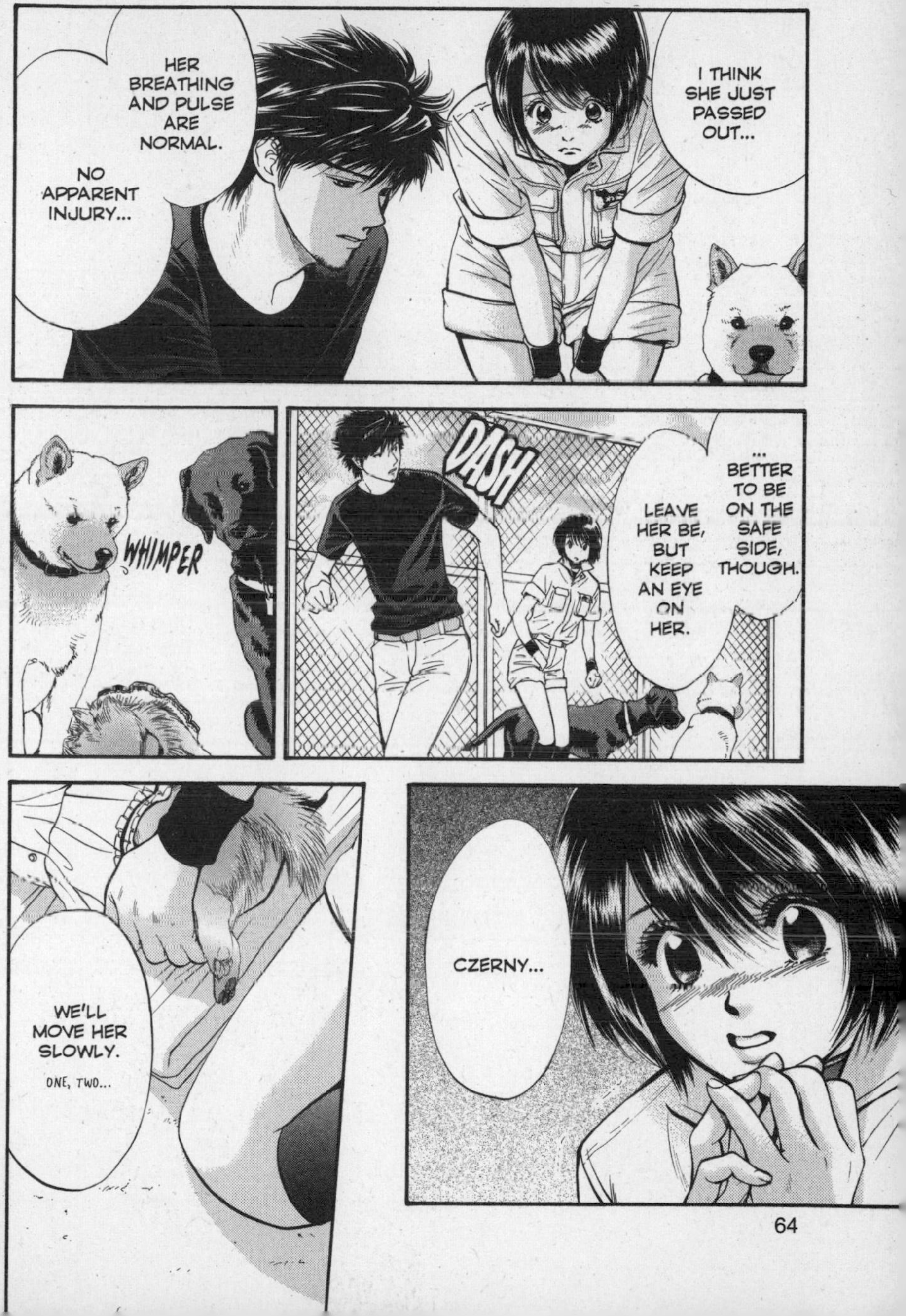
I THINK SHE JUST PASSED OUT...
HER BREATHING AND PULSE ARE NORMAL.
NO APPARENT INJURY...
DASH
... BETTER TO BE ON THE SAFE SIDE, THOUGH.
LEAVE HER BE, BUT KEEP AN EYE ON HER.
WHIMPER
CZERNY...
WE'LL MOVE HER SLOWLY.
ONE, TWO...

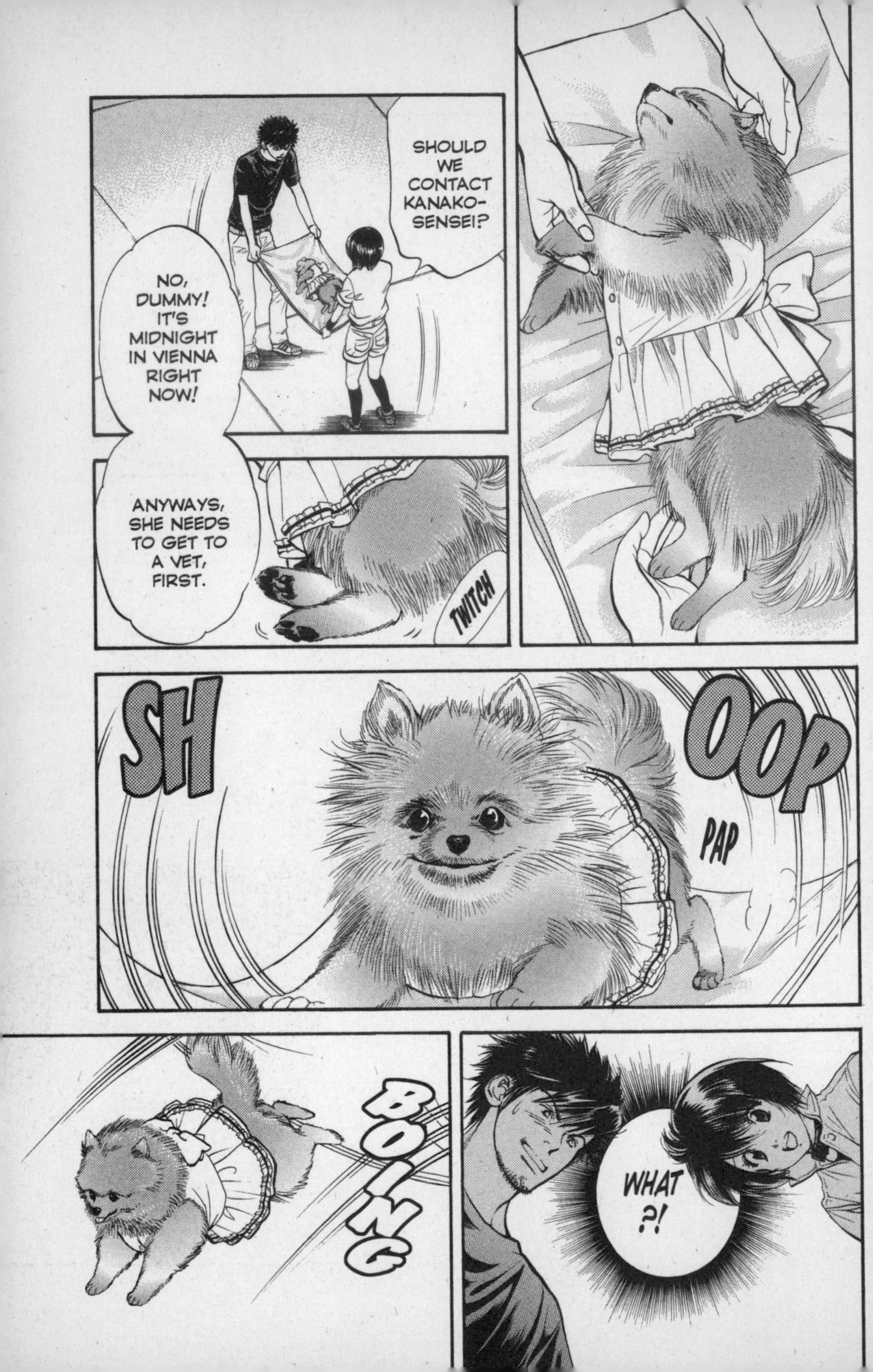
SHOULD WE CONTACT KANAKO-SENSEI?
NO, DUMMY! IT'S MIDNIGHT IN VIENNA RIGHT NOW!
ANYWAYS, SHE NEEDS TO GET TO A VET, FIRST.
TWITCH
SH
OOP
PAP
WHAT ?!
BOING

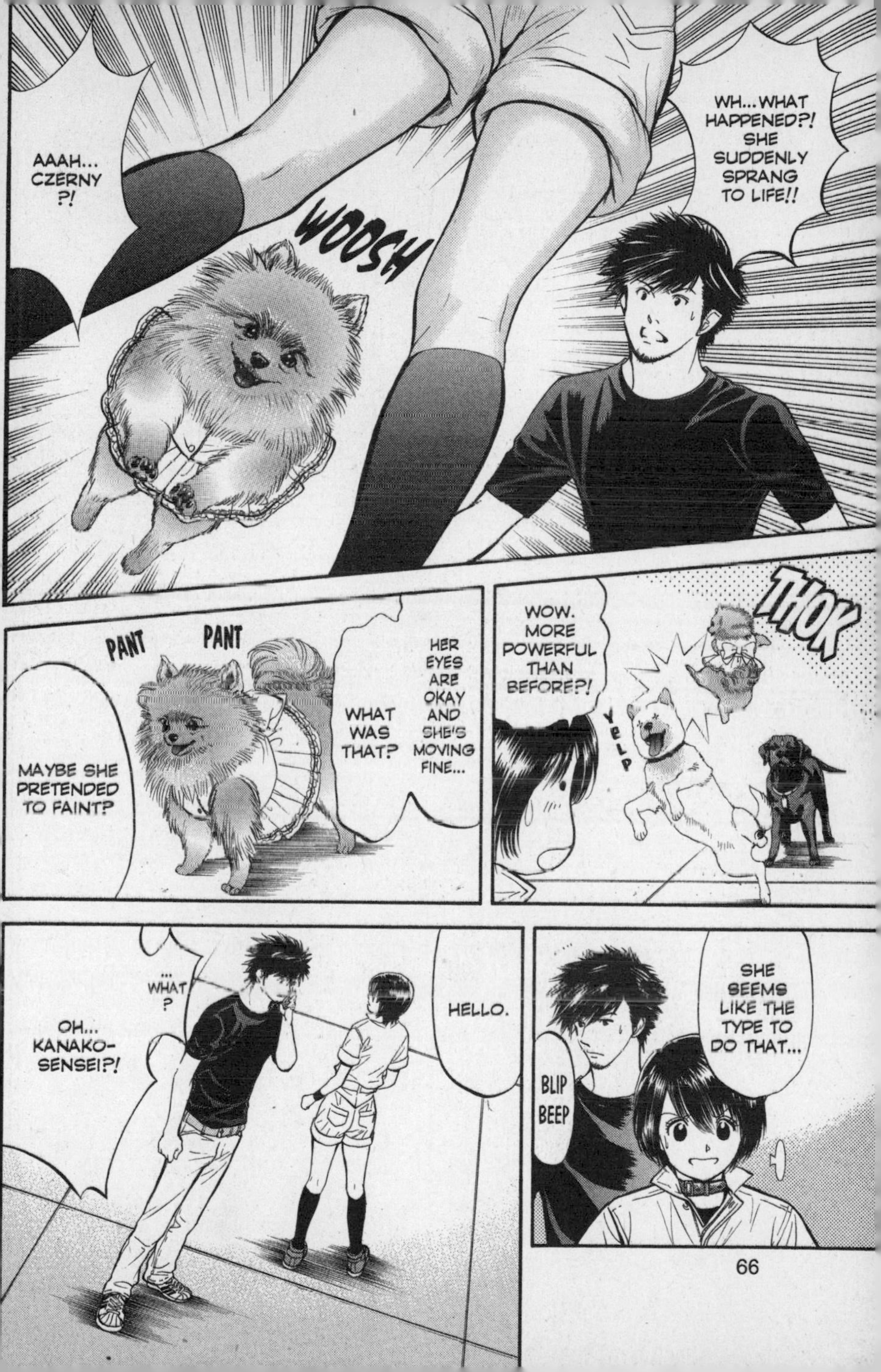
WH...WHAT HAPPENED?! SHE SUDDENLY SPRANG TO LIFE!!
WOOSH
AAAH... CZERNY ?!
THOK
WOW. MORE POWERFUL THAN BEFORE?!
YELP
HER EYES ARE OKAY AND SHE'S MOVING FINE...
WHAT WAS THAT?
PANT
PANT
MAYBE SHE PRETENDED TO FAINT?
SHE SEEMS LIKE THE TYPE TO DO THAT...
...
BLIP BEEP
!
HELLO.
... WHAT ?
OH... KANAKO-SENSEI?!

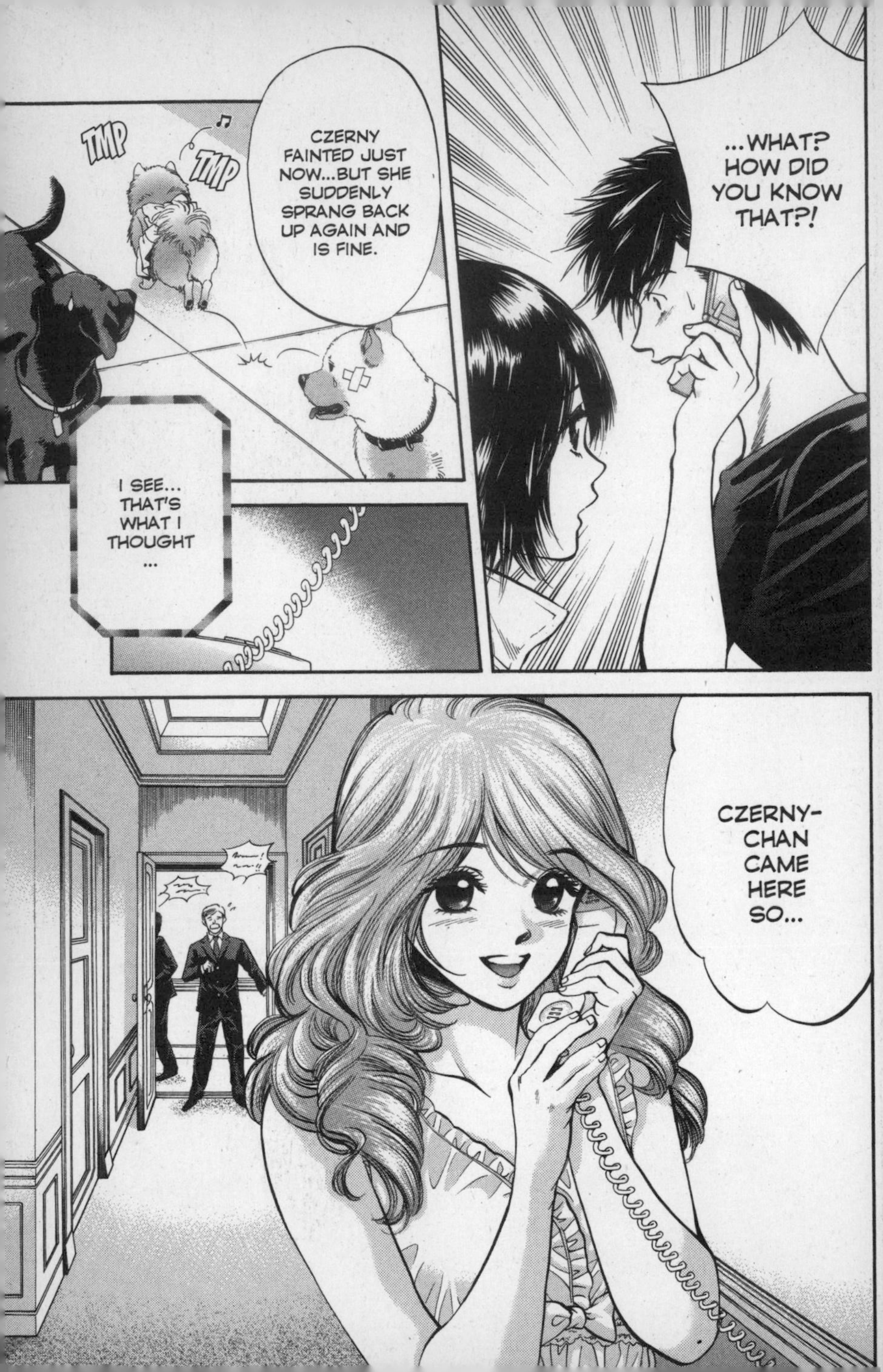
...WHAT? HOW DID YOU KNOW THAT?!
TMP
TMP
CZERNY FAINTED JUST NOW...BUT SHE SUDDENLY SPRANG BACK UP AGAIN AND IS FINE.
I SEE... THAT'S WHAT I THOUGHT ...
CZERNY-CHAN CAME HERE SO...

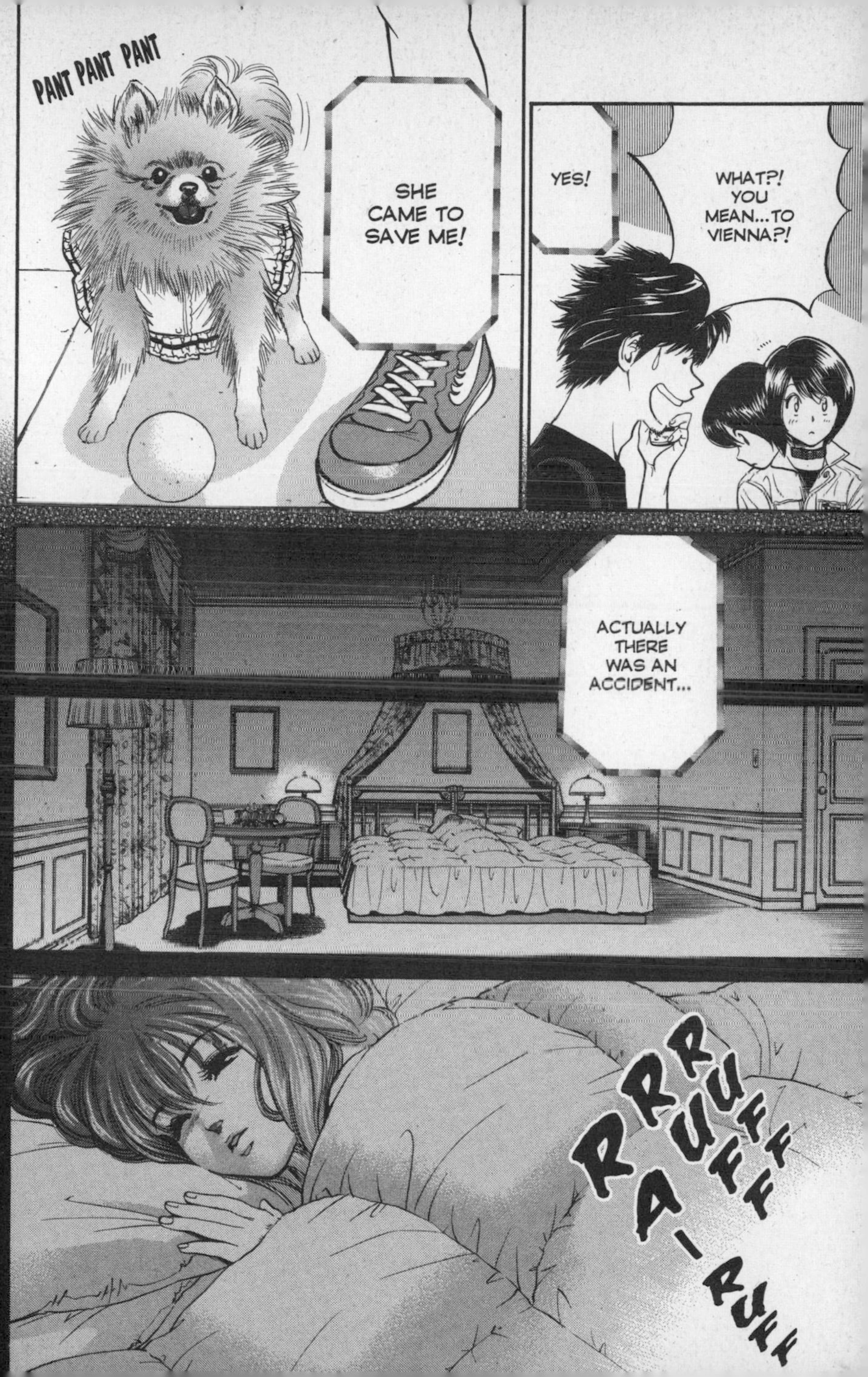
WHAT?! YOU MEAN...TO VIENNA?!
YES!
SHE CAME TO SAVE ME!
PANT PANT PANT
ACTUALLY THERE WAS AN ACCIDENT...
RRRUFF UFF A-RUFF

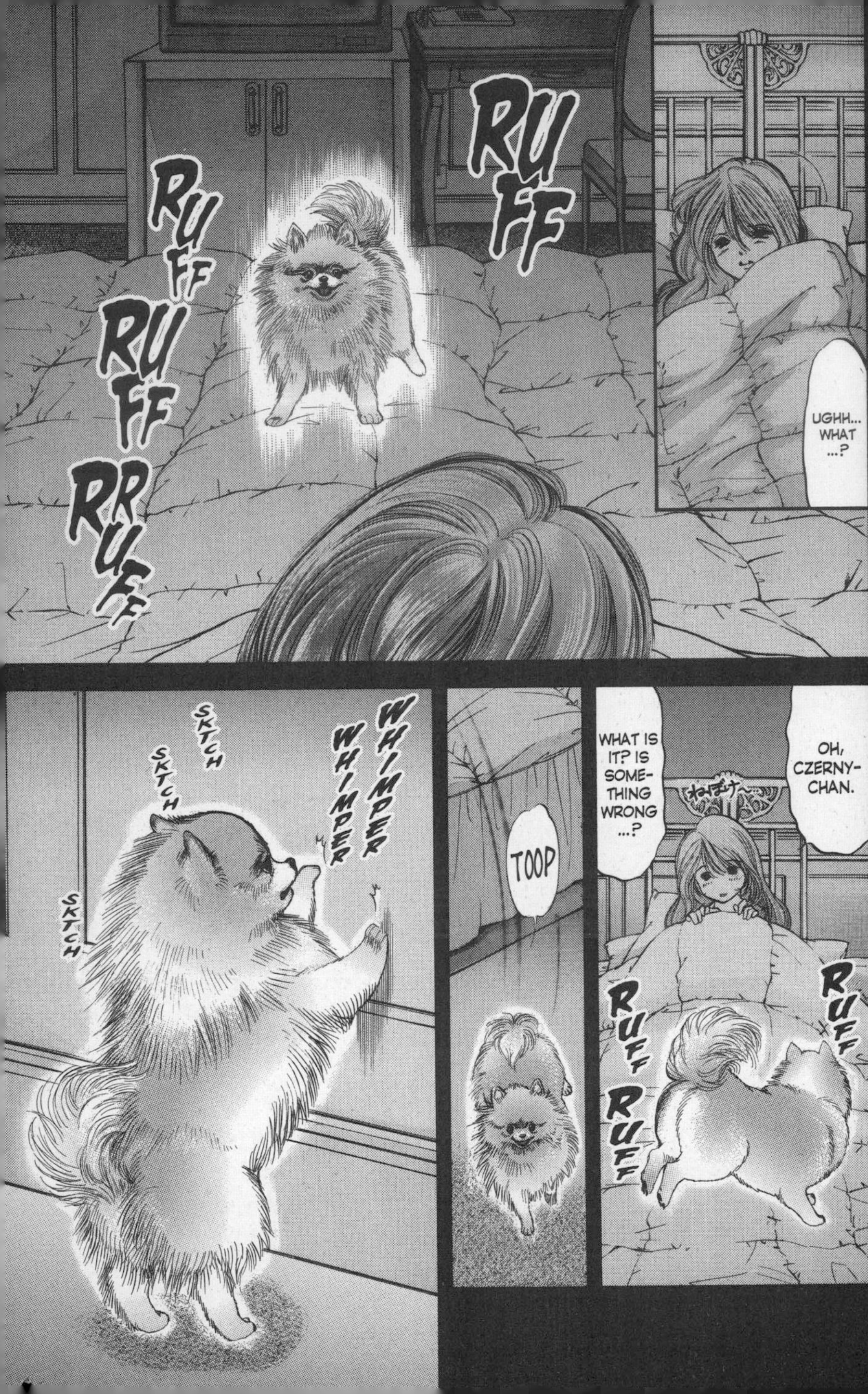
UGHH... WHAT ...?
RUFF
RUFF
RUFF
RRUFF
OH, CZERNY-CHAN.
WHAT IS IT? IS SOME-THING WRONG ...?
RUFF
RUFF
RUFF
TOOP
WHIMPER
WHIMPER
SKTCH
SKTCH
SKTCH

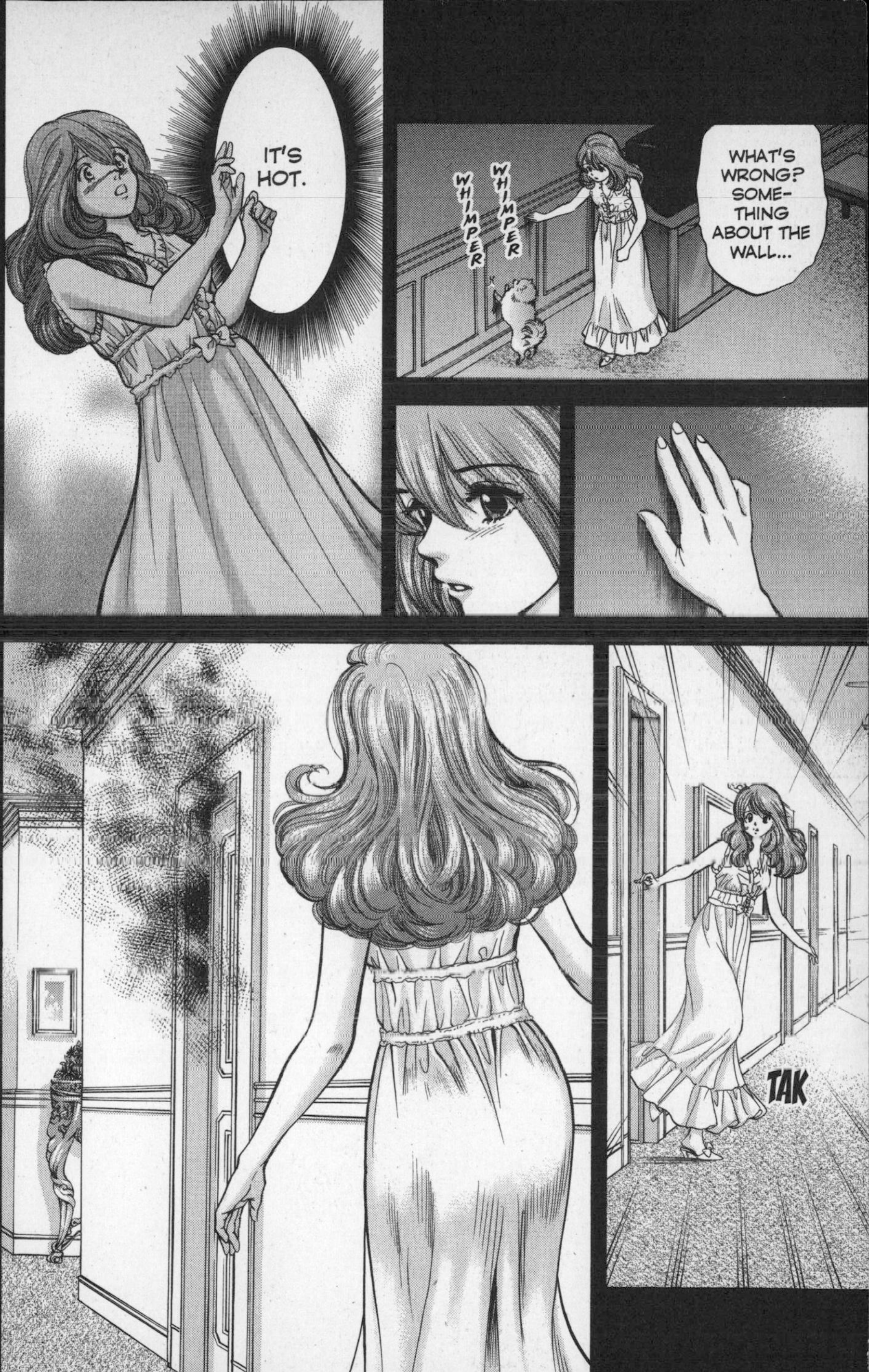
WHAT'S WRONG? SOME-THING ABOUT THE WALL...
WHIMPER
WHIMPER
IT'S HOT.
TAK

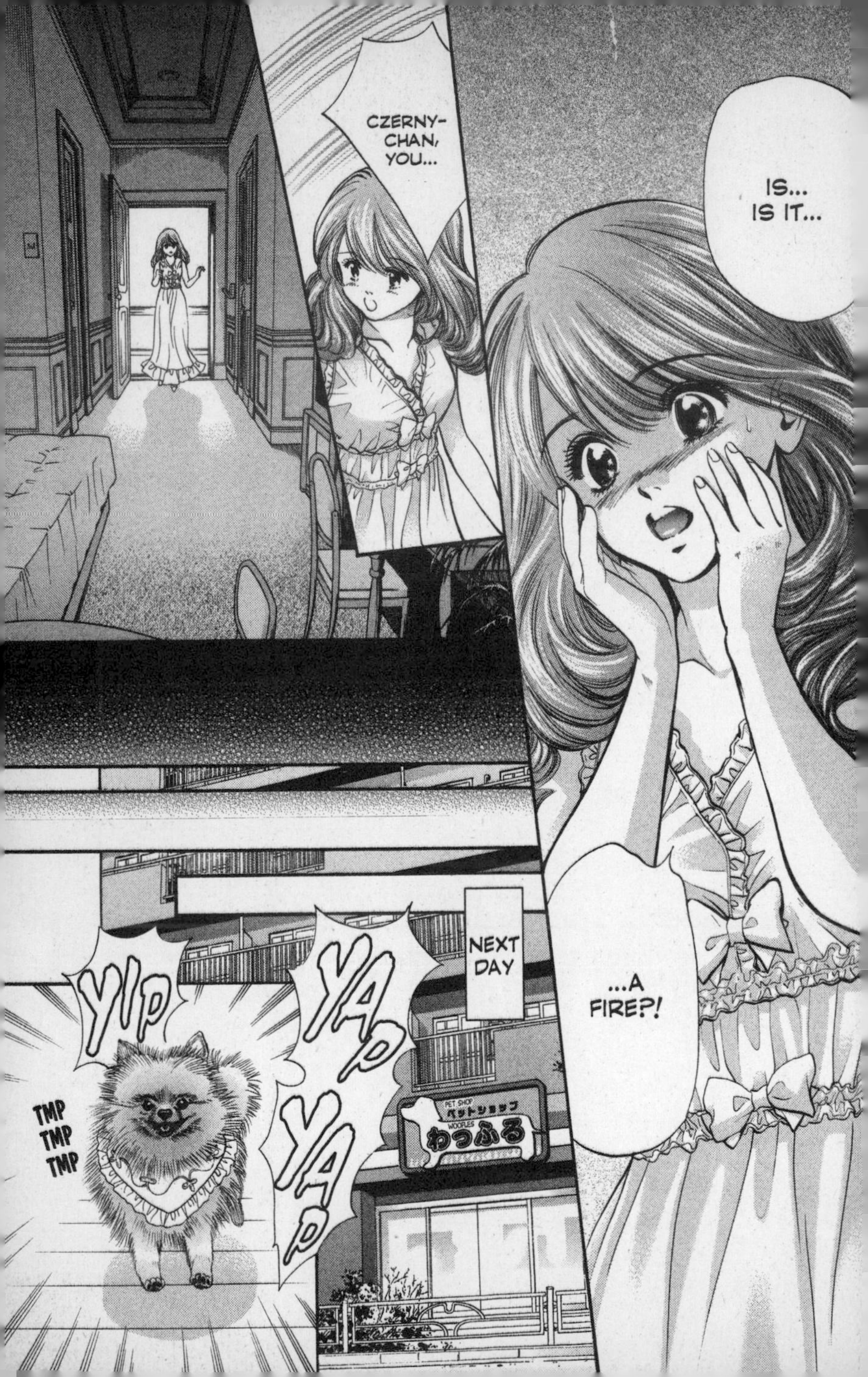
IS... IS IT...
...A FIRE?!
CZERNY-CHAN, YOU...
NEXT DAY
YAP YAP
YIP
TMP TMP TMP
PET SHOP
ペットショップ
WOOFLES
わっふる

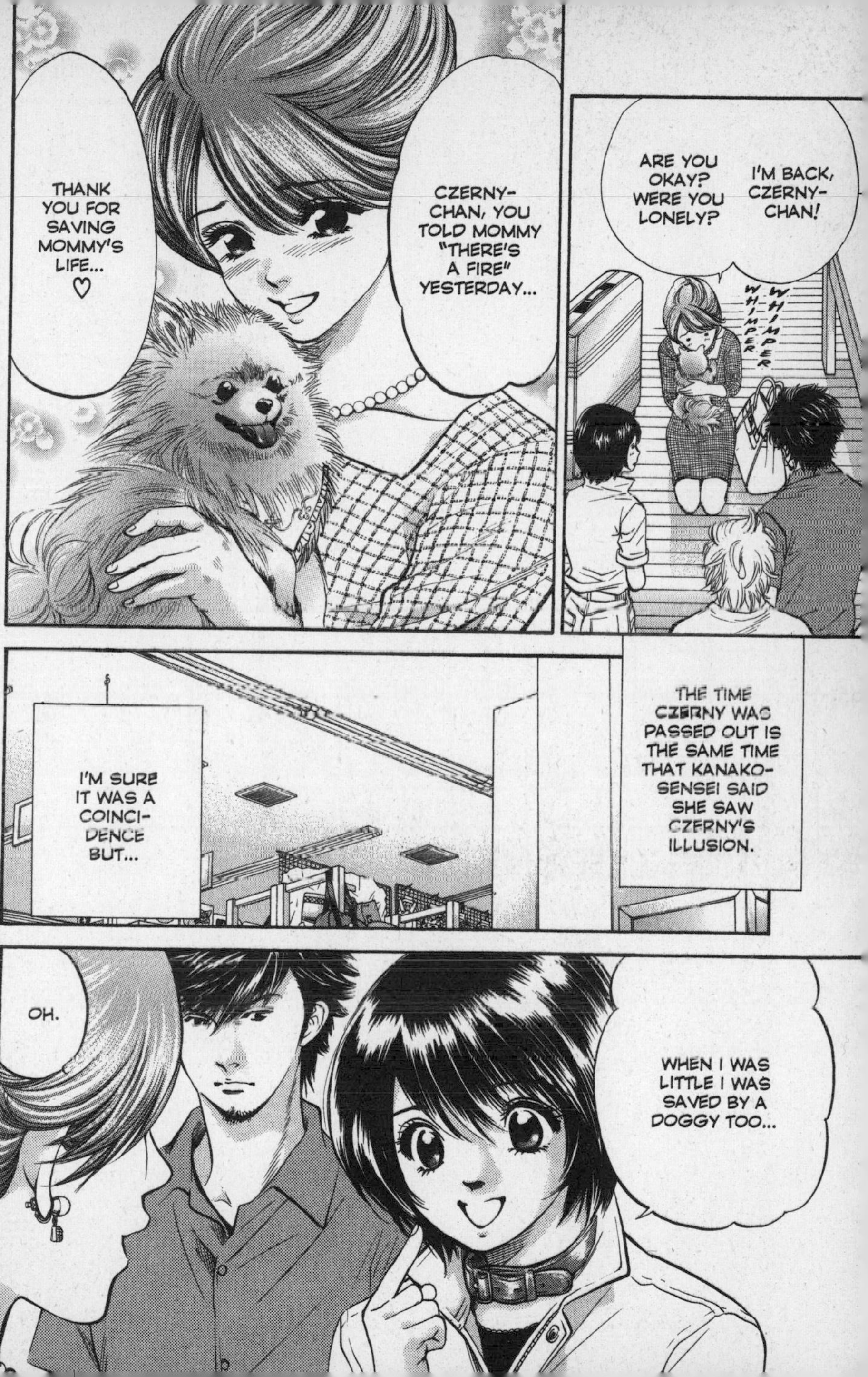
I'M BACK, CZERNY-CHAN!
ARE YOU OKAY? WERE YOU LONELY?
WHIMPER WHIMPER
CZERNY-CHAN, YOU TOLD MOMMY "THERE'S A FIRE" YESTERDAY...
THANK YOU FOR SAVING MOMMY'S LIFE... ♡
THE TIME CZERNY WAS PASSED OUT IS THE SAME TIME THAT KANAKO-SENSEI SAID SHE SAW CZERNY'S ILLUSION.
I'M SURE IT WAS A COINCIDENCE BUT...
WHEN I WAS LITTLE I WAS SAVED BY A DOGGY TOO...
OH.

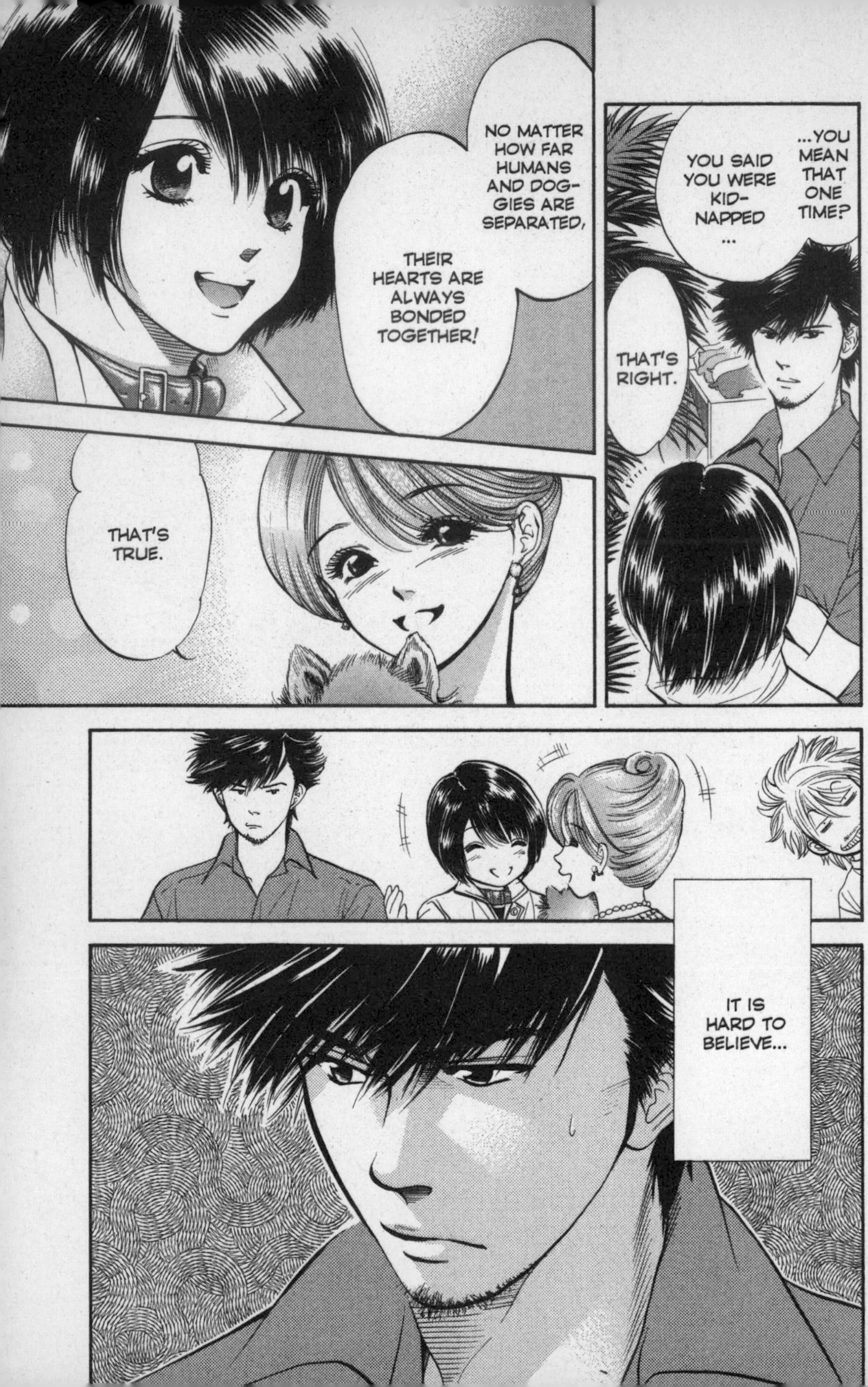
...YOU MEAN THAT ONE TIME?
YOU SAID YOU WERE KID-NAPPED ...
THAT'S RIGHT.
NO MATTER HOW FAR HUMANS AND DOG-GIES ARE SEPARATED,
THEIR HEARTS ARE ALWAYS BONDED TOGETHER!
THAT'S TRUE.
IT IS HARD TO BELIEVE...

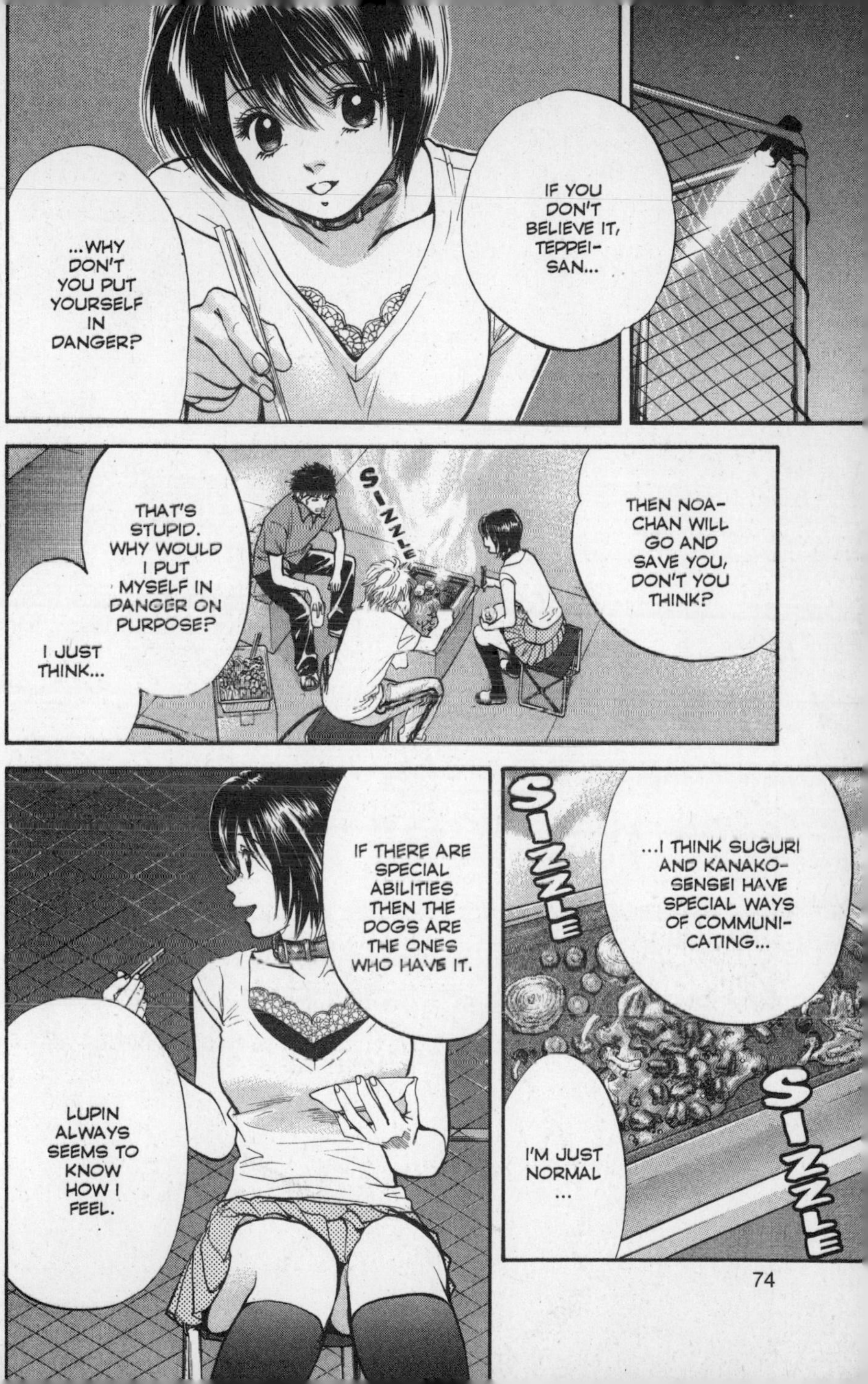
IF YOU DON'T BELIEVE IT, TEPPEI-SAN...
...WHY DON'T YOU PUT YOURSELF IN DANGER?
THEN NOA-CHAN WILL GO AND SAVE YOU, DON'T YOU THINK?
SIZZLE
THAT'S STUPID. WHY WOULD I PUT MYSELF IN DANGER ON PURPOSE?
I JUST THINK...
SIZZLE
...I THINK SUGURI AND KANAKO-SENSEI HAVE SPECIAL WAYS OF COMMUNICATING...
SIZZLE
I'M JUST NORMAL ...
IF THERE ARE SPECIAL ABILITIES THEN THE DOGS ARE THE ONES WHO HAVE IT.
LUPIN ALWAYS SEEMS TO KNOW HOW I FEEL.

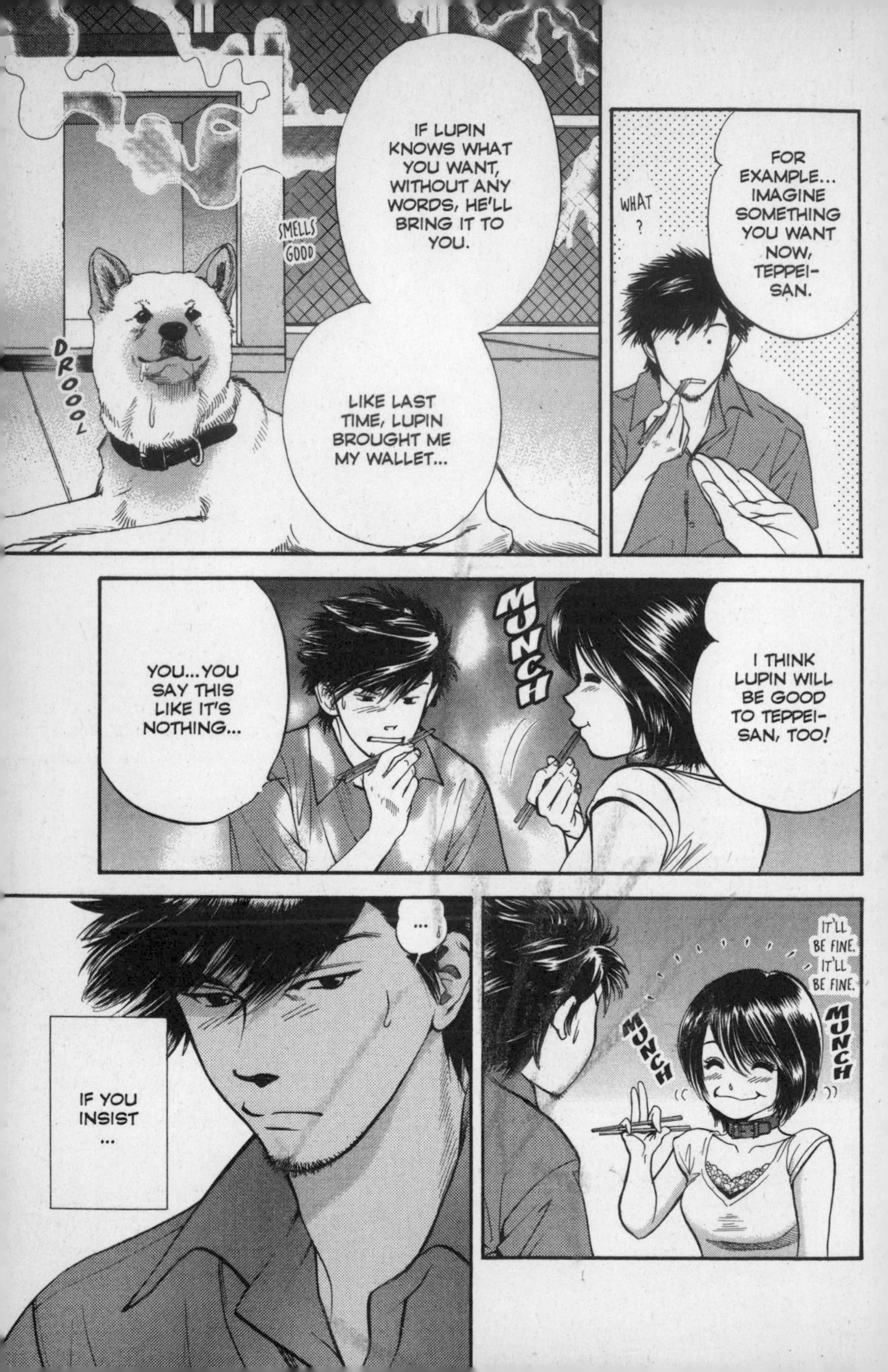
FOR EXAMPLE... IMAGINE SOMETHING YOU WANT NOW, TEPPEI-SAN.
WHAT ?
IF LUPIN KNOWS WHAT YOU WANT, WITHOUT ANY WORDS, HE'LL BRING IT TO YOU.
SMELLS GOOD
LIKE LAST TIME, LUPIN BROUGHT ME MY WALLET...
DROOOL
I THINK LUPIN WILL BE GOOD TO TEPPEI-SAN, TOO!
MUNCH
YOU...YOU SAY THIS LIKE IT'S NOTHING...
IT'LL BE FINE. IT'LL BE FINE.
MUNCH
MUNCH
...
IF YOU INSIST ...

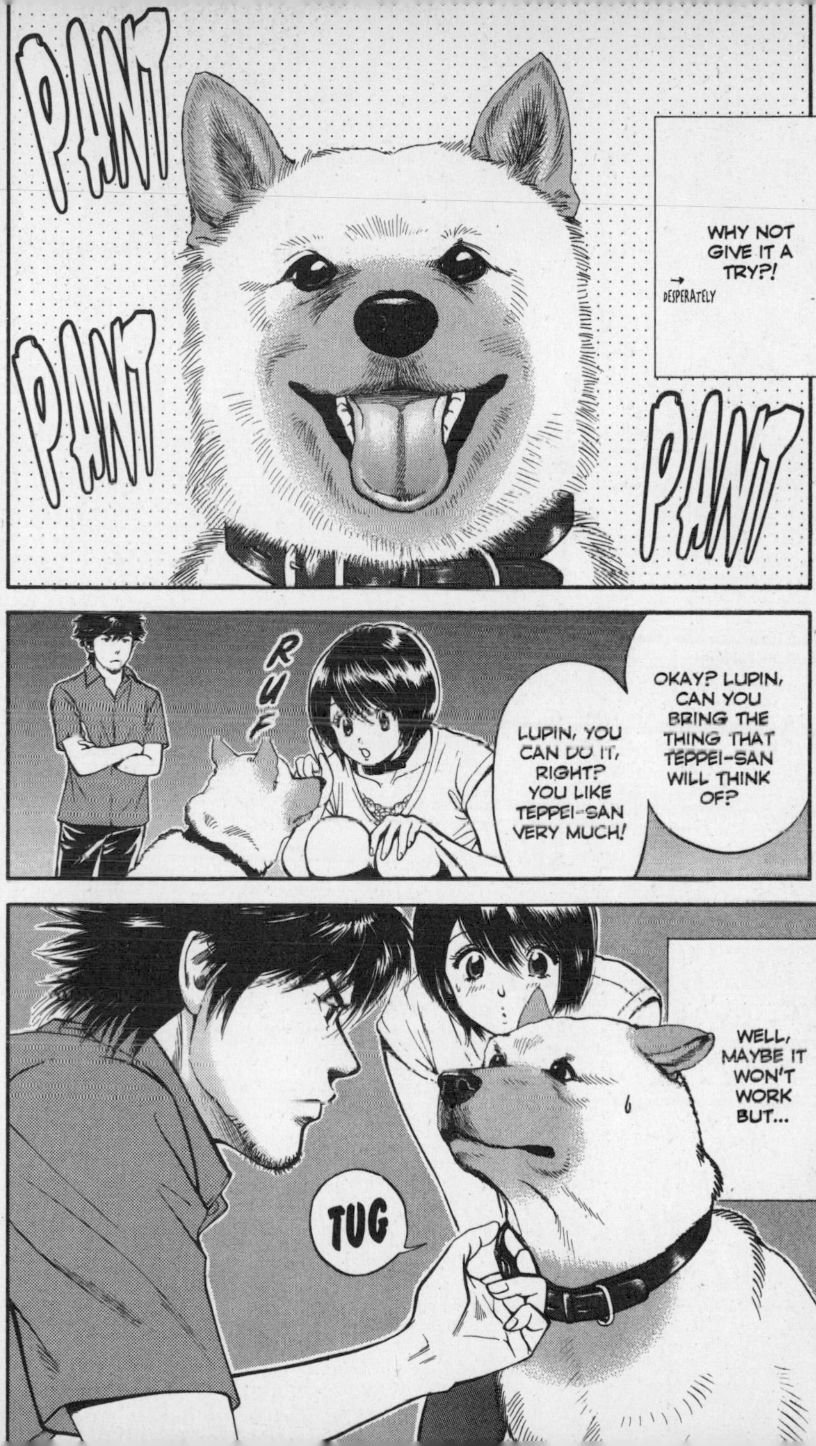
WHY NOT GIVE IT A TRY?!
DESPERATELY
PANT
PANT
PANT
OKAY? LUPIN, CAN YOU BRING THE THING THAT TEPPEI-SAN WILL THINK OF?
LUPIN, YOU CAN DO IT, RIGHT? YOU LIKE TEPPEI-SAN VERY MUCH!
RUF
WELL, MAYBE IT WON'T WORK BUT...
TUG

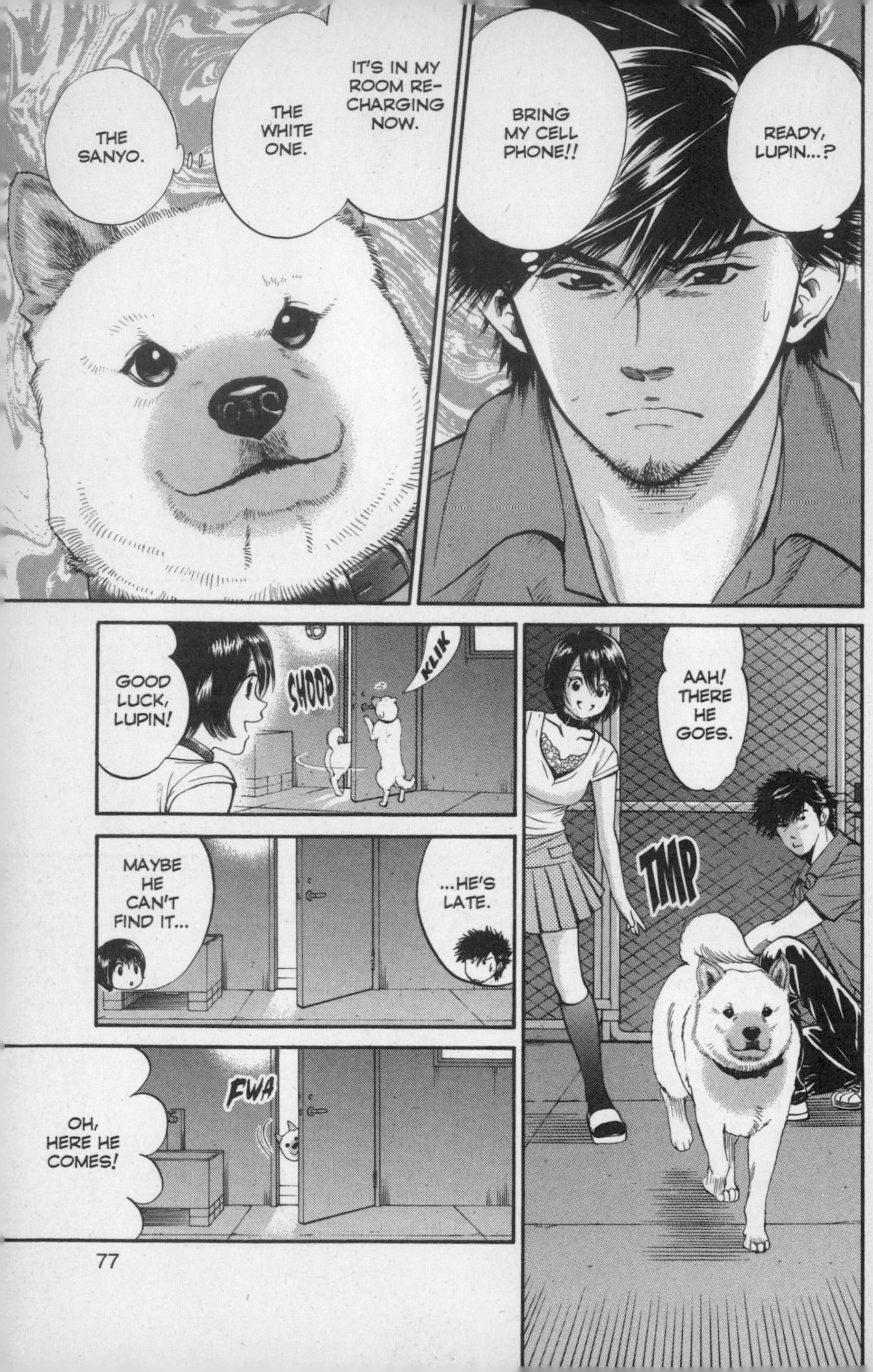
READY, LUPIN...?
BRING MY CELL PHONE!!
IT'S IN MY ROOM RE-CHARGING NOW.
THE WHITE ONE.
THE SANYO.
AAH! THERE HE GOES.
TMP
KLIK
SHOOP
GOOD LUCK, LUPIN!
...HE'S LATE.
MAYBE HE CAN'T FIND IT...
FWA
OH, HERE HE COMES!

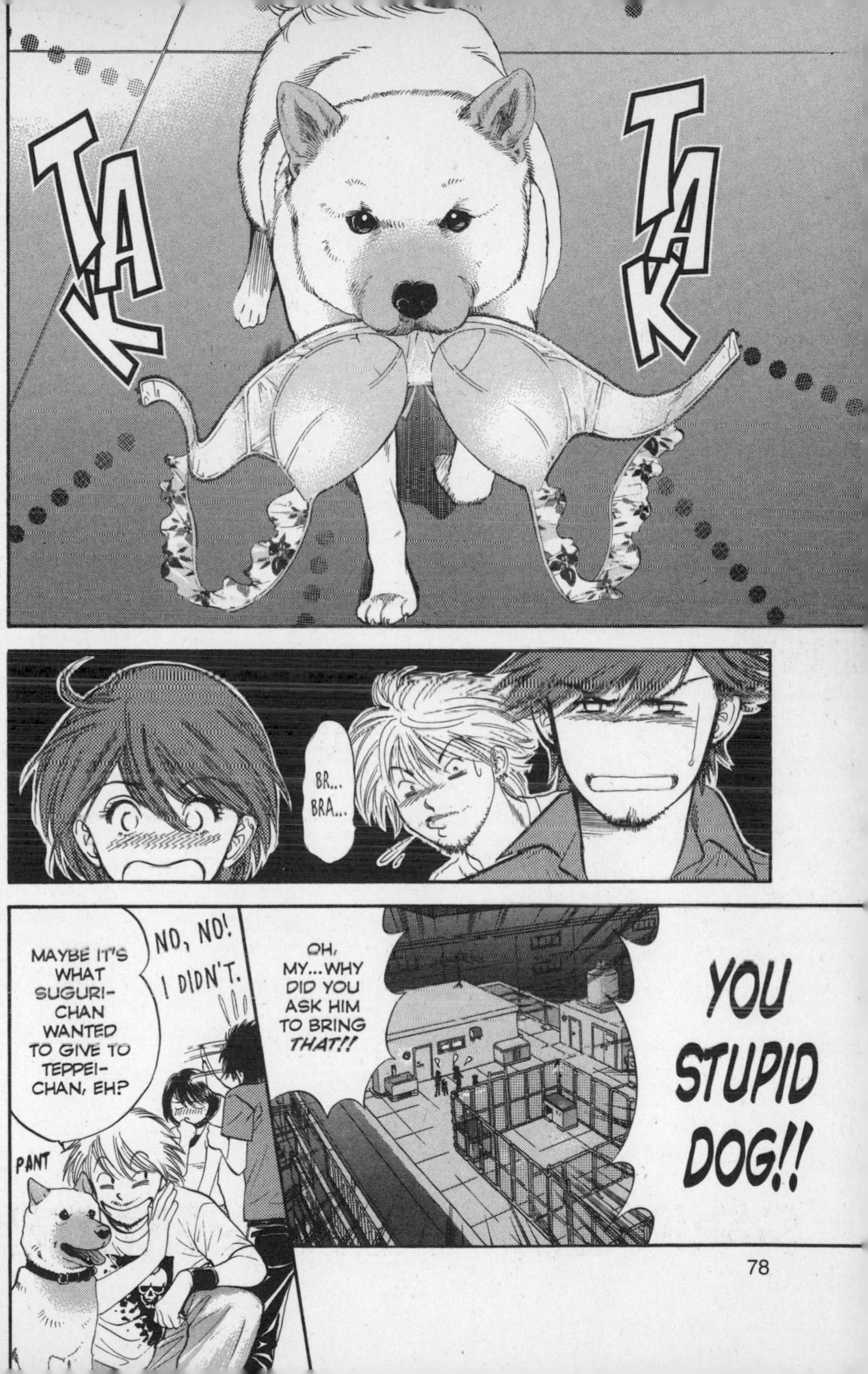
TAK
TAK
BR... BRA...
YOU STUPID DOG!!
OH, MY...WHY DID YOU ASK HIM TO BRING THAT!!
NO, NO! I DIDN'T.
MAYBE IT'S WHAT SUGURI-CHAN WANTED TO GIVE TO TEPPEI-CHAN, EH?
PANT

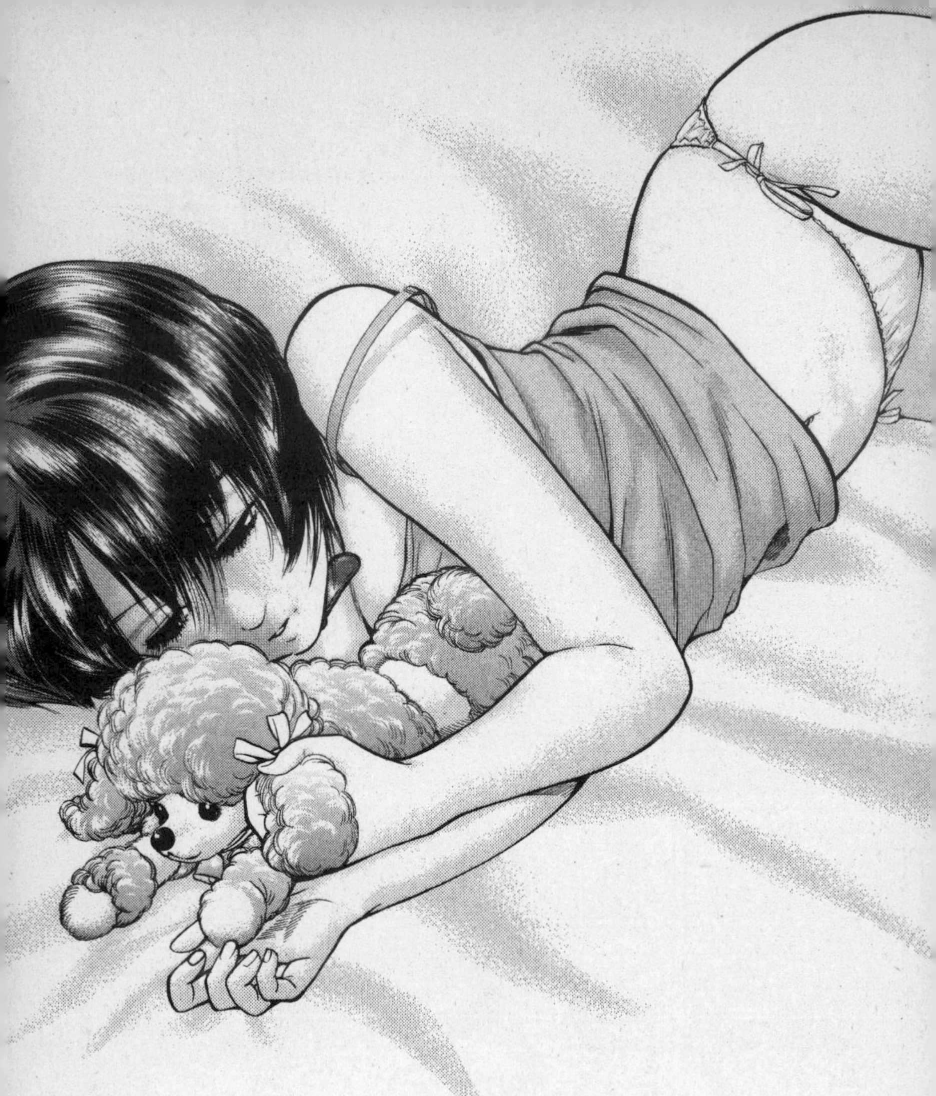

CHAPTER 24:

SUGURI LEARNS ABOUT NIGHTLIFE!

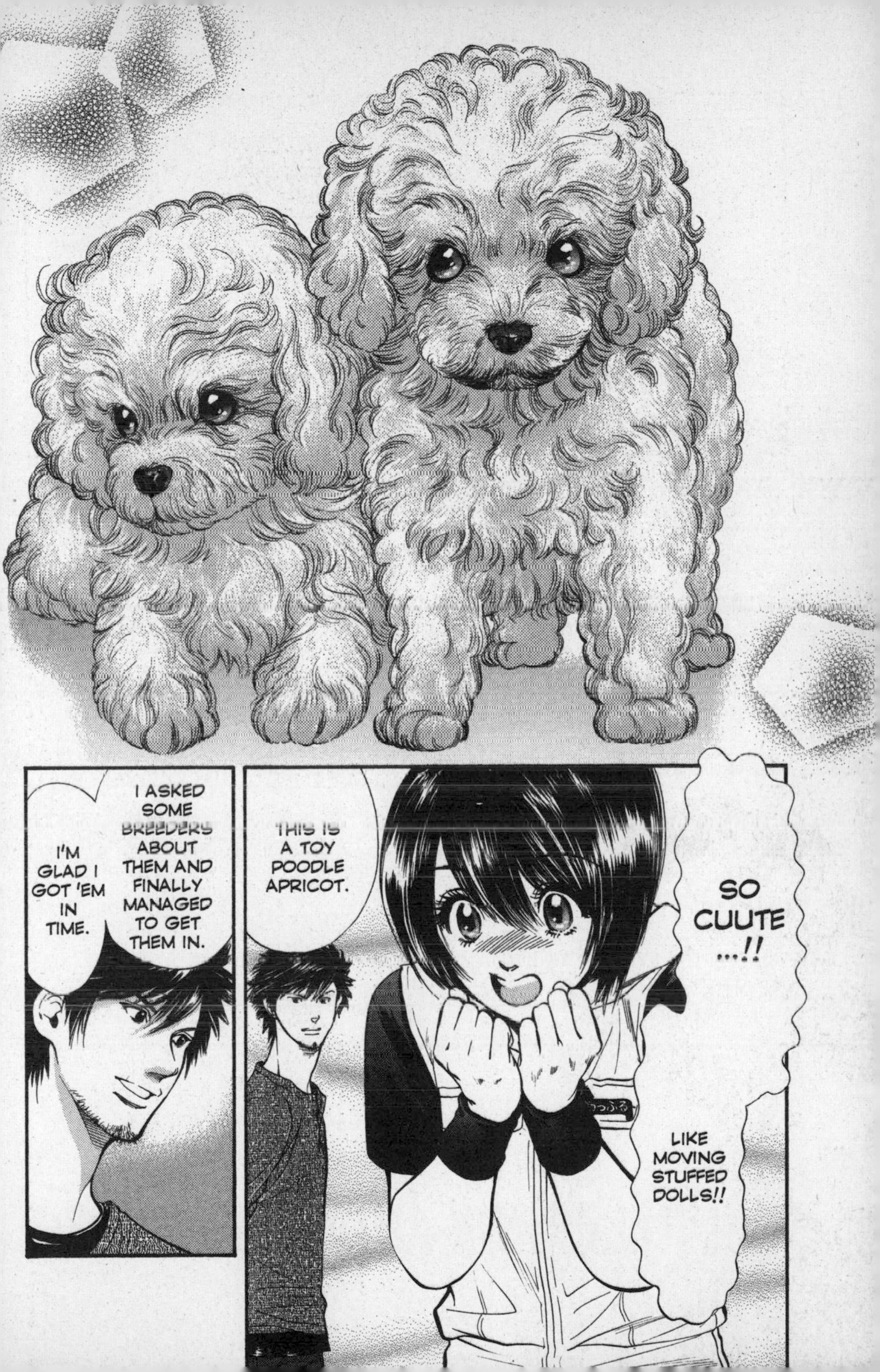
SO CUUTE ...!!
LIKE MOVING STUFFED DOLLS!!
THIS IS A TOY POODLE APRICOT.
I ASKED SOME BREEDERS ABOUT THEM AND FINALLY MANAGED TO GET THEM IN.
I'M GLAD I GOT 'EM IN TIME.

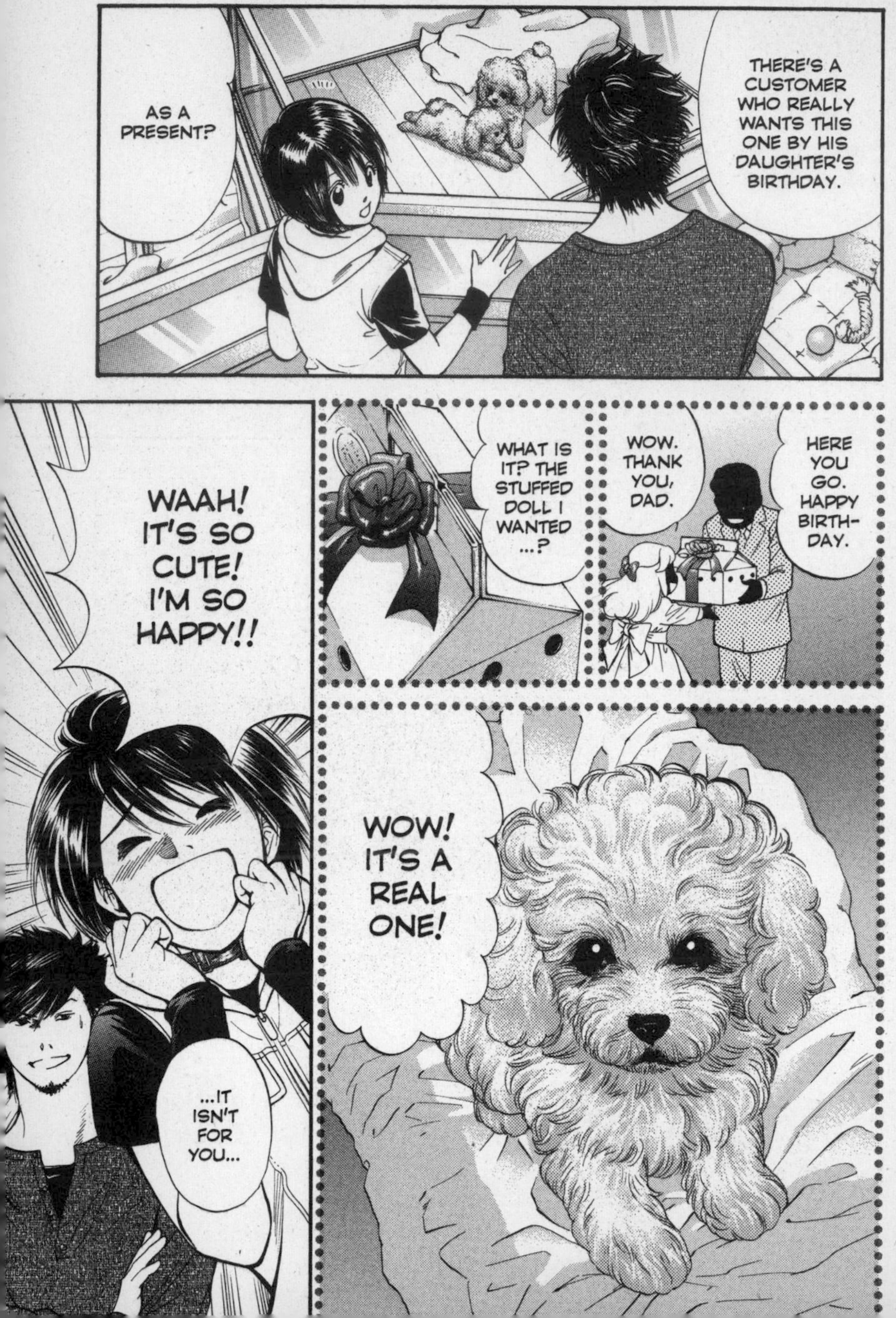
THERE'S A CUSTOMER WHO REALLY WANTS THIS ONE BY HIS DAUGHTER'S BIRTHDAY.
AS A PRESENT?
HERE YOU GO. HAPPY BIRTH-DAY.
WOW. THANK YOU, DAD.
WHAT IS IT? THE STUFFED DOLL I WANTED ...?
WOW! IT'S A REAL ONE!
WAAH! IT'S SO CUTE! I'M SO HAPPY!!
...IT ISN'T FOR YOU...

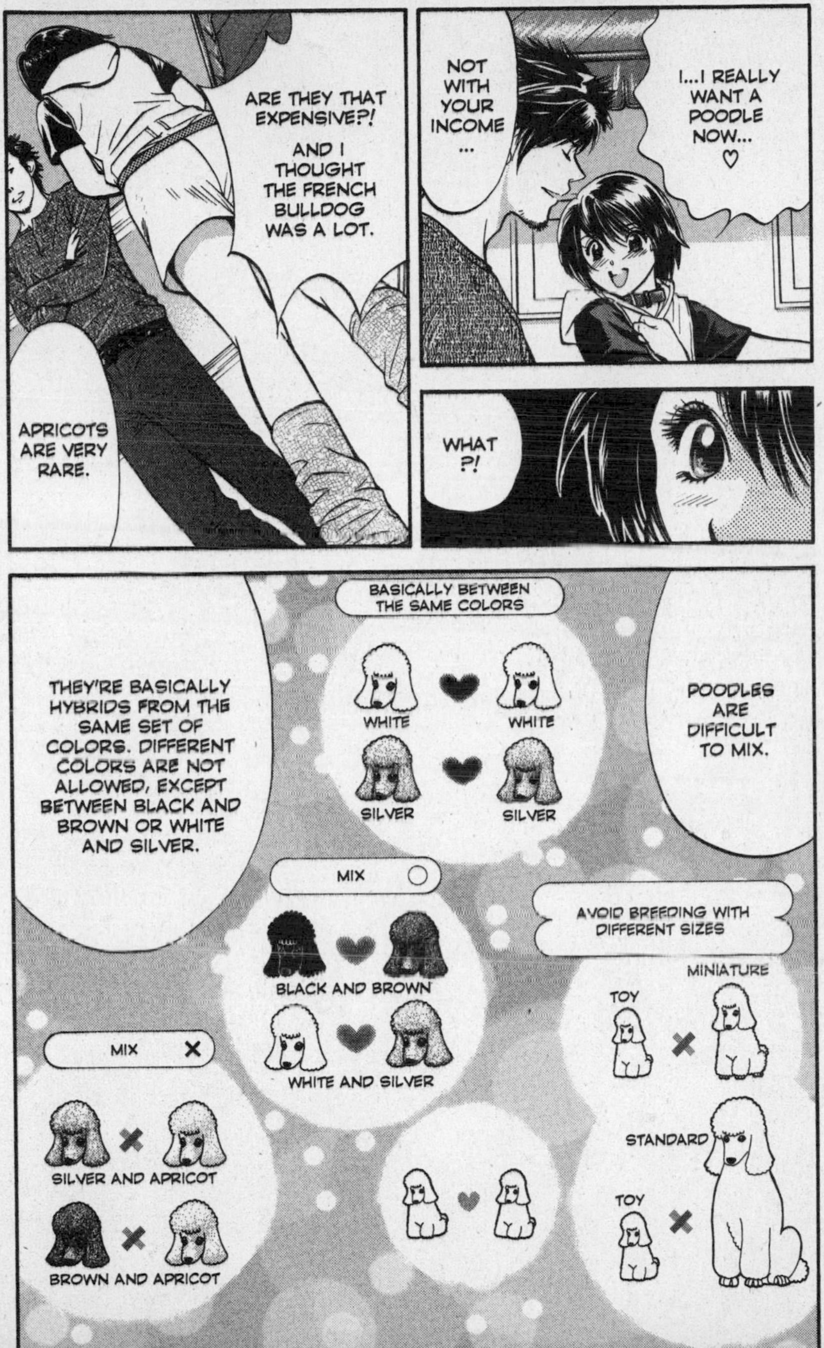
I...I REALLY WANT A POODLE NOW... ♡
NOT WITH YOUR INCOME...
WHAT?!
ARE THEY THAT EXPENSIVE?!
AND I THOUGHT THE FRENCH BULLDOG WAS A LOT.
APRICOTS ARE VERY RARE.
POODLES ARE DIFFICULT TO MIX.
BASICALLY BETWEEN THE SAME COLORS
WHITE
WHITE
SILVER
SILVER
THEY'RE BASICALLY HYBRIDS FROM THE SAME SET OF COLORS. DIFFERENT COLORS ARE NOT ALLOWED, EXCEPT BETWEEN BLACK AND BROWN OR WHITE AND SILVER.
AVOID BREEDING WITH DIFFERENT SIZES
MINIATURE
TOY
STANDARD
TOY
MIX ○
BLACK AND BROWN
WHITE AND SILVER
MIX ✕
SILVER AND APRICOT
BROWN AND APRICOT

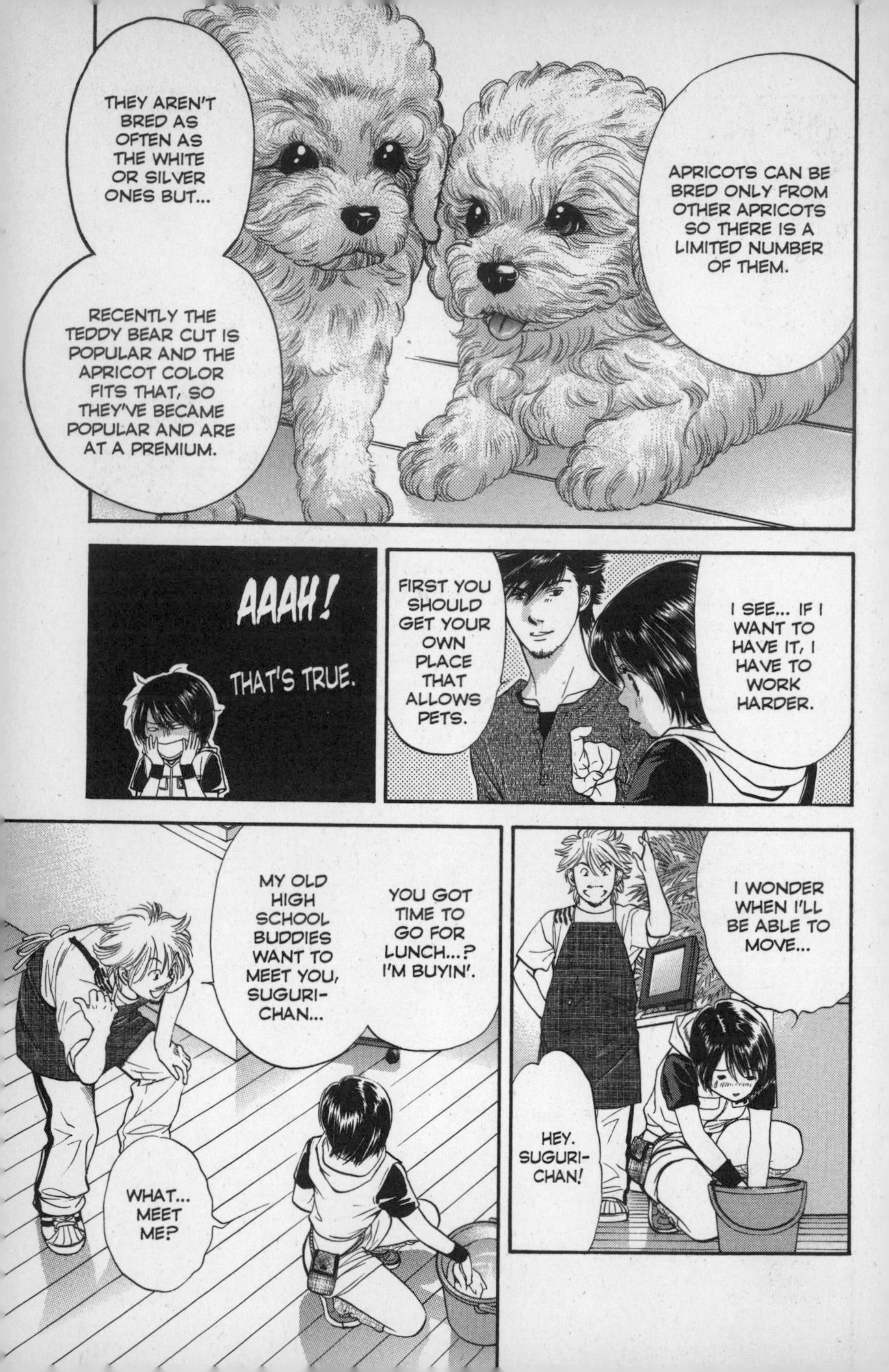
APRICOTS CAN BE BRED ONLY FROM OTHER APRICOTS SO THERE IS A LIMITED NUMBER OF THEM.
THEY AREN'T BRED AS OFTEN AS THE WHITE OR SILVER ONES BUT...
RECENTLY THE TEDDY BEAR CUT IS POPULAR AND THE APRICOT COLOR FITS THAT, SO THEY'VE BECAME POPULAR AND ARE AT A PREMIUM.
I SEE... IF I WANT TO HAVE IT, I HAVE TO WORK HARDER.
FIRST YOU SHOULD GET YOUR OWN PLACE THAT ALLOWS PETS.
AAAH!
THAT'S TRUE.
I WONDER WHEN I'LL BE ABLE TO MOVE...
HEY. SUGURI-CHAN!
YOU GOT TIME TO GO FOR LUNCH...? I'M BUYIN'.
MY OLD HIGH SCHOOL BUDDIES WANT TO MEET YOU, SUGURI-CHAN...
WHAT... MEET ME?

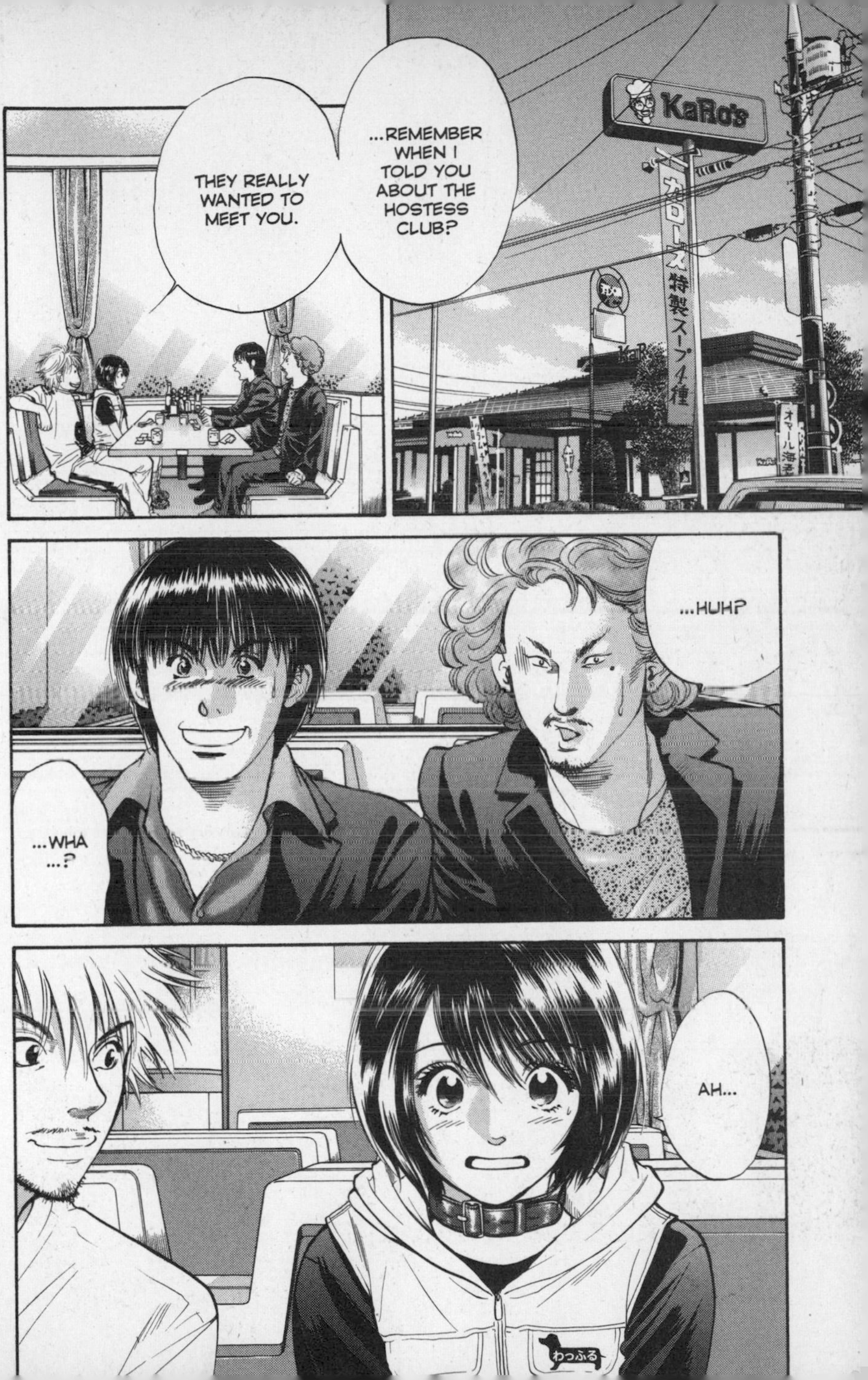
KaRo's
...REMEMBER WHEN I TOLD YOU ABOUT THE HOSTESS CLUB?
THEY REALLY WANTED TO MEET YOU.
...HUH?
...WHA ...?
AH...
わっふる

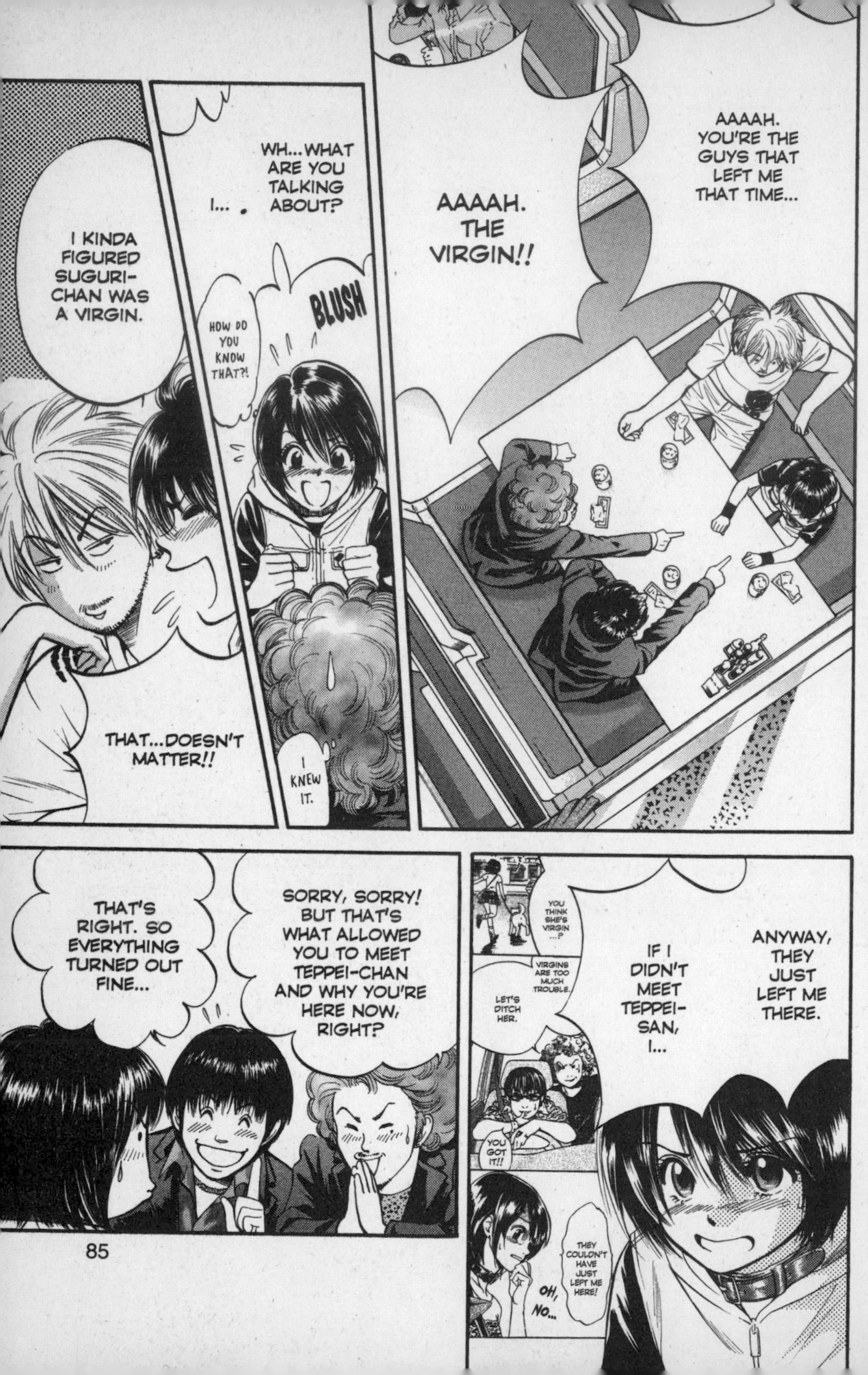
AAAAH. YOU'RE THE GUYS THAT LEFT ME THAT TIME...
AAAAH. THE VIRGIN!!
WH...WHAT ARE YOU TALKING ABOUT?
I...
BLUSH
HOW DO YOU KNOW THAT?!
I KNEW IT.
I KINDA FIGURED SUGURI-CHAN WAS A VIRGIN.
THAT...DOESN'T MATTER!!
ANYWAY, THEY JUST LEFT ME THERE.
IF I DIDN'T MEET TEPPEI-SAN, I...
YOU THINK SHE'S VIRGIN ...?
VIRGINS ARE TOO MUCH TROUBLE.
LET'S DITCH HER.
YOU GOT IT!!
THEY COULDN'T HAVE JUST LEFT ME HERE!
OH, NO...
SORRY, SORRY! BUT THAT'S WHAT ALLOWED YOU TO MEET TEPPEI-CHAN AND WHY YOU'RE HERE NOW, RIGHT?
THAT'S RIGHT. SO EVERYTHING TURNED OUT FINE...

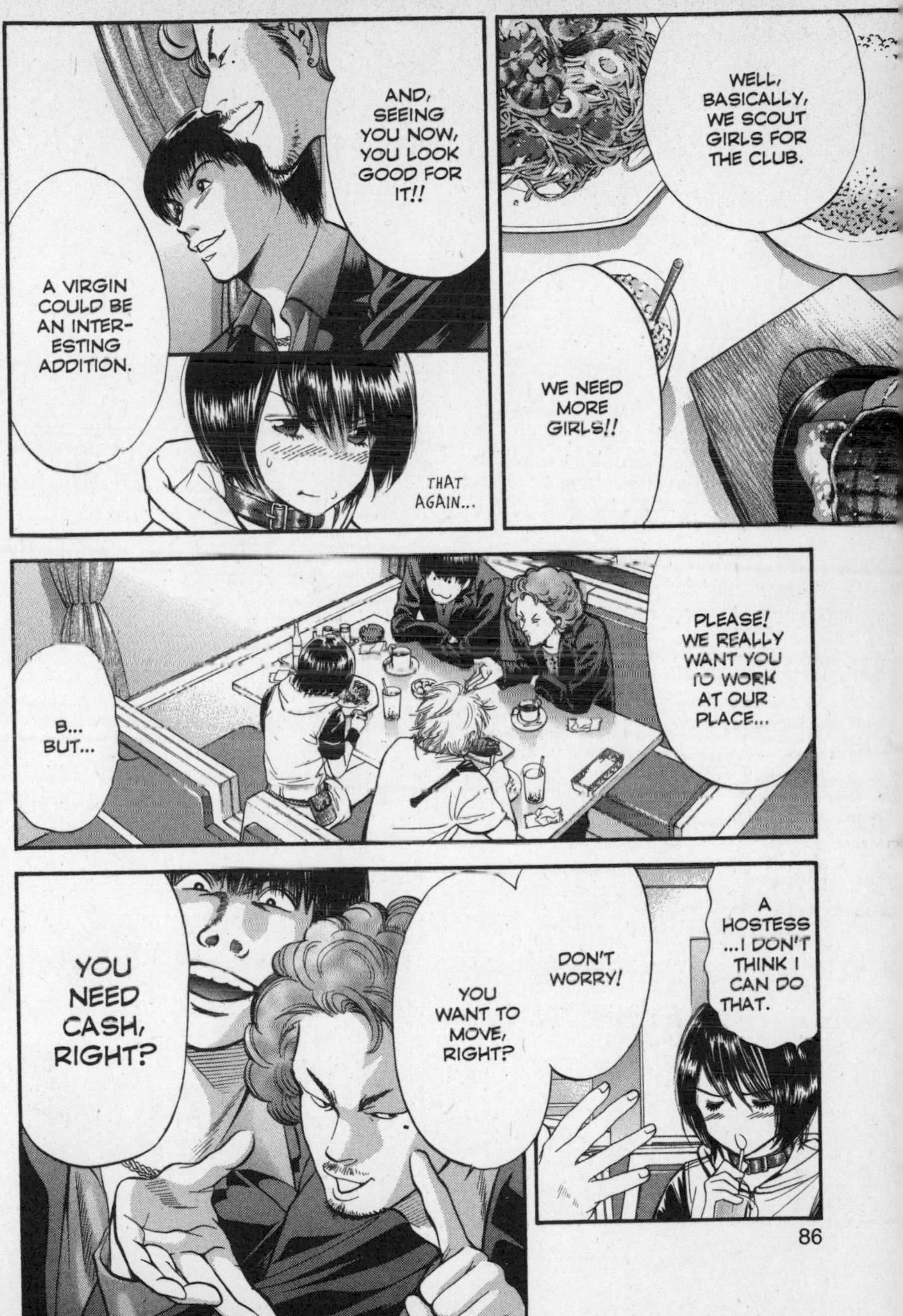
WELL, BASICALLY, WE SCOUT GIRLS FOR THE CLUB.
WE NEED MORE GIRLS!!
AND, SEEING YOU NOW, YOU LOOK GOOD FOR IT!!
A VIRGIN COULD BE AN INTER-ESTING ADDITION.
THAT AGAIN...
PLEASE! WE REALLY WANT YOU TO WORK AT OUR PLACE...
B... BUT...
A HOSTESS ...I DON'T THINK I CAN DO THAT.
DON'T WORRY!
YOU WANT TO MOVE, RIGHT?
YOU NEED CASH, RIGHT?

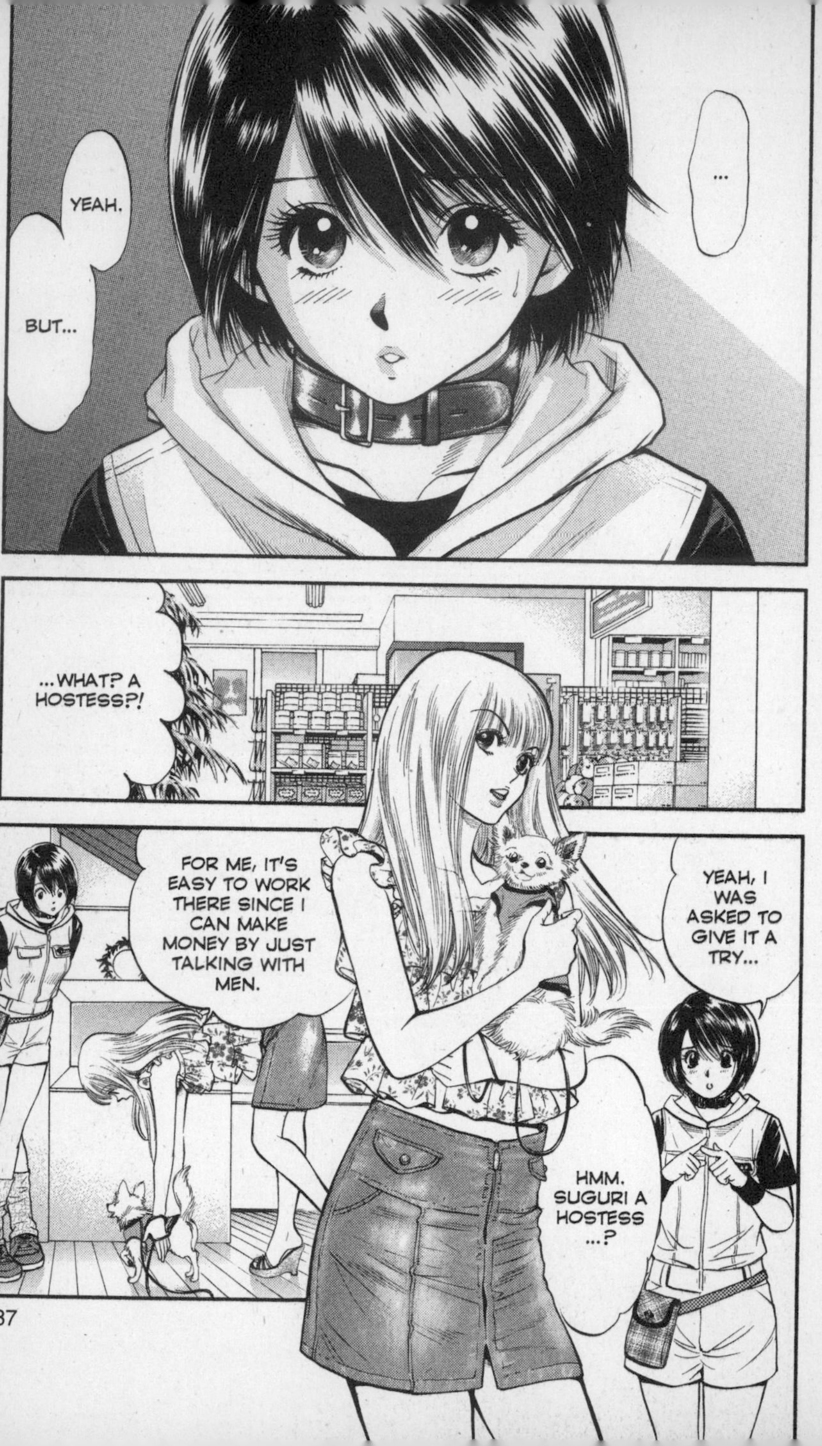
...
YEAH.
BUT...
...WHAT? A HOSTESS?!
YEAH, I WAS ASKED TO GIVE IT A TRY...
HMM. SUGURI A HOSTESS ...?
FOR ME, IT'S EASY TO WORK THERE SINCE I CAN MAKE MONEY BY JUST TALKING WITH MEN.
W...WELL, CHIZURU-CHAN.

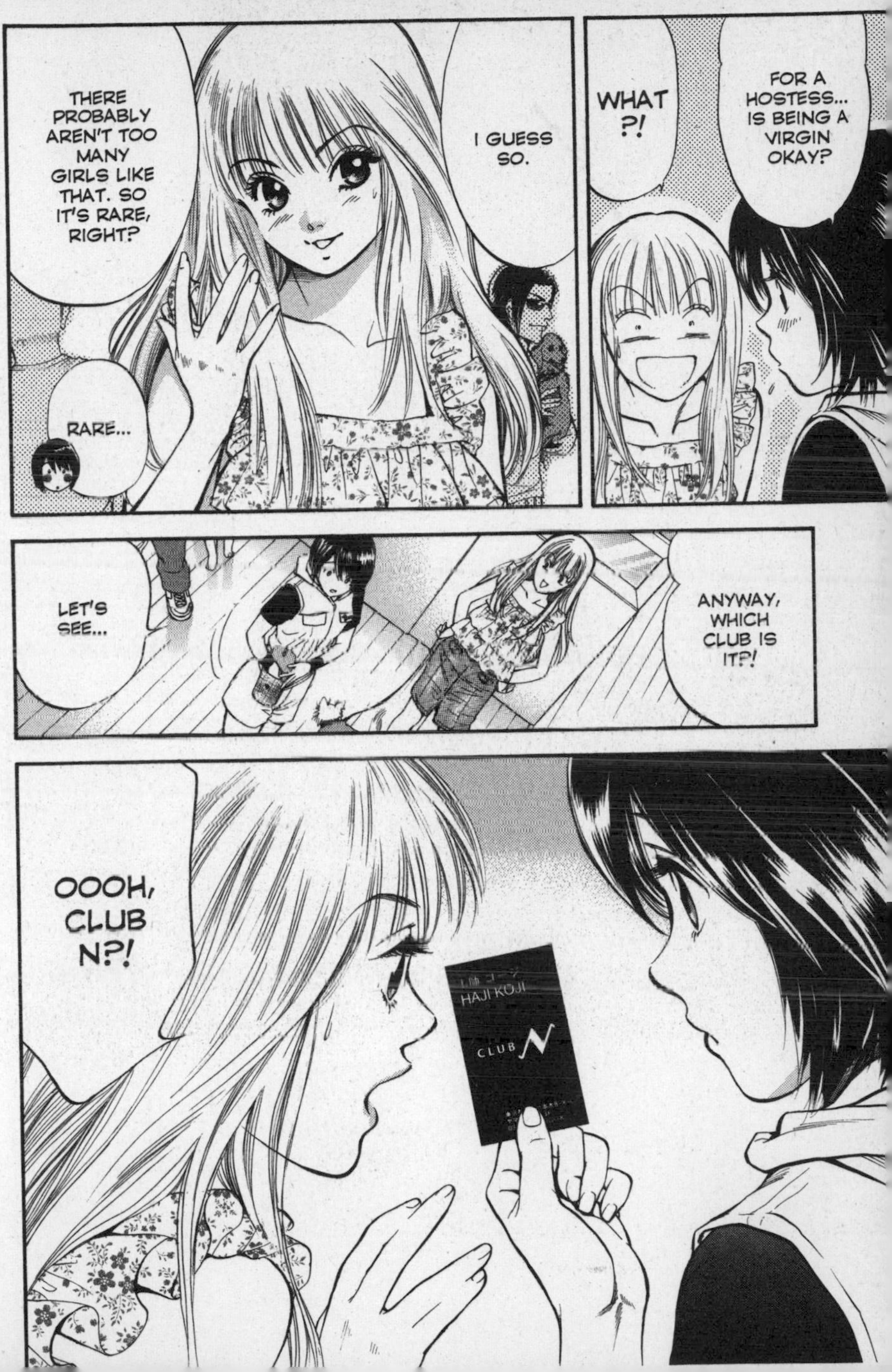
FOR A HOSTESS... IS BEING A VIRGIN OKAY?
WHAT?!
I GUESS SO.
THERE PROBABLY AREN'T TOO MANY GIRLS LIKE THAT. SO IT'S RARE, RIGHT?
RARE...
ANYWAY, WHICH CLUB IS IT?!
LET'S SEE...
OOOH, CLUB N?!
HAJI KOJI
CLUB N

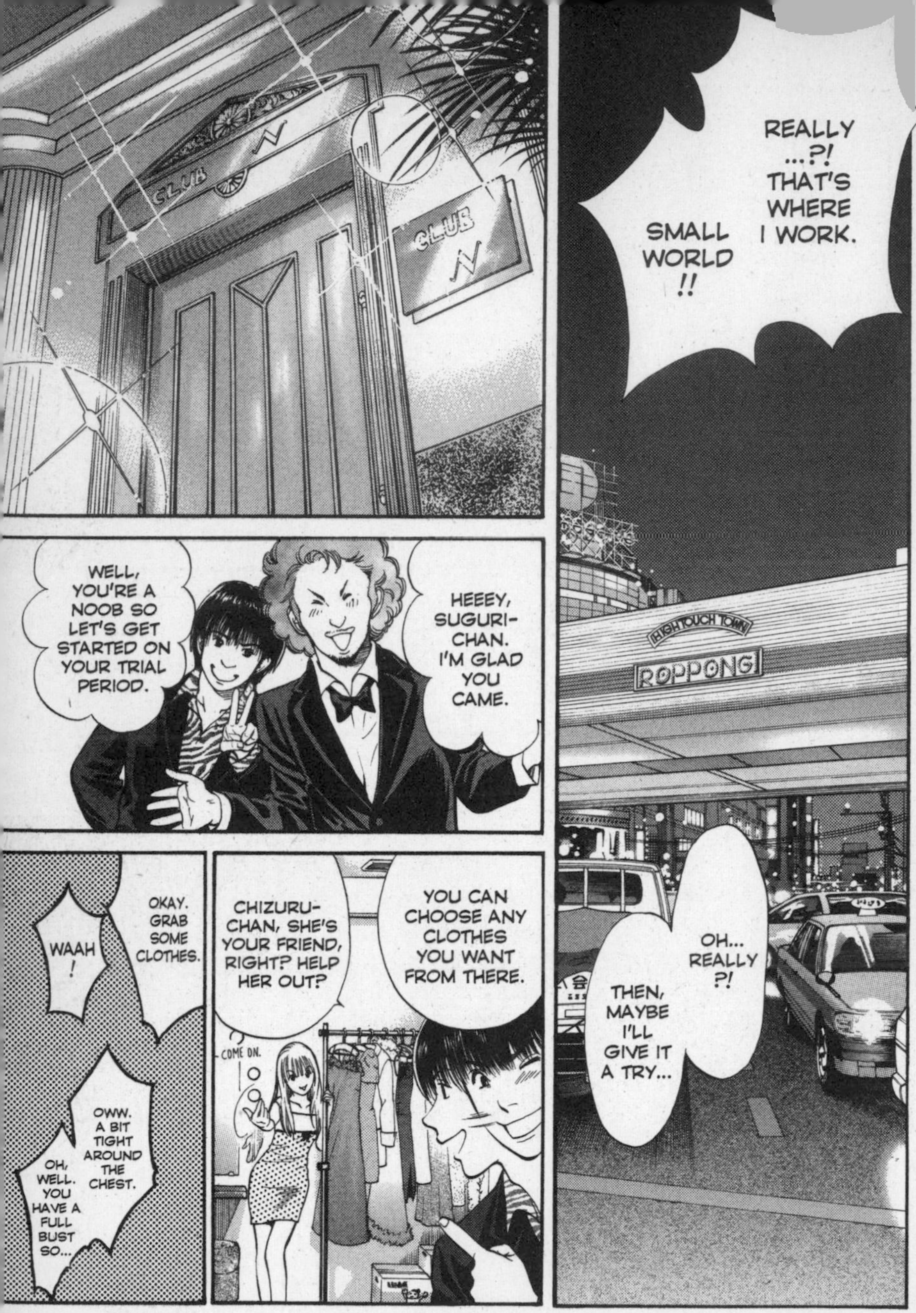
REALLY ...?! THAT'S WHERE I WORK.
SMALL WORLD !!
OH... REALLY ?!
THEN, MAYBE I'LL GIVE IT A TRY...
CLUB
CLUB
HIGH TOUCH TOWN
ROPPONGI
HEEEY, SUGURI-CHAN. I'M GLAD YOU CAME.
WELL, YOU'RE A NOOB SO LET'S GET STARTED ON YOUR TRIAL PERIOD.
YOU CAN CHOOSE ANY CLOTHES YOU WANT FROM THERE.
CHIZURU-CHAN, SHE'S YOUR FRIEND, RIGHT? HELP HER OUT?
COME ON.
OKAY. GRAB SOME CLOTHES.
WAAH!
OWW. A BIT TIGHT AROUND THE CHEST.
OH, WELL. YOU HAVE A FULL BUST SO...

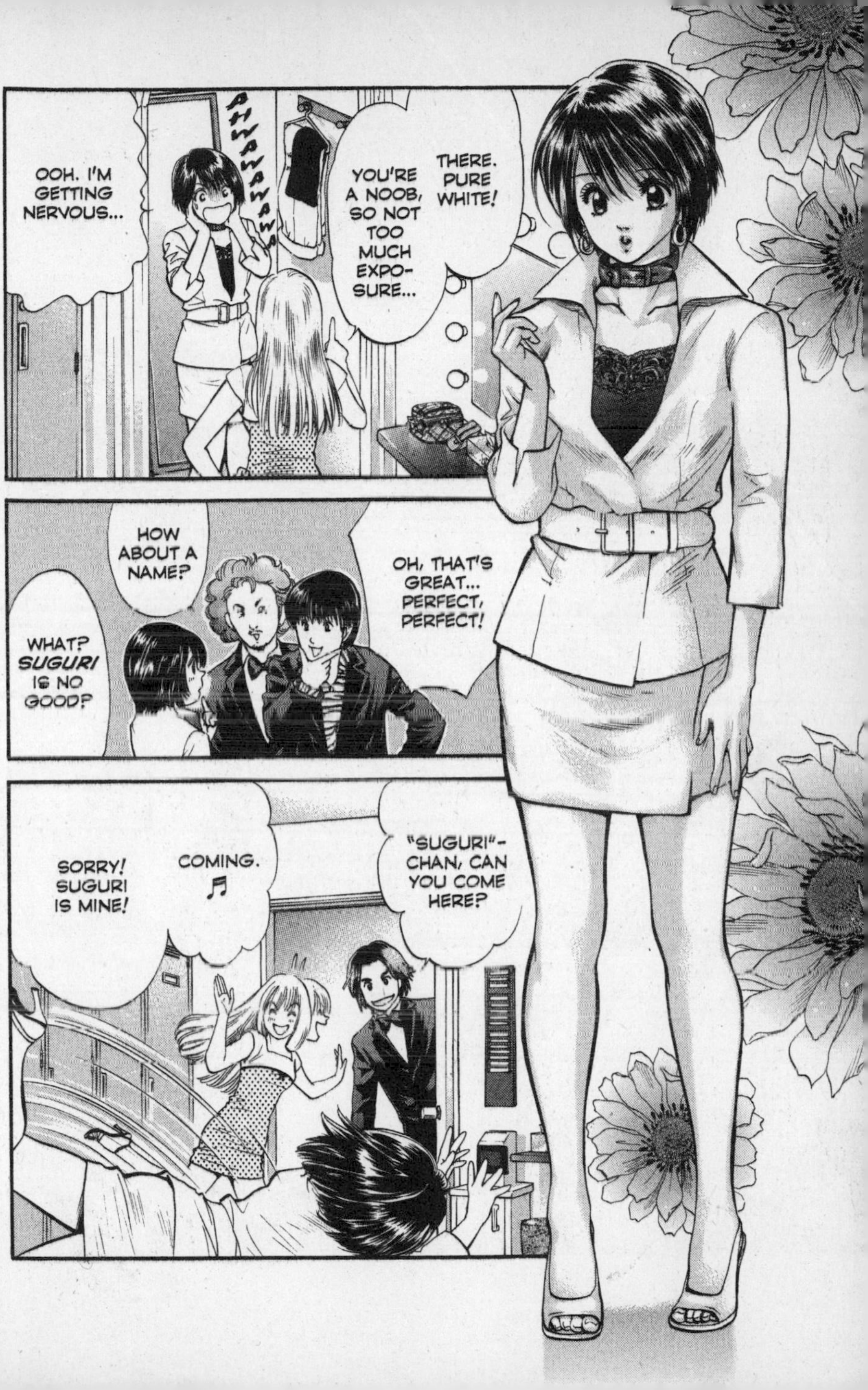
THERE. PURE WHITE!
YOU'RE A NOOB, SO NOT TOO MUCH EXPOSURE...
AHWAWAWAWA
OOH. I'M GETTING NERVOUS...
OH, THAT'S GREAT... PERFECT, PERFECT!
HOW ABOUT A NAME?
WHAT? *SUGURI* IS NO GOOD?
"SUGURI"-CHAN, CAN YOU COME HERE?
COMING. ♫
SORRY! SUGURI IS MINE!

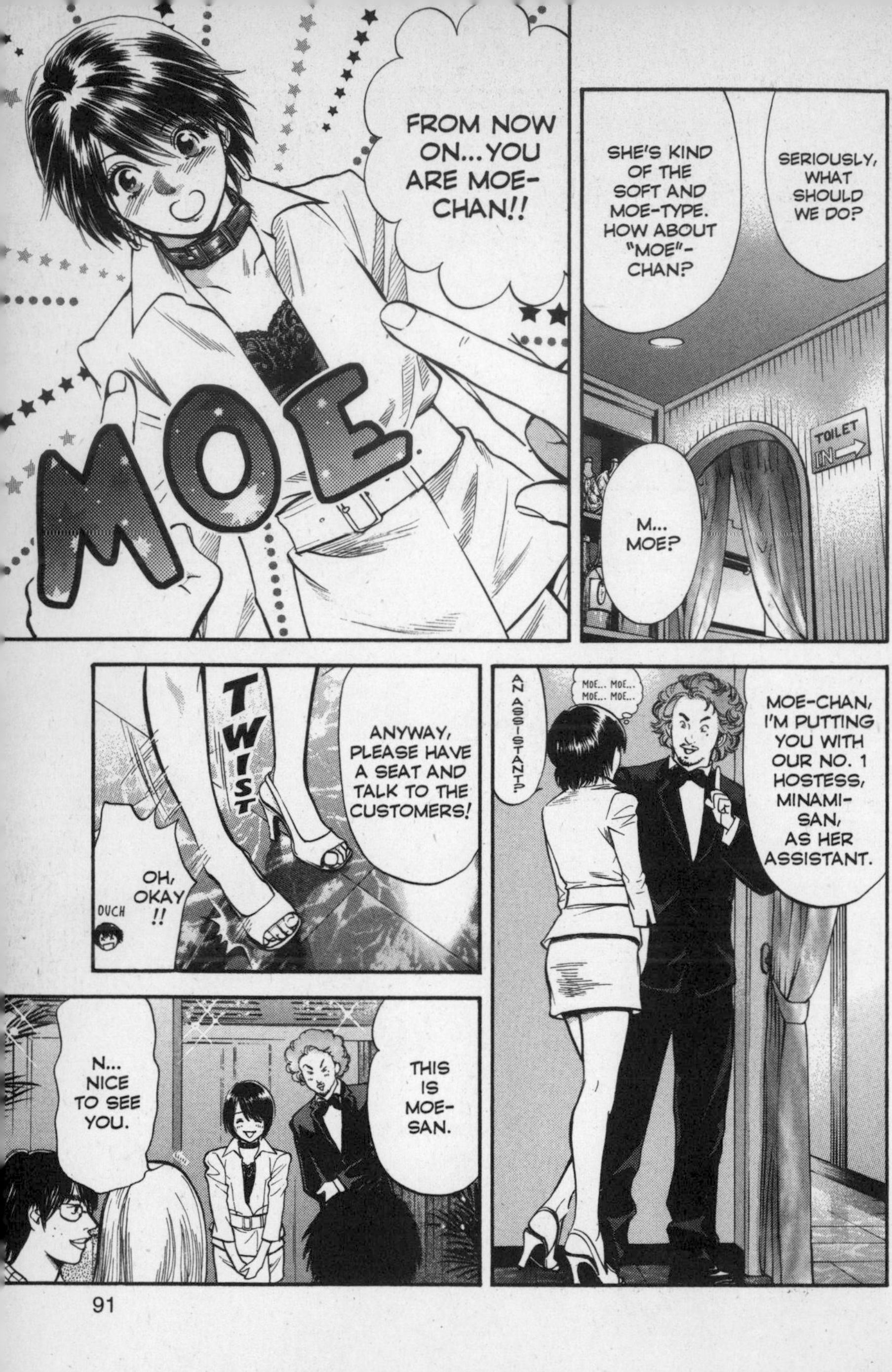
SERIOUSLY, WHAT SHOULD WE DO?
SHE'S KIND OF THE SOFT AND MOE-TYPE. HOW ABOUT "MOE"-CHAN?
M... MOE?
TOILET IN
FROM NOW ON...YOU ARE MOE-CHAN!!
MOE
MOE-CHAN, I'M PUTTING YOU WITH OUR NO. 1 HOSTESS, MINAMI-SAN, AS HER ASSISTANT.
MOE... MOE... MOE... MOE...
AN ASSISTANT!?
ANYWAY, PLEASE HAVE A SEAT AND TALK TO THE CUSTOMERS!
TWIST
OH, OKAY!!
OUCH
THIS IS MOE-SAN.
N... NICE TO SEE YOU.

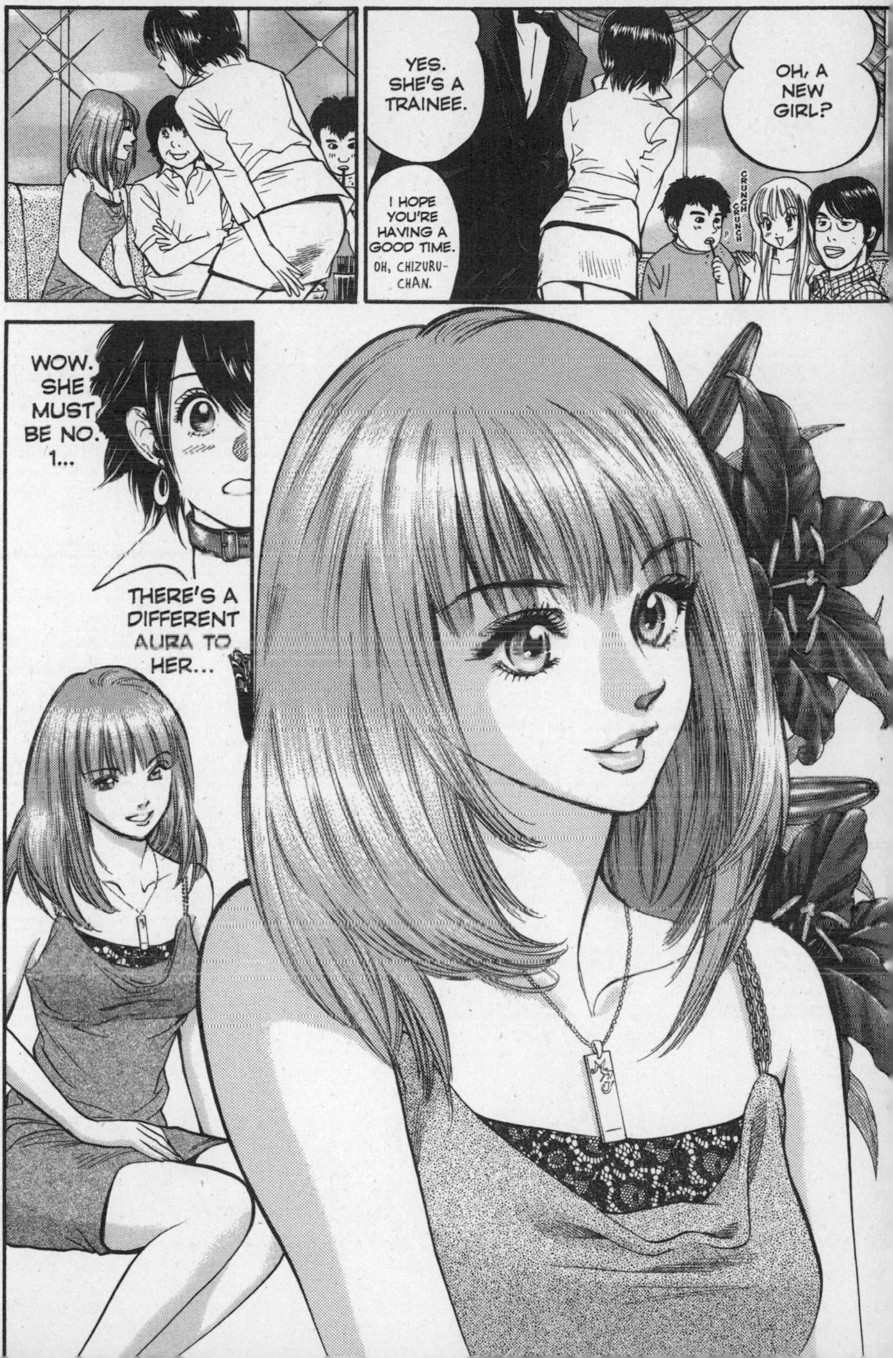
OH, A NEW GIRL?
CRUNCH CRUNCH
YES. SHE'S A TRAINEE.
I HOPE YOU'RE HAVING A GOOD TIME.
OH, CHIZURU-CHAN.
WOW. SHE MUST BE NO. 1...
THERE'S A DIFFERENT AURA TO HER...

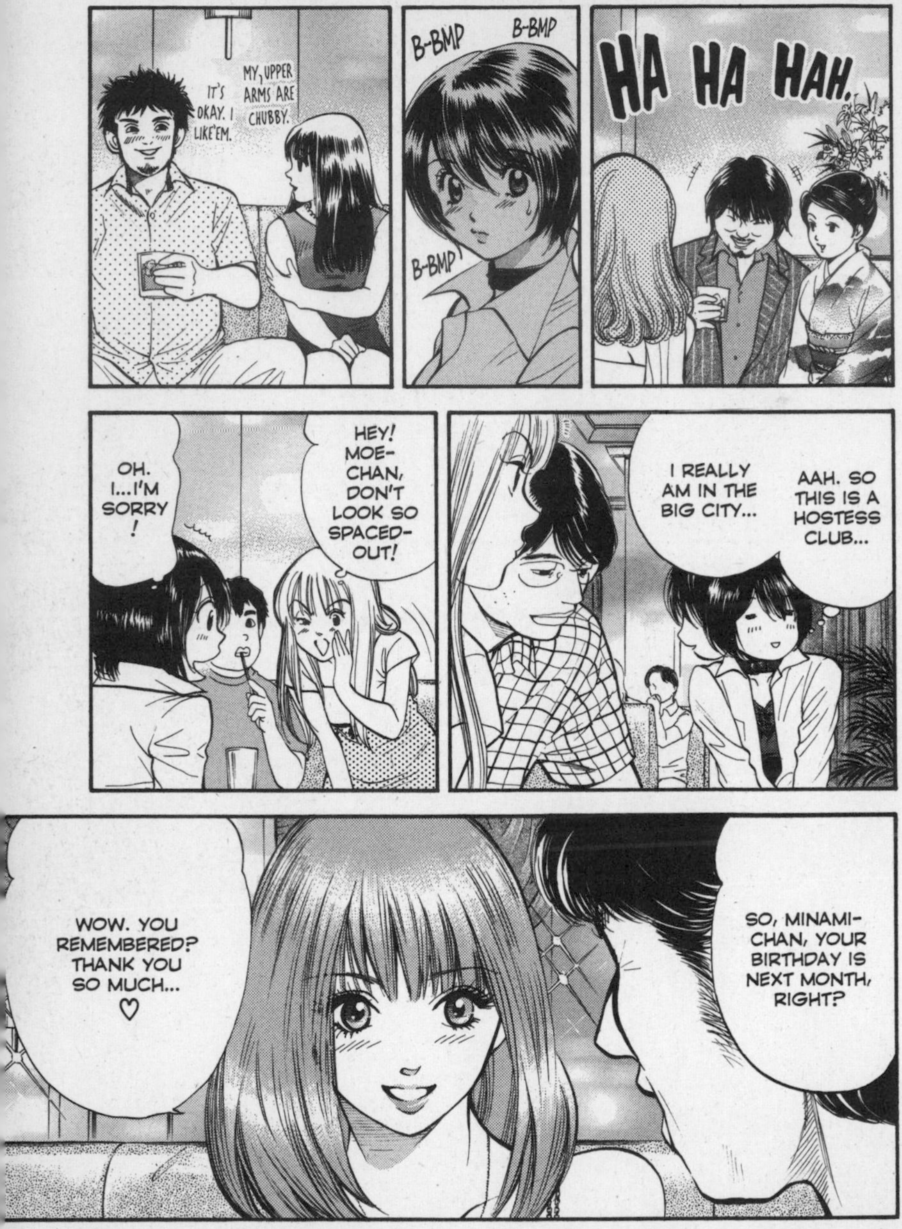
HA HA HAH.
B-BMP
B-BMP
B-BMP
MY, UPPER ARMS ARE CHUBBY.
IT'S OKAY. I LIKE'EM.
AAH. SO THIS IS A HOSTESS CLUB...
I REALLY AM IN THE BIG CITY...
HEY! MOE-CHAN, DON'T LOOK SO SPACED-OUT!
OH. I...I'M SORRY!
SO, MINAMI-CHAN, YOUR BIRTHDAY IS NEXT MONTH, RIGHT?
WOW. YOU REMEMBERED? THANK YOU SO MUCH... ♡

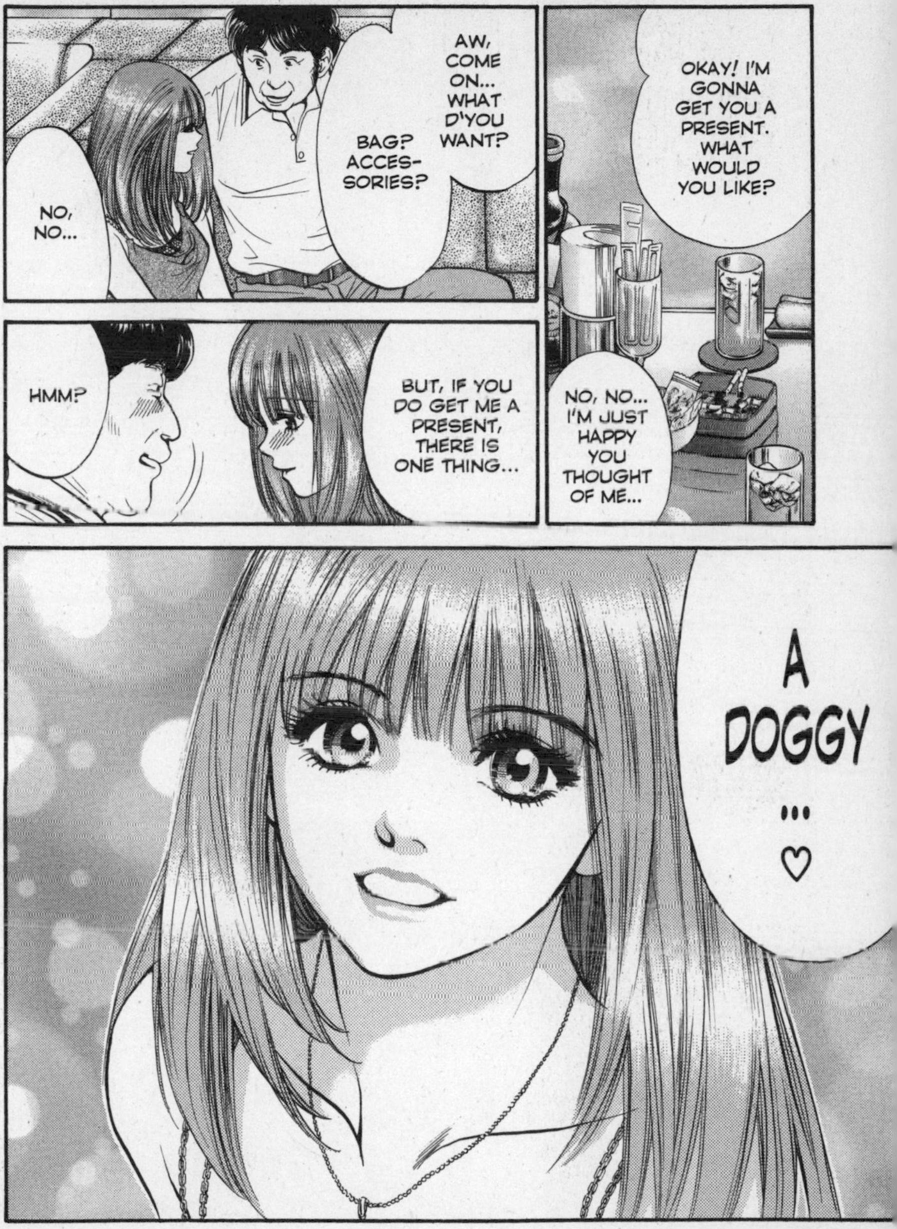
OKAY! I'M GONNA GET YOU A PRESENT. WHAT WOULD YOU LIKE?
NO, NO... I'M JUST HAPPY YOU THOUGHT OF ME...
AW, COME ON... WHAT D'YOU WANT?
BAG? ACCES-SORIES?
NO, NO...
BUT, IF YOU DO GET ME A PRESENT, THERE IS ONE THING...
HMM?
A DOGGY ... ♡

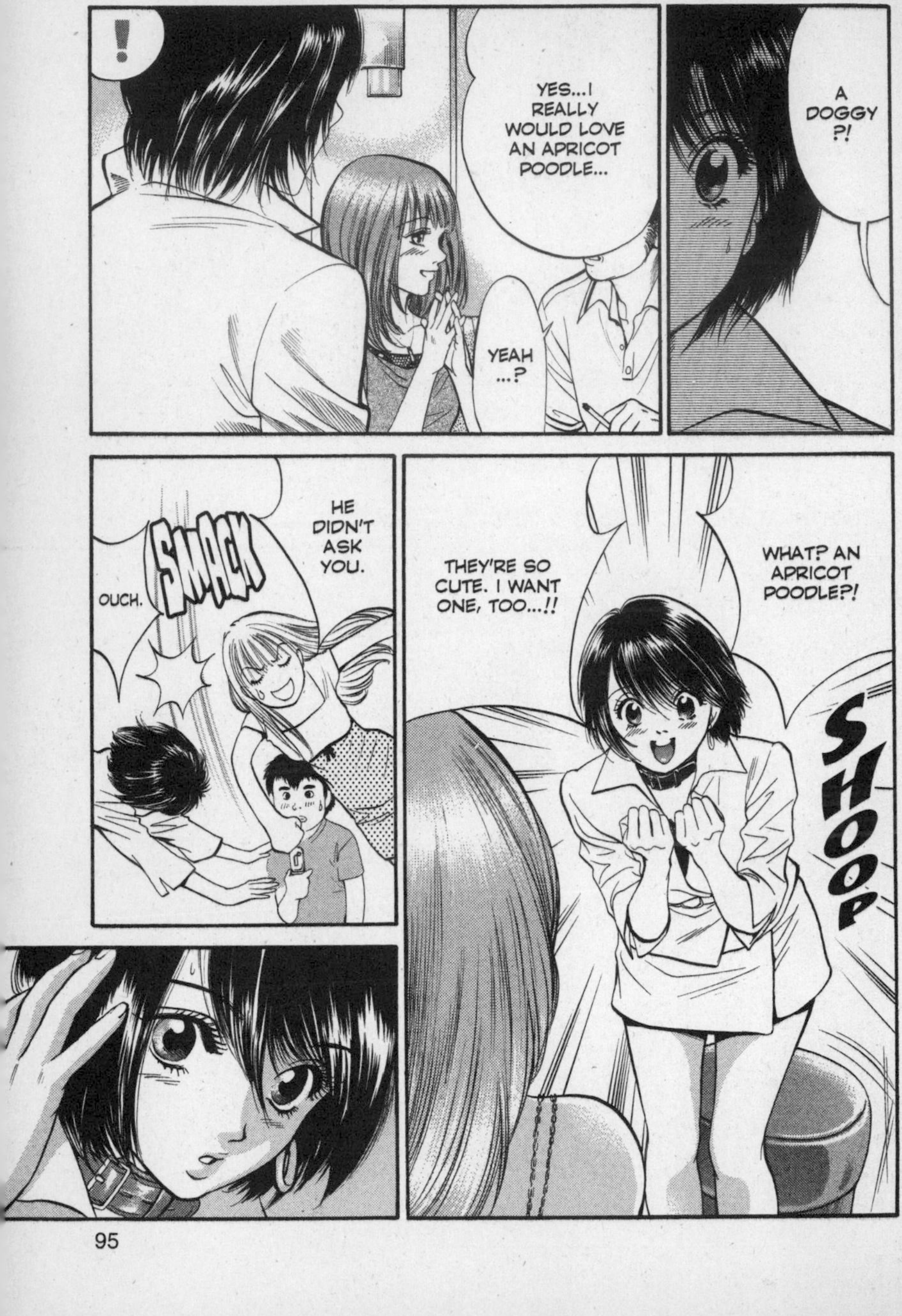
A DOGGY ?!
YES...I REALLY WOULD LOVE AN APRICOT POODLE...
YEAH ...?
!
WHAT? AN APRICOT POODLE?!
THEY'RE SO CUTE. I WANT ONE, TOO...!!
SHOOP
HE DIDN'T ASK YOU.
SMACK
OUCH.

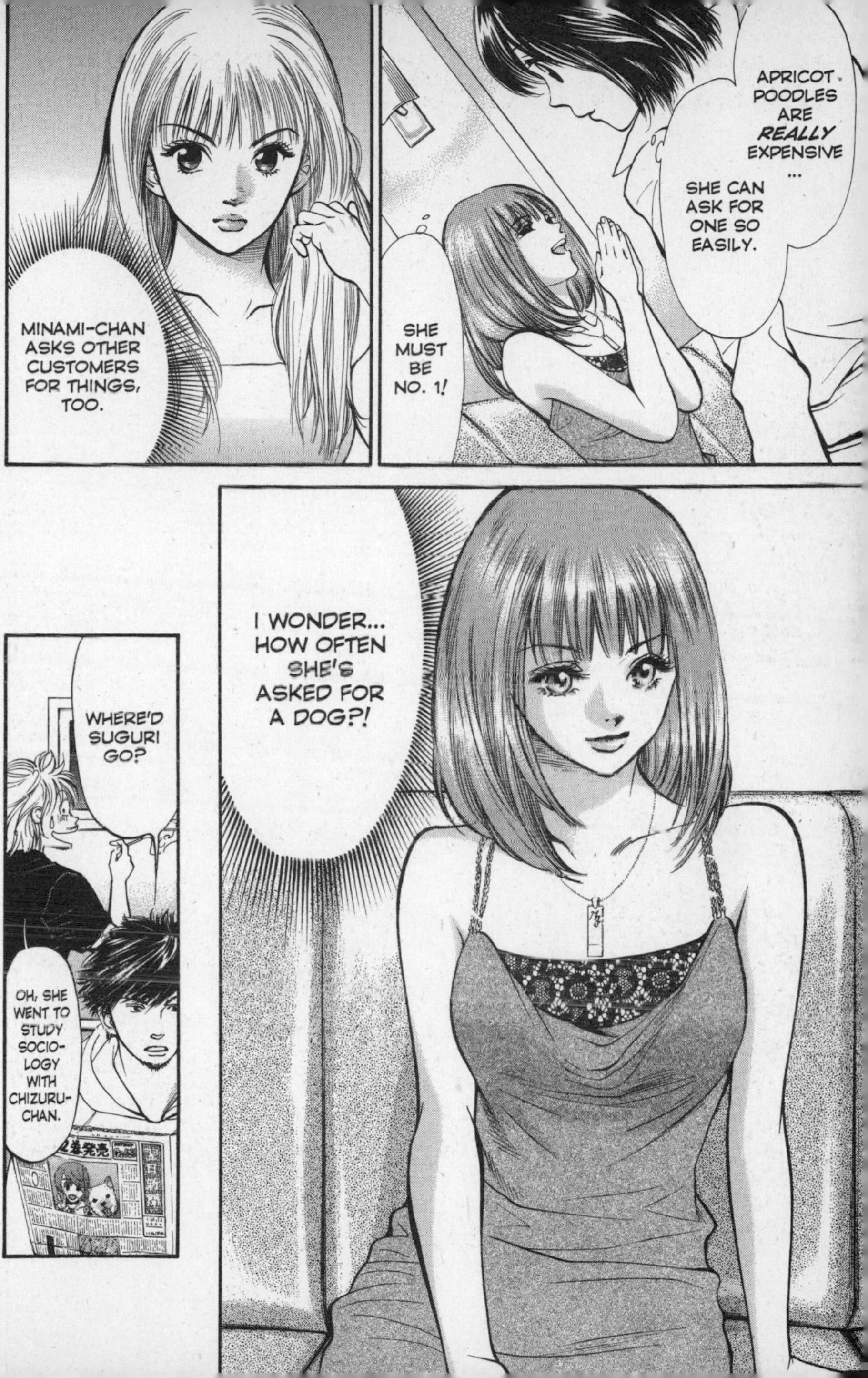
APRICOT POODLES ARE *REALLY* EXPENSIVE ...
SHE CAN ASK FOR ONE SO EASILY.
SHE MUST BE NO. 1!
MINAMI-CHAN ASKS OTHER CUSTOMERS FOR THINGS, TOO.
I WONDER... HOW OFTEN SHE'S ASKED FOR A DOG?!
WHERE'D SUGURI GO?
OH, SHE WENT TO STUDY SOCIO-LOGY WITH CHIZURU-CHAN.

CHAPTER 25: THE WHEREABOUTS OF THE PRESENTS

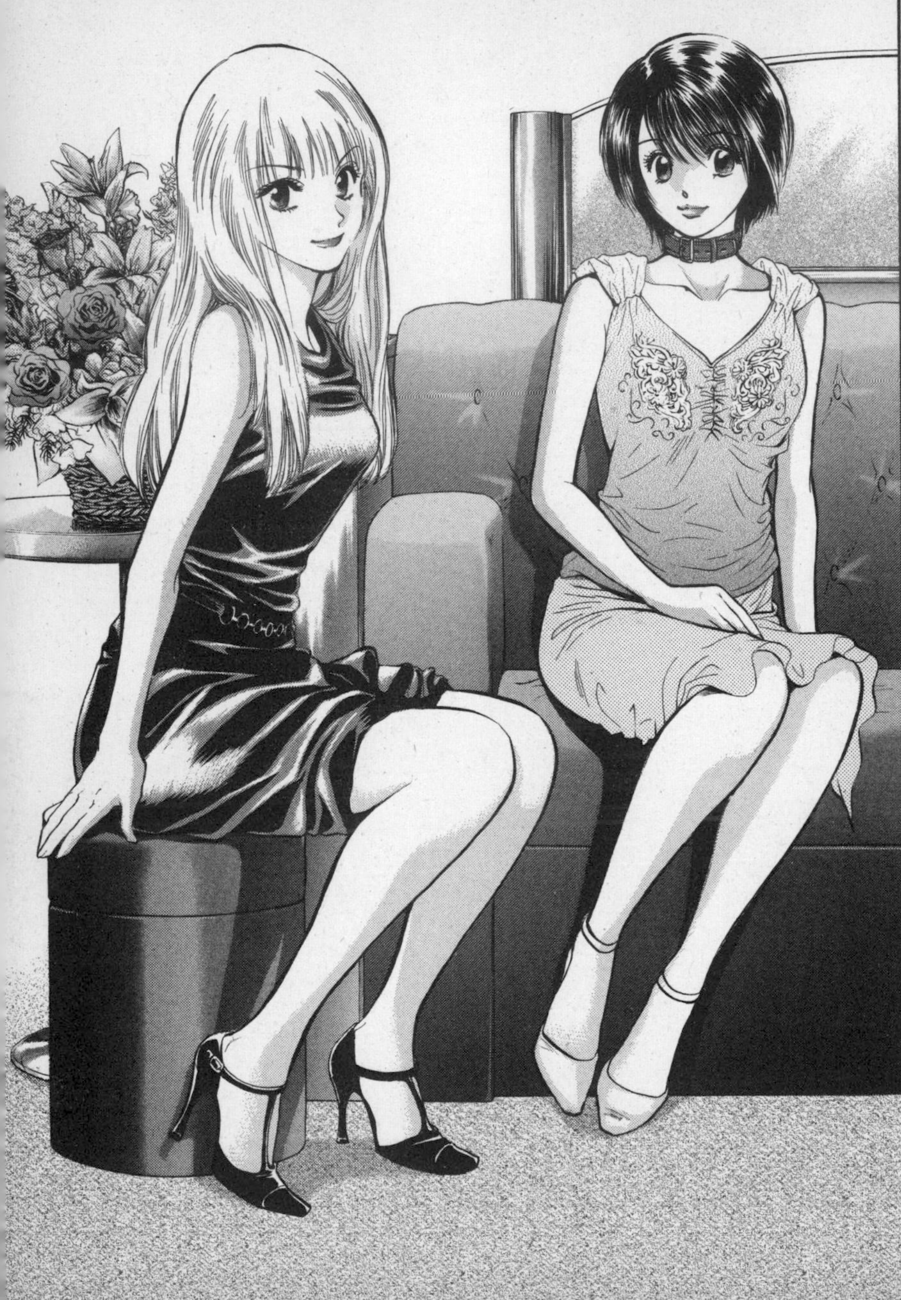

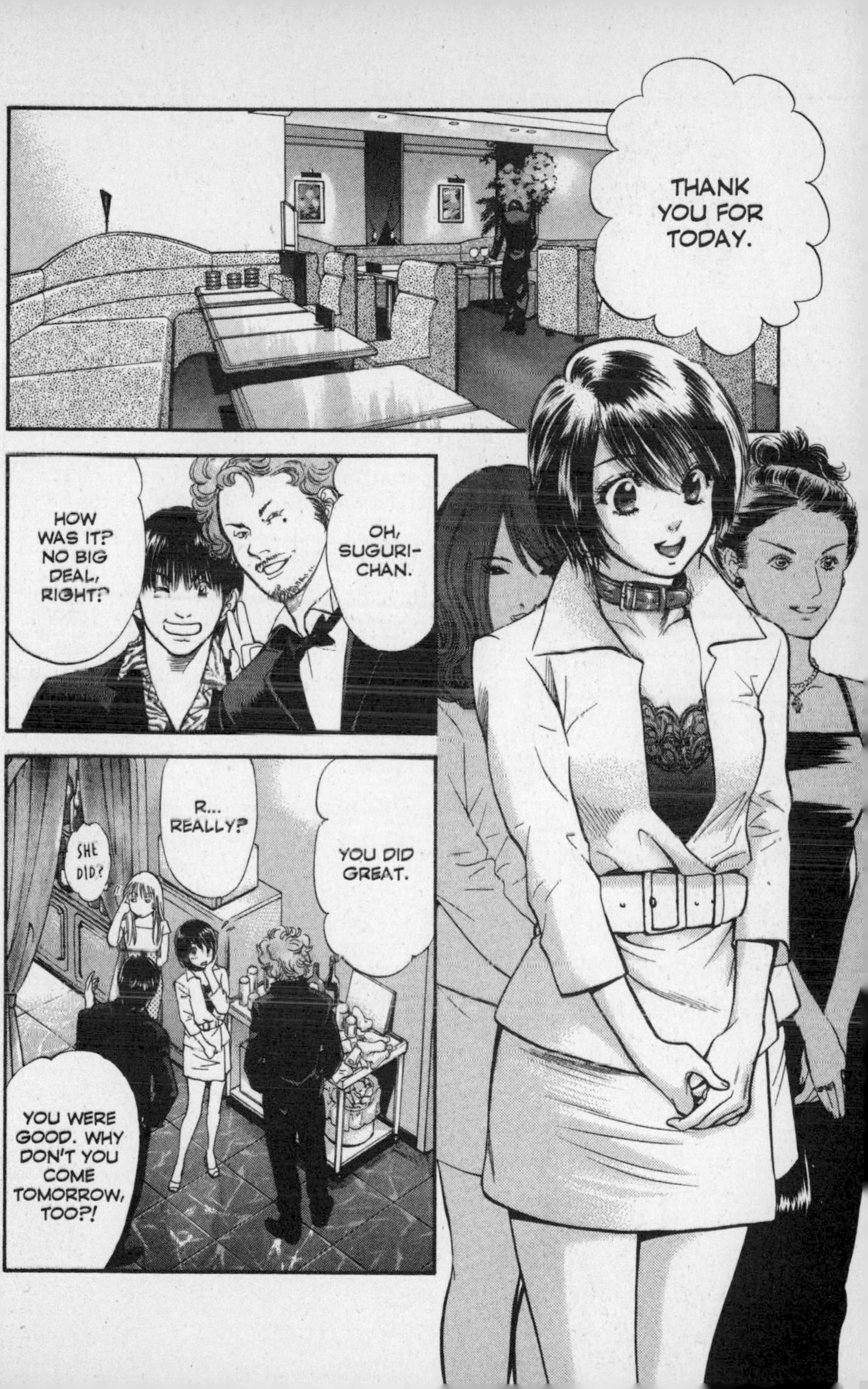
THANK YOU FOR TODAY.
OH, SUGURI-CHAN.
HOW WAS IT? NO BIG DEAL, RIGHT?
YOU DID GREAT.
R... REALLY?
SHE DID?
YOU WERE GOOD. WHY DON'T YOU COME TOMORROW, TOO?!

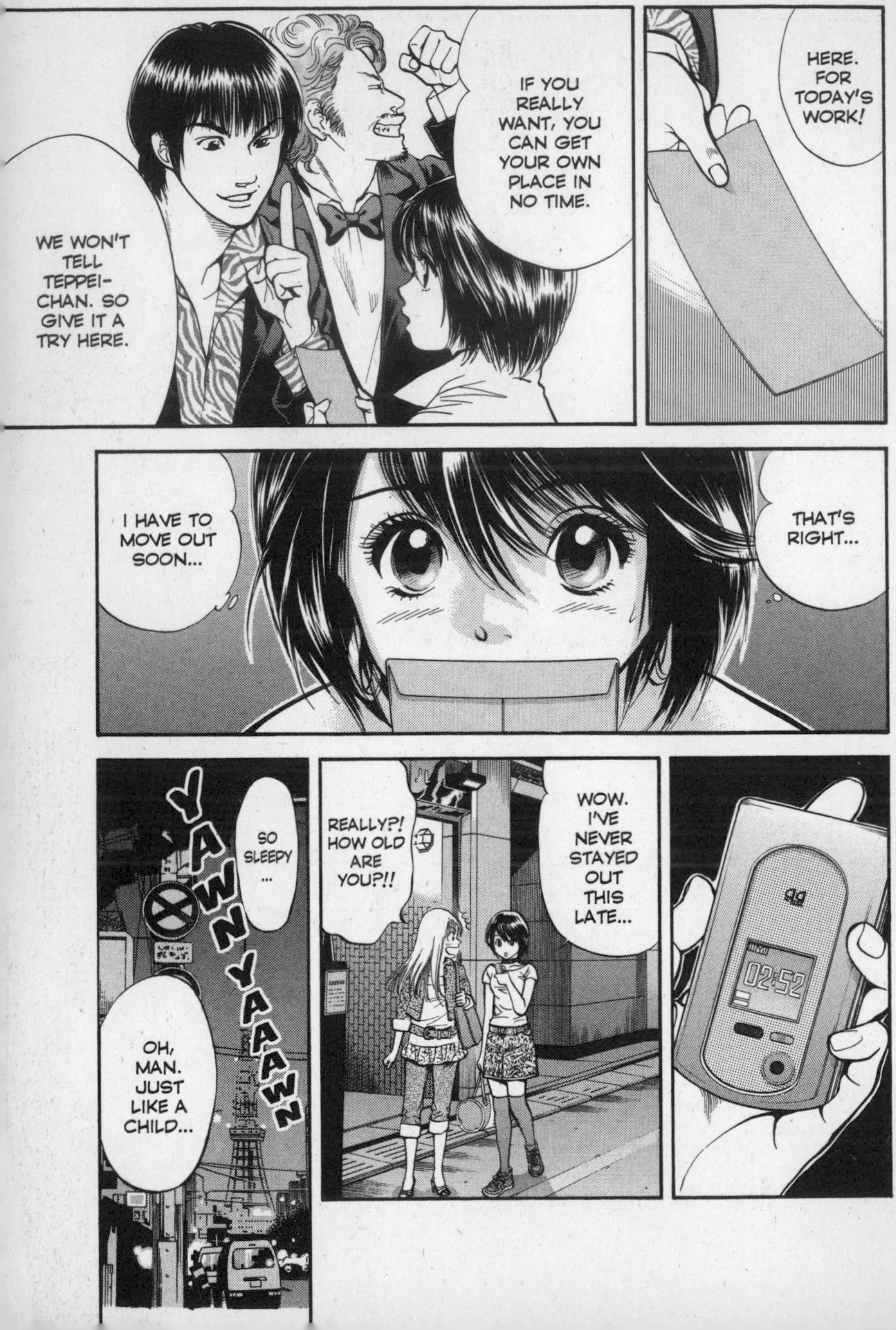
HERE. FOR TODAY'S WORK!
IF YOU REALLY WANT, YOU CAN GET YOUR OWN PLACE IN NO TIME.
WE WON'T TELL TEPPEI-CHAN. SO GIVE IT A TRY HERE.
THAT'S RIGHT...
I HAVE TO MOVE OUT SOON...
02:52
WOW. I'VE NEVER STAYED OUT THIS LATE...
REALLY?! HOW OLD ARE YOU?!!
SO SLEEPY...
YAWN
YAAAAWN
OH, MAN. JUST LIKE A CHILD...

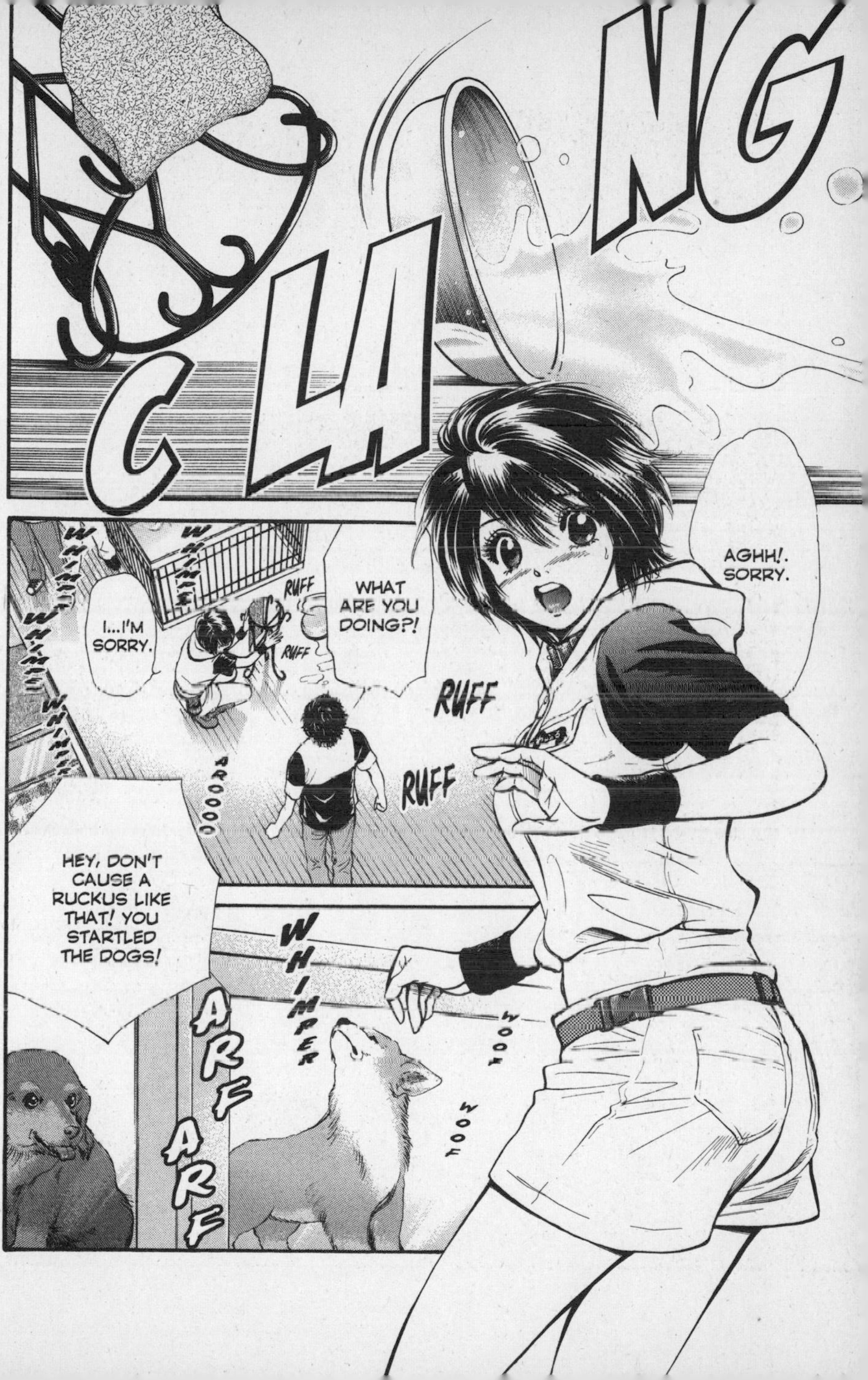
CLANG
AGHH!. SORRY.
WHAT ARE YOU DOING?!
RUFF
RUFF
RUFF
RUFF
I...I'M SORRY.
WHIMPER
WHIMPER
WHIMPER
WHIMPER
AROOOO
HEY, DON'T CAUSE A RUCKUS LIKE THAT! YOU STARTLED THE DOGS!
WOOF
WOOF
WHIMPER
ARF
ARF

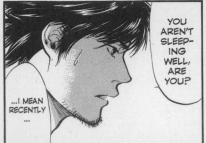

YOU AREN'T SLEEPING WELL, ARE YOU?

...I MEAN RECENTLY...

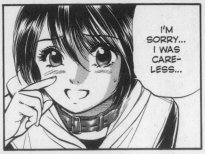

I'M SORRY... I WAS CARELESS...

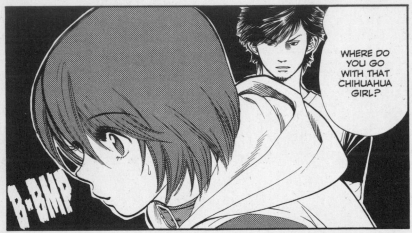

WHERE DO YOU GO WITH THAT CHIHUAHUA GIRL?

B-BMP

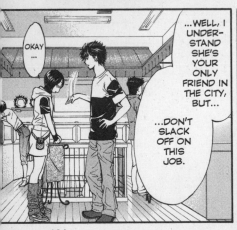

OKAY...

...WELL, I UNDERSTAND SHE'S YOUR ONLY FRIEND IN THE CITY, BUT...

...DON'T SLACK OFF ON THIS JOB.

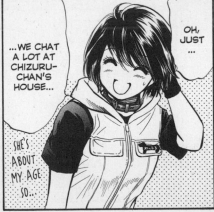

...WE CHAT A LOT AT CHIZURU-CHAN'S HOUSE...

OH, JUST...

SHE'S ABOUT MY AGE SO...

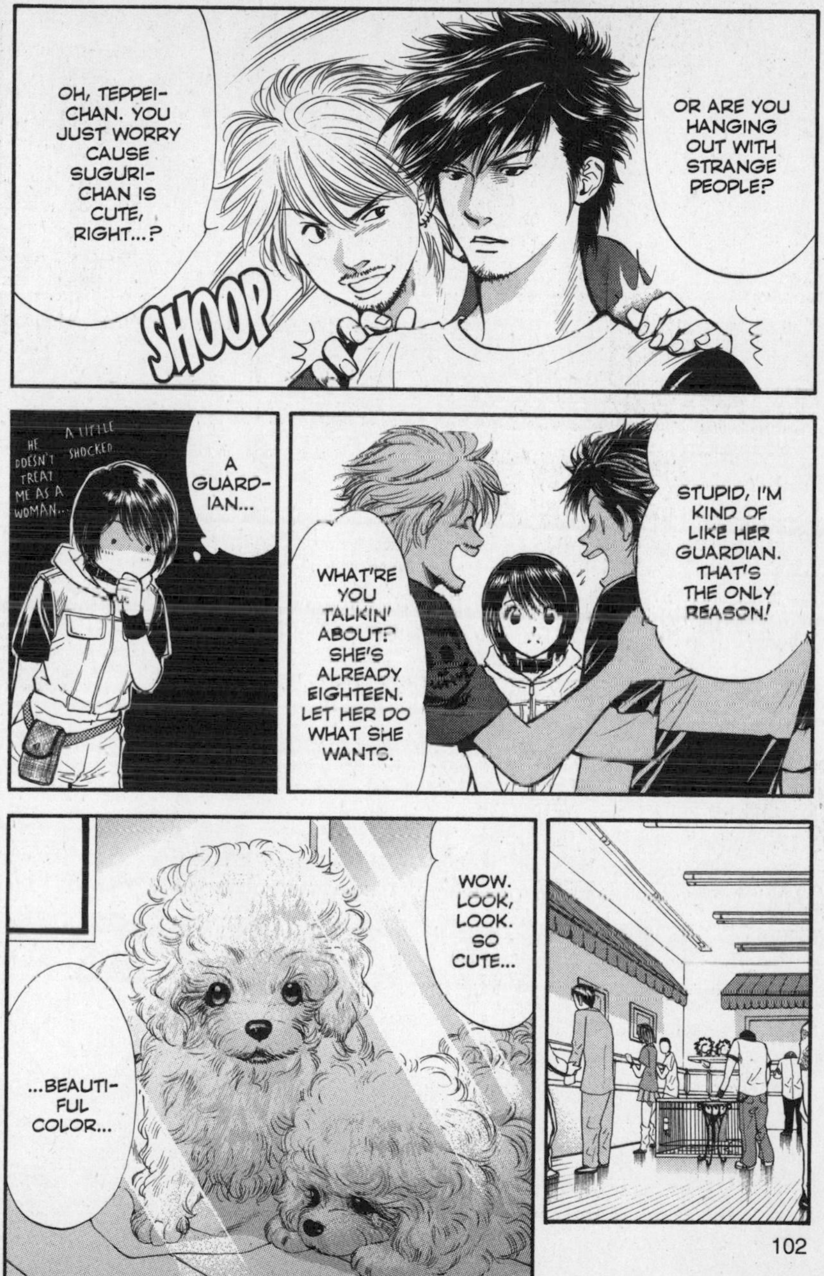
OR ARE YOU HANGING OUT WITH STRANGE PEOPLE?
OH, TEPPEI-CHAN. YOU JUST WORRY CAUSE SUGURI-CHAN IS CUTE, RIGHT...?
SHOOP
STUPID, I'M KIND OF LIKE HER GUARDIAN. THAT'S THE ONLY REASON!
WHAT'RE YOU TALKIN' ABOUT? SHE'S ALREADY EIGHTEEN. LET HER DO WHAT SHE WANTS.
A GUARDIAN...
A LITTLE SHOCKED...
HE DOESN'T TREAT ME AS A WOMAN...
WOW. LOOK, LOOK. SO CUTE...
...BEAUTIFUL COLOR...

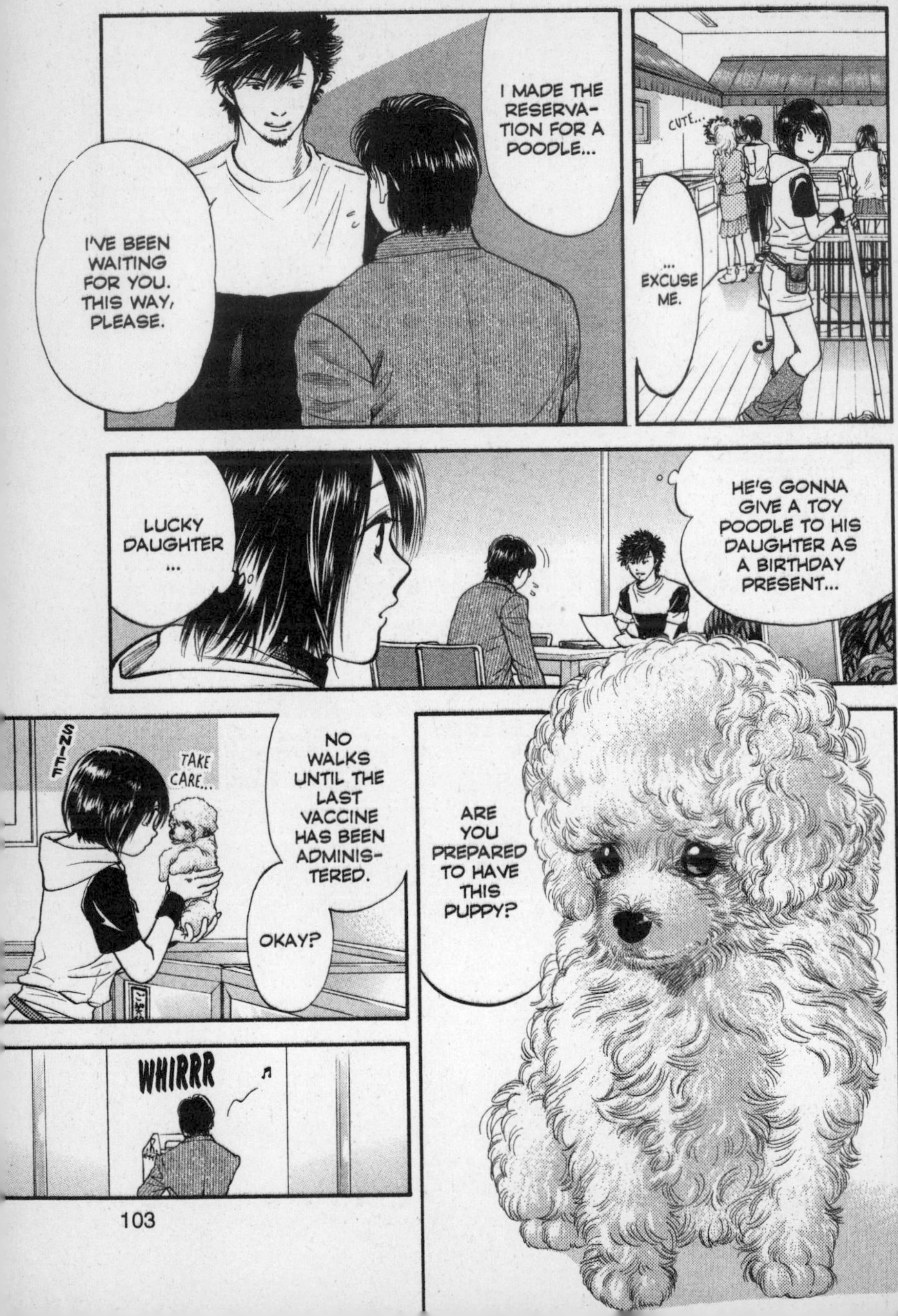
CUTE...
...EXCUSE ME.
I MADE THE RESERVATION FOR A POODLE...
I'VE BEEN WAITING FOR YOU. THIS WAY, PLEASE.
HE'S GONNA GIVE A TOY POODLE TO HIS DAUGHTER AS A BIRTHDAY PRESENT...
LUCKY DAUGHTER...
ARE YOU PREPARED TO HAVE THIS PUPPY?
NO WALKS UNTIL THE LAST VACCINE HAS BEEN ADMINISTERED.
OKAY?
TAKE CARE...
SNIFF
WHIRRR

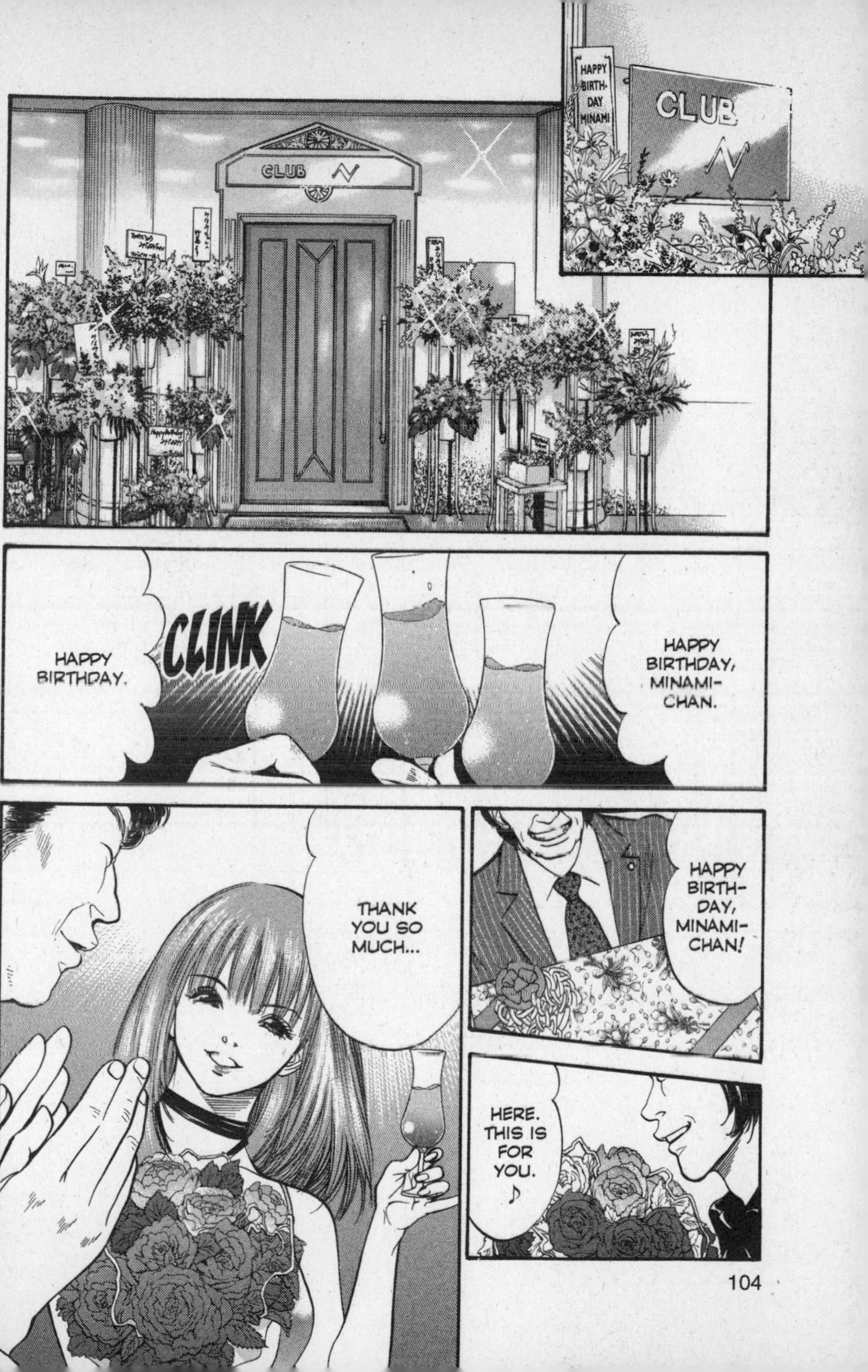
HAPPY BIRTH-DAY MINAMI
CLUB
CLUB
HAPPY BIRTHDAY, MINAMI-CHAN.
CLINK
HAPPY BIRTHDAY.
HAPPY BIRTH-DAY, MINAMI-CHAN!
HERE. THIS IS FOR YOU. ♪
THANK YOU SO MUCH...

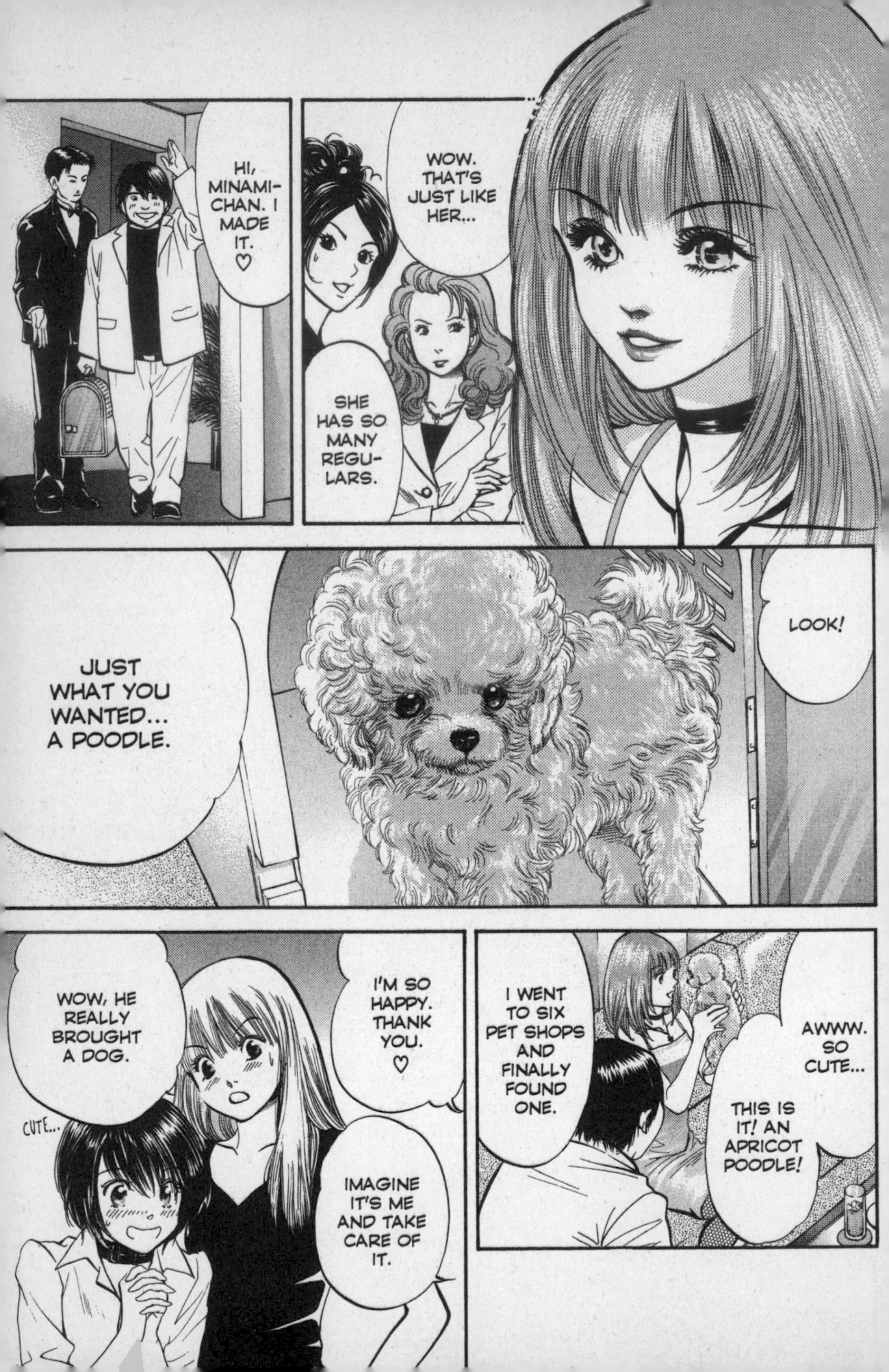
...
WOW. THAT'S JUST LIKE HER...
SHE HAS SO MANY REGULARS.
HI, MINAMI-CHAN. I MADE IT. ♡
LOOK!
JUST WHAT YOU WANTED... A POODLE.
AWWW. SO CUTE...
THIS IS IT! AN APRICOT POODLE!
I WENT TO SIX PET SHOPS AND FINALLY FOUND ONE.
I'M SO HAPPY. THANK YOU. ♡
IMAGINE IT'S ME AND TAKE CARE OF IT.
WOW, HE REALLY BROUGHT A DOG.
CUTE...

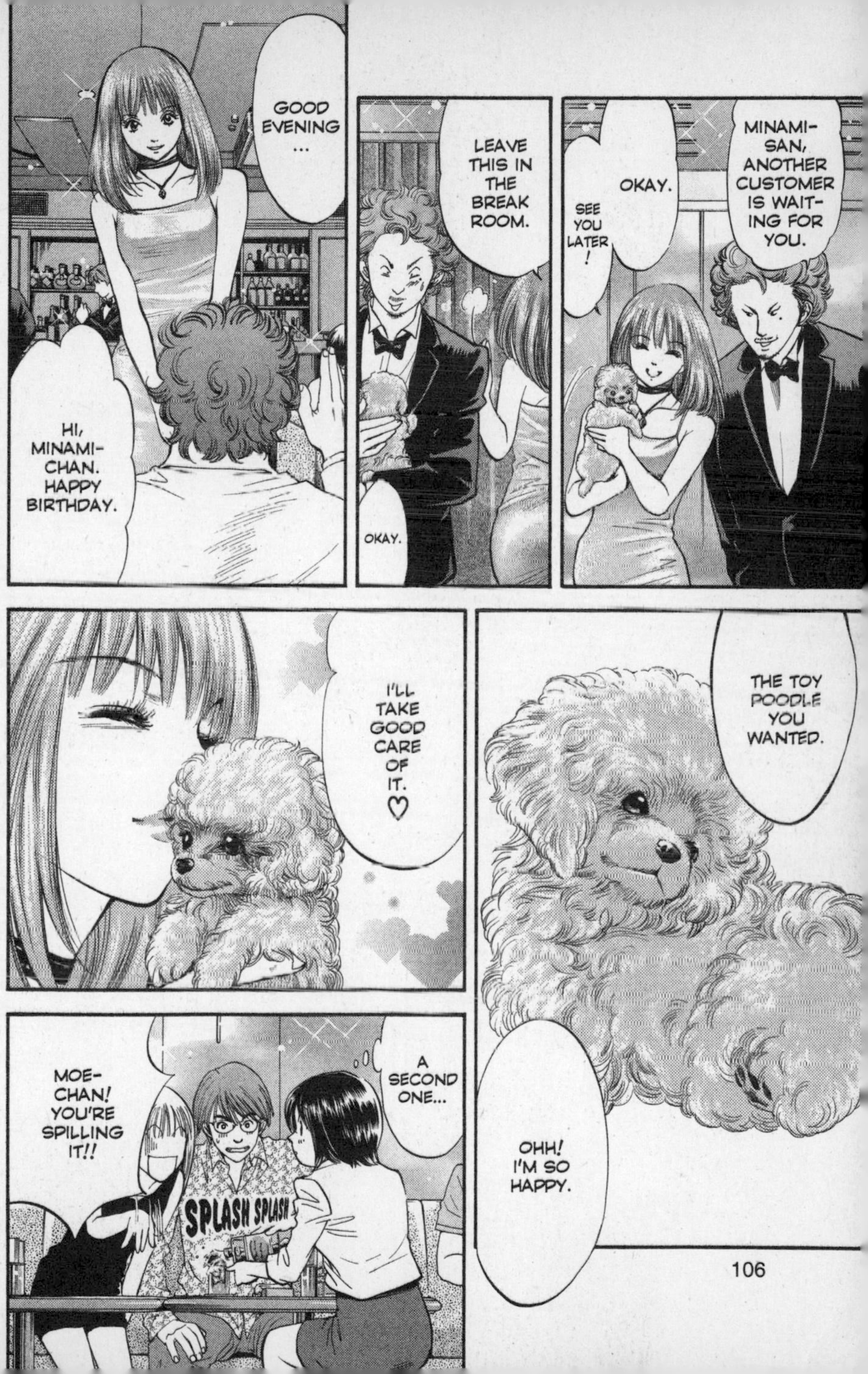
MINAMI-SAN, ANOTHER CUSTOMER IS WAITING FOR YOU.
OKAY.
SEE YOU LATER!
LEAVE THIS IN THE BREAK ROOM.
OKAY.
GOOD EVENING...
HI, MINAMI-CHAN. HAPPY BIRTHDAY.
THE TOY POODLE YOU WANTED.
OHH! I'M SO HAPPY.
I'LL TAKE GOOD CARE OF IT. ♡
A SECOND ONE...
MOE-CHAN! YOU'RE SPILLING IT!!
SPLASH SPLASH

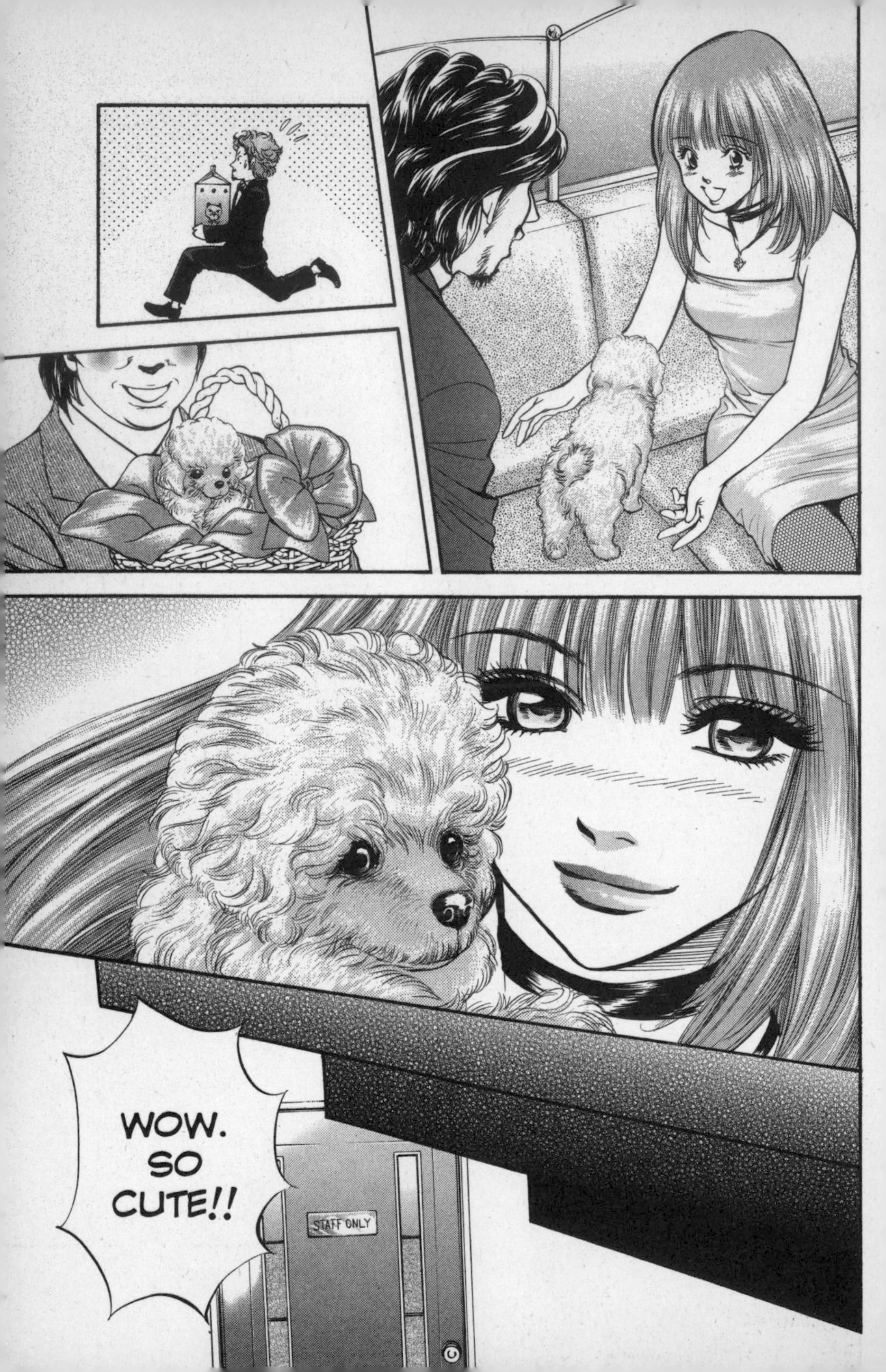
WOW. SO CUTE!!
STAFF ONLY

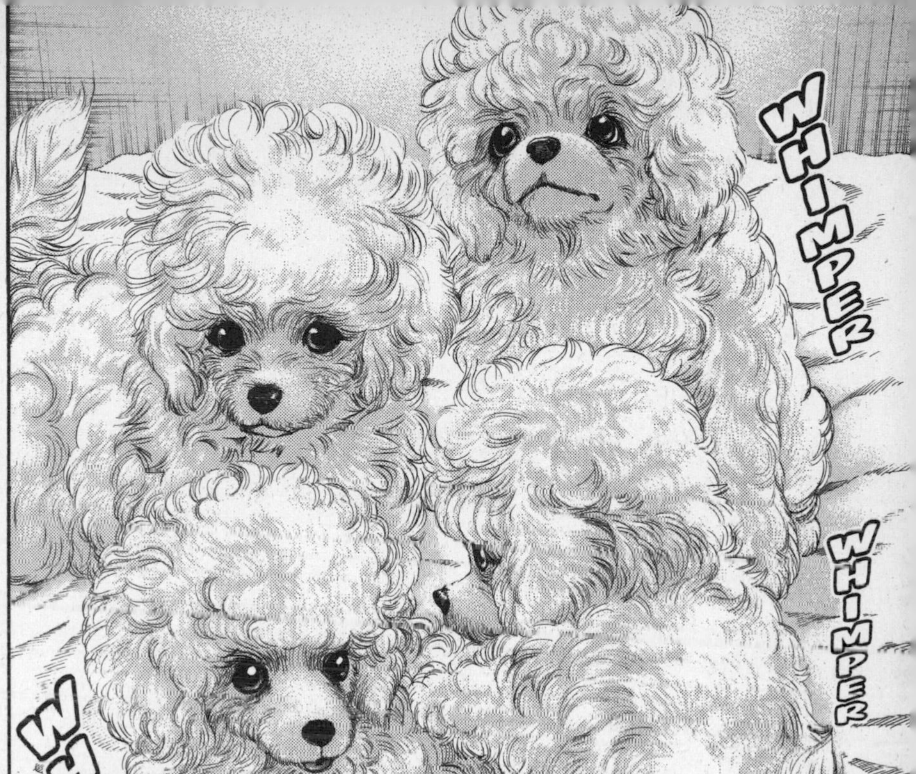
WHIMPER
WHIMPER
WHIMPER
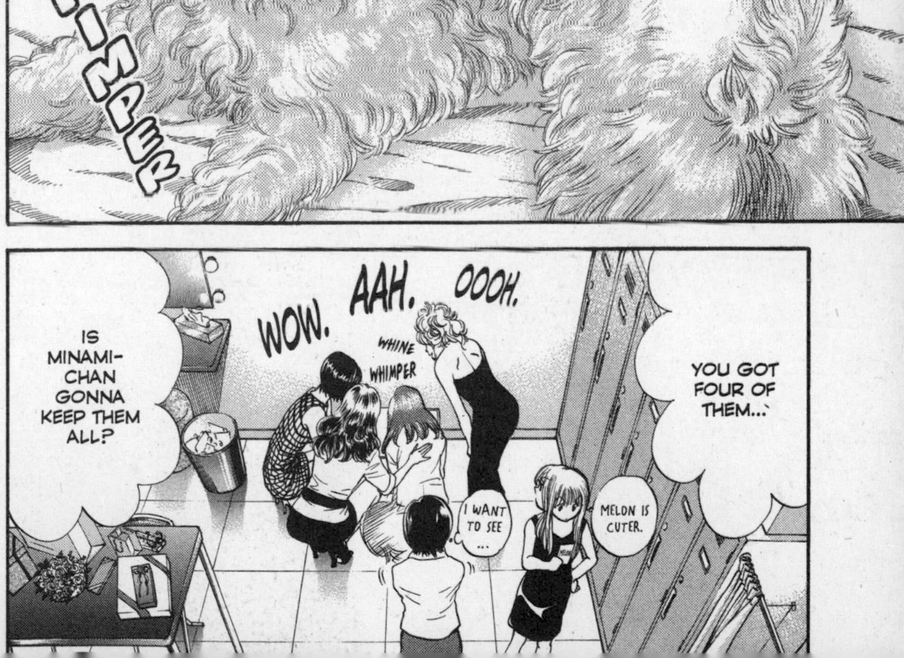
YOU GOT FOUR OF THEM...
OOOH.
AAH.
WOW.
WHINE
WHIMPER
IS MINAMI-CHAN GONNA KEEP THEM ALL?
MELON IS CUTER.
I WANT TO SEE ...

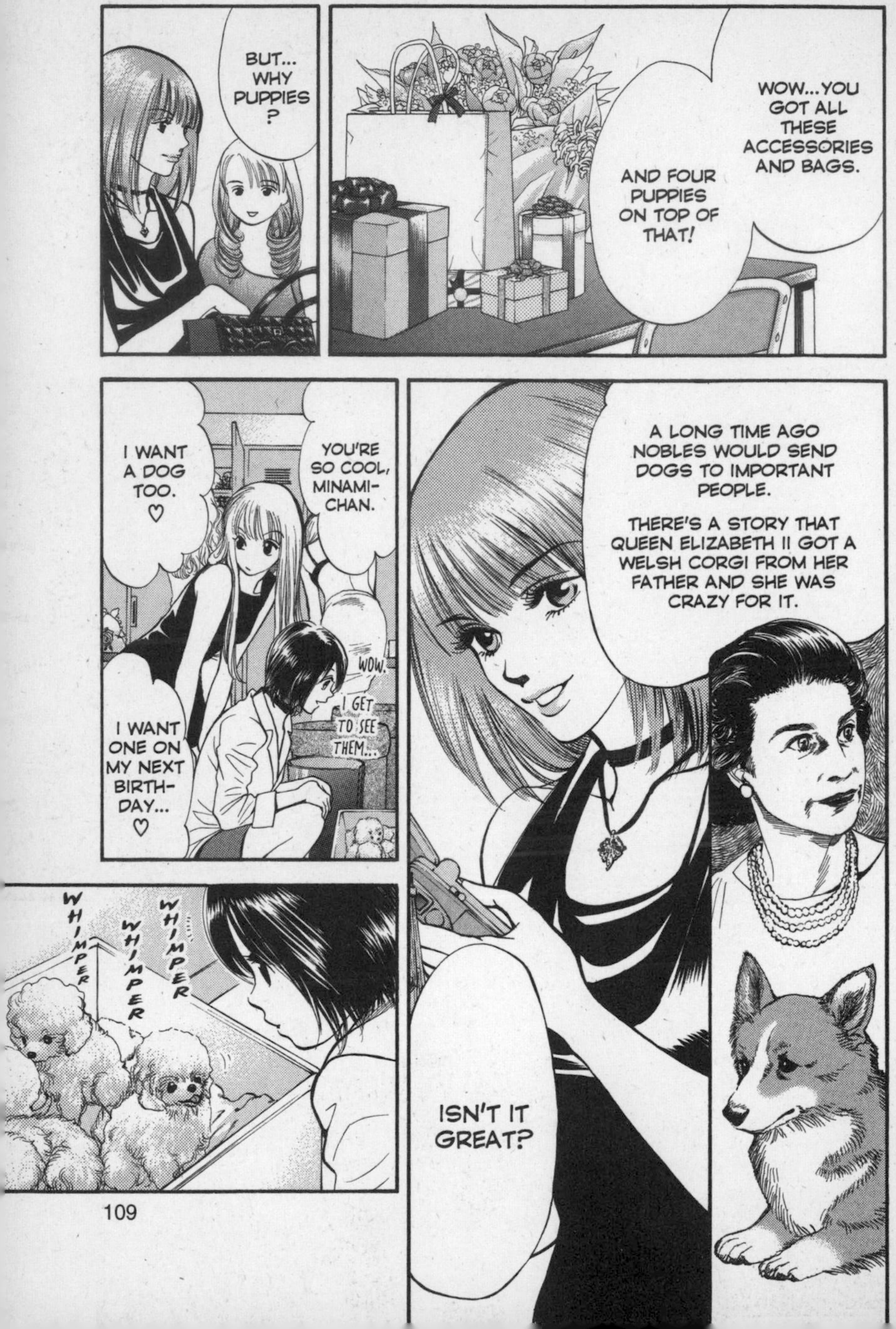

WOW...YOU GOT ALL THESE ACCESSORIES AND BAGS.
AND FOUR PUPPIES ON TOP OF THAT!
BUT... WHY PUPPIES?
A LONG TIME AGO NOBLES WOULD SEND DOGS TO IMPORTANT PEOPLE.
THERE'S A STORY THAT QUEEN ELIZABETH II GOT A WELSH CORGI FROM HER FATHER AND SHE WAS CRAZY FOR IT.
ISN'T IT GREAT?
YOU'RE SO COOL, MINAMI-CHAN.
I WANT A DOG TOO. ♡
WOW.
I GET TO SEE THEM...
I WANT ONE ON MY NEXT BIRTHDAY... ♡
WHIMPER
WHIMPER
WHIMPER

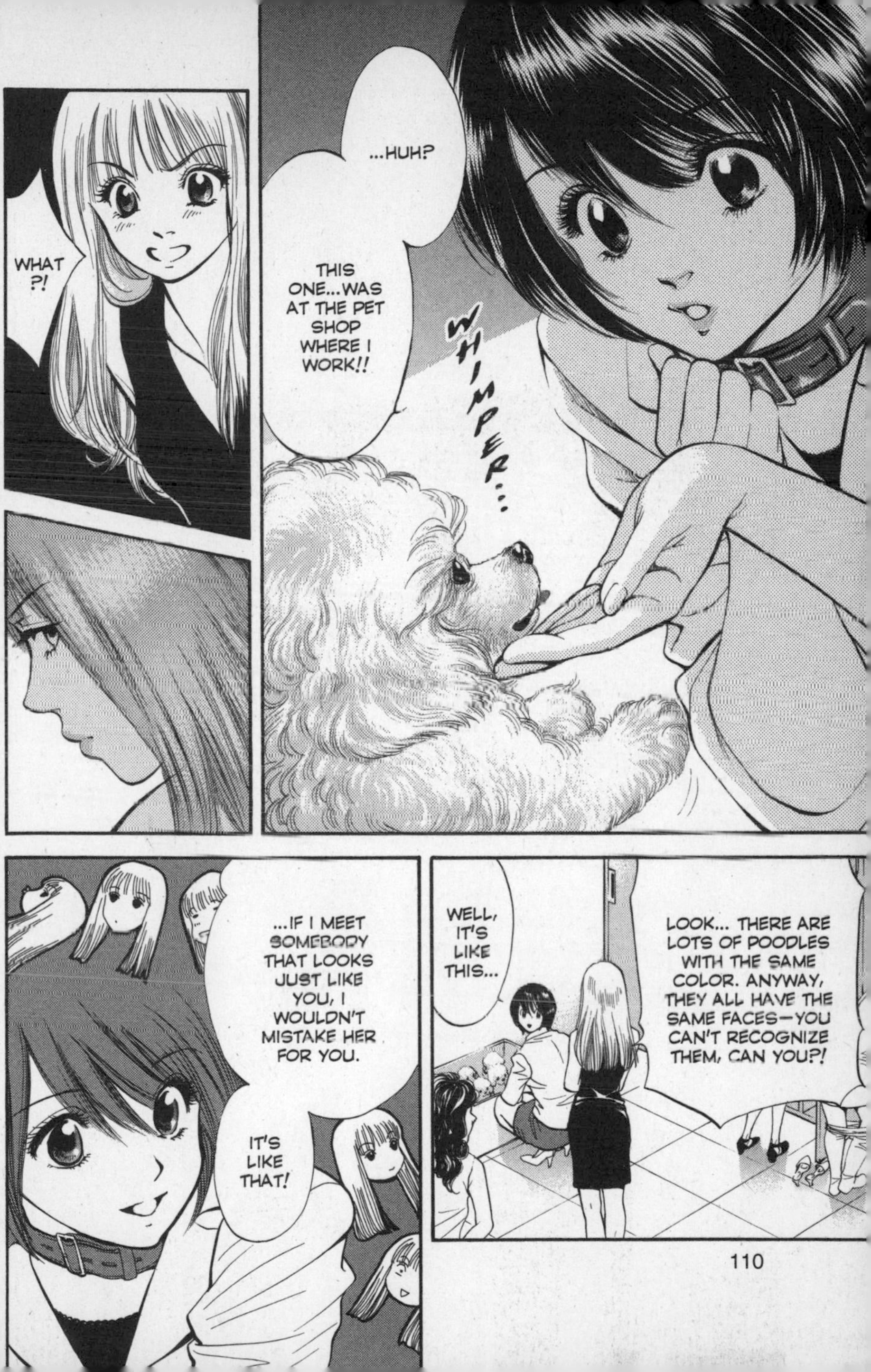
...HUH?
THIS ONE...WAS AT THE PET SHOP WHERE I WORK!!
WHIMPER...
WHAT ?!
LOOK... THERE ARE LOTS OF POODLES WITH THE SAME COLOR. ANYWAY, THEY ALL HAVE THE SAME FACES—YOU CAN'T RECOGNIZE THEM, CAN YOU?!
WELL, IT'S LIKE THIS...
...IF I MEET SOMEBODY THAT LOOKS JUST LIKE YOU, I WOULDN'T MISTAKE HER FOR YOU.
IT'S LIKE THAT!

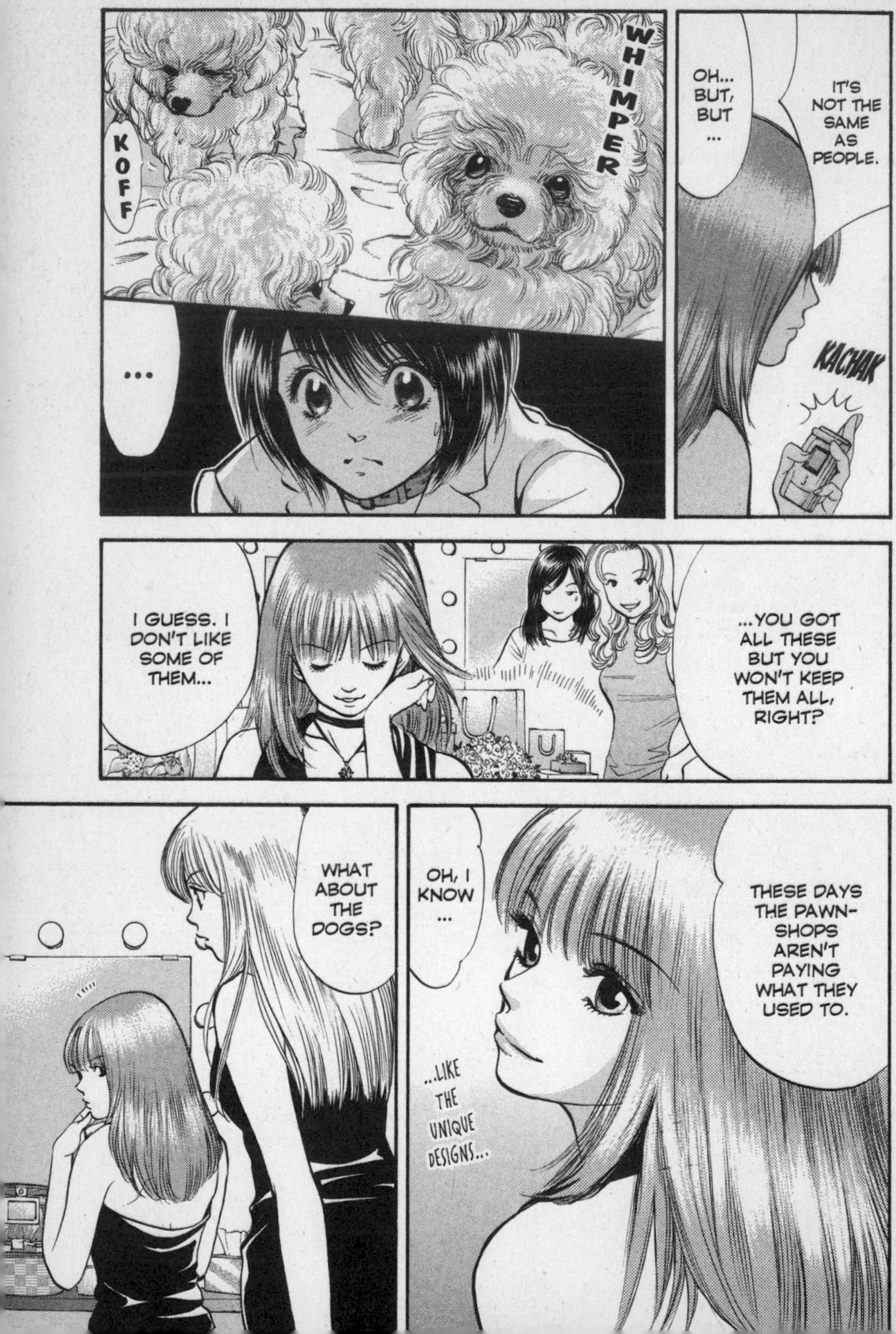
IT'S NOT THE SAME AS PEOPLE.
OH... BUT, BUT ...
KACHAK
WHIMPER
KOFF
...
...YOU GOT ALL THESE BUT YOU WON'T KEEP THEM ALL, RIGHT?
I GUESS. I DON'T LIKE SOME OF THEM...
THESE DAYS THE PAWN-SHOPS AREN'T PAYING WHAT THEY USED TO.
...LIKE THE UNIQUE DESIGNS...
OH, I KNOW ...
WHAT ABOUT THE DOGS?

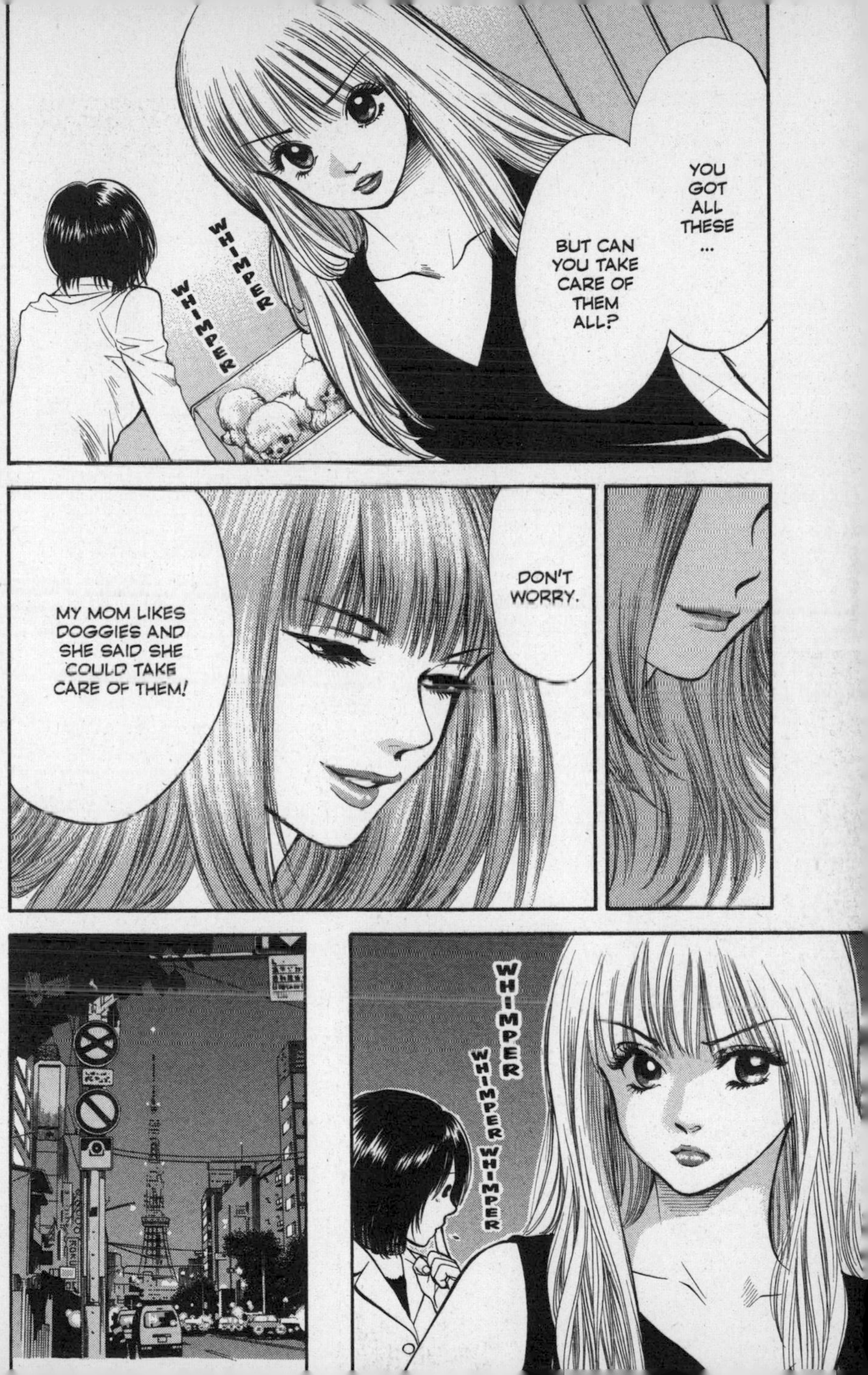
YOU GOT ALL THESE ...
BUT CAN YOU TAKE CARE OF THEM ALL?
WHIMPER
WHIMPER
DON'T WORRY.
MY MOM LIKES DOGGIES AND SHE SAID SHE COULD TAKE CARE OF THEM!
WHIMPER
WHIMPER WHIMPER
WHIMPER

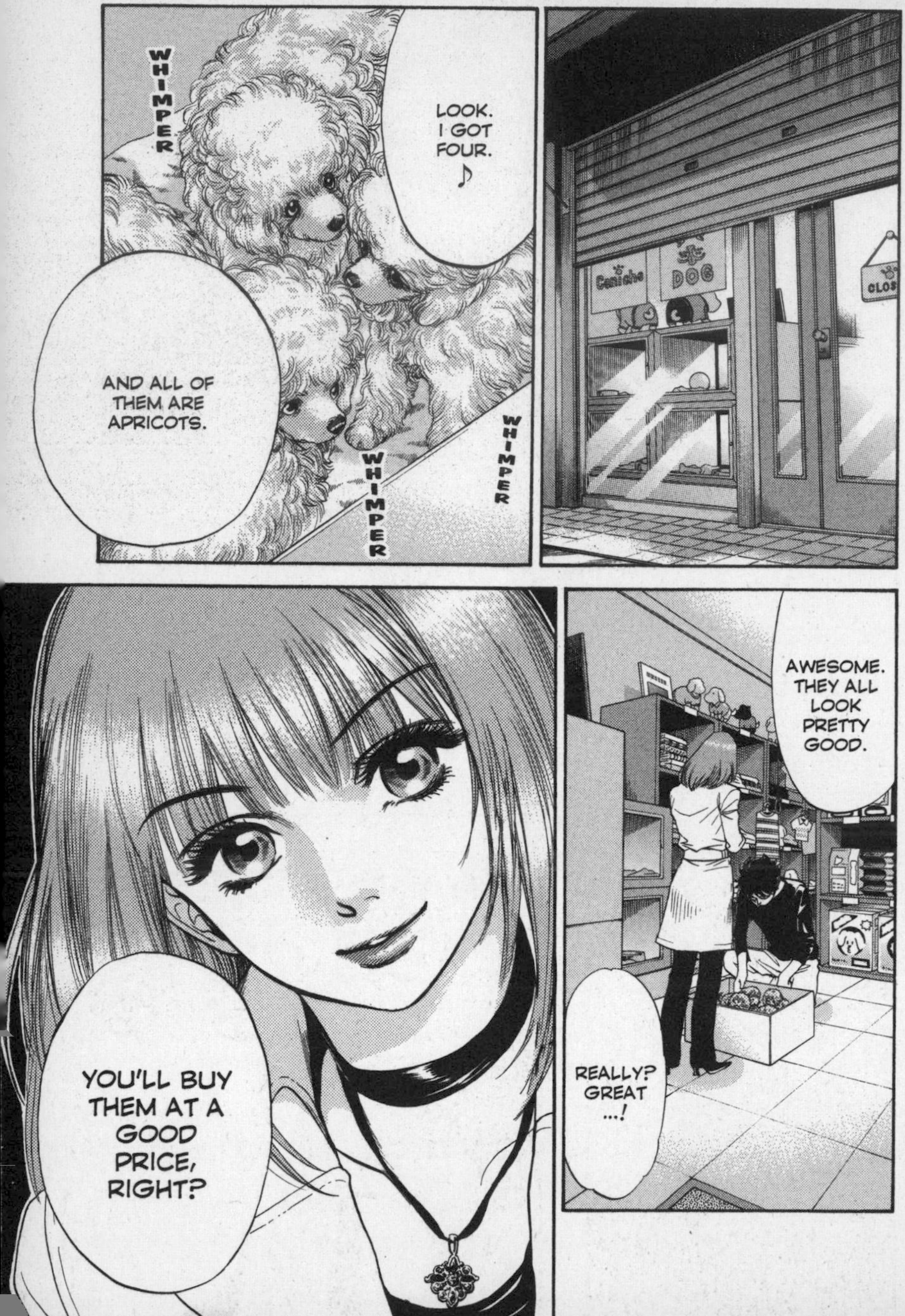
Caniche
DOG
CLOS
LOOK. I GOT FOUR. ♪
WHIMPER
AND ALL OF THEM ARE APRICOTS.
WHIMPER
WHIMPER
AWESOME. THEY ALL LOOK PRETTY GOOD.
REALLY? GREAT ...!
YOU'LL BUY THEM AT A GOOD PRICE, RIGHT?

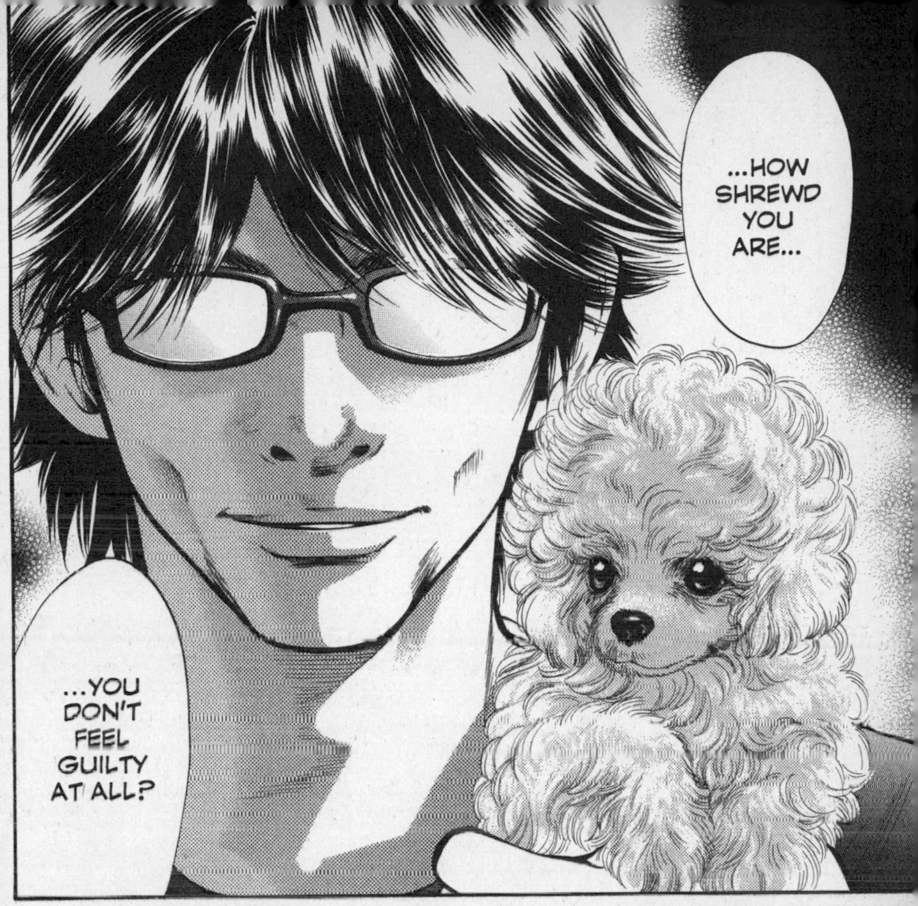
...HOW SHREWD YOU ARE...
...YOU DON'T FEEL GUILTY AT ALL?

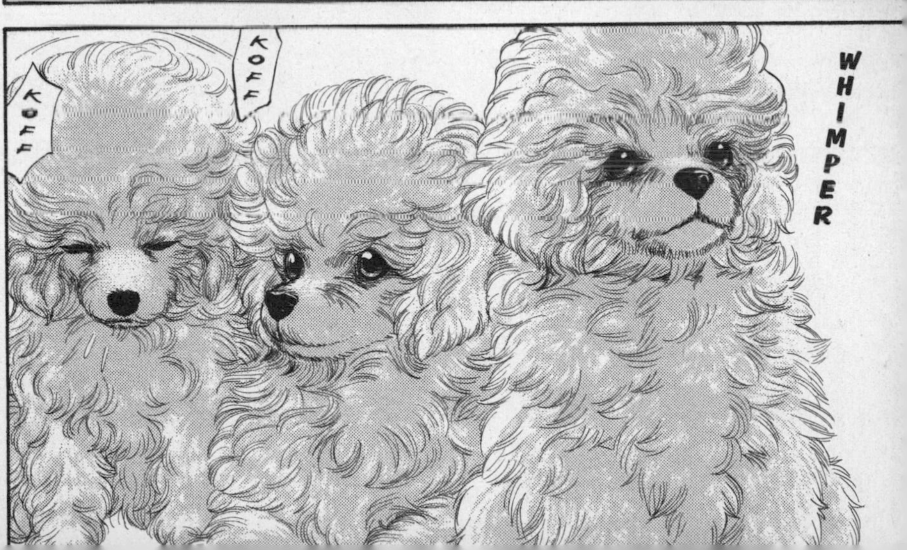
WHIMPER
KOFF
KOFF

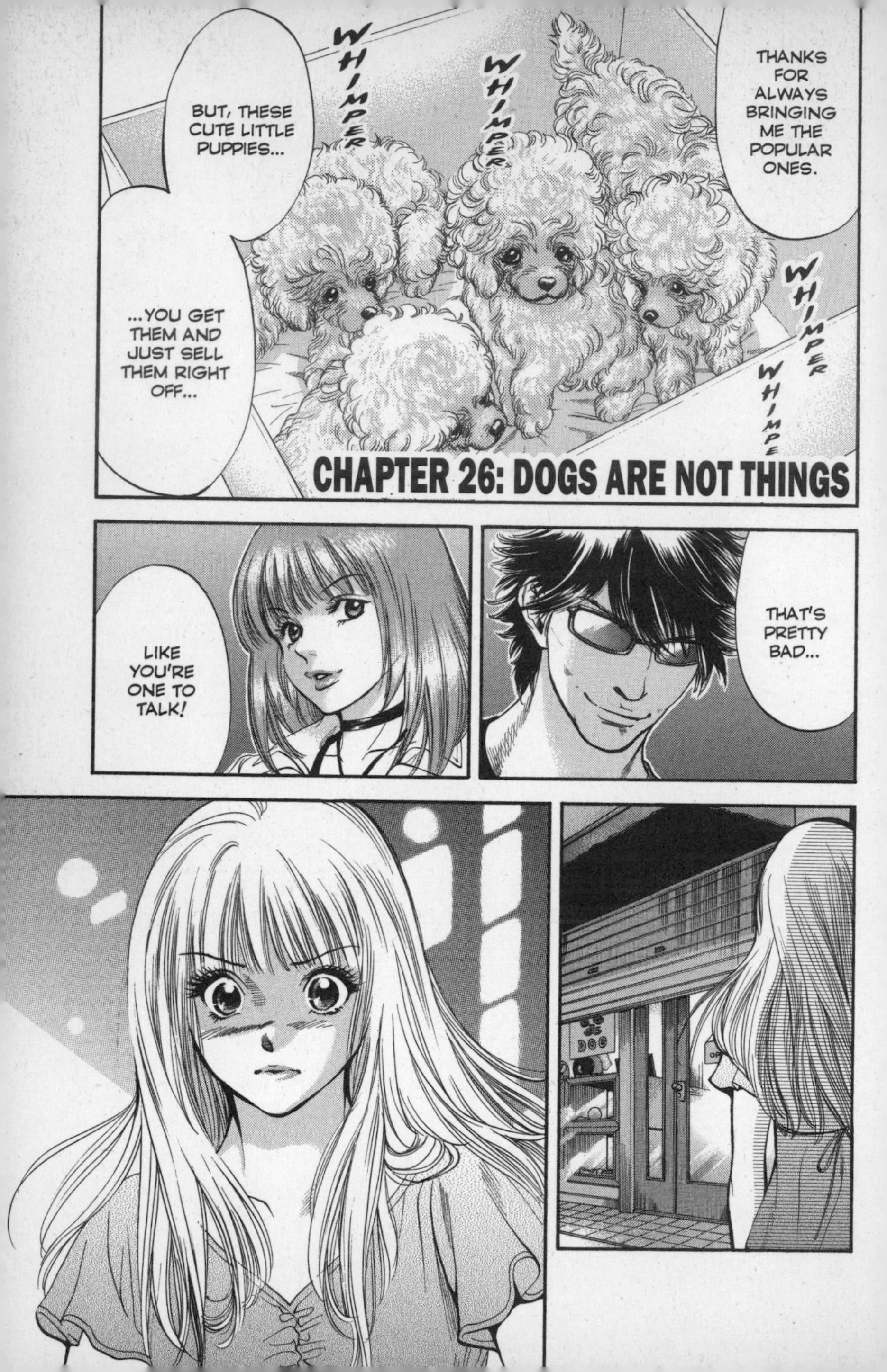
THANKS FOR ALWAYS BRINGING ME THE POPULAR ONES.
WHIMPER
WHIMPE
WHIMPER
WHIMPER
BUT, THESE CUTE LITTLE PUPPIES...
...YOU GET THEM AND JUST SELL THEM RIGHT OFF...
CHAPTER 26: DOGS ARE NOT THINGS
THAT'S PRETTY BAD...
LIKE YOU'RE ONE TO TALK!
DOG

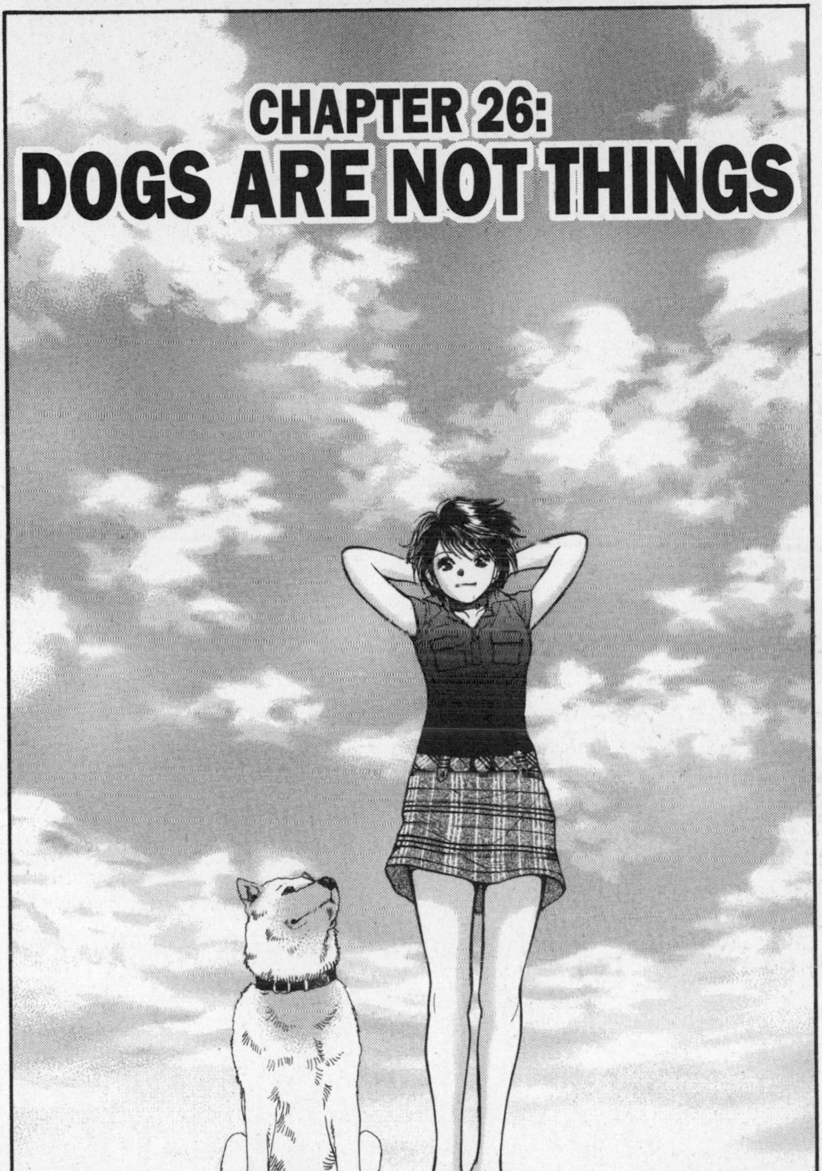
CHAPTER 26:
DOGS ARE NOT THINGS

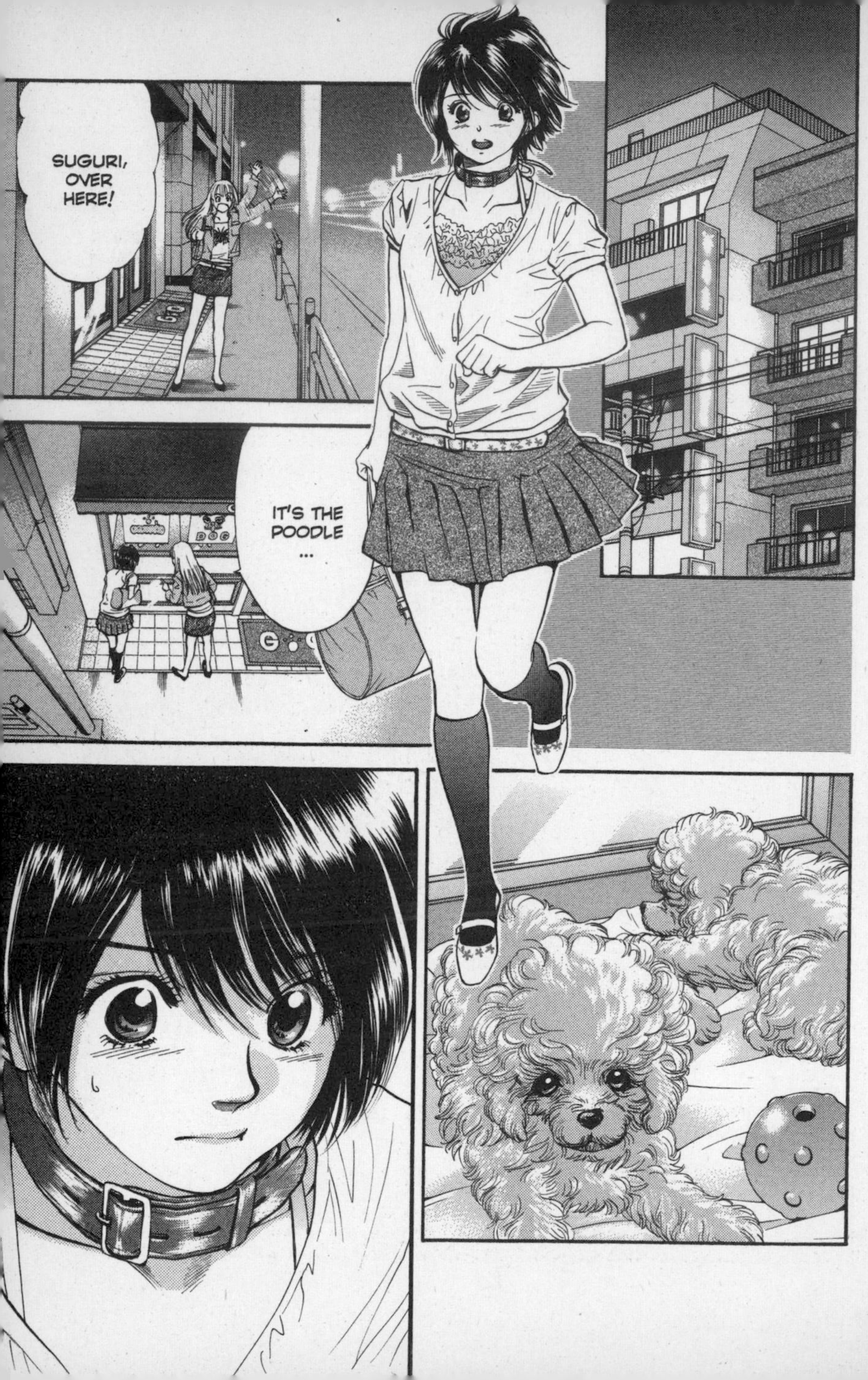
SUGURI, OVER HERE!
IT'S THE POODLE ...

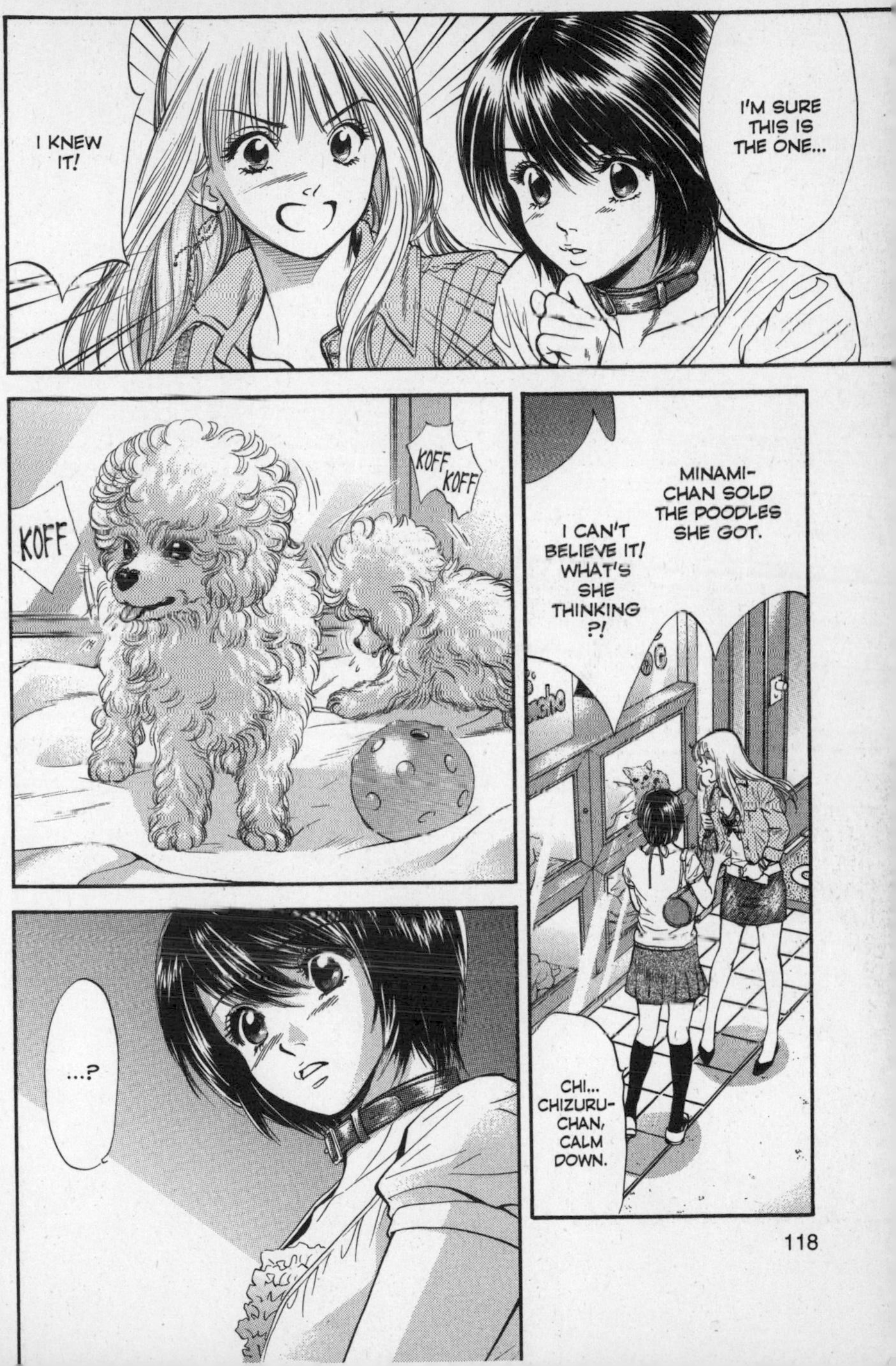
I'M SURE THIS IS THE ONE...
I KNEW IT!
MINAMI-CHAN SOLD THE POODLES SHE GOT.
I CAN'T BELIEVE IT! WHAT'S SHE THINKING?!
CHI... CHIZURU-CHAN, CALM DOWN.
KOFF KOFF
KOFF
...?

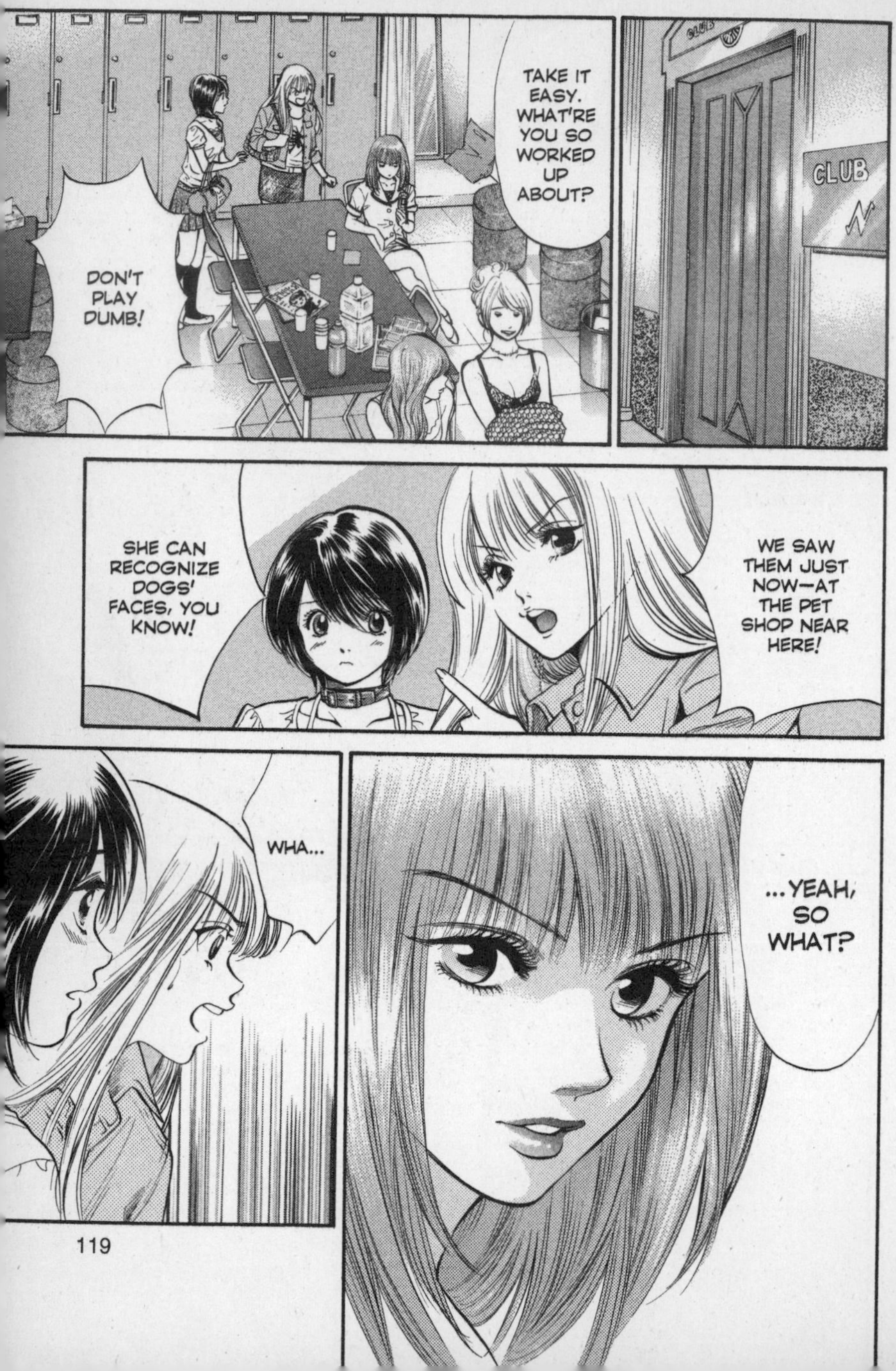
TAKE IT EASY. WHAT'RE YOU SO WORKED UP ABOUT?
DON'T PLAY DUMB!
WE SAW THEM JUST NOW—AT THE PET SHOP NEAR HERE!
SHE CAN RECOGNIZE DOGS' FACES, YOU KNOW!
...YEAH, SO WHAT?
WHA...

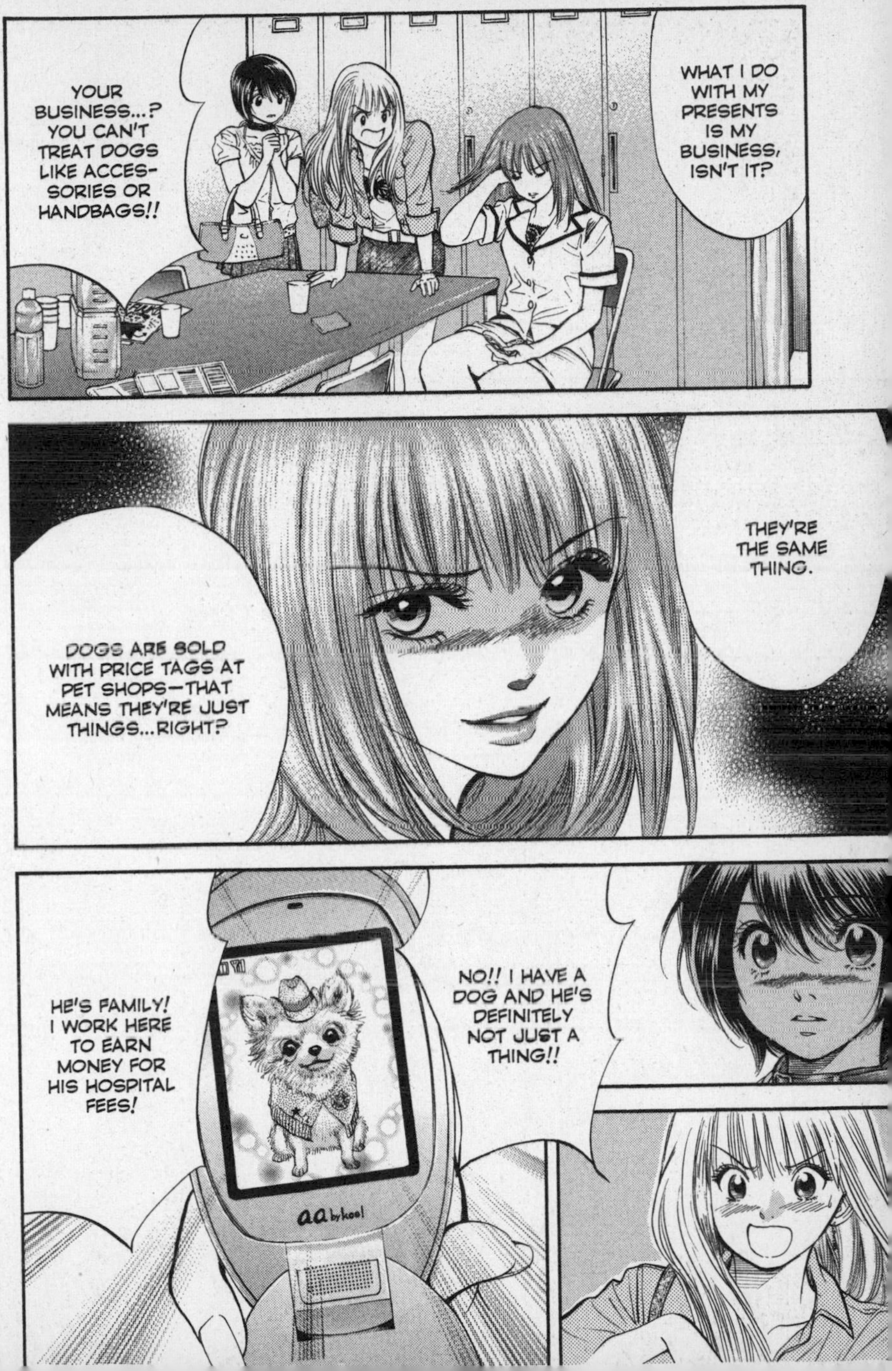
WHAT I DO WITH MY PRESENTS IS MY BUSINESS, ISN'T IT?
YOUR BUSINESS...? YOU CAN'T TREAT DOGS LIKE ACCES-SORIES OR HANDBAGS!!
THEY'RE THE SAME THING.
DOGS ARE SOLD WITH PRICE TAGS AT PET SHOPS—THAT MEANS THEY'RE JUST THINGS...RIGHT?
NO!! I HAVE A DOG AND HE'S DEFINITELY NOT JUST A THING!!
HE'S FAMILY! I WORK HERE TO EARN MONEY FOR HIS HOSPITAL FEES!
aa by kool

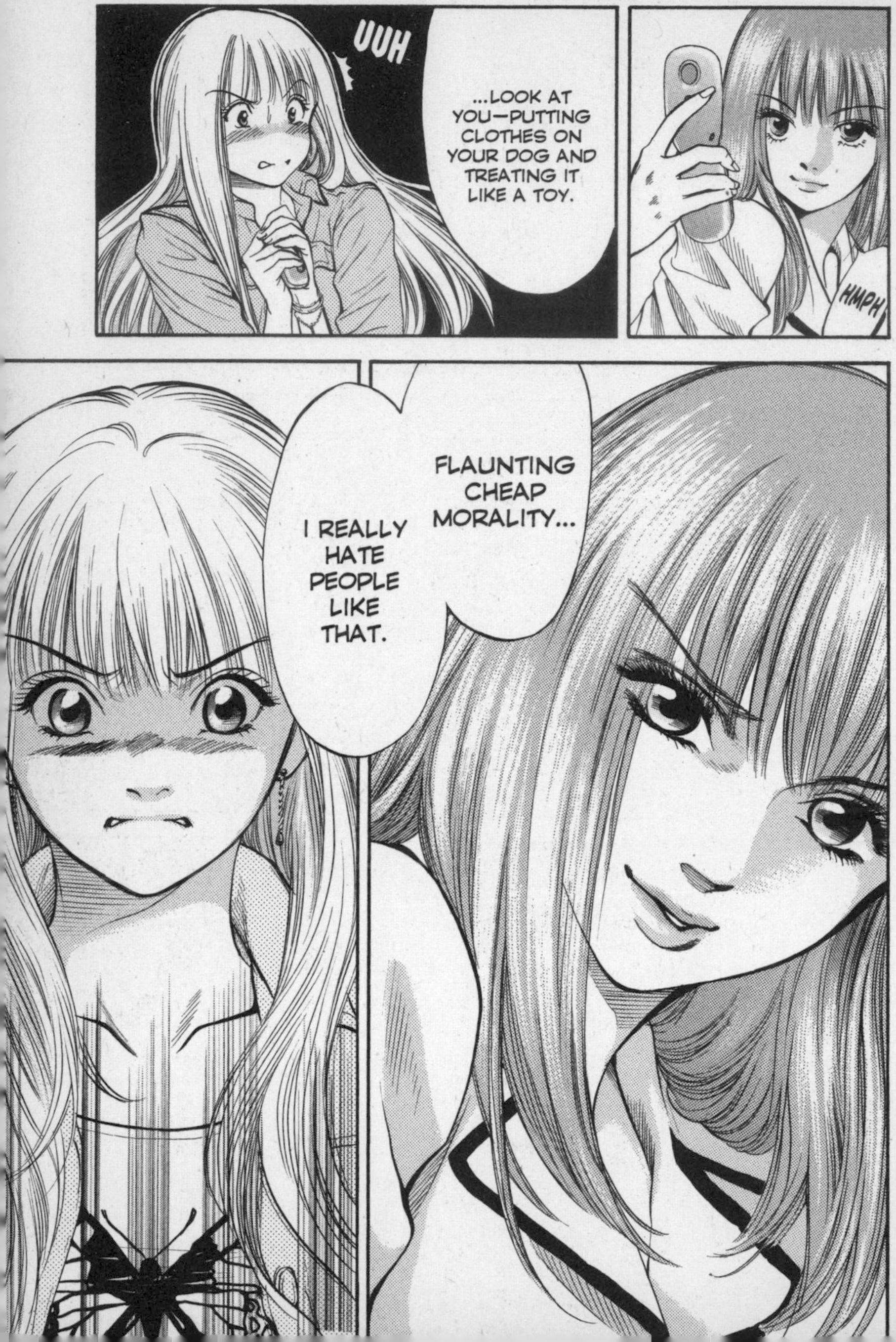
HMPH
UUH
...LOOK AT YOU—PUTTING CLOTHES ON YOUR DOG AND TREATING IT LIKE A TOY.
FLAUNTING CHEAP MORALITY...
I REALLY HATE PEOPLE LIKE THAT.

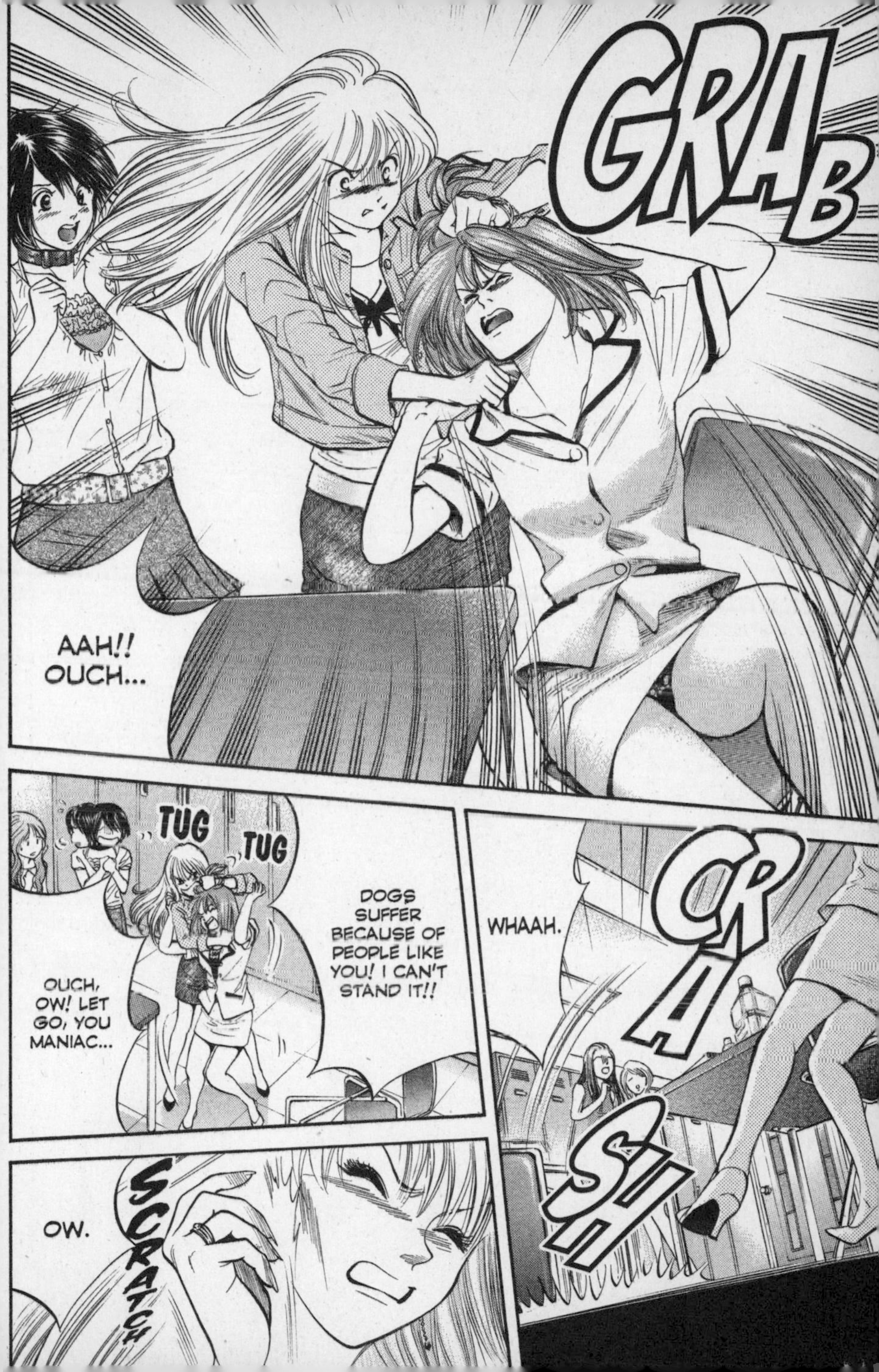
GRAB
AAH!! OUCH...
CRASH
WHAAH.
TUG
TUG
DOGS SUFFER BECAUSE OF PEOPLE LIKE YOU! I CAN'T STAND IT!!
OUCH, OW! LET GO, YOU MANIAC...
SCRATCH
OW.

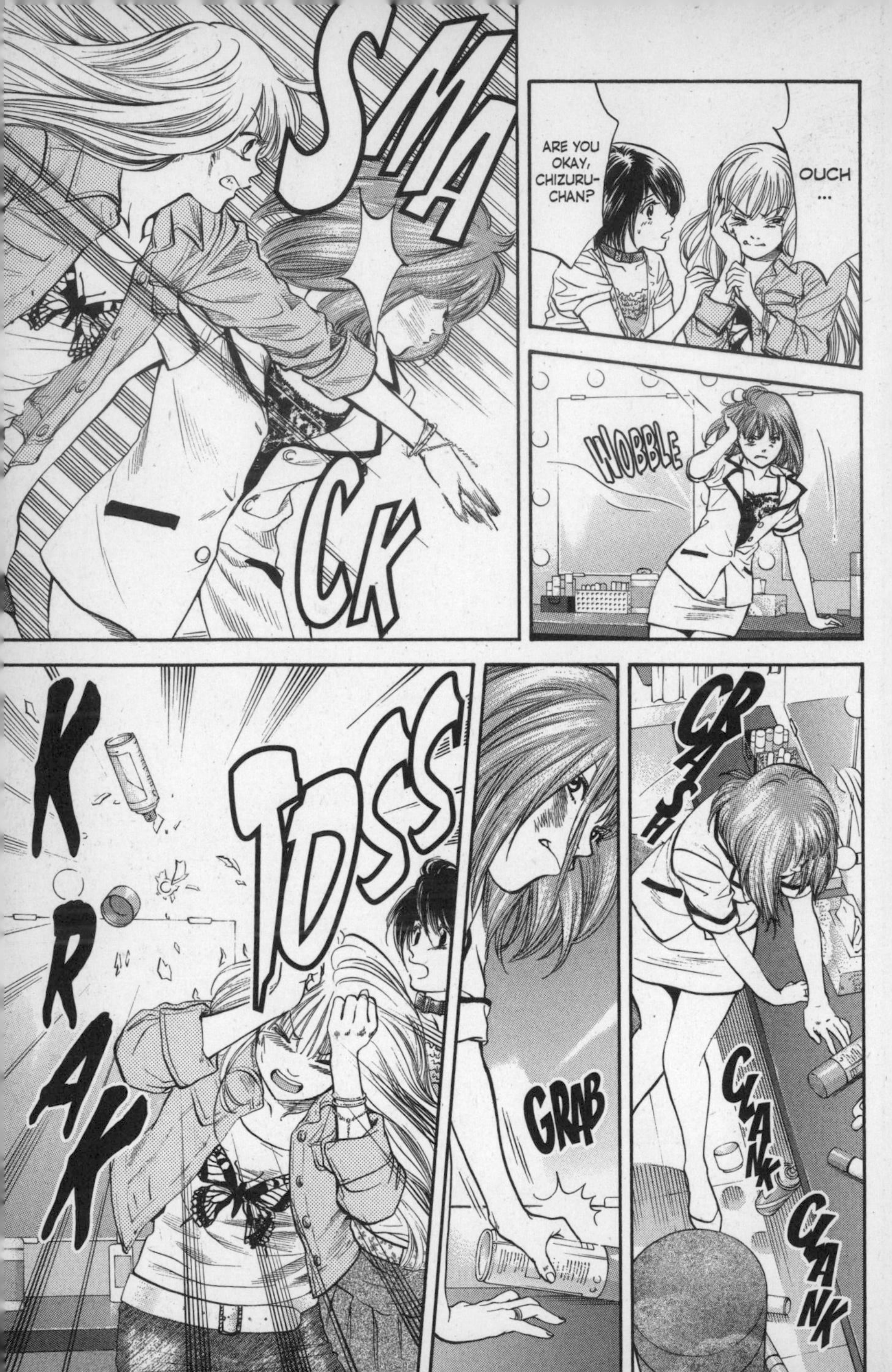
OUCH ...
ARE YOU OKAY, CHIZURU-CHAN?
WOBBLE
SMACK
CRASH
CLANK
CLANK
GRAB
TOSS
KRAK

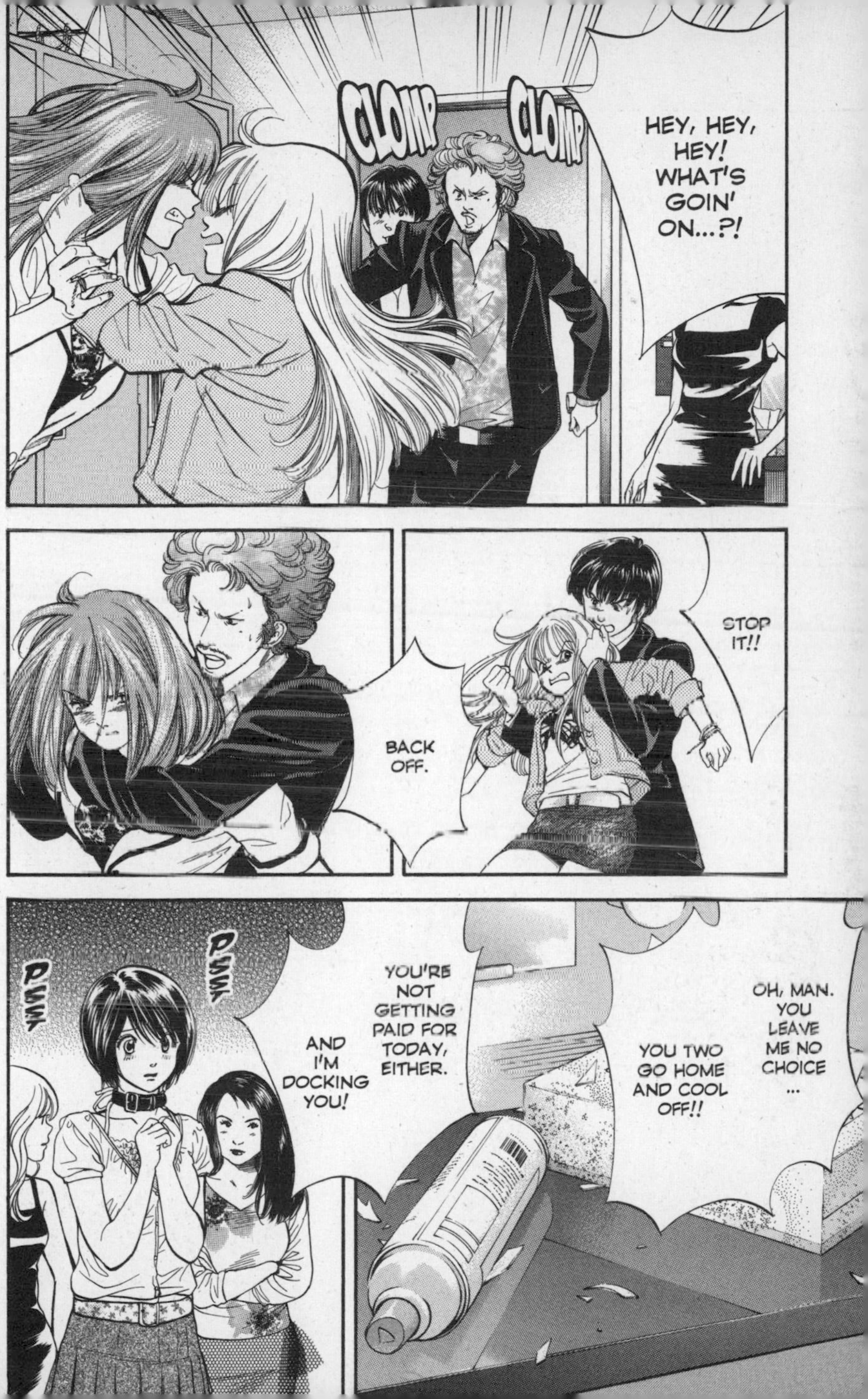
CLOMP
CLOMP
HEY, HEY, HEY! WHAT'S GOIN' ON...?!
STOP IT!!
BACK OFF.
OH, MAN. YOU LEAVE ME NO CHOICE ...
YOU TWO GO HOME AND COOL OFF!!
YOU'RE NOT GETTING PAID FOR TODAY, EITHER.
AND I'M DOCKING YOU!

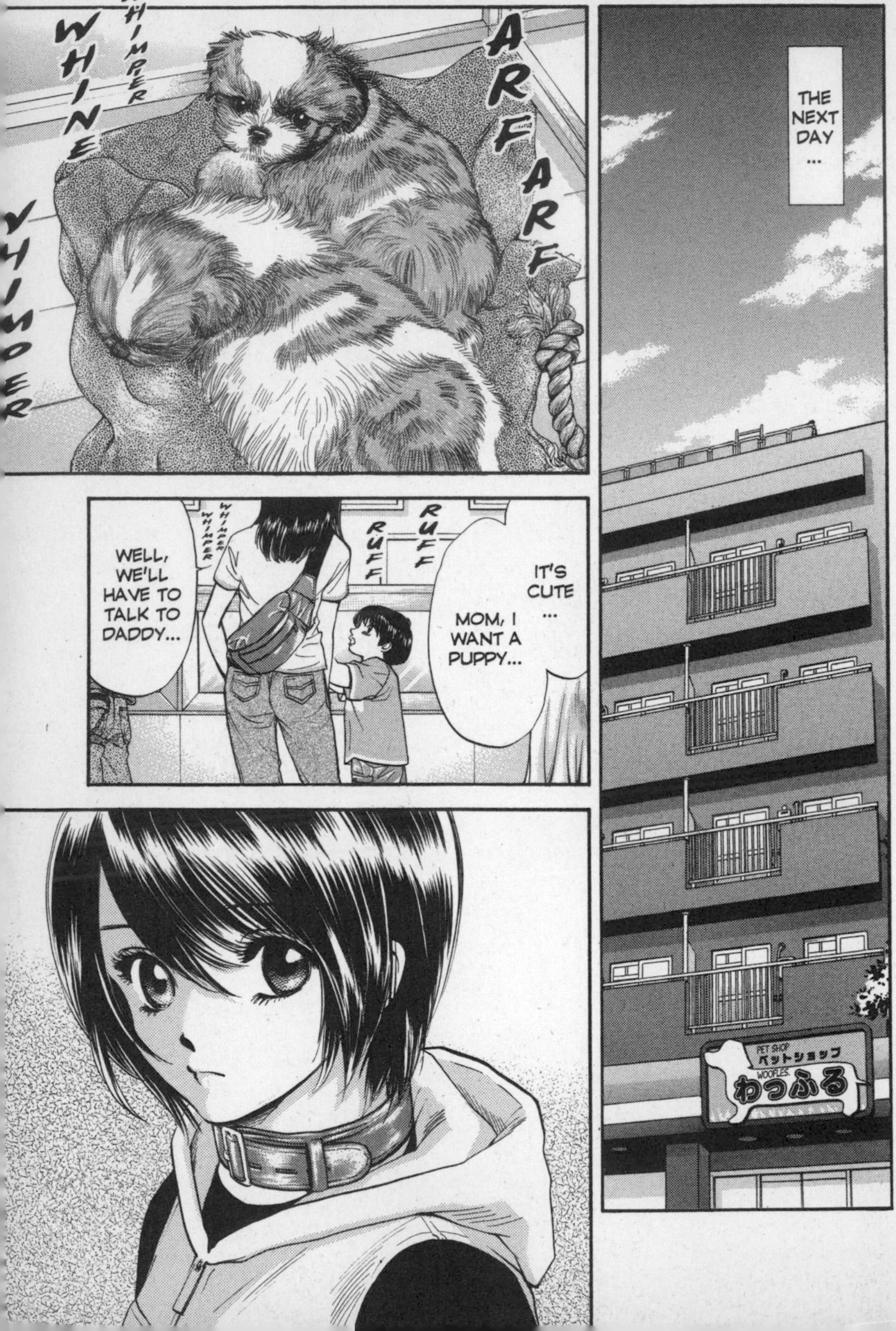

THE NEXT DAY ...
PET SHOP
ペットショップ
WOOFLES
わっふる
ARF ARF
WHIMPER
WHINE
RUFF RUFF
WHIMPER WHIMPER
IT'S CUTE ...
MOM, I WANT A PUPPY...
WELL, WE'LL HAVE TO TALK TO DADDY...

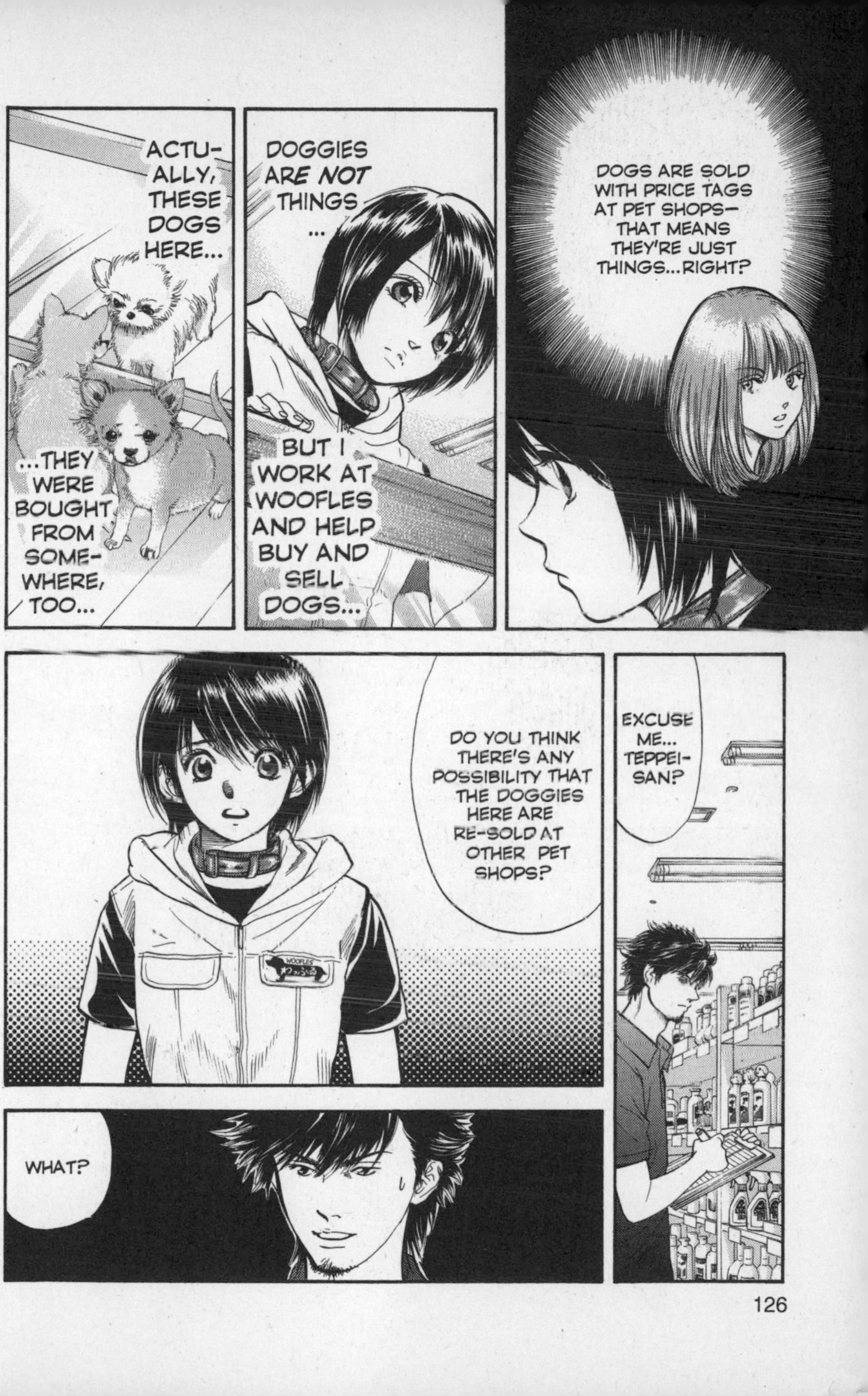
DOGS ARE SOLD WITH PRICE TAGS AT PET SHOPS— THAT MEANS THEY'RE JUST THINGS...RIGHT?
DOGGIES ARE *NOT* THINGS ...
BUT I WORK AT WOOFLES AND HELP BUY AND SELL DOGS...
ACTU-ALLY, THESE DOGS HERE...
...THEY WERE BOUGHT FROM SOME-WHERE, TOO...
EXCUSE ME... TEPPEI-SAN?
DO YOU THINK THERE'S ANY POSSIBILITY THAT THE DOGGIES HERE ARE RE-SOLD AT OTHER PET SHOPS?
WHAT?

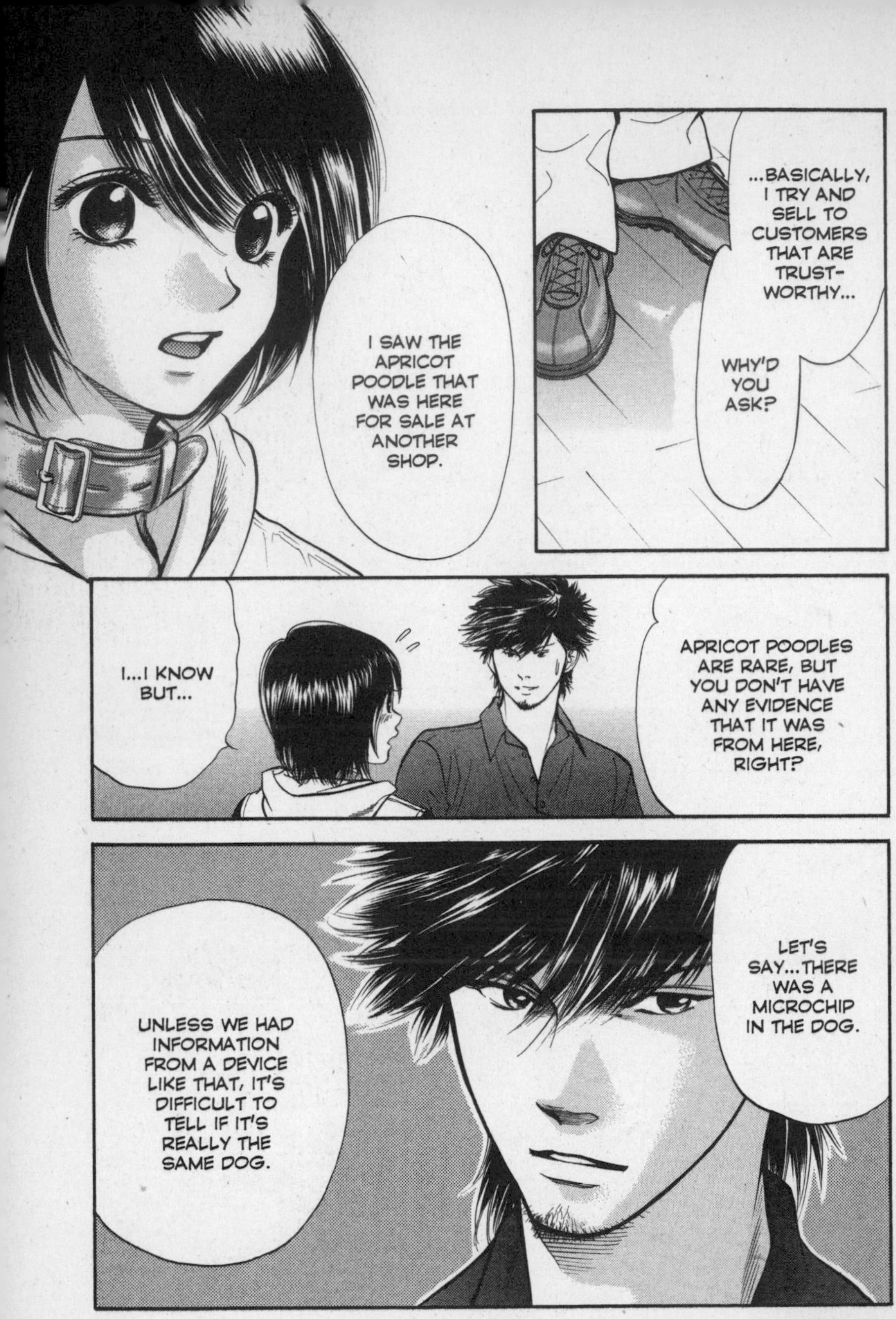
...BASICALLY, I TRY AND SELL TO CUSTOMERS THAT ARE TRUST-WORTHY...
WHY'D YOU ASK?
I SAW THE APRICOT POODLE THAT WAS HERE FOR SALE AT ANOTHER SHOP.
APRICOT POODLES ARE RARE, BUT YOU DON'T HAVE ANY EVIDENCE THAT IT WAS FROM HERE, RIGHT?
I...I KNOW BUT...
LET'S SAY...THERE WAS A MICROCHIP IN THE DOG.
UNLESS WE HAD INFORMATION FROM A DEVICE LIKE THAT, IT'S DIFFICULT TO TELL IF IT'S REALLY THE SAME DOG.

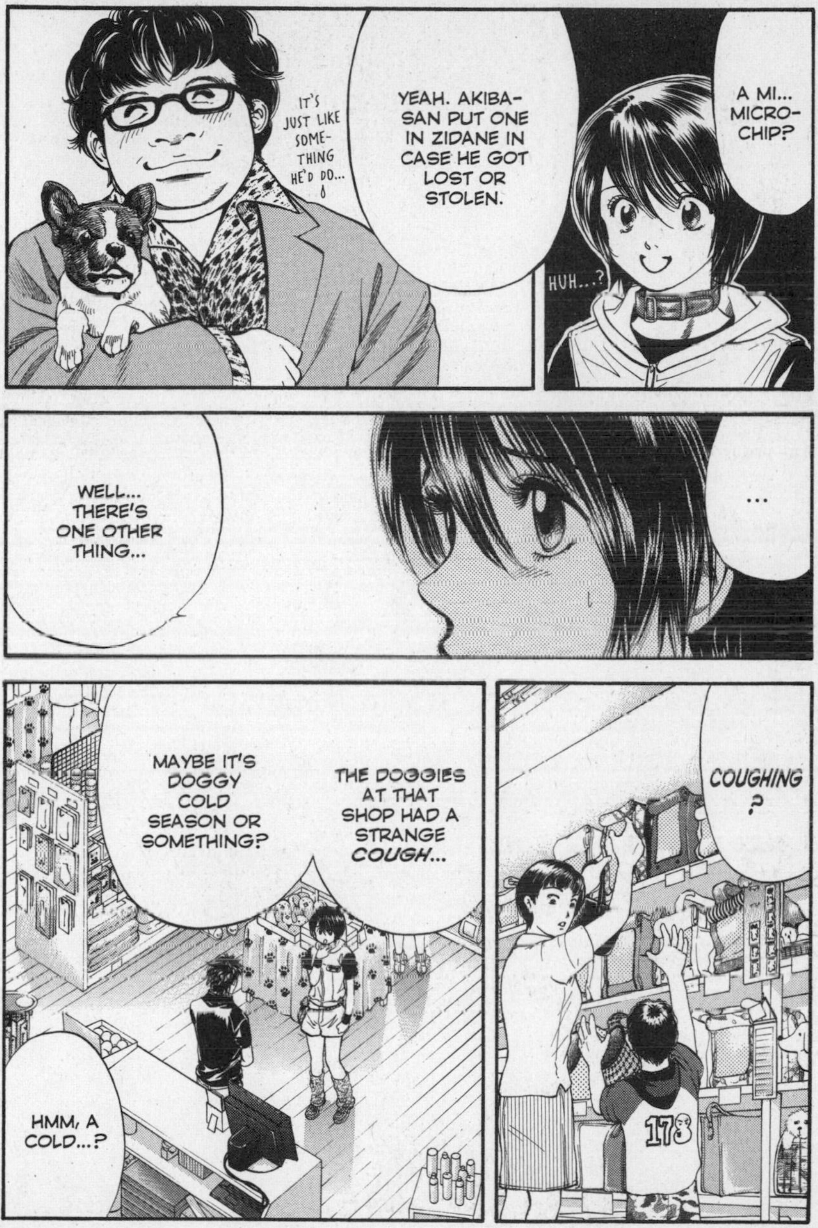
A MI... MICRO-CHIP?
HUH...?
YEAH. AKIBA-SAN PUT ONE IN ZIDANE IN CASE HE GOT LOST OR STOLEN.
IT'S JUST LIKE SOME-THING HE'D DO...
...
WELL... THERE'S ONE OTHER THING...
COUGHING?
THE DOGGIES AT THAT SHOP HAD A STRANGE *COUGH*...
MAYBE IT'S DOGGY COLD SEASON OR SOMETHING?
HMM, A COLD...?

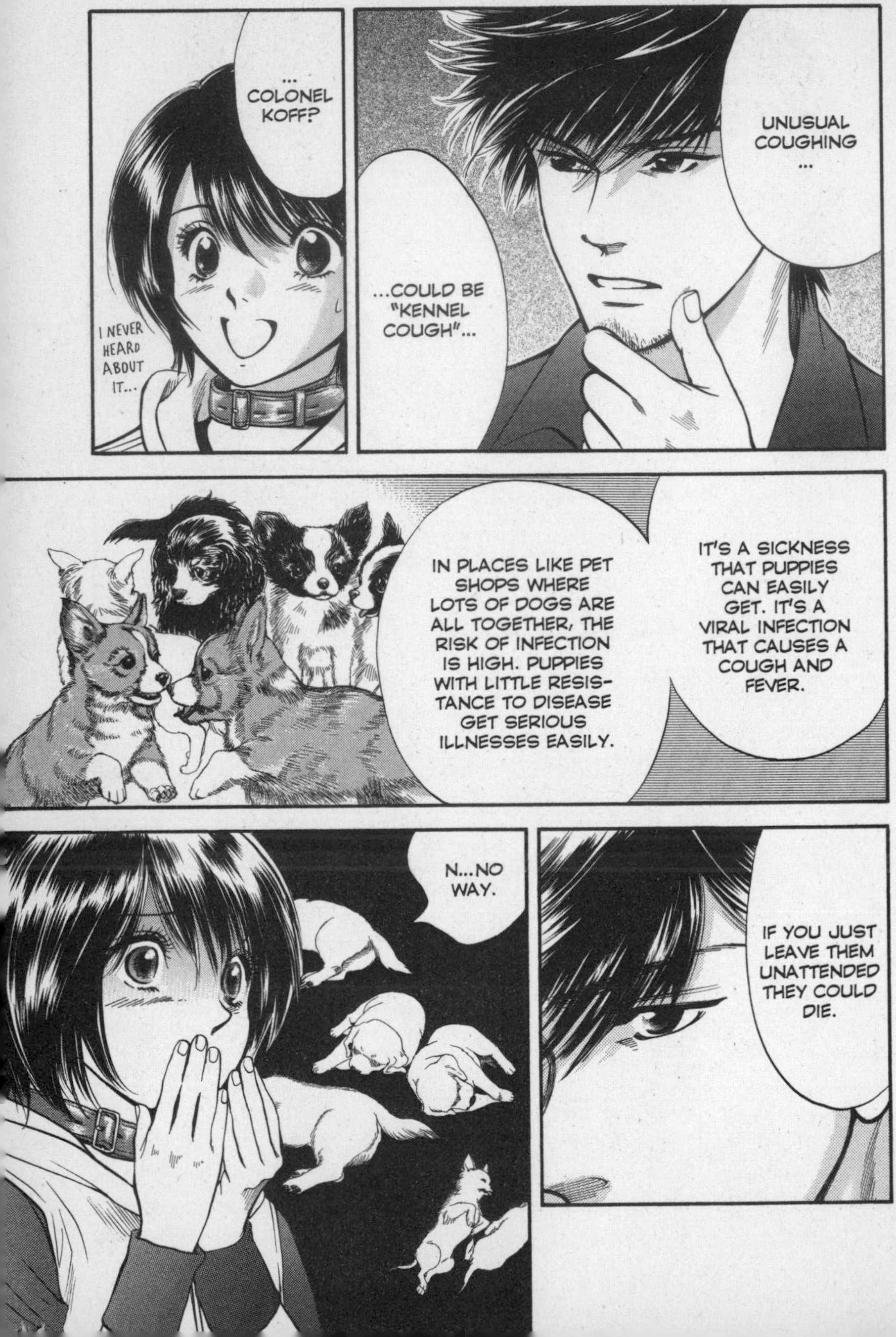
UNUSUAL COUGHING ...
...COULD BE "KENNEL COUGH"...
... COLONEL KOFF?
I NEVER HEARD ABOUT IT...
IT'S A SICKNESS THAT PUPPIES CAN EASILY GET. IT'S A VIRAL INFECTION THAT CAUSES A COUGH AND FEVER.
IN PLACES LIKE PET SHOPS WHERE LOTS OF DOGS ARE ALL TOGETHER, THE RISK OF INFECTION IS HIGH. PUPPIES WITH LITTLE RESIS-TANCE TO DISEASE GET SERIOUS ILLNESSES EASILY.
IF YOU JUST LEAVE THEM UNATTENDED THEY COULD DIE.
N...NO WAY.

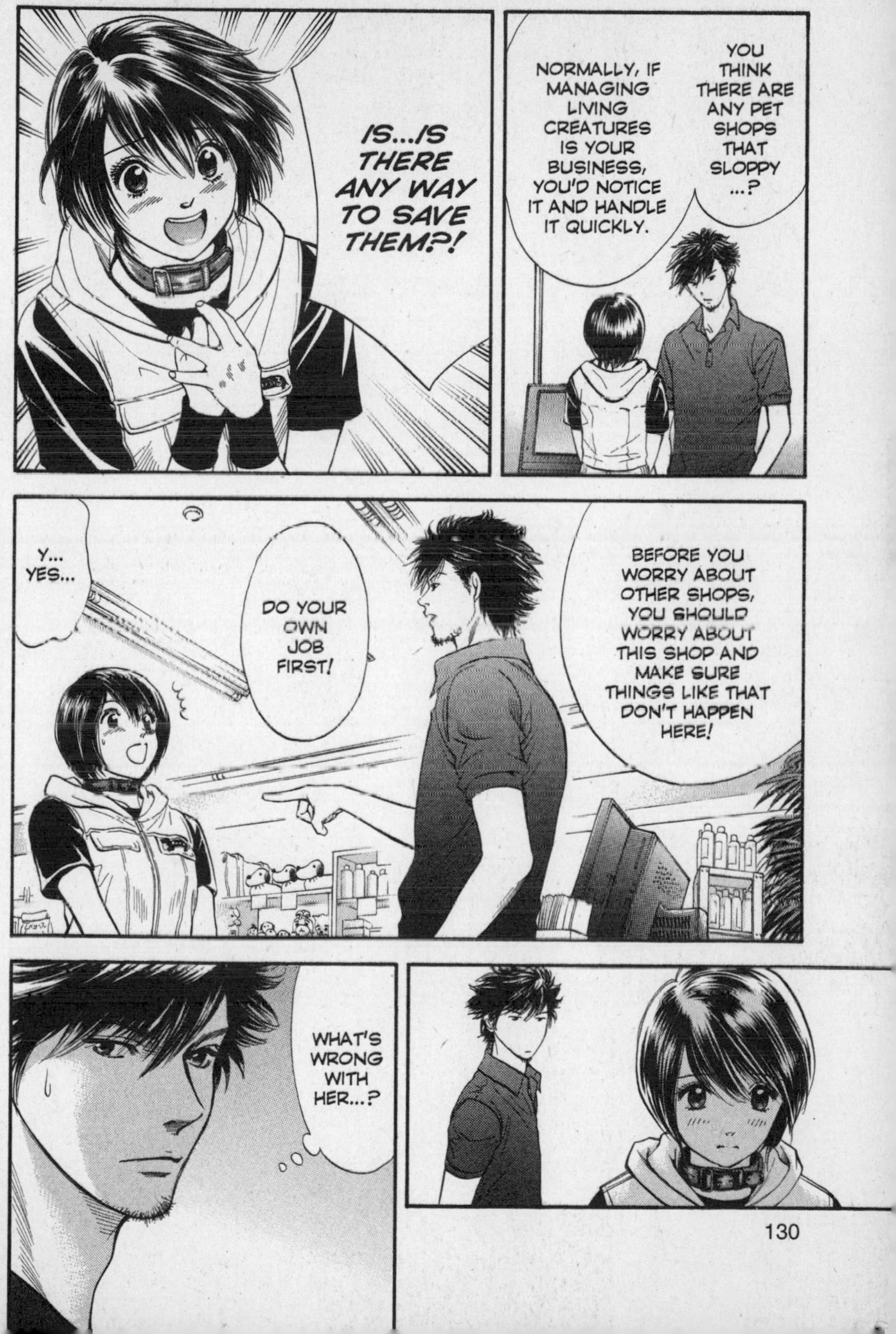
YOU THINK THERE ARE ANY PET SHOPS THAT SLOPPY ...?
NORMALLY, IF MANAGING LIVING CREATURES IS YOUR BUSINESS, YOU'D NOTICE IT AND HANDLE IT QUICKLY.
IS...IS THERE ANY WAY TO SAVE THEM?!
BEFORE YOU WORRY ABOUT OTHER SHOPS, YOU SHOULD WORRY ABOUT THIS SHOP AND MAKE SURE THINGS LIKE THAT DON'T HAPPEN HERE!
DO YOUR OWN JOB FIRST!
Y... YES...
WHAT'S WRONG WITH HER...?

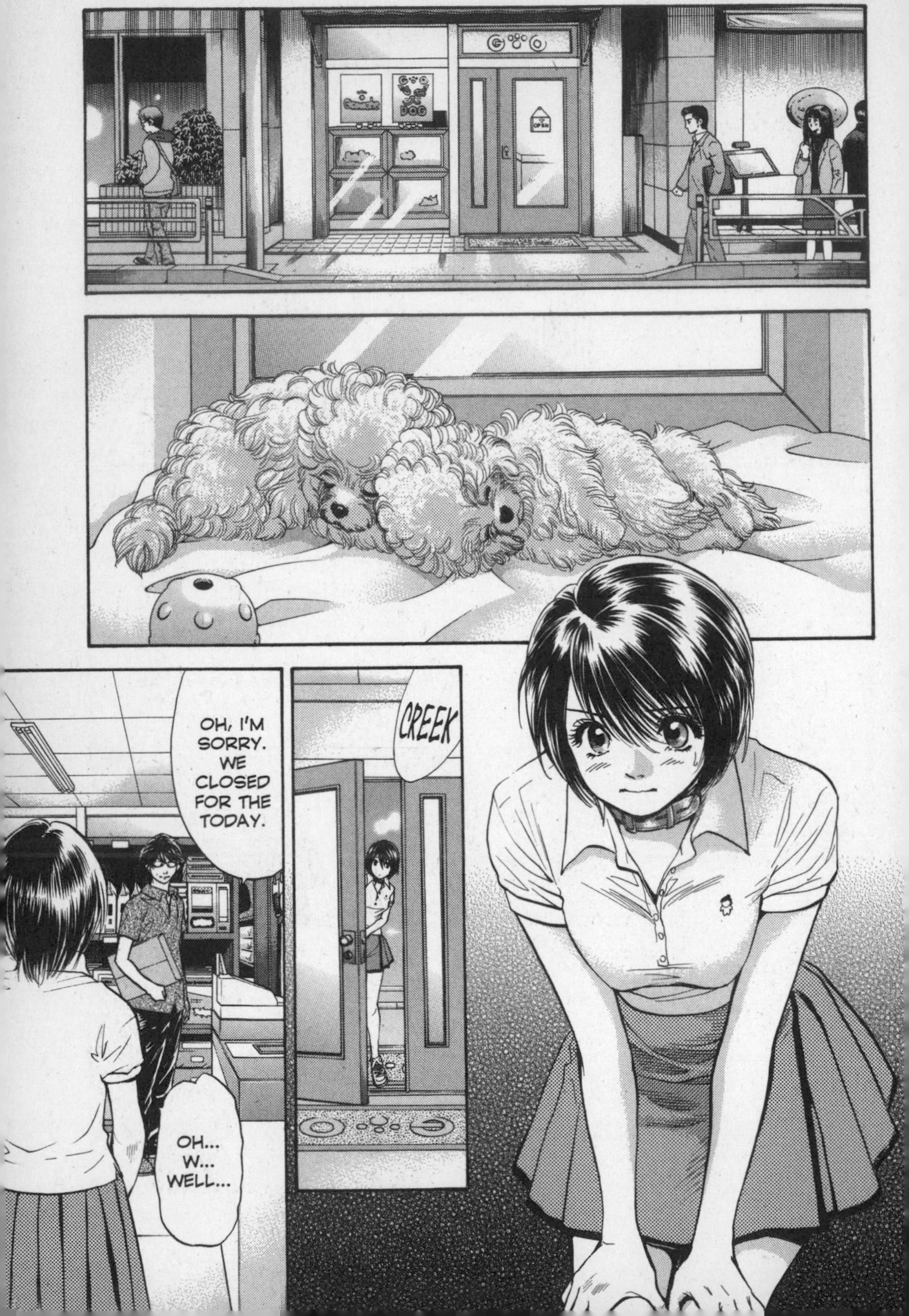
CREEK
OH, I'M SORRY. WE CLOSED FOR THE TODAY.
OH... W... WELL...

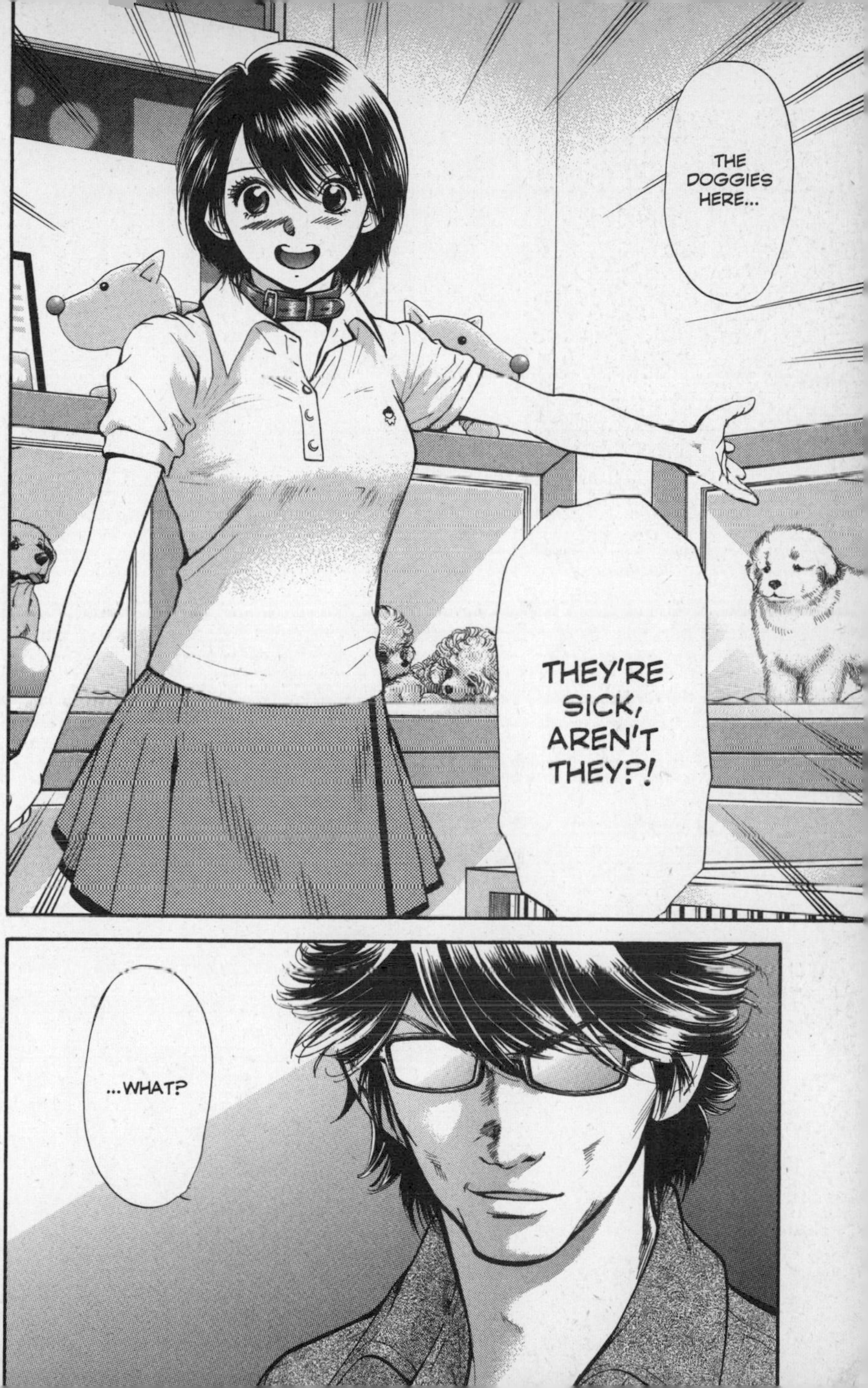
THE DOGGIES HERE...
THEY'RE SICK, AREN'T THEY?!
...WHAT?

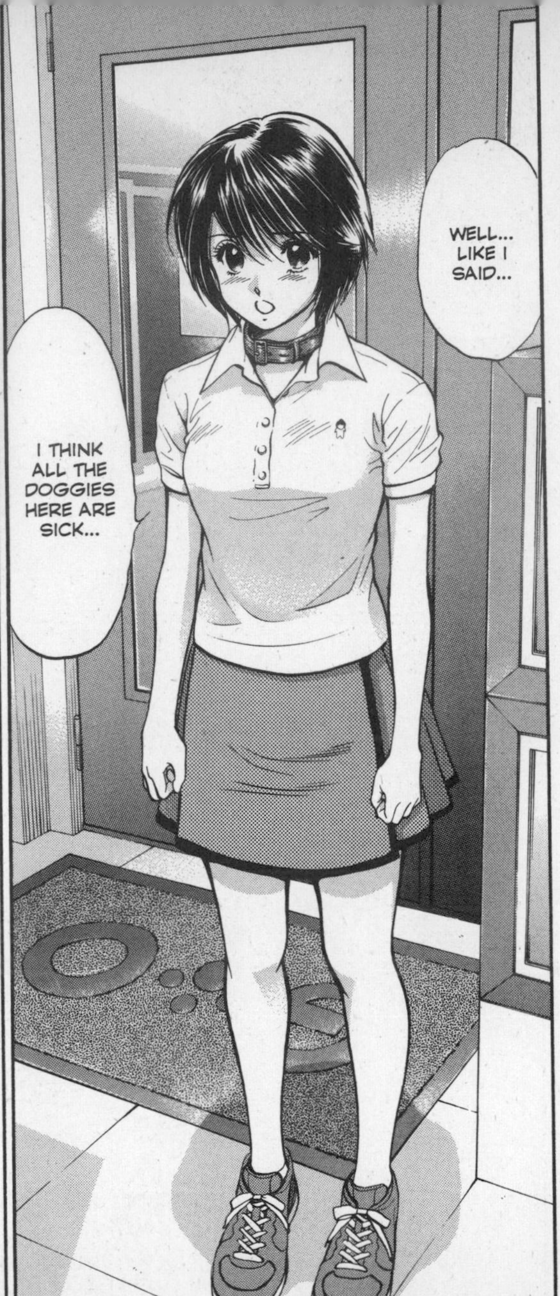
WELL... LIKE I SAID...
I THINK ALL THE DOGGIES HERE ARE SICK...

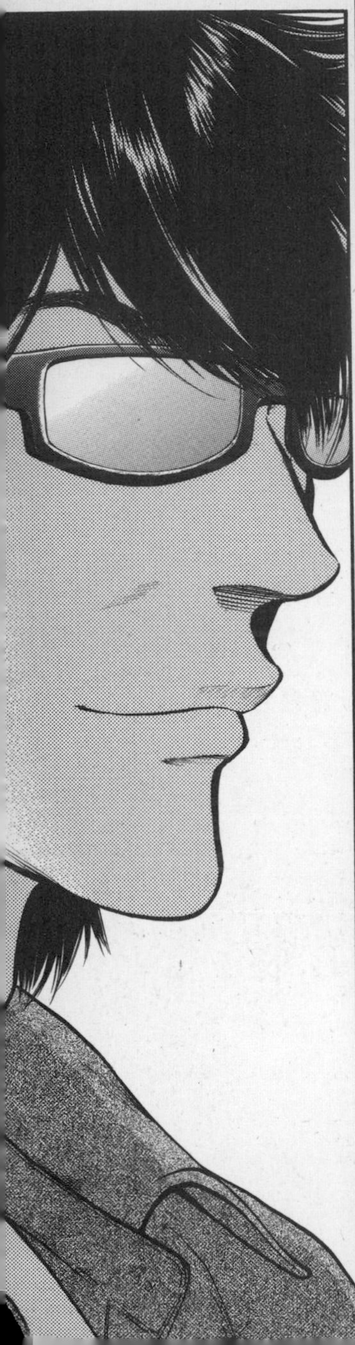

CHAPTER 27: OPERATION: SAVE THE DOGS

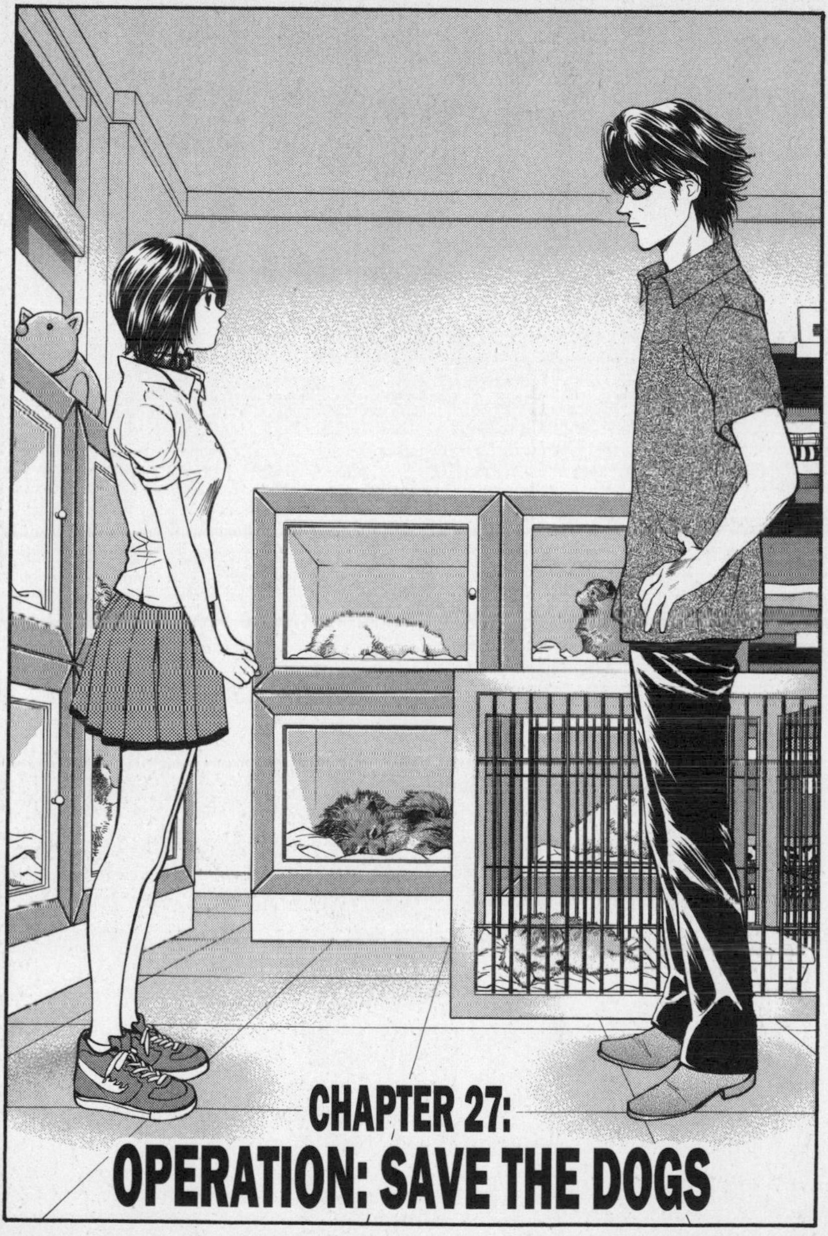
CHAPTER 27:
OPERATION: SAVE THE DOGS

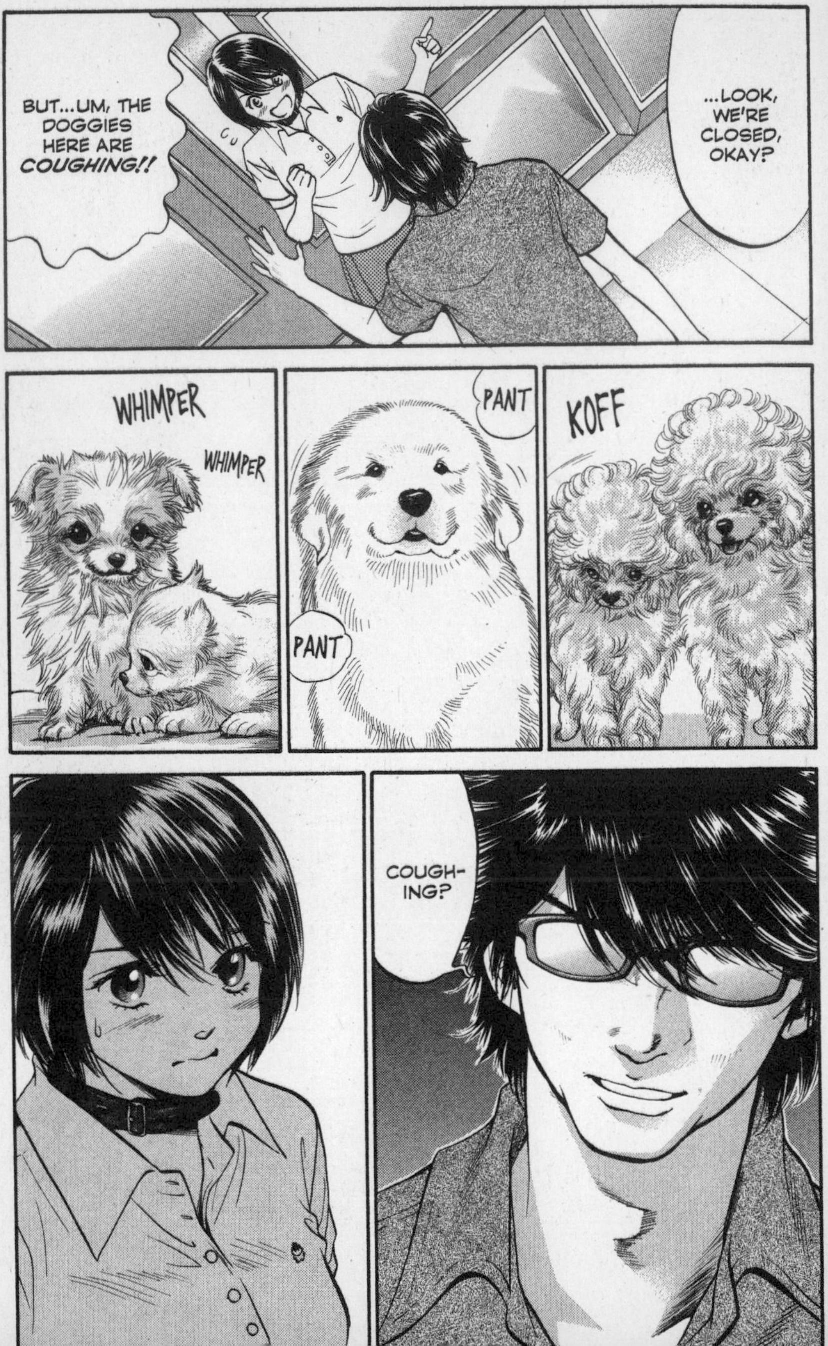
...LOOK, WE'RE CLOSED, OKAY?
BUT...UM, THE DOGGIES HERE ARE *COUGHING!!*
KOFF
PANT
PANT
WHIMPER
WHIMPER
COUGH-ING?

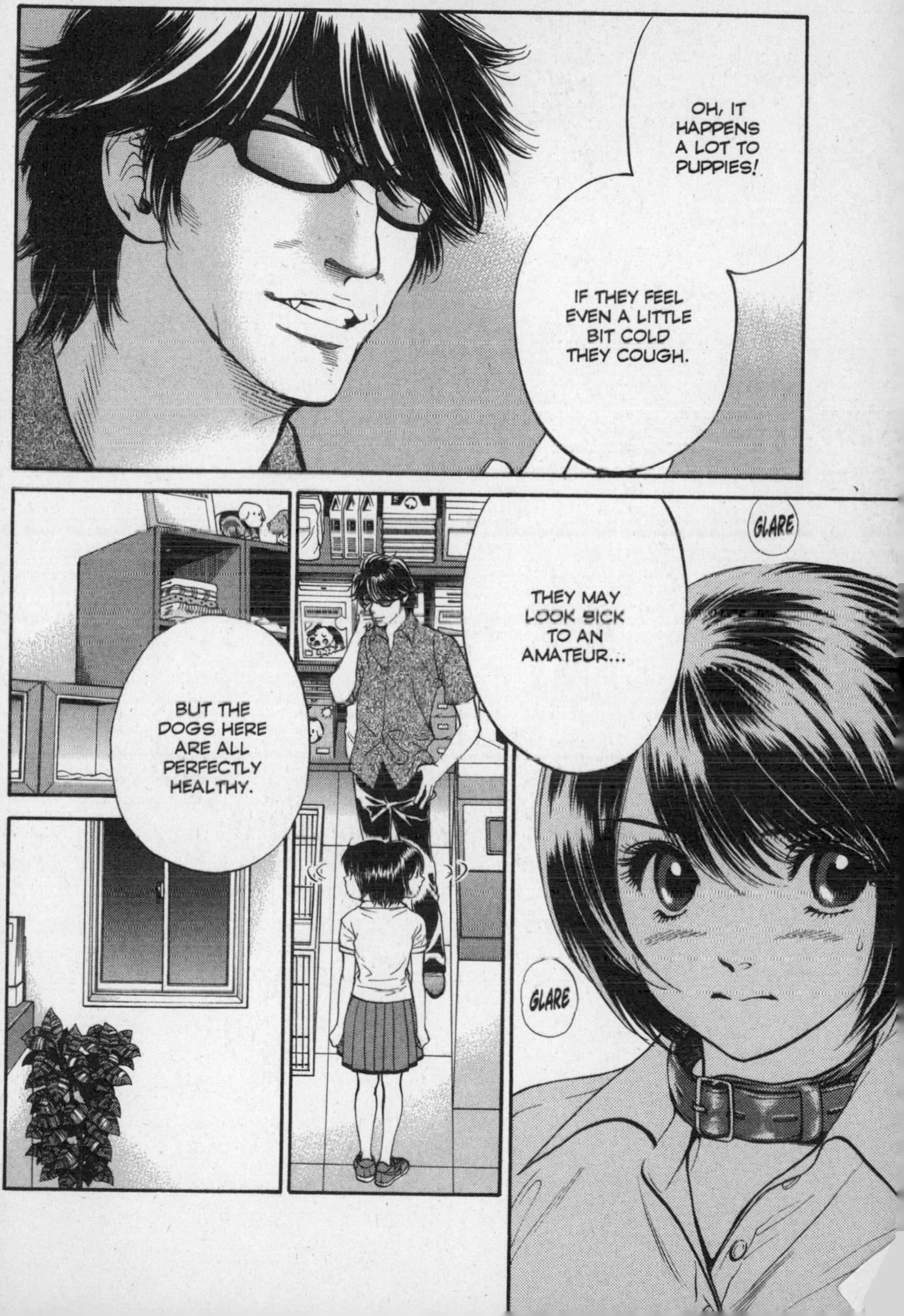
OH, IT HAPPENS A LOT TO PUPPIES!
IF THEY FEEL EVEN A LITTLE BIT COLD THEY COUGH.
GLARE
THEY MAY LOOK SICK TO AN AMATEUR...
GLARE
BUT THE DOGS HERE ARE ALL PERFECTLY HEALTHY.

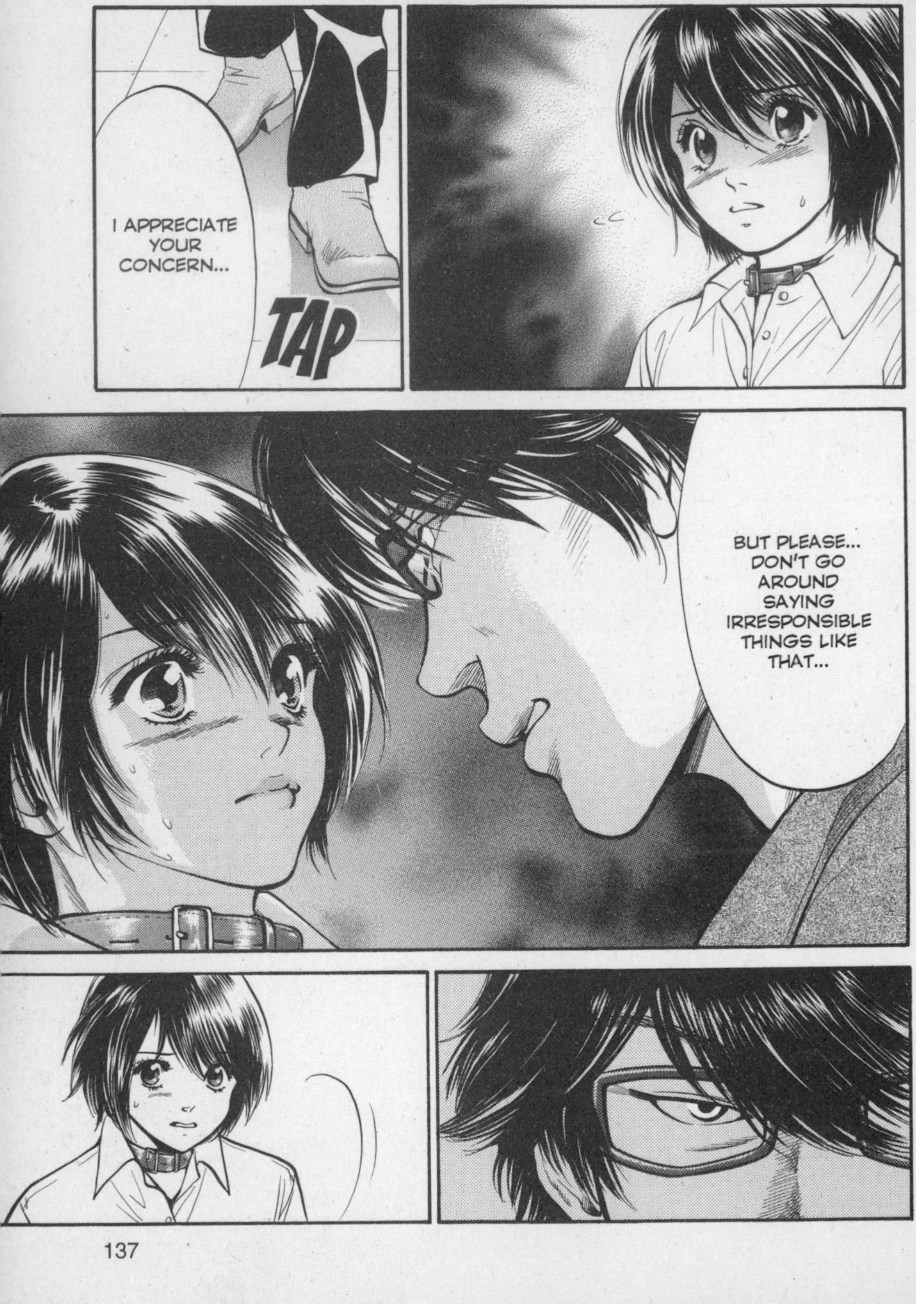
I APPRECIATE YOUR CONCERN...
TAP
BUT PLEASE... DON'T GO AROUND SAYING IRRESPONSIBLE THINGS LIKE THAT...

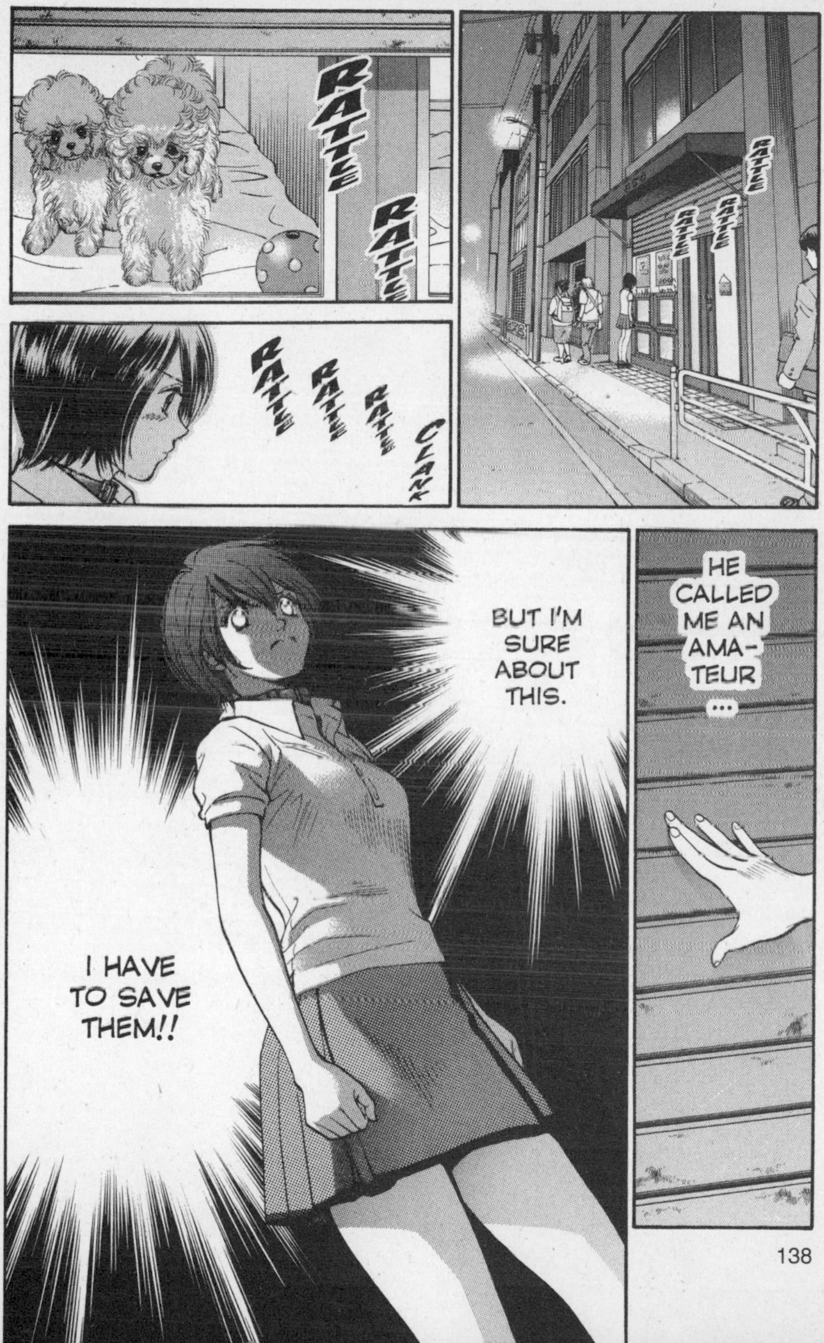
RATTLE
RATTLE
RATTLE
RATTLE
RATTLE
RATTLE
RATTLE
RATTLE
CLANK
HE CALLED ME AN AMATEUR...
BUT I'M SURE ABOUT THIS.
I HAVE TO SAVE THEM!!

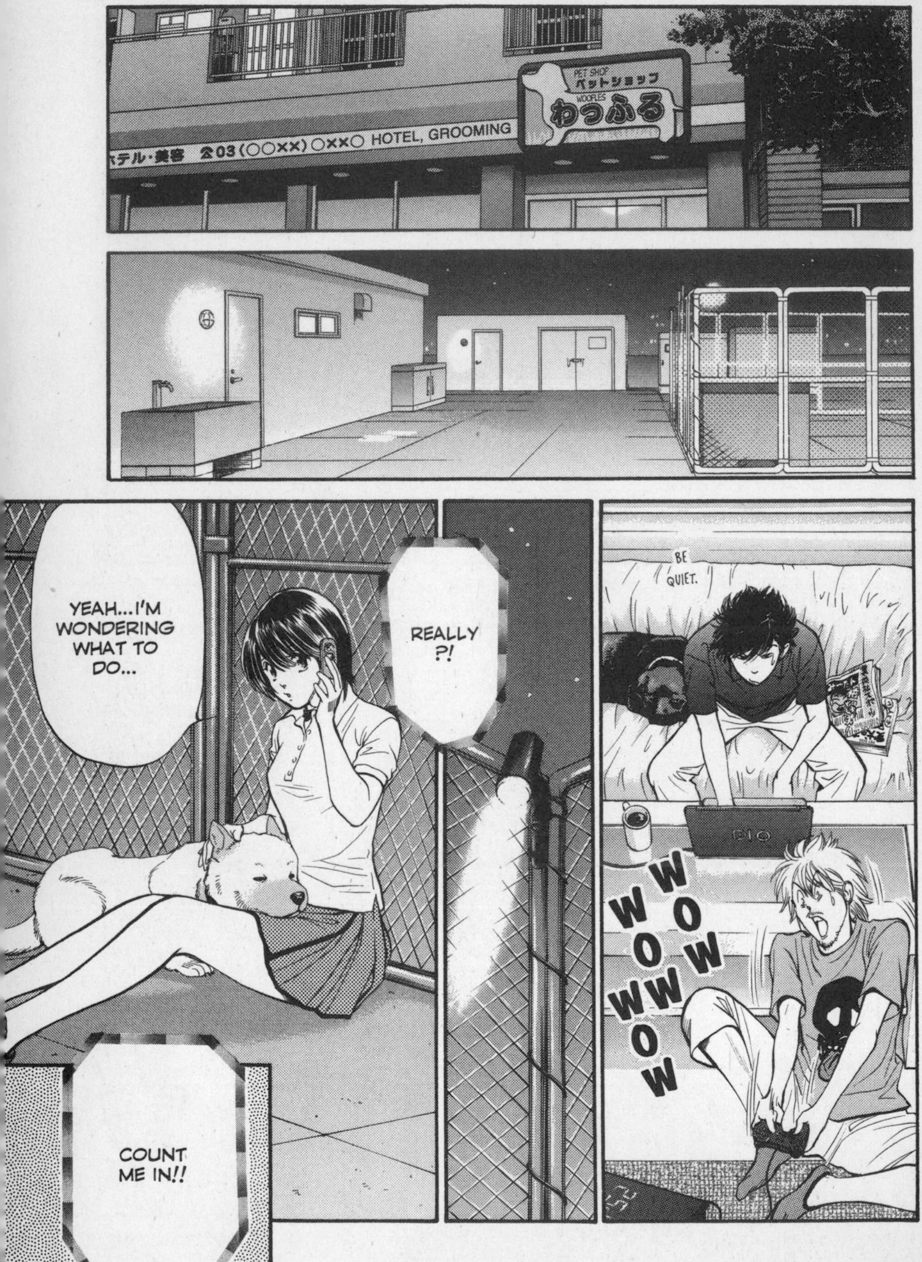
PET SHOP
ペットショップ
WOOFLES
わっふる
ホテル・美容 ☎03(○○××)○××○ HOTEL, GROOMING
BE QUIET.
WOW WOW WOW WOW
REALLY?!
YEAH...I'M WONDERING WHAT TO DO...
COUNT ME IN!!

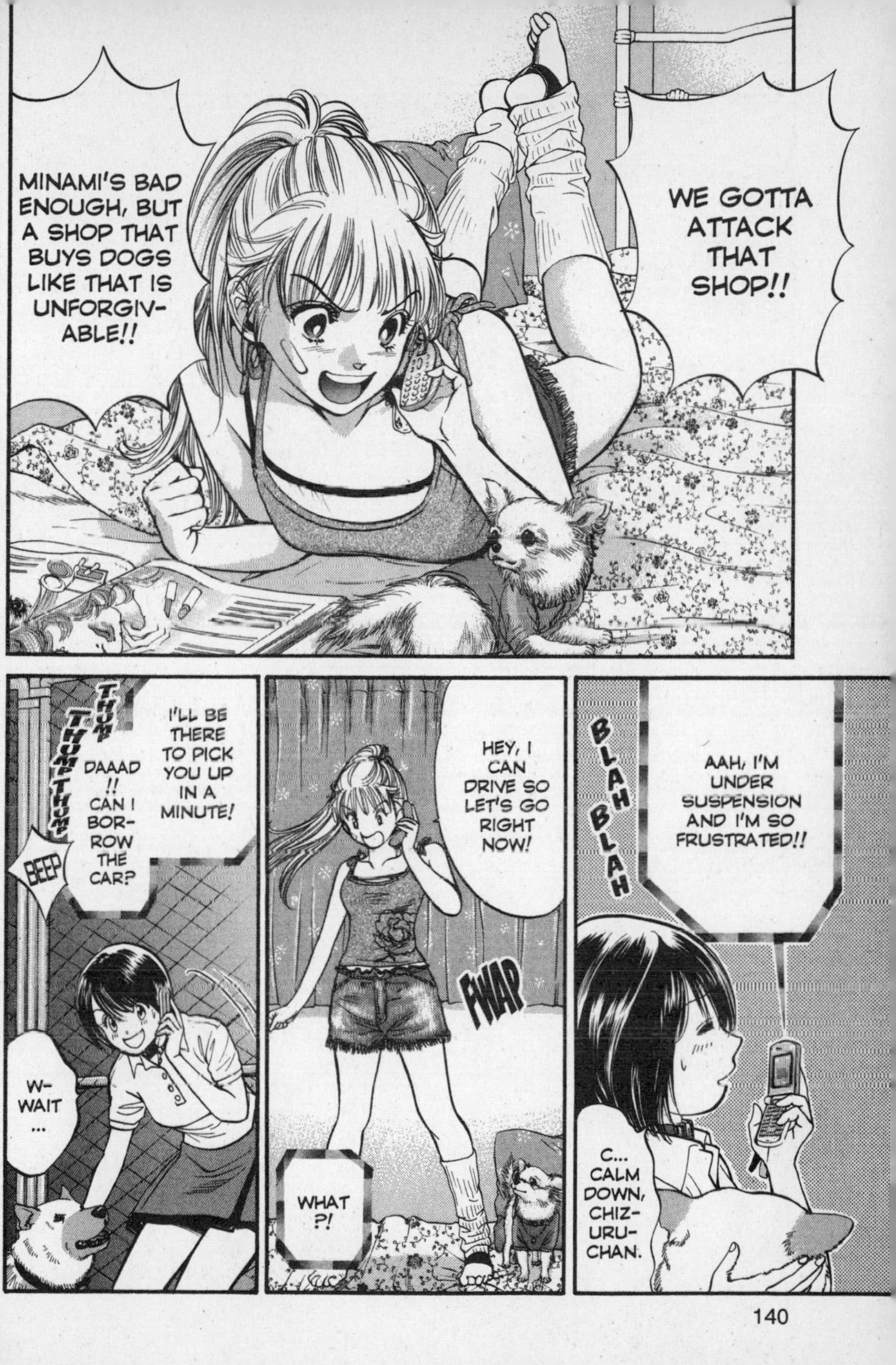

WE GOTTA ATTACK THAT SHOP!!
MINAMI'S BAD ENOUGH, BUT A SHOP THAT BUYS DOGS LIKE THAT IS UNFORGIVABLE!!
AAH, I'M UNDER SUSPENSION AND I'M SO FRUSTRATED!!
BLAH BLAH
C... CALM DOWN, CHIZURU-CHAN.
HEY, I CAN DRIVE SO LET'S GO RIGHT NOW!
PWAP
WHAT?!
I'LL BE THERE TO PICK YOU UP IN A MINUTE!
THUMP THUMP THUMP THUMP
DAAAD!! CAN I BORROW THE CAR?
BEEP
W-WAIT ...

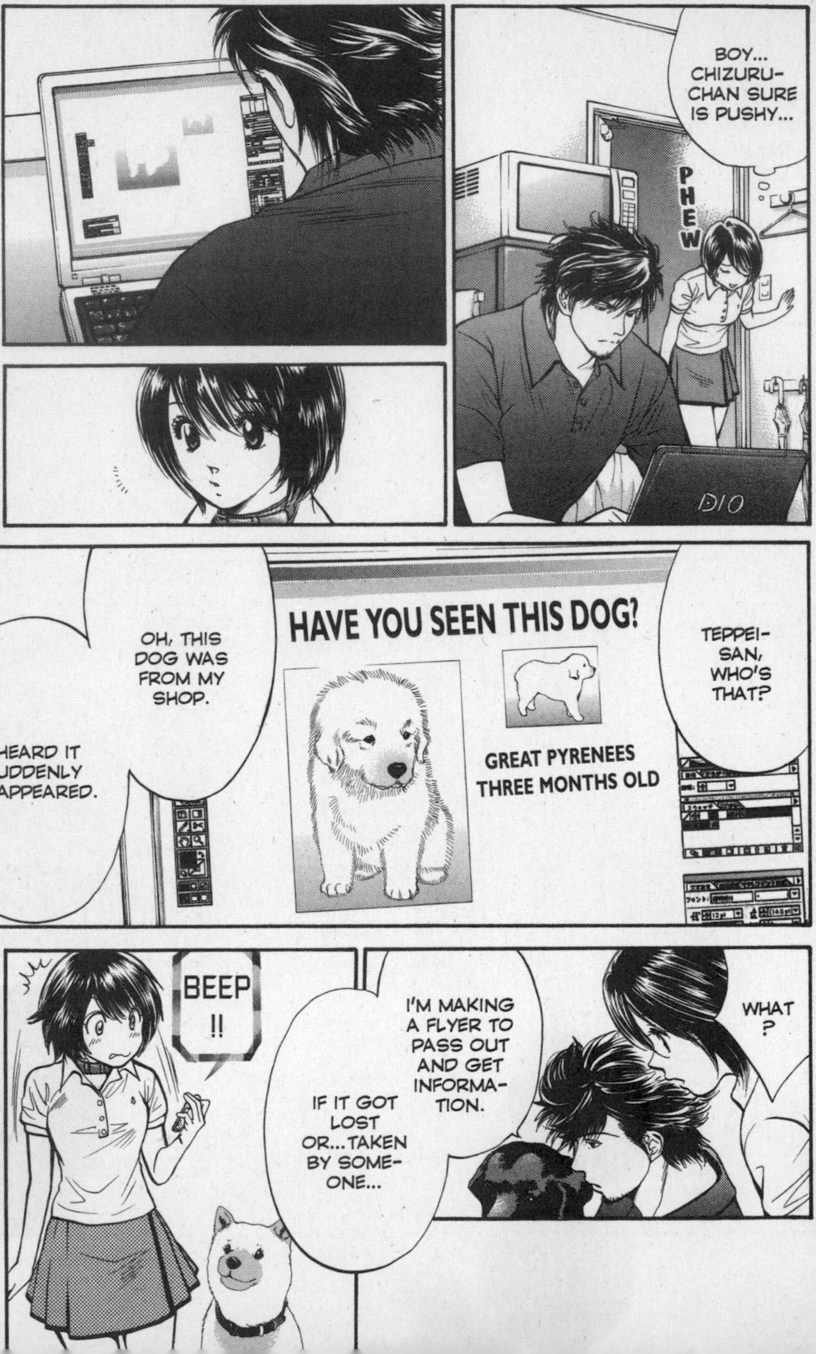
BOY... CHIZURU-CHAN SURE IS PUSHY...
PHEW
DIO
TEPPEI-SAN, WHO'S THAT?
HAVE YOU SEEN THIS DOG?
GREAT PYRENEES
THREE MONTHS OLD
OH, THIS DOG WAS FROM MY SHOP.
I HEARD IT SUDDENLY DISAPPEARED.
WHAT?
I'M MAKING A FLYER TO PASS OUT AND GET INFORMA-TION.
IF IT GOT LOST OR...TAKEN BY SOME-ONE...
BEEP !!

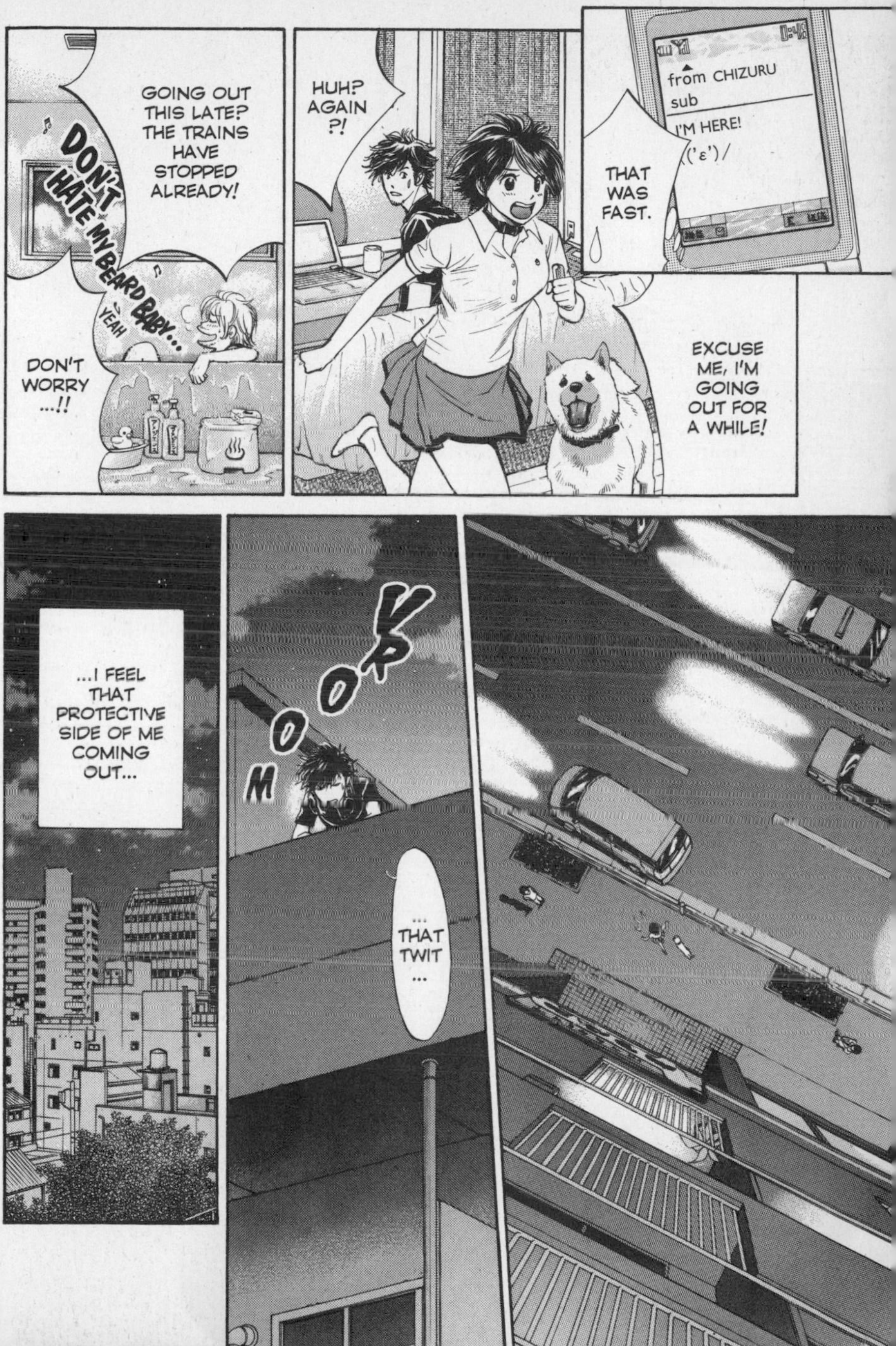
from CHIZURU
sub
I'M HERE!
('ε')/
THAT WAS FAST.
EXCUSE ME, I'M GOING OUT FOR A WHILE!
HUH? AGAIN?!
GOING OUT THIS LATE? THE TRAINS HAVE STOPPED ALREADY!
DON'T HATE MY BEARD BABY...
YEAH
DON'T WORRY ...!!
VROOOM
...THAT TWIT...
...I FEEL THAT PROTECTIVE SIDE OF ME COMING OUT...

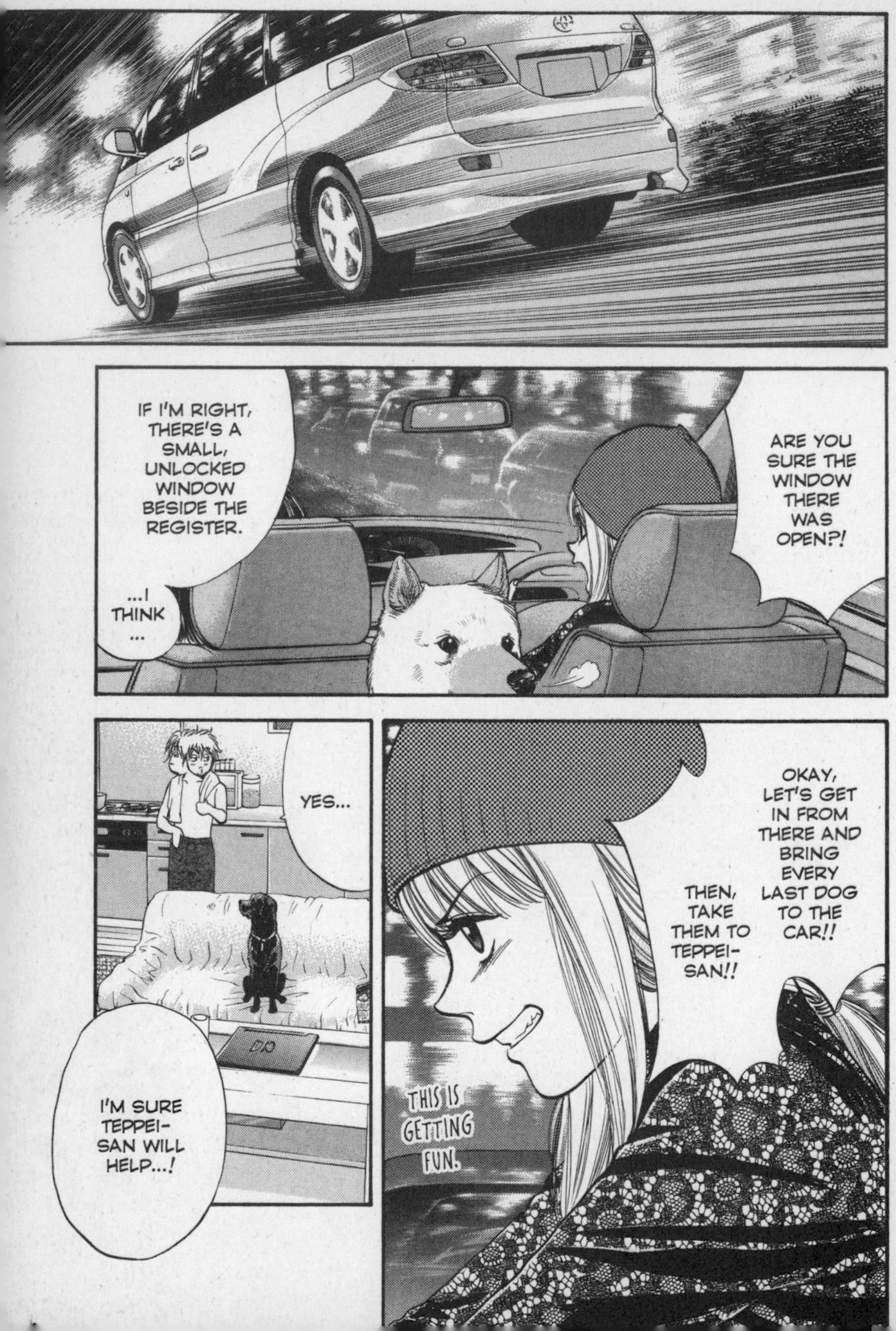
ARE YOU SURE THE WINDOW THERE WAS OPEN?!
IF I'M RIGHT, THERE'S A SMALL, UNLOCKED WINDOW BESIDE THE REGISTER.
...I THINK ...
OKAY, LET'S GET IN FROM THERE AND BRING EVERY LAST DOG TO THE CAR!!
THEN, TAKE THEM TO TEPPEI-SAN!!
THIS IS GETTING FUN.
YES...
I'M SURE TEPPEI-SAN WILL HELP...!

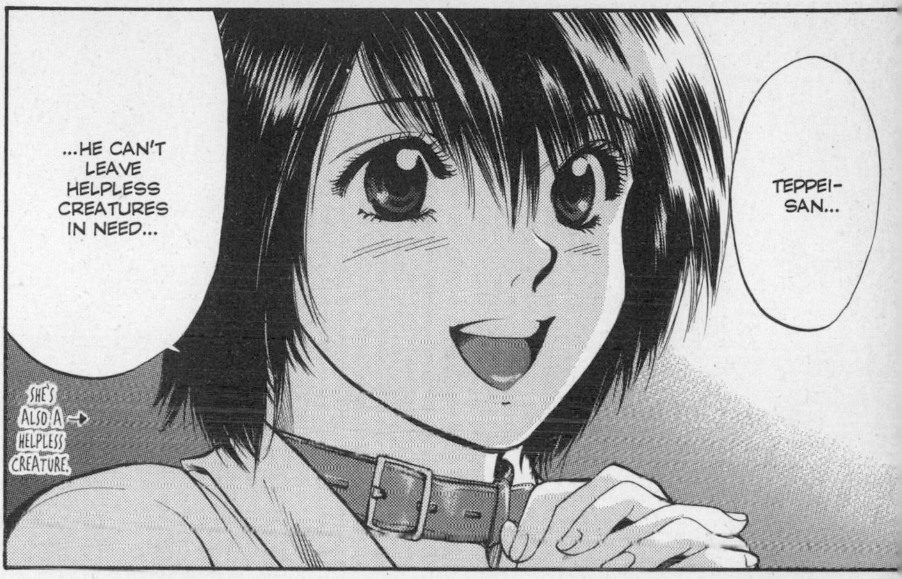
TEPPEI-SAN...
...HE CAN'T LEAVE HELPLESS CREATURES IN NEED...
SHE'S ALSO A → HELPLESS CREATURE.

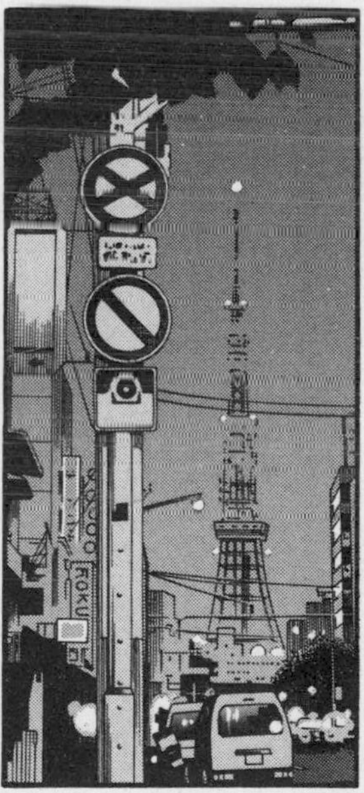

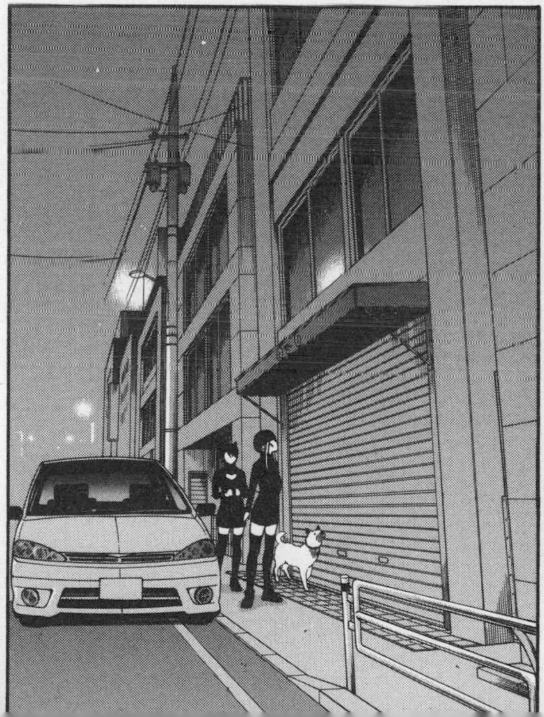

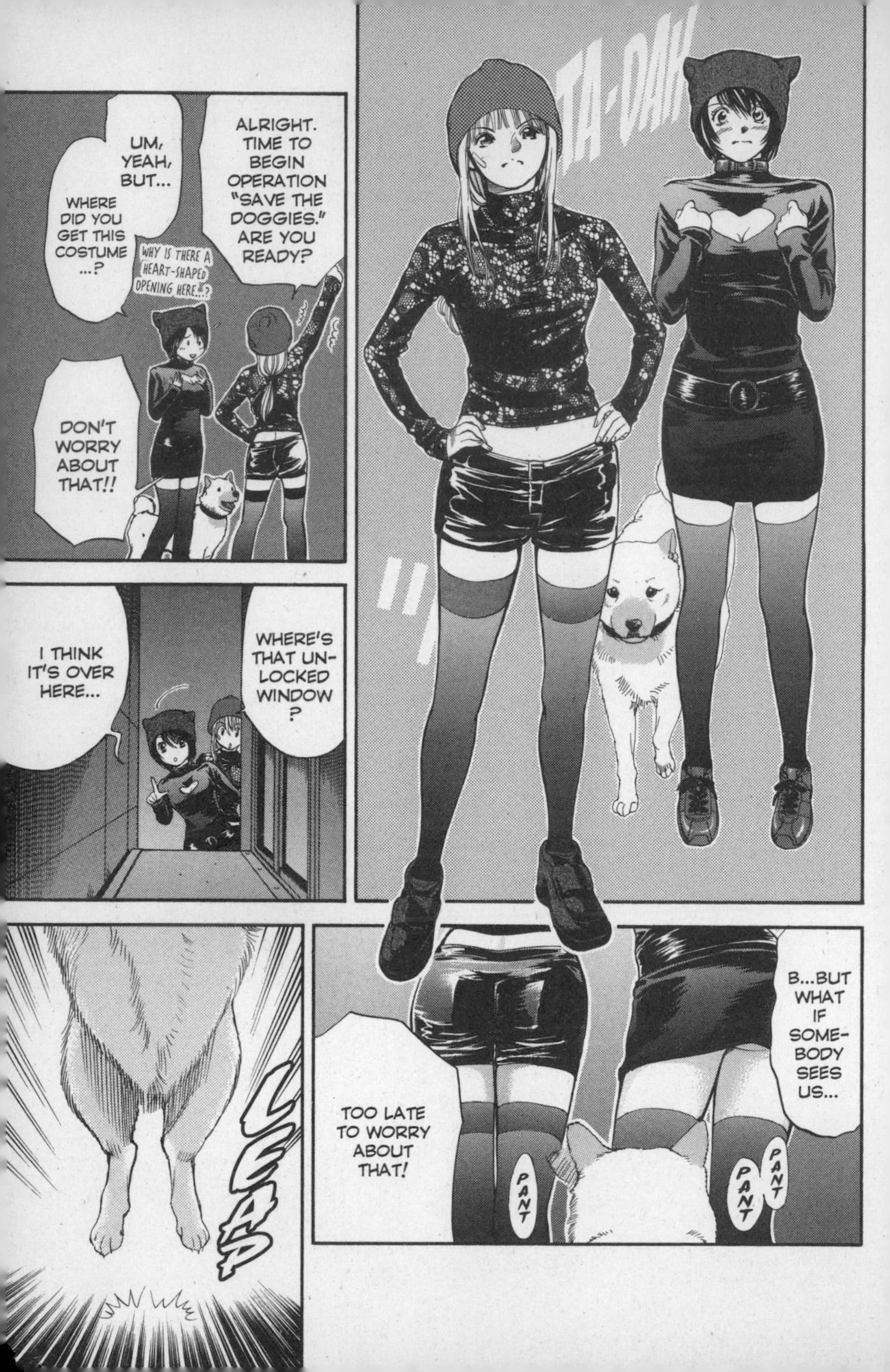
TA-DAH
ALRIGHT. TIME TO BEGIN OPERATION "SAVE THE DOGGIES." ARE YOU READY?
UM, YEAH, BUT...
WHERE DID YOU GET THIS COSTUME ...?
WHY IS THERE A HEART-SHAPED OPENING HERE...?
DON'T WORRY ABOUT THAT!!
WHERE'S THAT UN-LOCKED WINDOW ?
I THINK IT'S OVER HERE...
B...BUT WHAT IF SOME-BODY SEES US...
PANT
PANT
PANT
TOO LATE TO WORRY ABOUT THAT!
PANT
LEAP

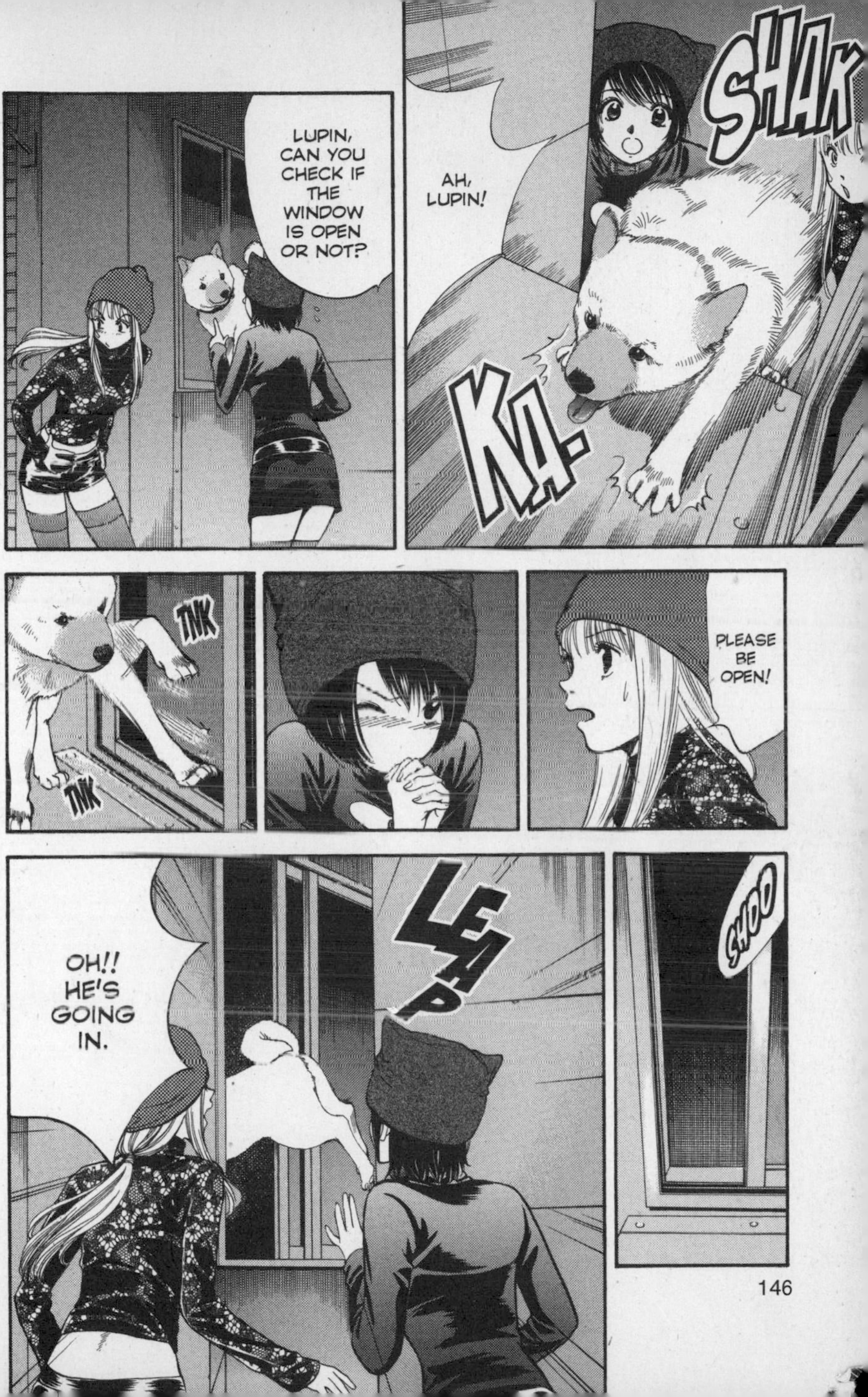
SHAK
AH, LUPIN!
KA.
LUPIN, CAN YOU CHECK IF THE WINDOW IS OPEN OR NOT?
PLEASE BE OPEN!
TNK
TNK
SHOO
LEAP
OH!! HE'S GOING IN.

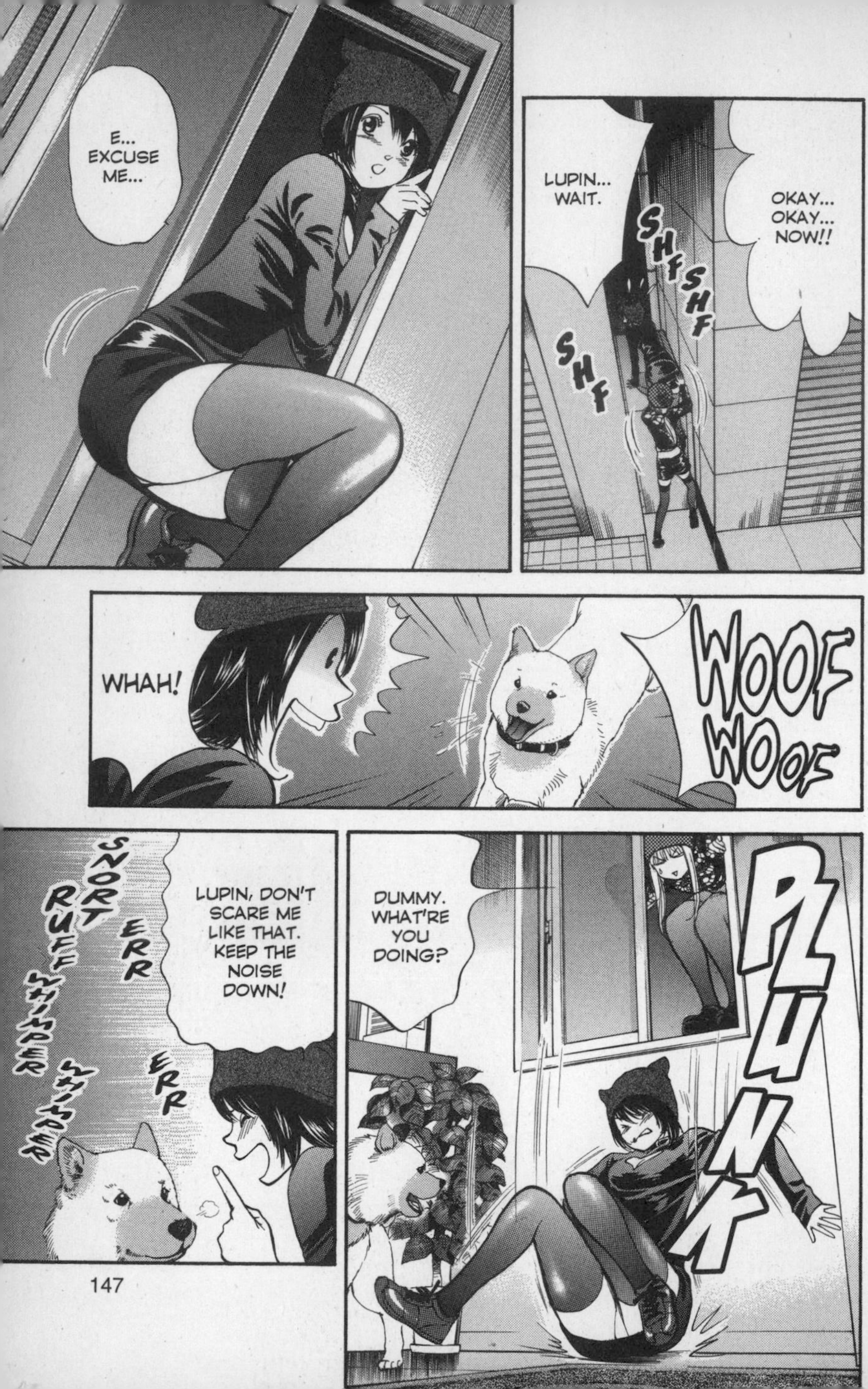
OKAY... OKAY... NOW!!
LUPIN... WAIT.
SHF SHF
SHF
E... EXCUSE ME...
WOOF WOOF
WHAH!
PLUNK
DUMMY. WHAT'RE YOU DOING?
LUPIN, DON'T SCARE ME LIKE THAT. KEEP THE NOISE DOWN!
ERR
ERR
SNORT
RUFF
WHIMPER WHIMPER

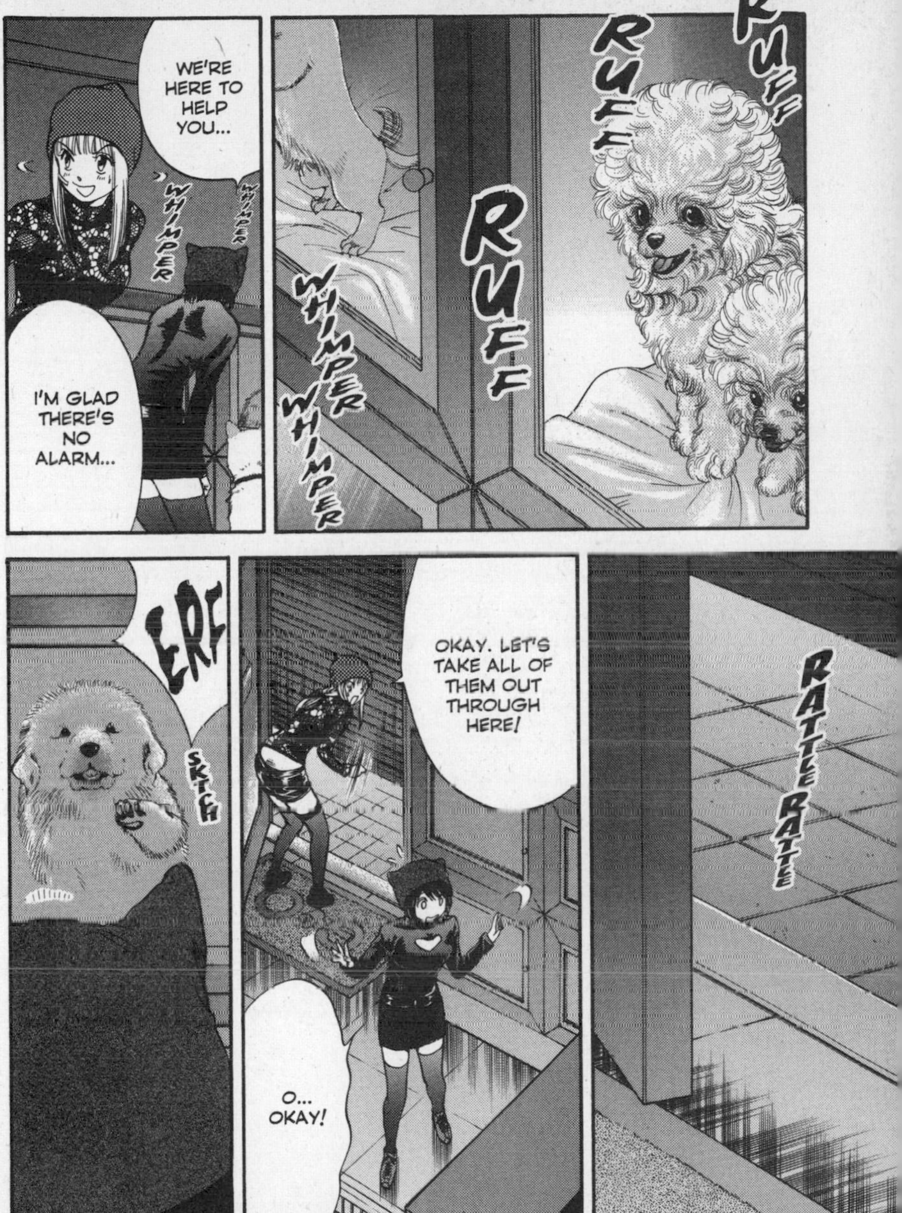
RUFF
RUFF
RUFF
WHIMPER
WHIMPER
WHIMPER
WHIMPER
WE'RE HERE TO HELP YOU...
I'M GLAD THERE'S NO ALARM...
RATTLE RATTLE
OKAY. LET'S TAKE ALL OF THEM OUT THROUGH HERE!
O... OKAY!
ERF
SKTCH

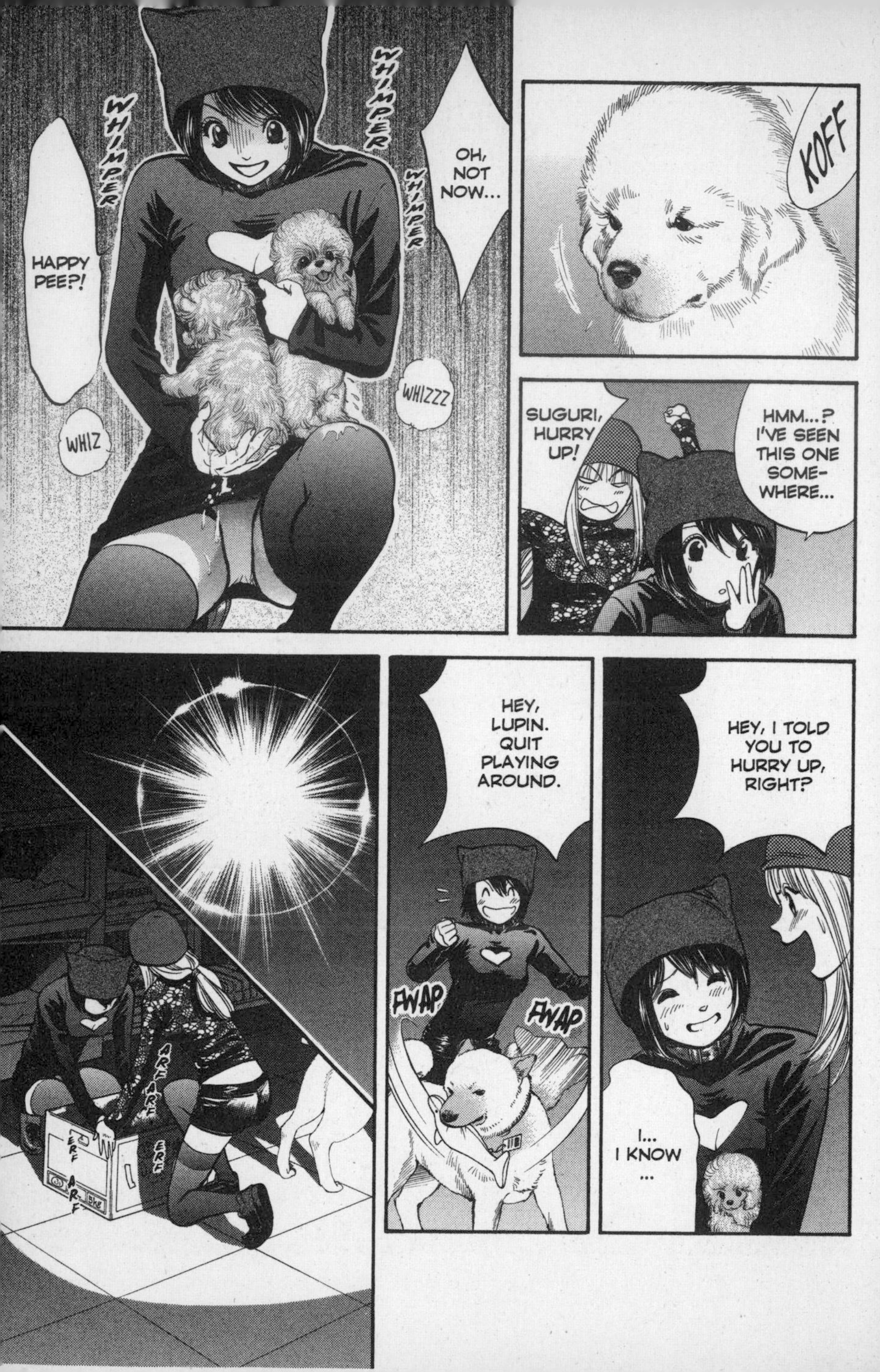
KOFF
HMM...? I'VE SEEN THIS ONE SOME-WHERE...
SUGURI, HURRY UP!
WHIMPER
OH, NOT NOW...
WHIMPER
WHIMPER
HAPPY PEE?!
WHIZZZ
WHIZ
HEY, I TOLD YOU TO HURRY UP, RIGHT?
I... I KNOW ...
HEY, LUPIN. QUIT PLAYING AROUND.
FWAP
FWAP
ARF ARF
ERF
ERF
ARF ARF

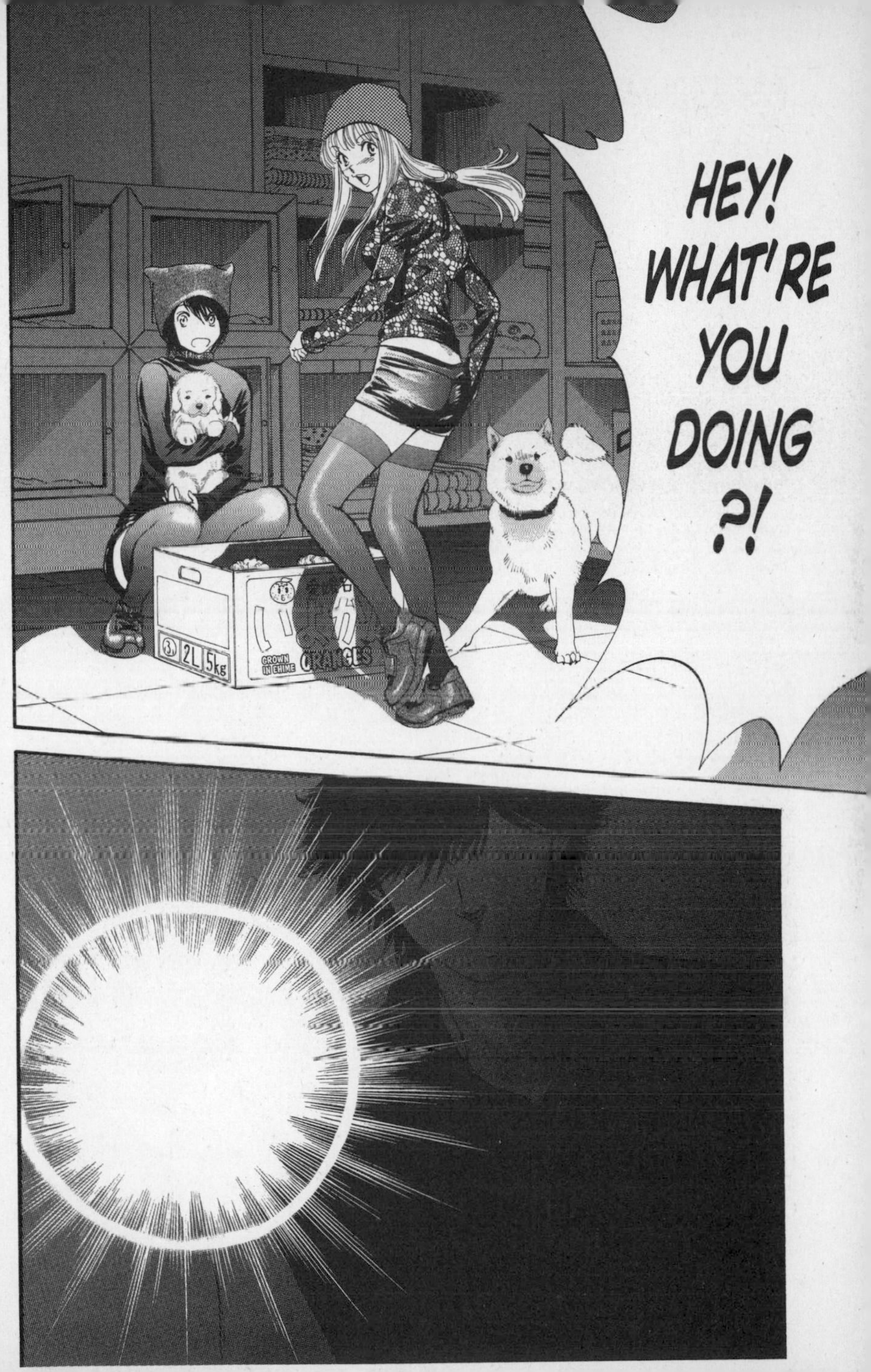
HEY! WHAT'RE YOU DOING ?!
3 2L 5kg
GROWN IN EHIME
ORANGES

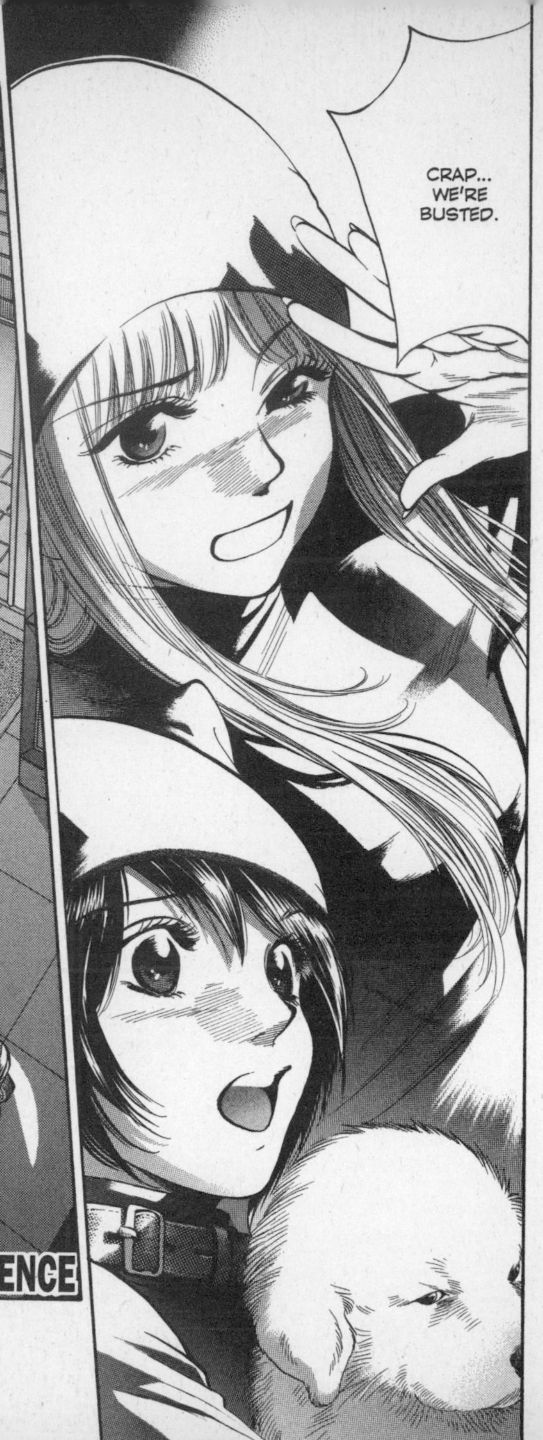
CRAP... WE'RE BUSTED.

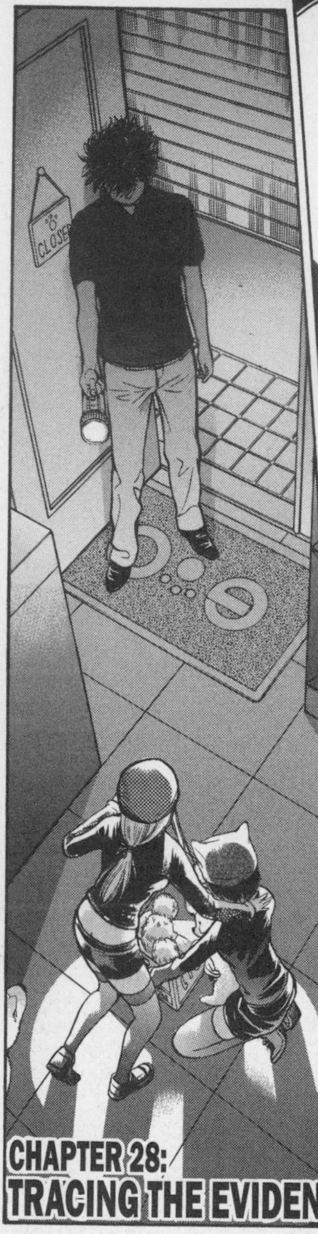

CHAPTER 28: TRACING THE EVIDENCE

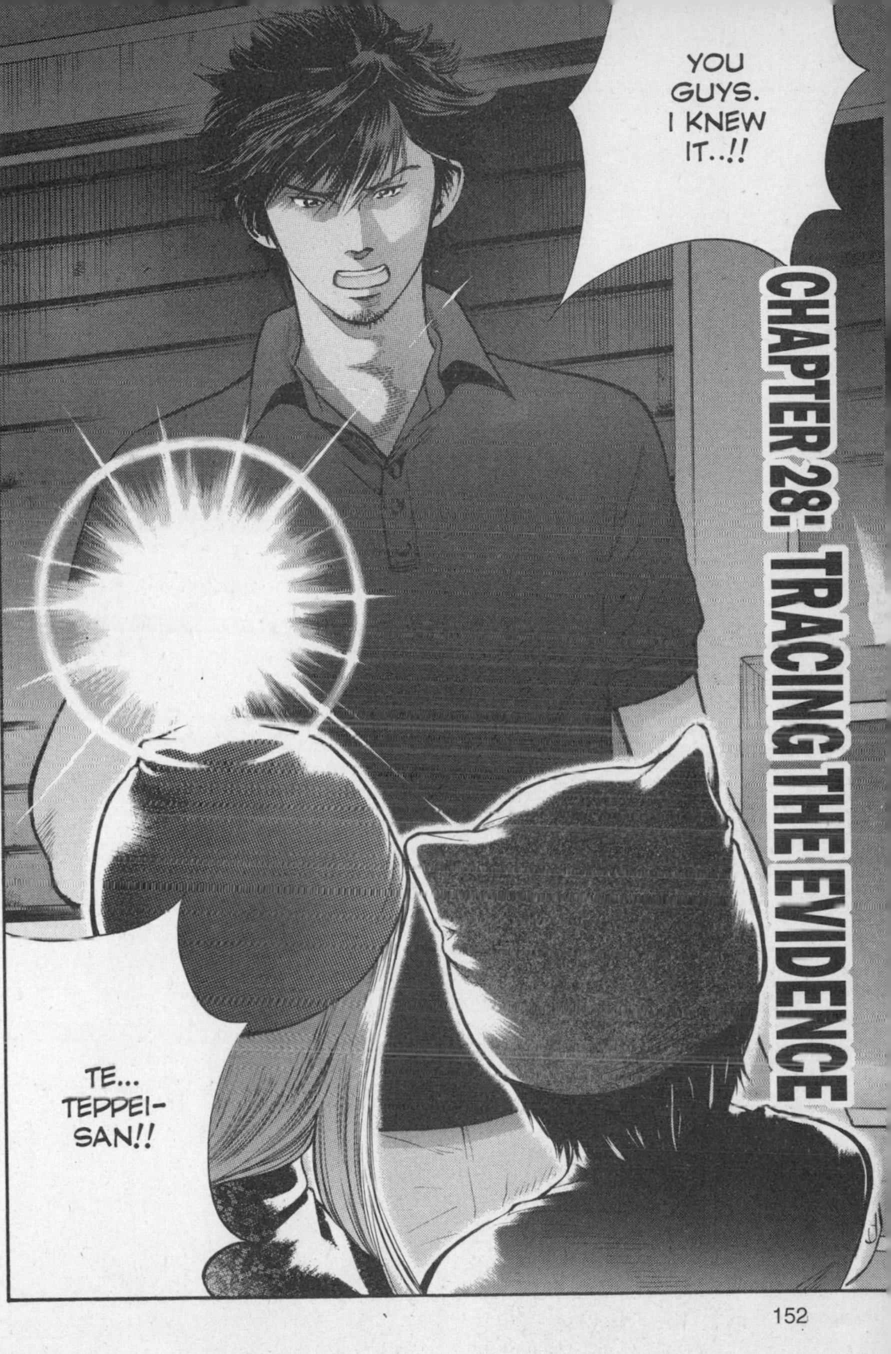
YOU GUYS. I KNEW IT..!!
CHAPTER 28: TRACING THE EVIDENCE
TE... TEPPEI-SAN!!

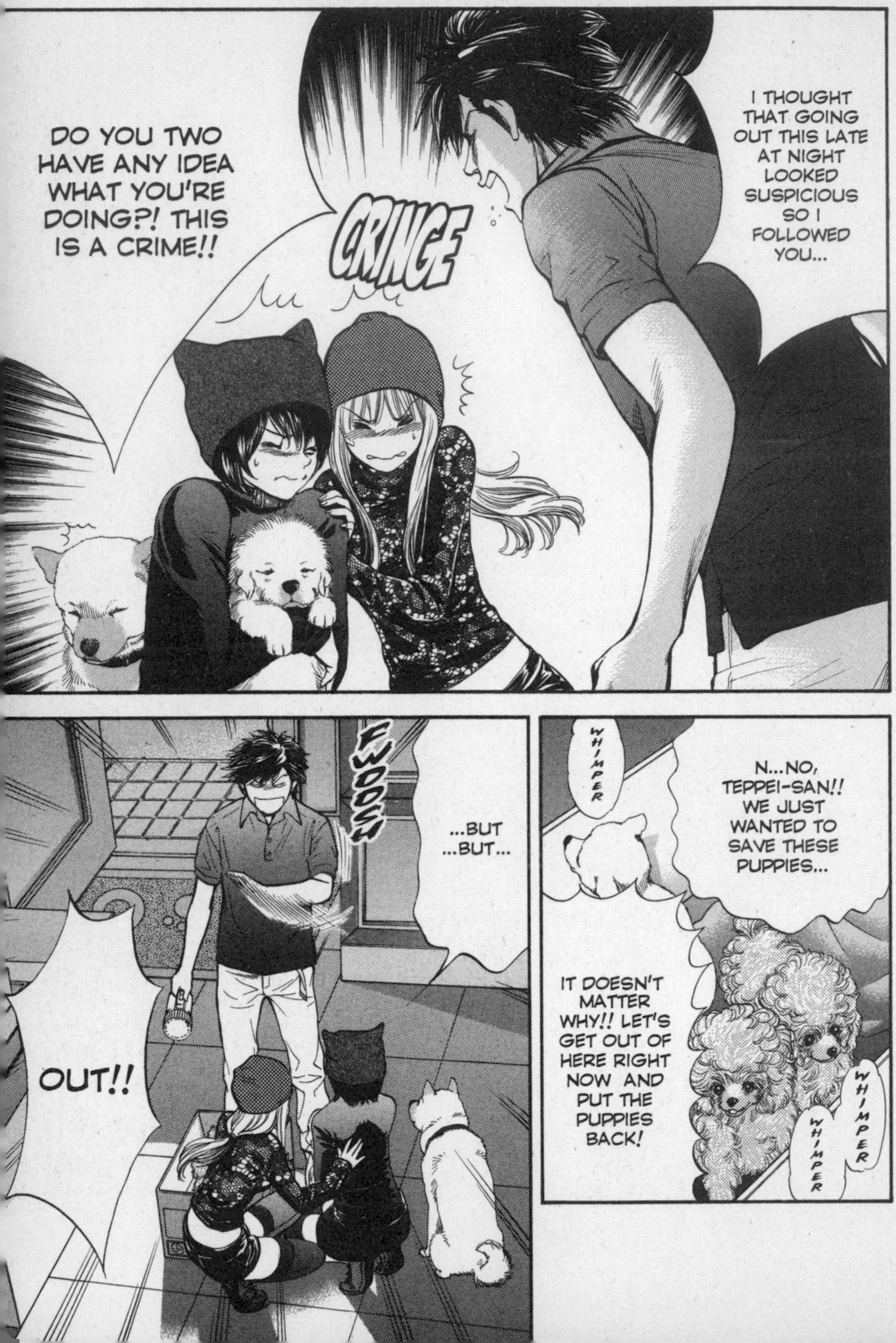
I THOUGHT THAT GOING OUT THIS LATE AT NIGHT LOOKED SUSPICIOUS SO I FOLLOWED YOU...
CRINGE
DO YOU TWO HAVE ANY IDEA WHAT YOU'RE DOING?! THIS IS A CRIME!!
N...NO, TEPPEI-SAN!! WE JUST WANTED TO SAVE THESE PUPPIES...
WHIMPER
IT DOESN'T MATTER WHY!! LET'S GET OUT OF HERE RIGHT NOW AND PUT THE PUPPIES BACK!
WHIMPER
WHIMPER
FWOOSH
...BUT ...BUT...
OUT!!

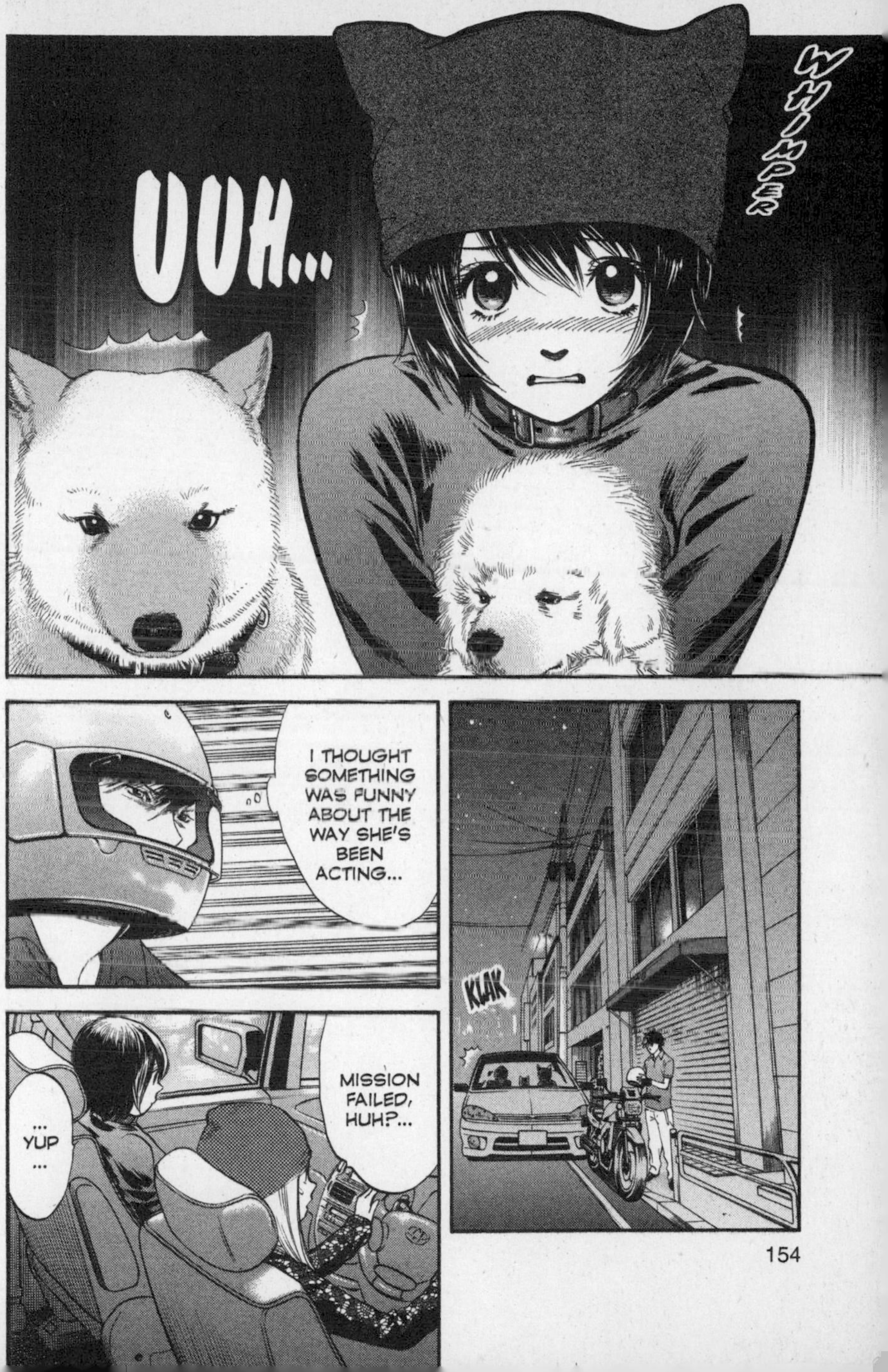
WHIMPER
UUH...
KLAK
I THOUGHT SOMETHING WAS FUNNY ABOUT THE WAY SHE'S BEEN ACTING...
MISSION FAILED, HUH?...
... YUP ...

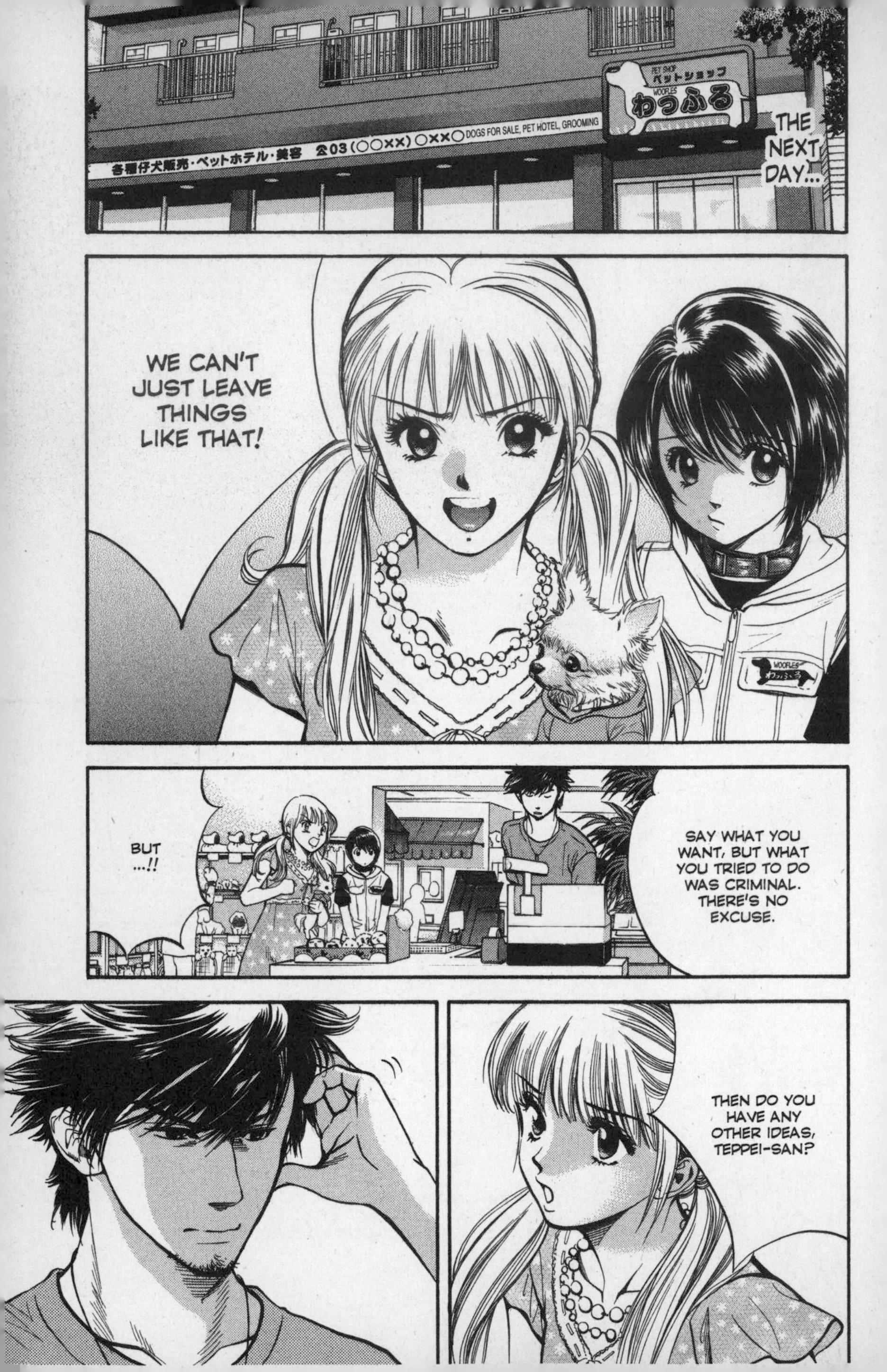
THE NEXT DAY...
PET SHOP ペットショップ
WOOFLES わっふる
DOGS FOR SALE, PET HOTEL, GROOMING
各種仔犬販売・ペットホテル・美容 ☎03(○○××)○××○
WE CAN'T JUST LEAVE THINGS LIKE THAT!
SAY WHAT YOU WANT, BUT WHAT YOU TRIED TO DO WAS CRIMINAL. THERE'S NO EXCUSE.
BUT ...!!
THEN DO YOU HAVE ANY OTHER IDEAS, TEPPEI-SAN?

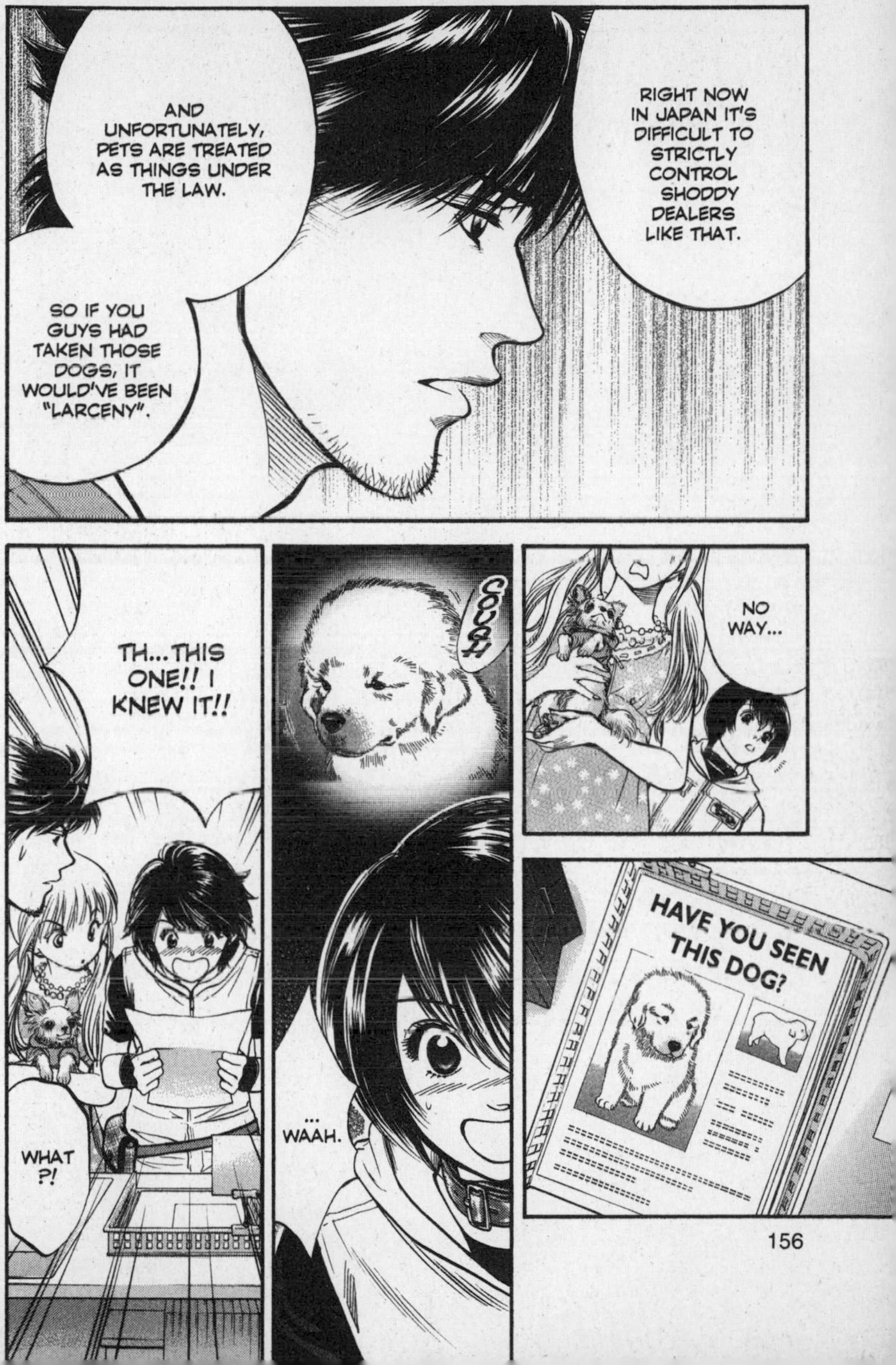
RIGHT NOW IN JAPAN IT'S DIFFICULT TO STRICTLY CONTROL SHODDY DEALERS LIKE THAT.
AND UNFORTUNATELY, PETS ARE TREATED AS THINGS UNDER THE LAW.
SO IF YOU GUYS HAD TAKEN THOSE DOGS, IT WOULD'VE BEEN "LARCENY".
NO WAY...
HAVE YOU SEEN THIS DOG?
COUGH
... WAAH.
TH...THIS ONE!! I KNEW IT!!
WHAT ?!

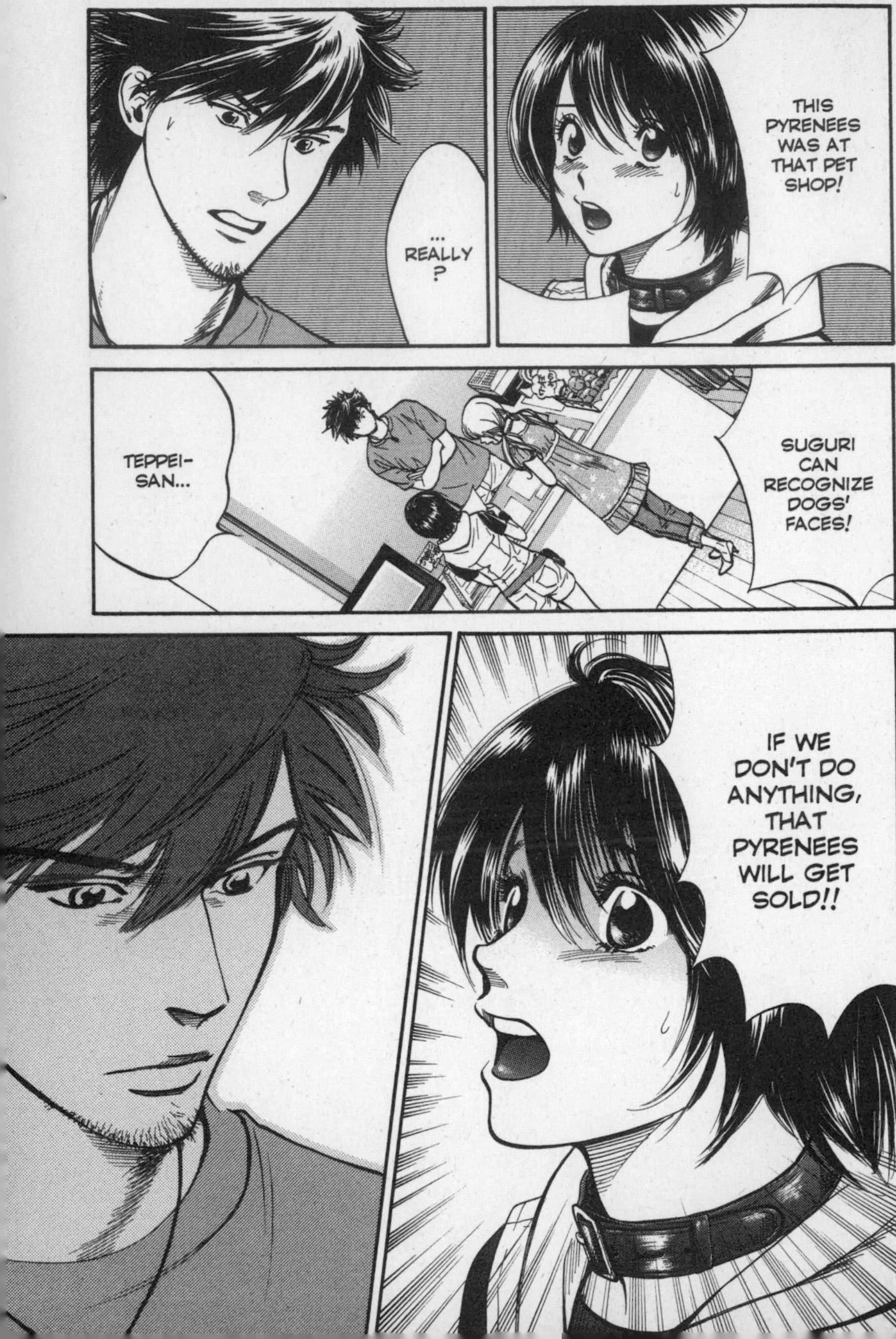
THIS PYRENEES WAS AT THAT PET SHOP!
...REALLY?
SUGURI CAN RECOGNIZE DOGS' FACES!
TEPPEI-SAN...
IF WE DON'T DO ANYTHING, THAT PYRENEES WILL GET SOLD!!

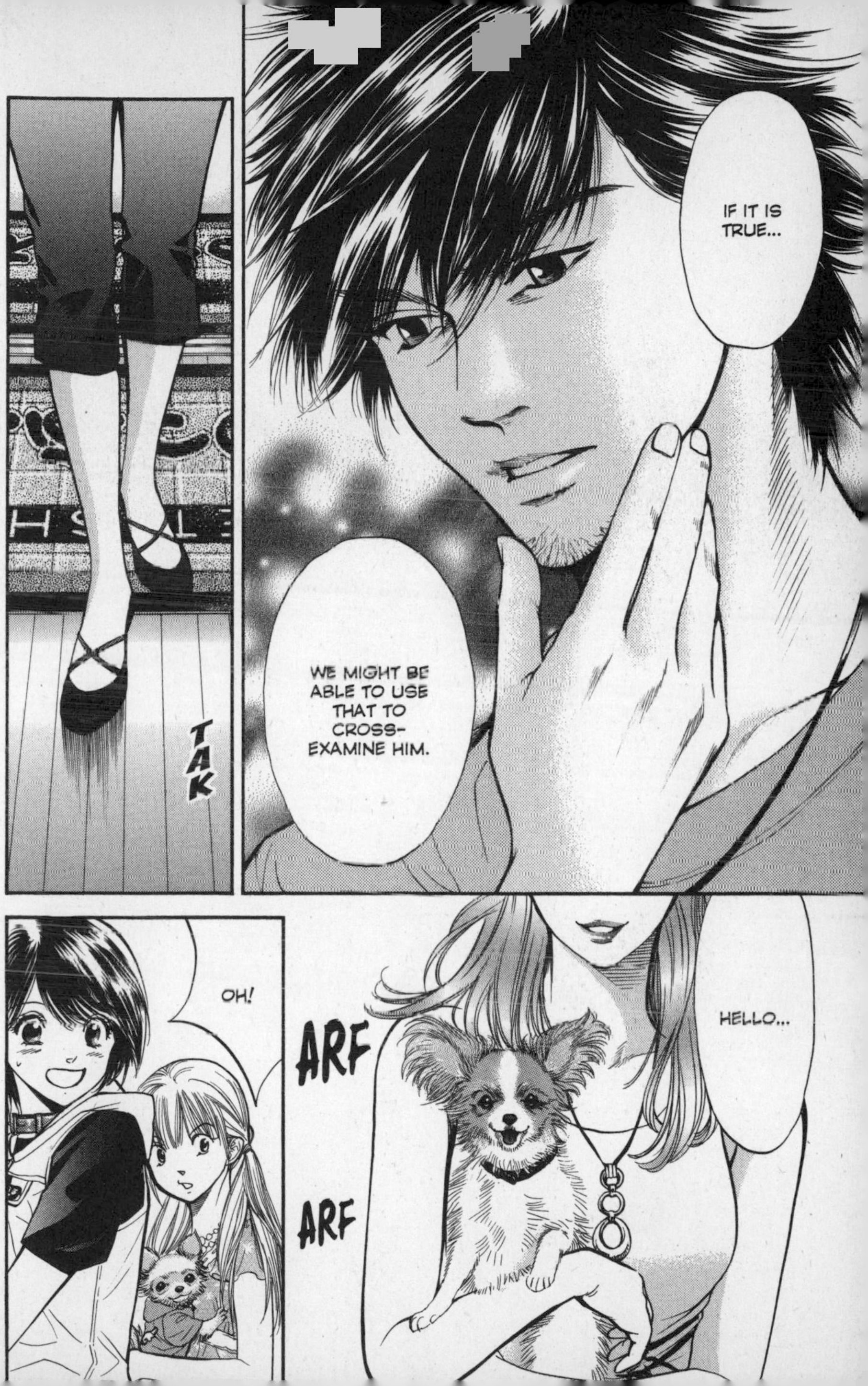
IF IT IS TRUE...
WE MIGHT BE ABLE TO USE THAT TO CROSS-EXAMINE HIM.
TAK
HELLO...
ARF
ARF
OH!

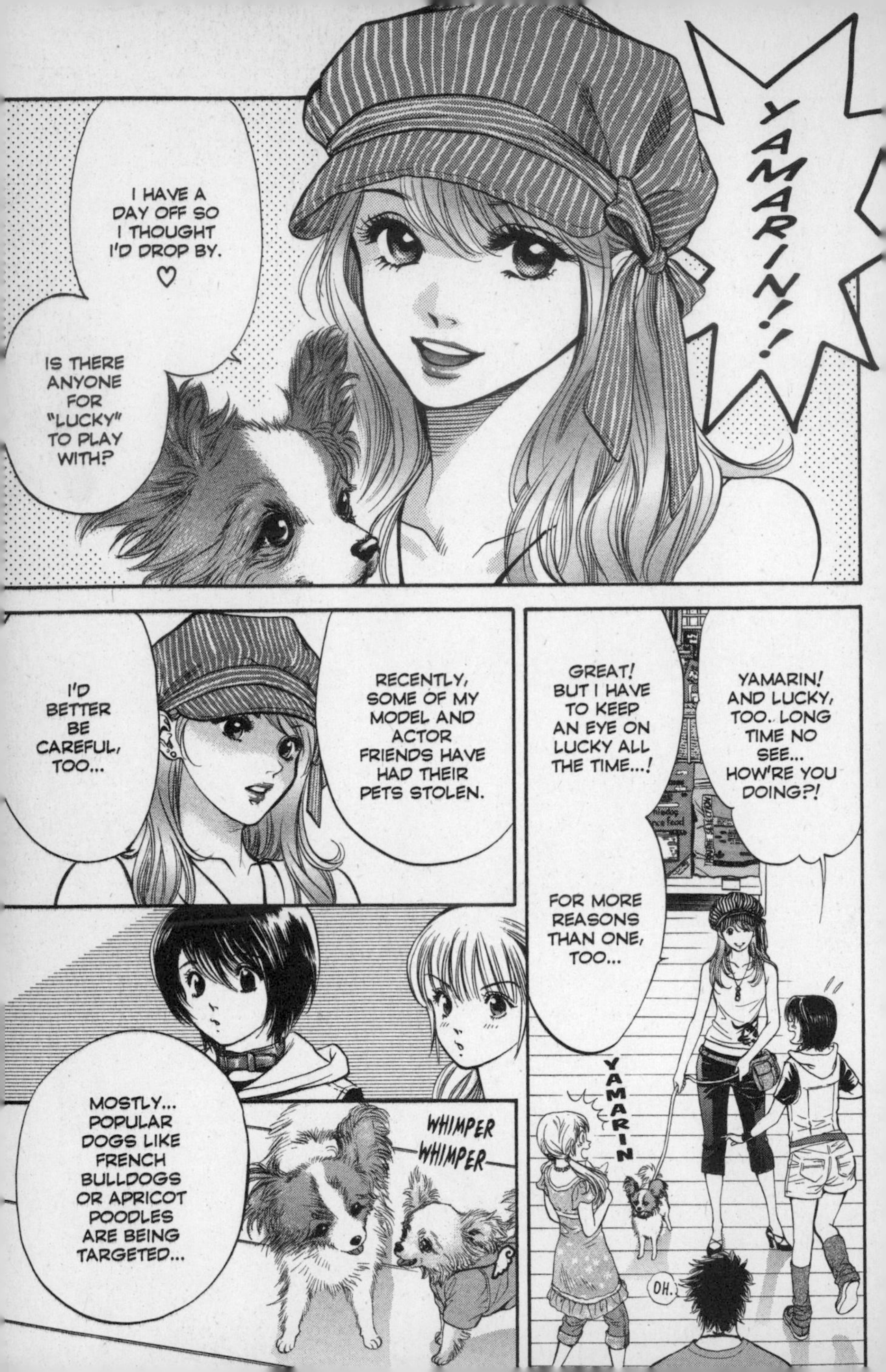
YAMARIN!!
I HAVE A DAY OFF SO I THOUGHT I'D DROP BY. ♡
IS THERE ANYONE FOR "LUCKY" TO PLAY WITH?
YAMARIN! AND LUCKY, TOO.. LONG TIME NO SEE... HOW'RE YOU DOING?!
GREAT! BUT I HAVE TO KEEP AN EYE ON LUCKY ALL THE TIME...!
FOR MORE REASONS THAN ONE, TOO...
YAMARIN
OH.
RECENTLY, SOME OF MY MODEL AND ACTOR FRIENDS HAVE HAD THEIR PETS STOLEN.
I'D BETTER BE CAREFUL, TOO...
MOSTLY... POPULAR DOGS LIKE FRENCH BULLDOGS OR APRICOT POODLES ARE BEING TARGETED...
WHIMPER WHIMPER

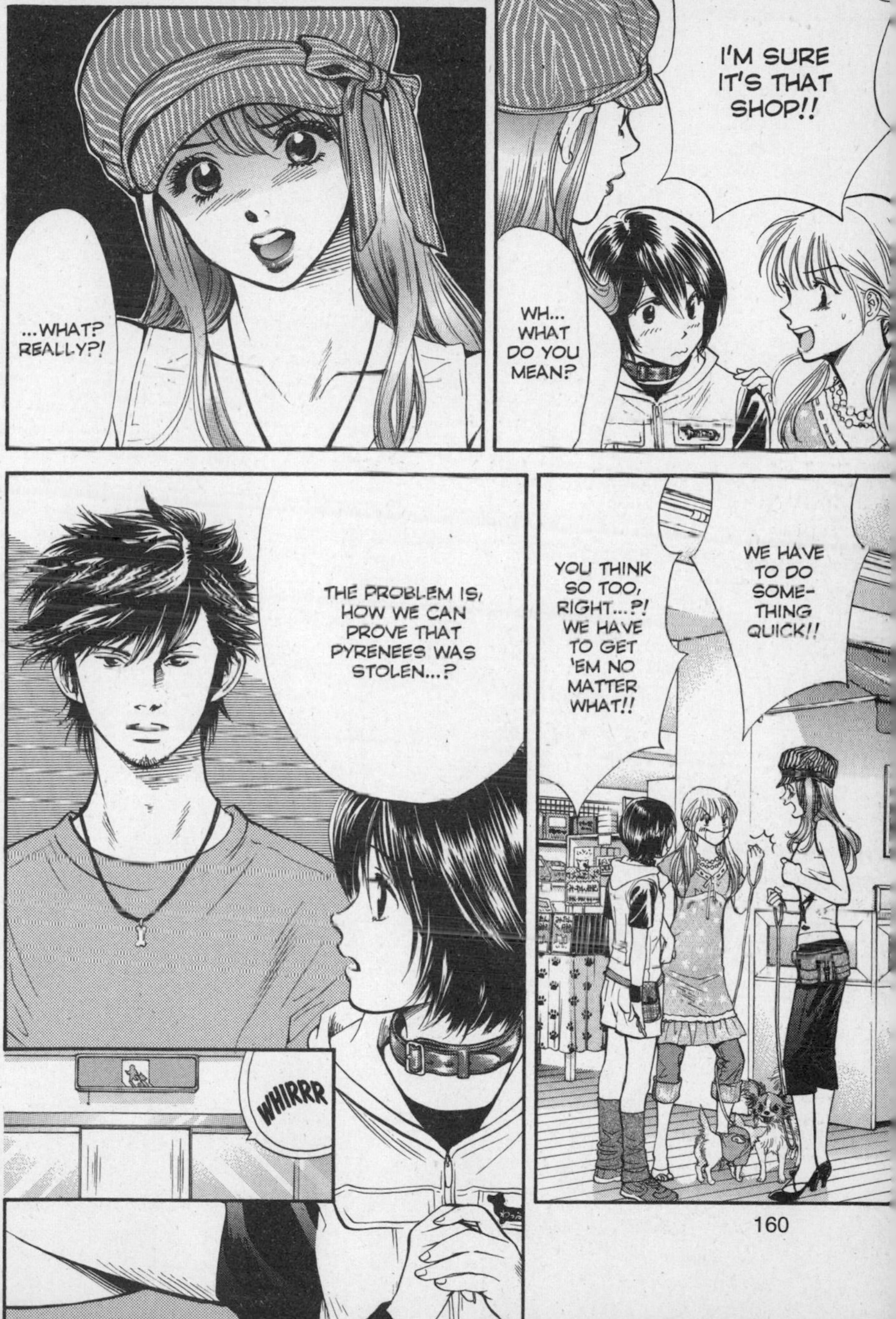
I'M SURE IT'S THAT SHOP!!
WH... WHAT DO YOU MEAN?
...WHAT? REALLY?!
WE HAVE TO DO SOME-THING QUICK!!
YOU THINK SO TOO, RIGHT...?! WE HAVE TO GET 'EM NO MATTER WHAT!!
THE PROBLEM IS, HOW WE CAN PROVE THAT PYRENEES WAS STOLEN...?
WHIRRR

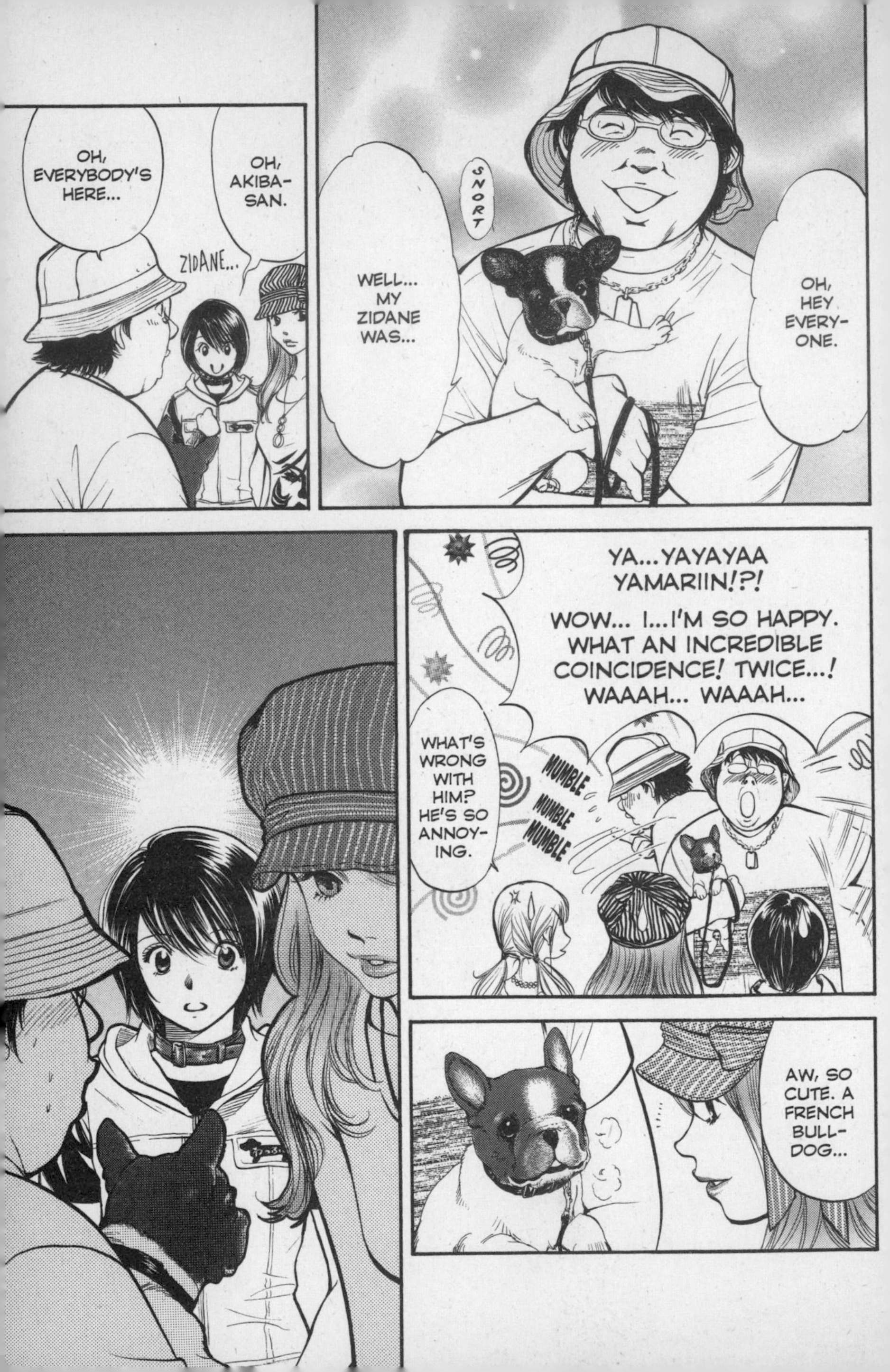
OH, HEY EVERY-ONE.
SNORT
WELL... MY ZIDANE WAS...
OH, AKIBA-SAN.
ZIDANE...
OH, EVERYBODY'S HERE...
YA...YAYAYAA YAMARIIN!?!
WOW... I...I'M SO HAPPY. WHAT AN INCREDIBLE COINCIDENCE! TWICE...! WAAAH... WAAAH...
MUMBLE MUMBLE MUMBLE
WHAT'S WRONG WITH HIM? HE'S SO ANNOY-ING.
AW, SO CUTE. A FRENCH BULL-DOG...

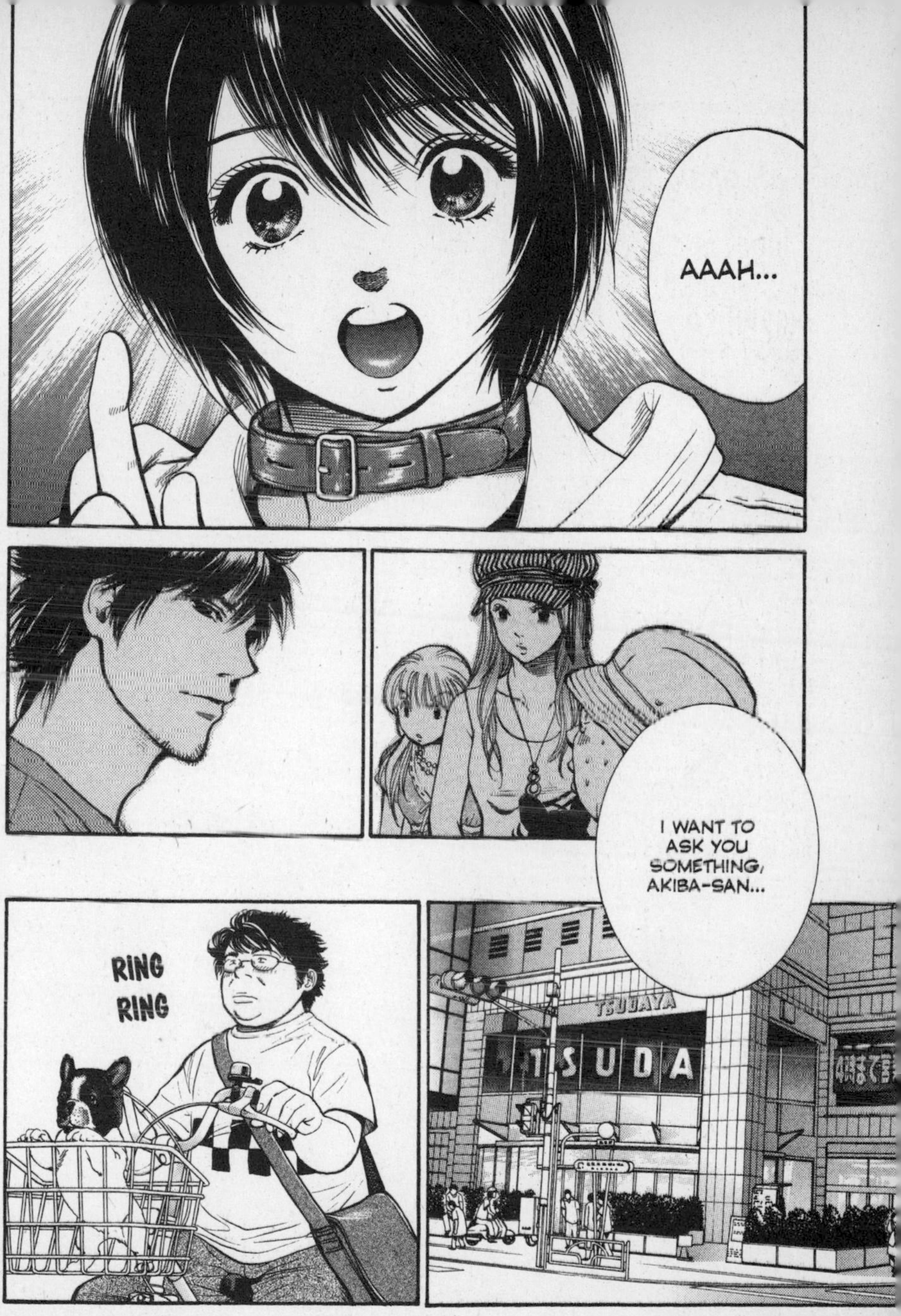
AAAH...
I WANT TO ASK YOU SOMETHING, AKIBA-SAN...
TSUDAYA
TSUDA
RING RING

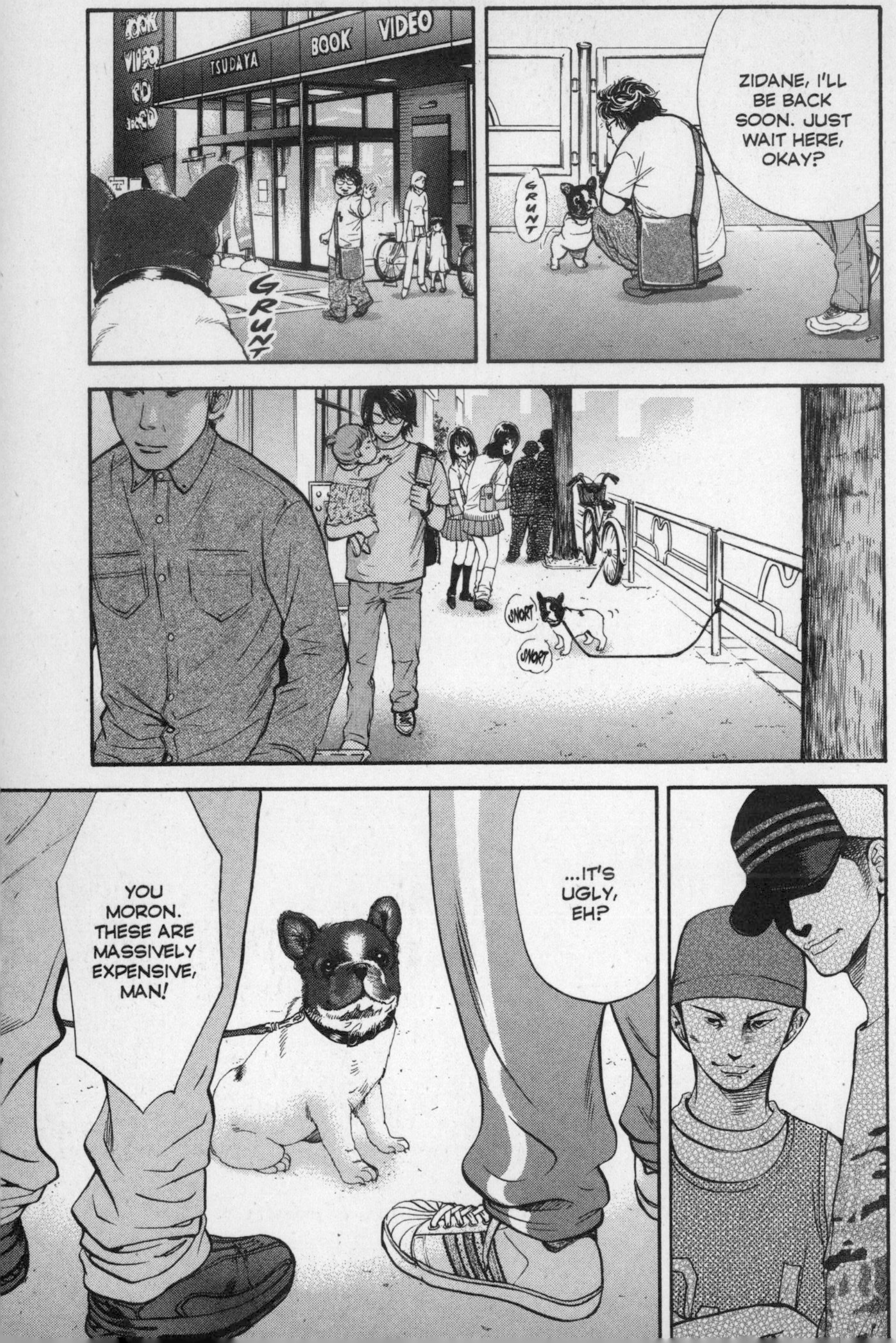
ZIDANE, I'LL BE BACK SOON. JUST WAIT HERE, OKAY?
GRUNT
BOOK
VIDEO
TSUDAYA
BOOK
VIDEO
GRUNT
SNORT
SNORT
...IT'S UGLY, EH?
YOU MORON. THESE ARE MASSIVELY EXPENSIVE, MAN!

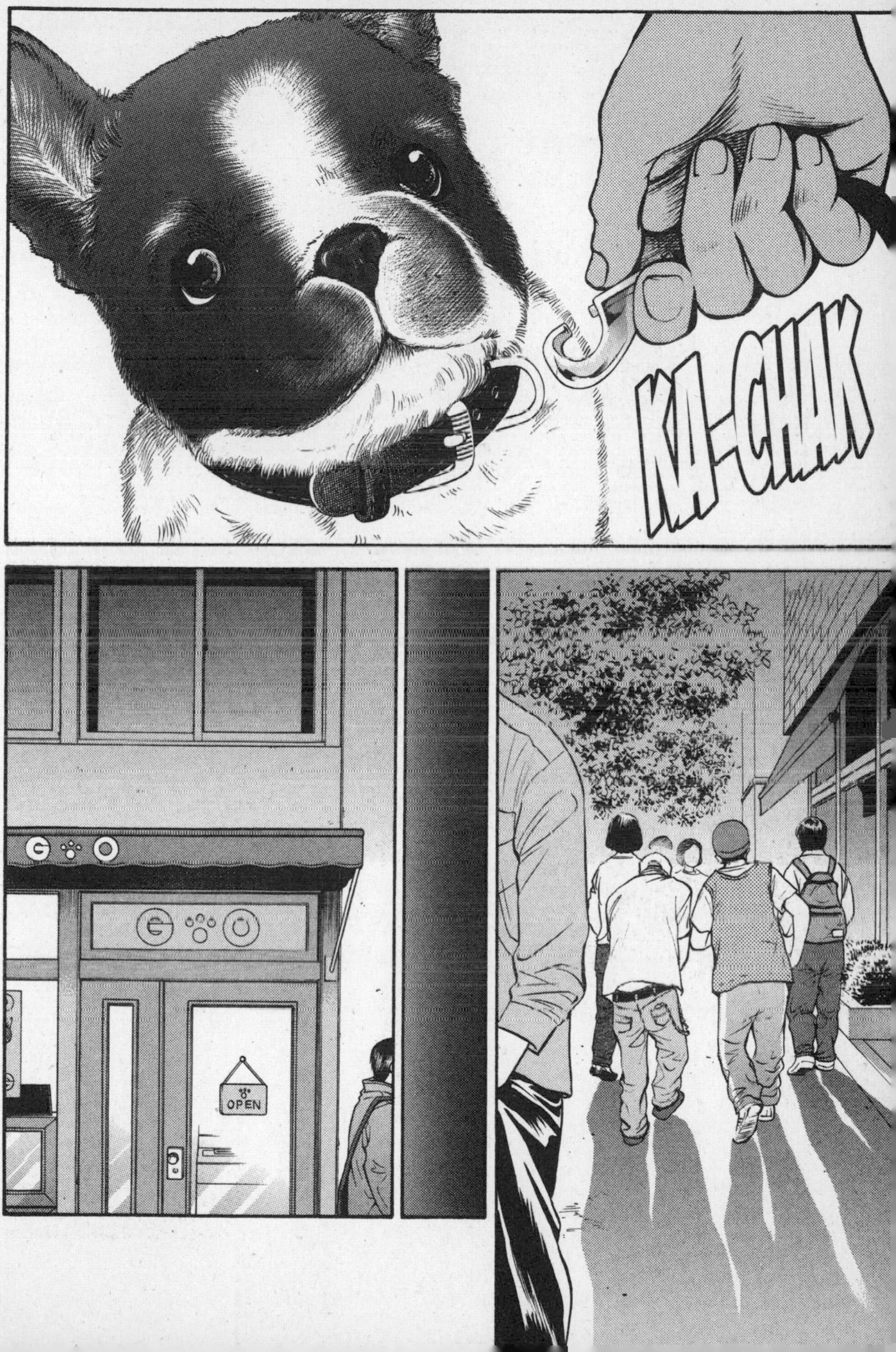
KA-CHAK
OPEN

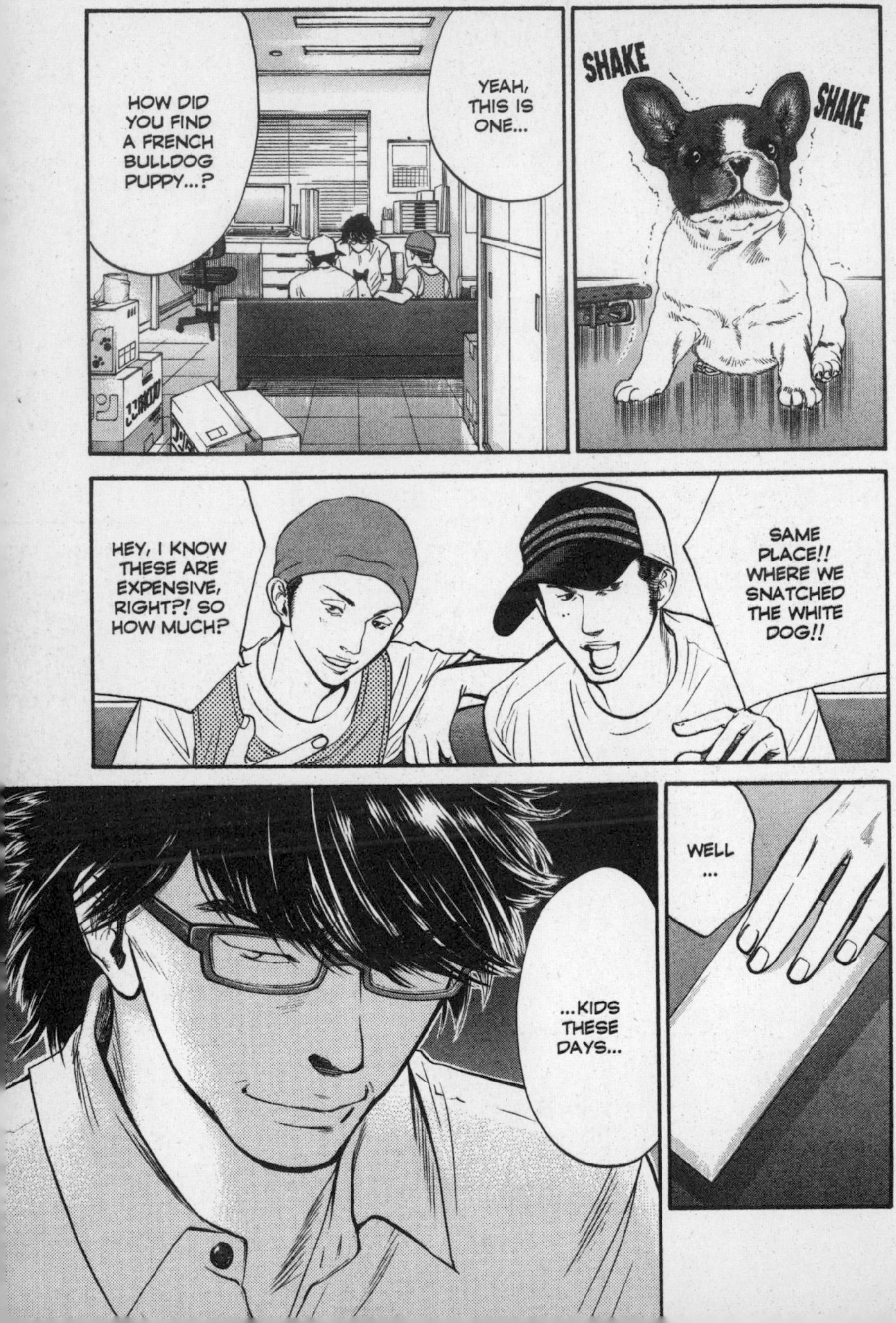
SHAKE
SHAKE
YEAH, THIS IS ONE...
HOW DID YOU FIND A FRENCH BULLDOG PUPPY...?
SAME PLACE!! WHERE WE SNATCHED THE WHITE DOG!!
HEY, I KNOW THESE ARE EXPENSIVE, RIGHT?! SO HOW MUCH?
WELL ...
...KIDS THESE DAYS...

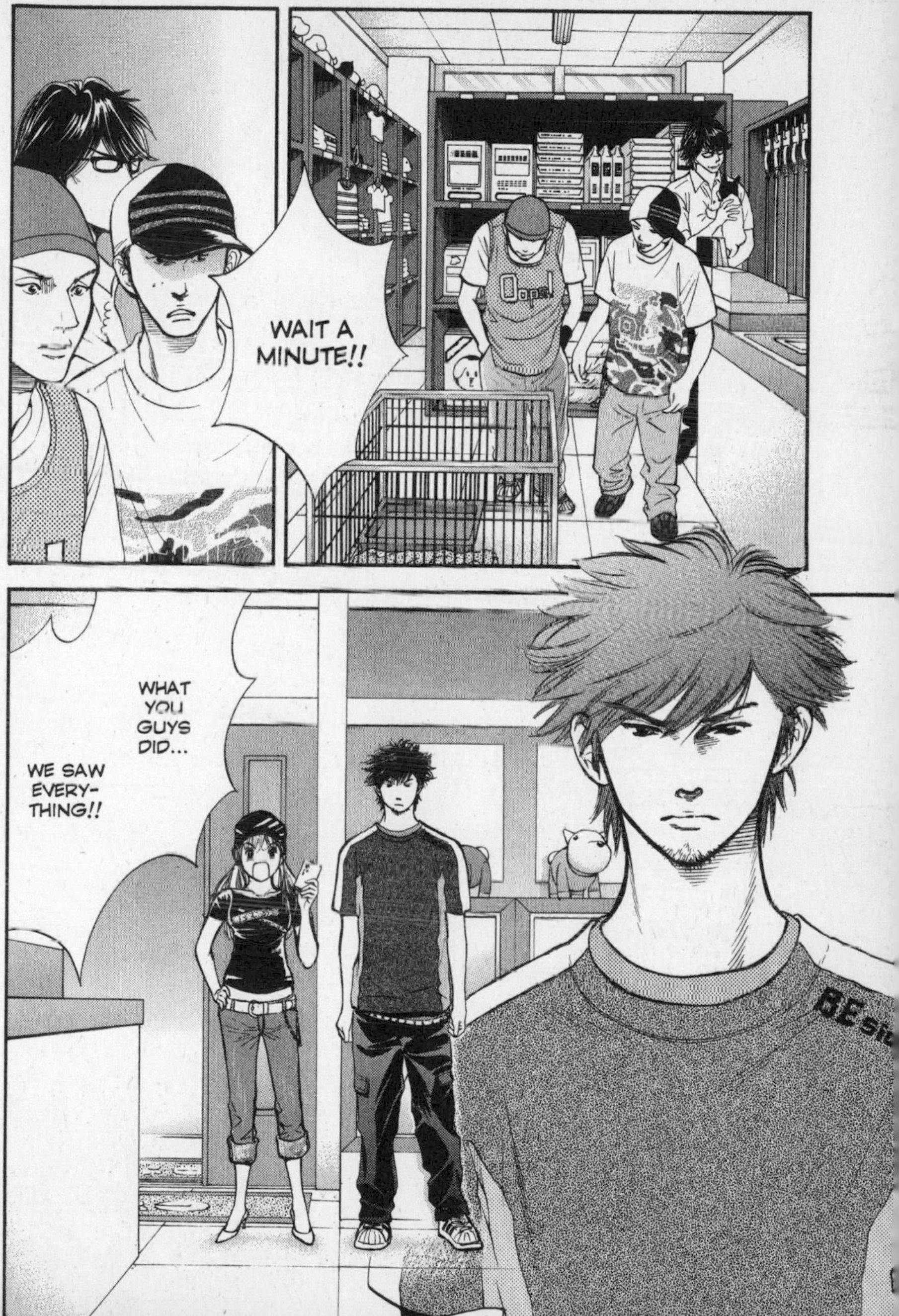
WAIT A MINUTE!!
WHAT YOU GUYS DID...
WE SAW EVERY-THING!!
BE sid

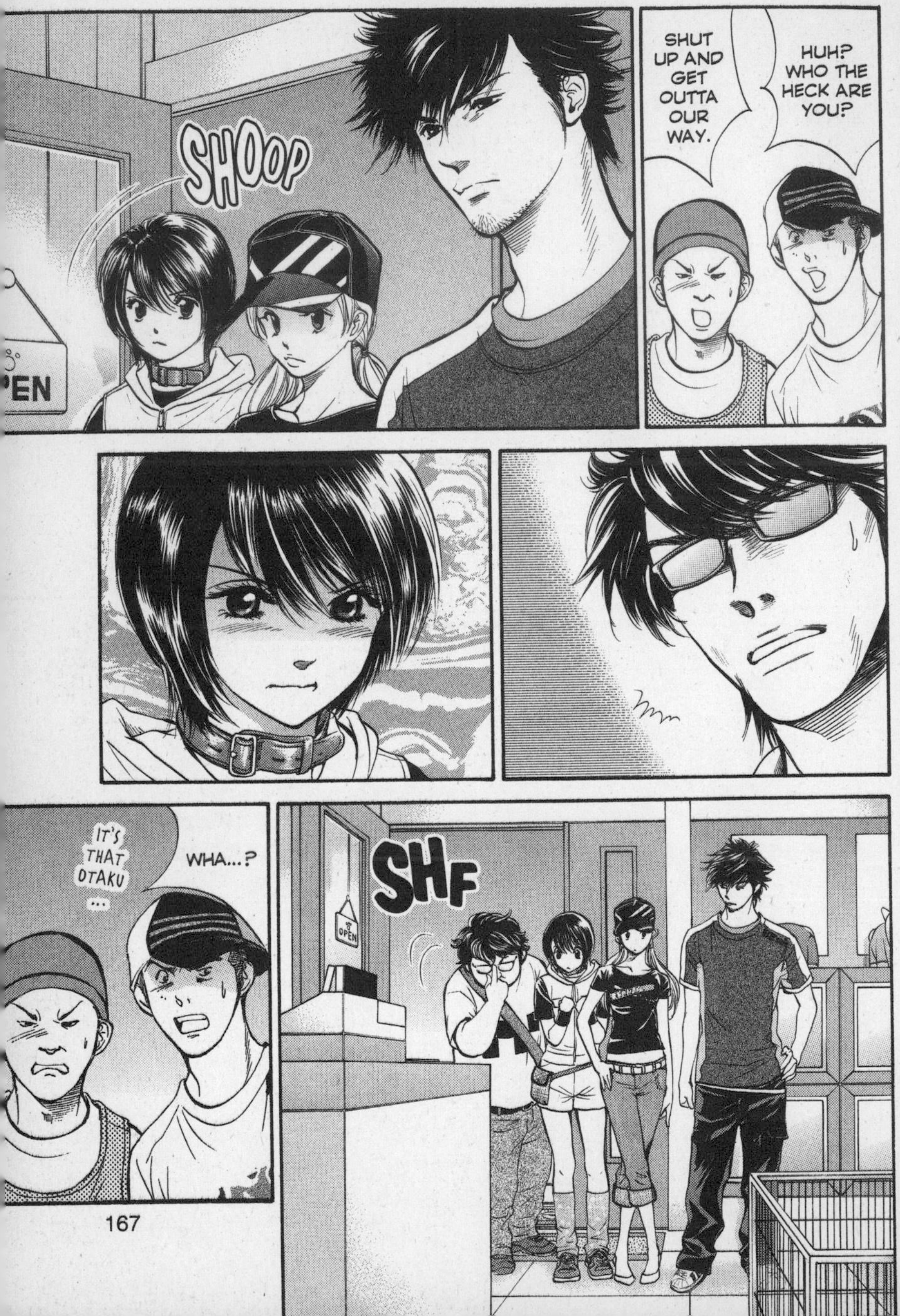
HUH? WHO THE HECK ARE YOU?
SHUT UP AND GET OUTTA OUR WAY.
SHOOP
Mm
SHF
WHA...?
IT'S THAT OTAKU ...

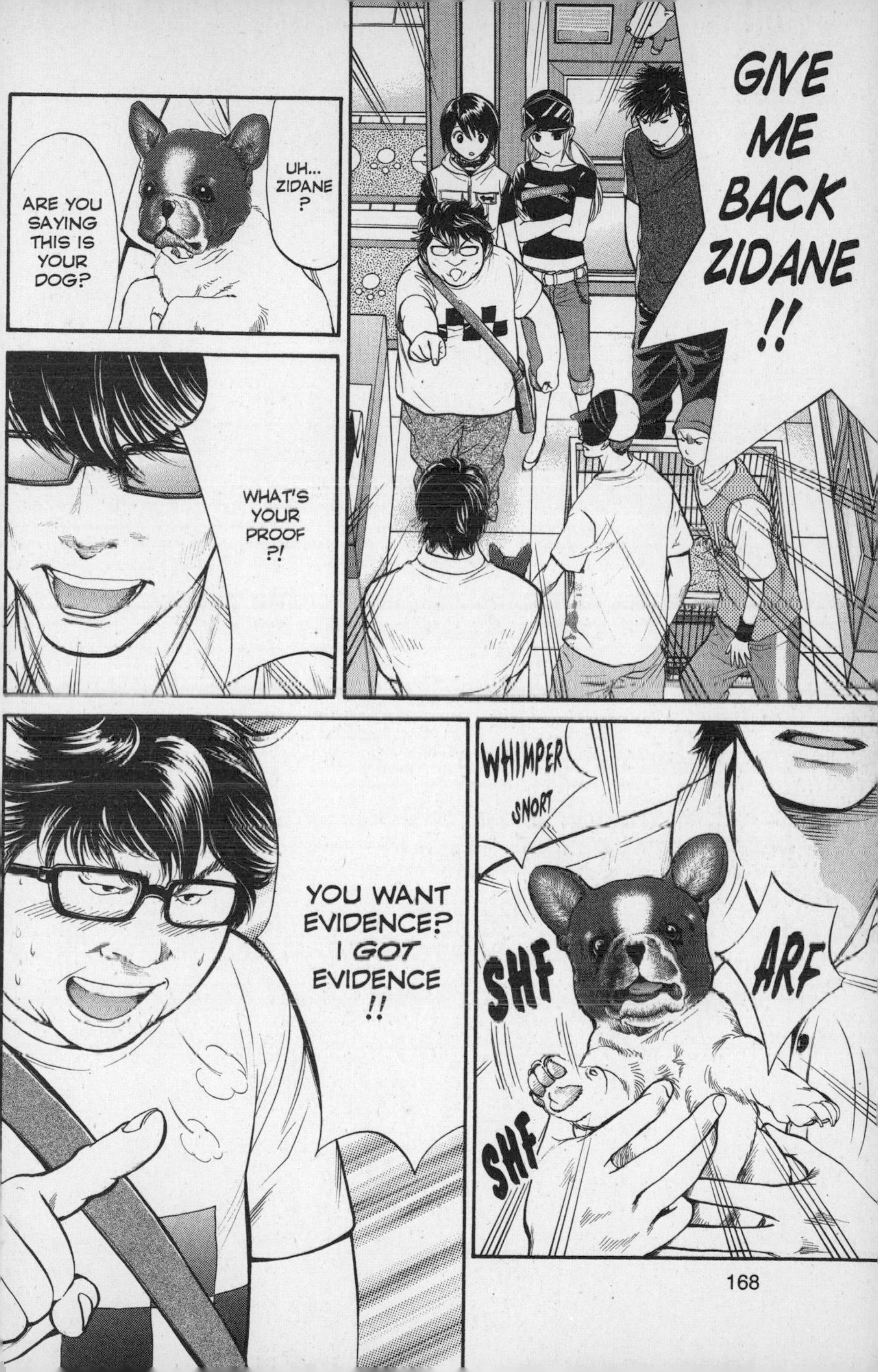
GIVE ME BACK ZIDANE !!
UH... ZIDANE ?
ARE YOU SAYING THIS IS YOUR DOG?
WHAT'S YOUR PROOF ?!
WHIMPER
SNORT
ARF
SHF
SHF
YOU WANT EVIDENCE? I GOT EVIDENCE !!

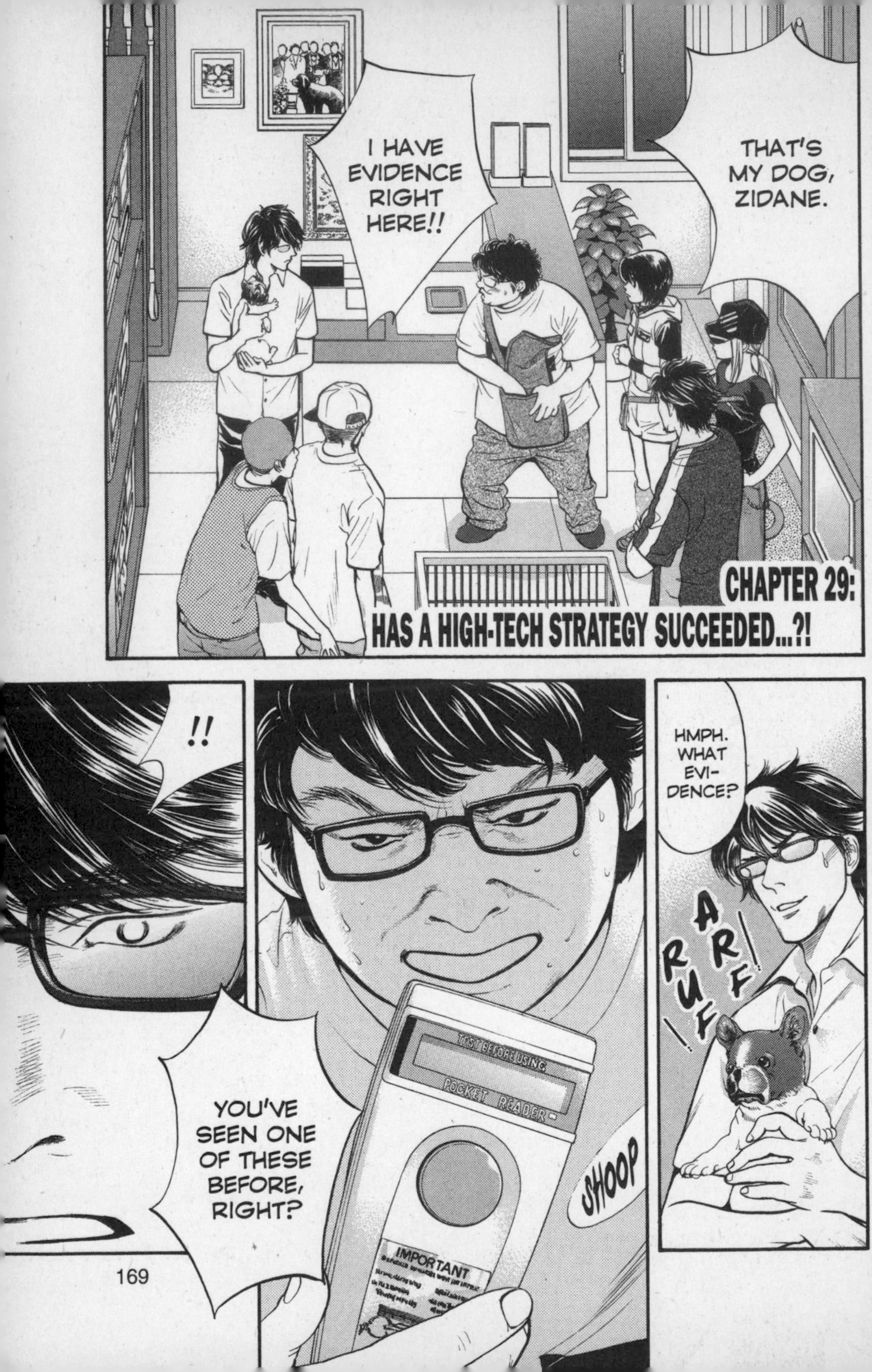
THAT'S MY DOG, ZIDANE.
I HAVE EVIDENCE RIGHT HERE!!
CHAPTER 29:
HAS A HIGH-TECH STRATEGY SUCCEEDED...?!
HMPH. WHAT EVI-DENCE?
ARF
RUF
SHOOP
TEST BEFORE USING
POCKET READER
IMPORTANT
YOU'VE SEEN ONE OF THESE BEFORE, RIGHT?
!!

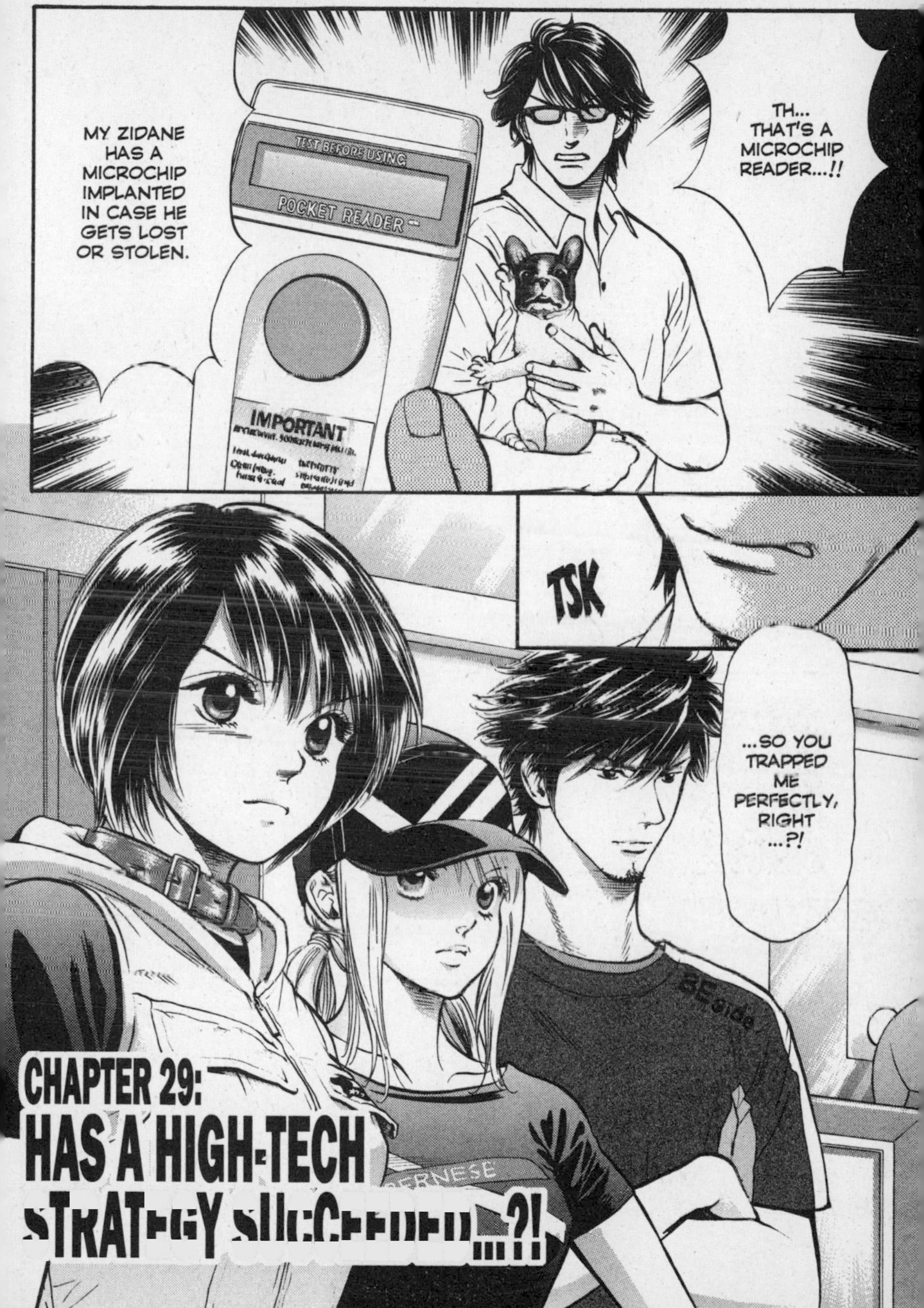
TH... THAT'S A MICROCHIP READER...!!
MY ZIDANE HAS A MICROCHIP IMPLANTED IN CASE HE GETS LOST OR STOLEN.
TEST BEFORE USING
POCKET READER
IMPORTANT
TSK
...SO YOU TRAPPED ME PERFECTLY, RIGHT ...?!
BEside

CHAPTER 29: HAS A HIGH-TECH STRATEGY SUCCEEDED...?!

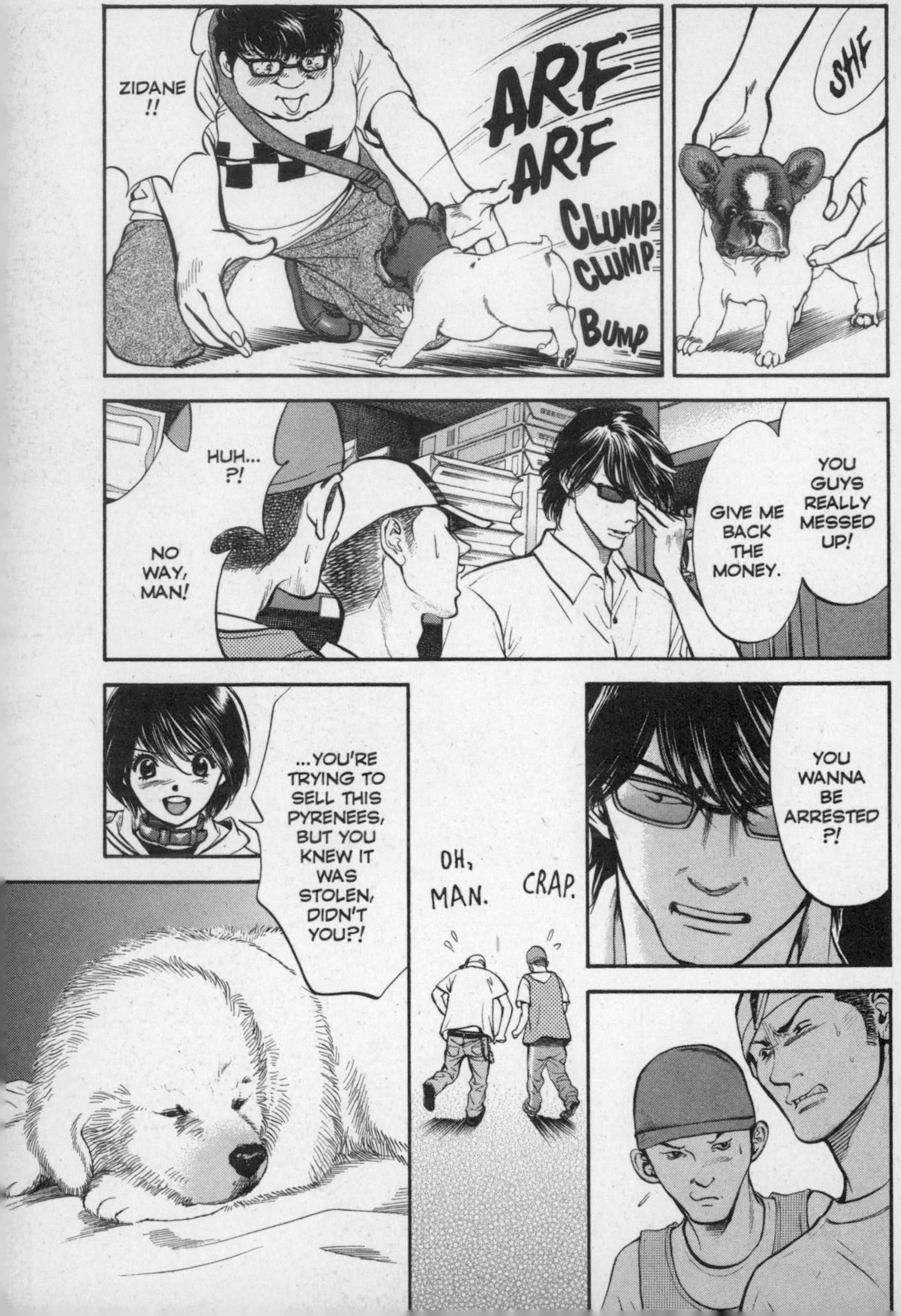
SHF
ARF
ARF
CLUMP
CLUMP
BUMP
ZIDANE!!
YOU GUYS REALLY MESSED UP!
GIVE ME BACK THE MONEY.
HUH...?!
NO WAY, MAN!
YOU WANNA BE ARRESTED?!
CRAP.
OH, MAN.
...YOU'RE TRYING TO SELL THIS PYRENEES, BUT YOU KNEW IT WAS STOLEN, DIDN'T YOU?!

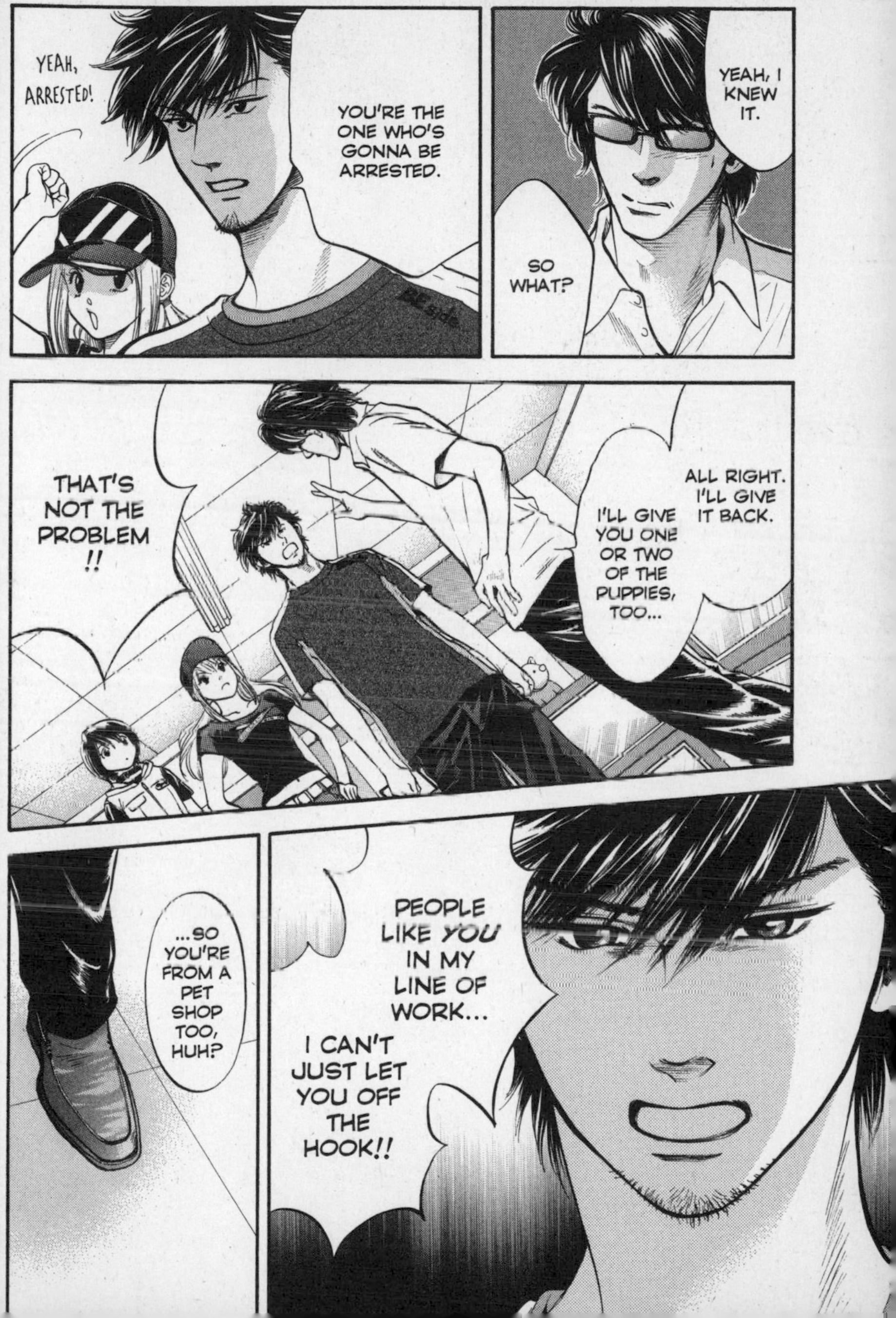
YEAH, I KNEW IT.
SO WHAT?
YOU'RE THE ONE WHO'S GONNA BE ARRESTED.
YEAH, ARRESTED!
ALL RIGHT. I'LL GIVE IT BACK.
I'LL GIVE YOU ONE OR TWO OF THE PUPPIES, TOO...
THAT'S NOT THE PROBLEM !!
PEOPLE LIKE *YOU* IN MY LINE OF WORK...
I CAN'T JUST LET YOU OFF THE HOOK!!
...SO YOU'RE FROM A PET SHOP TOO, HUH?

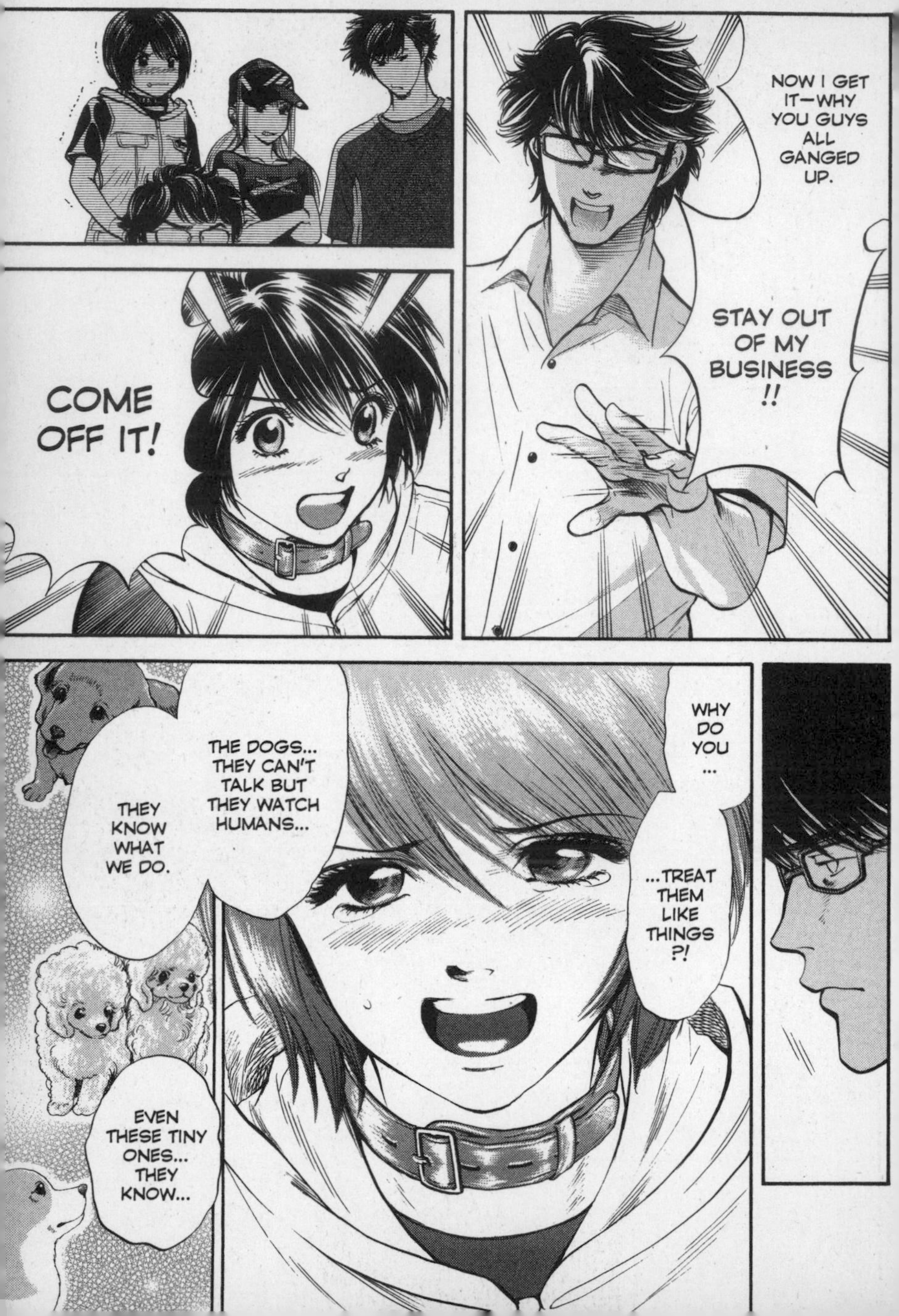
NOW I GET IT—WHY YOU GUYS ALL GANGED UP.
STAY OUT OF MY BUSINESS!!
COME OFF IT!
WHY DO YOU ...
...TREAT THEM LIKE THINGS?!
THE DOGS... THEY CAN'T TALK BUT THEY WATCH HUMANS...
THEY KNOW WHAT WE DO.
EVEN THESE TINY ONES... THEY KNOW...

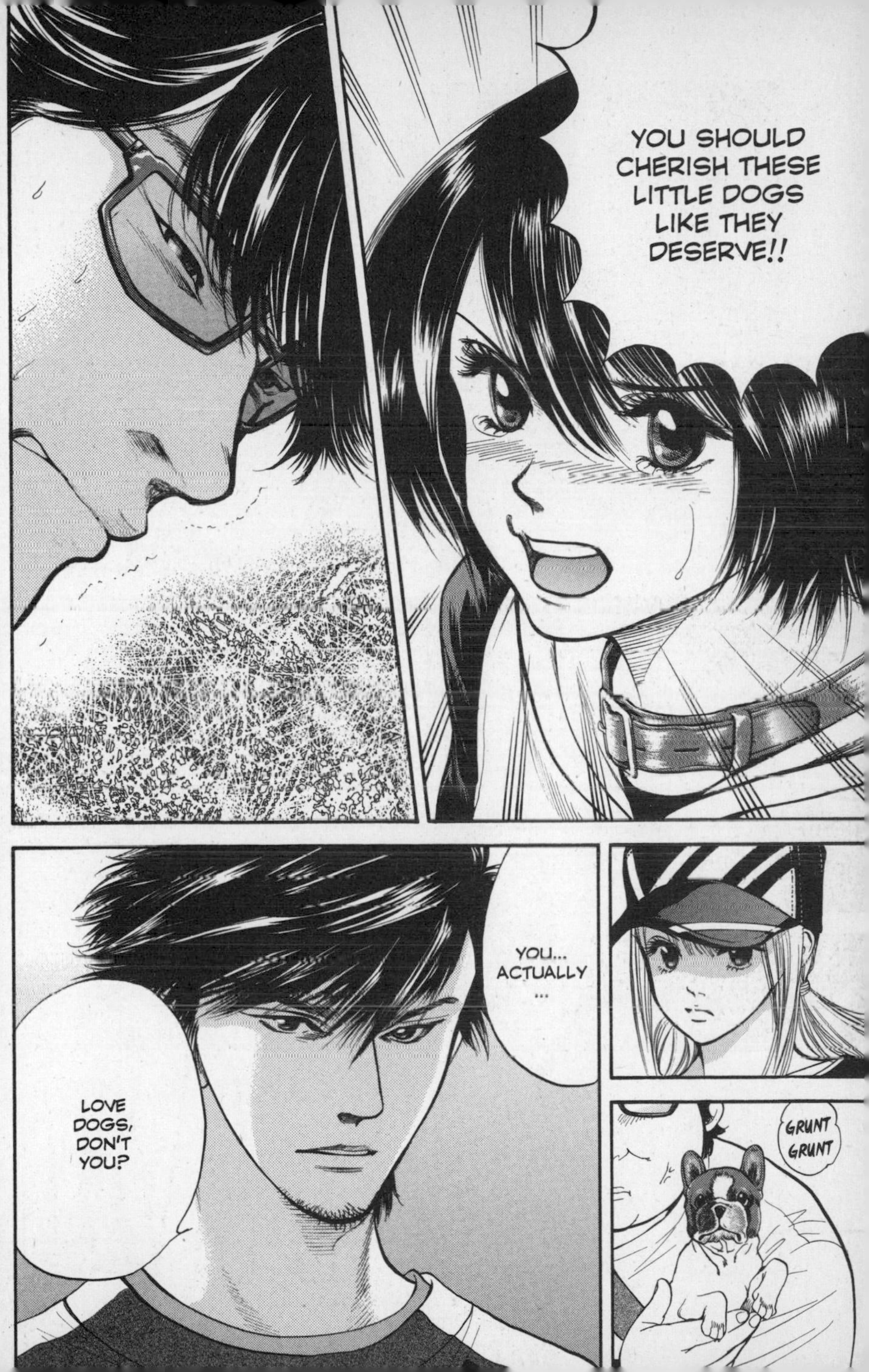
YOU SHOULD CHERISH THESE LITTLE DOGS LIKE THEY DESERVE!!
GRUNT GRUNT
YOU... ACTUALLY ...
LOVE DOGS, DON'T YOU?

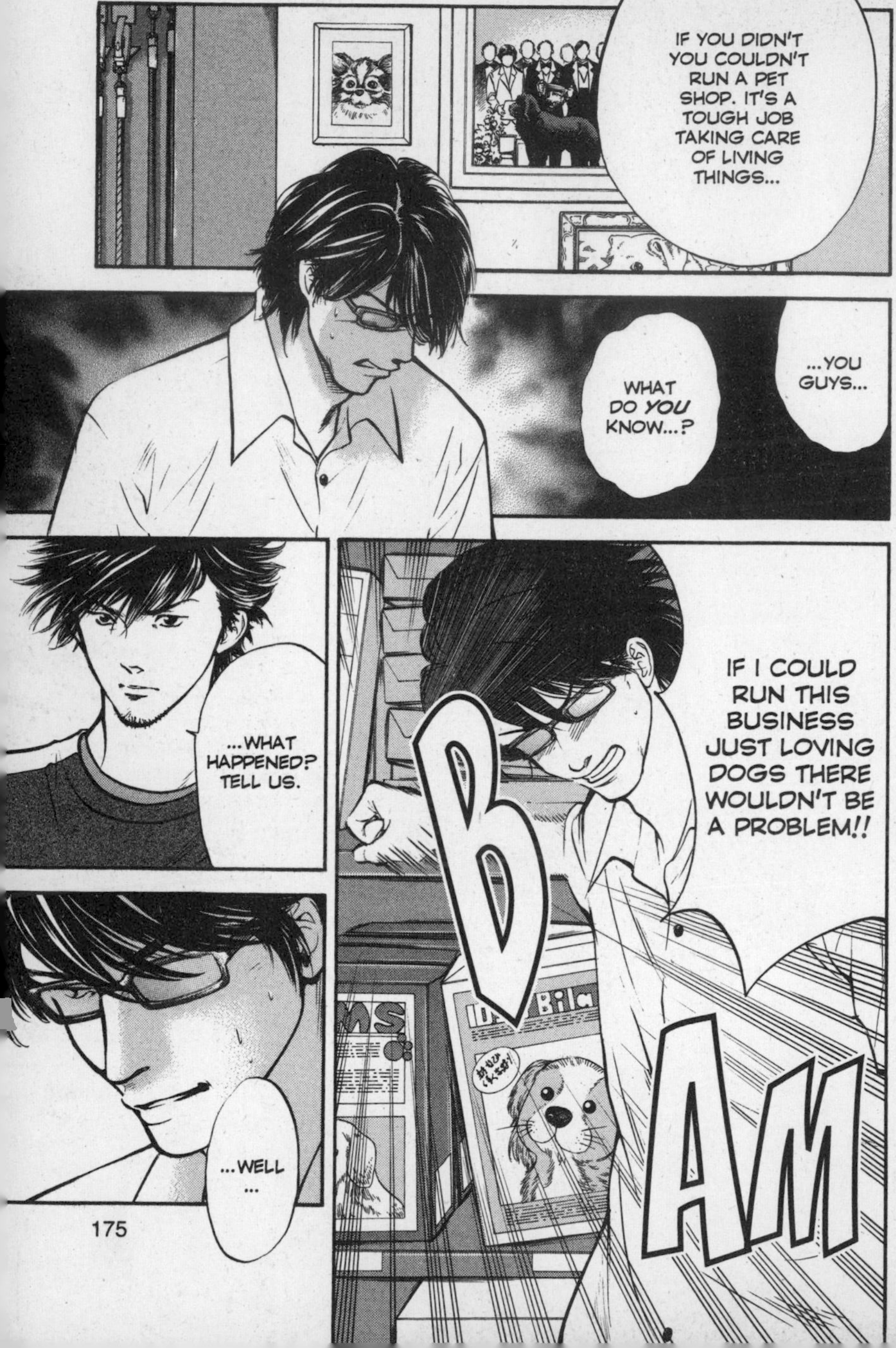
IF YOU DIDN'T YOU COULDN'T RUN A PET SHOP. IT'S A TOUGH JOB TAKING CARE OF LIVING THINGS...
...YOU GUYS...
WHAT DO *YOU* KNOW...?
IF I COULD RUN THIS BUSINESS JUST LOVING DOGS THERE WOULDN'T BE A PROBLEM!!
BAM
...WHAT HAPPENED? TELL US.
...WELL ...

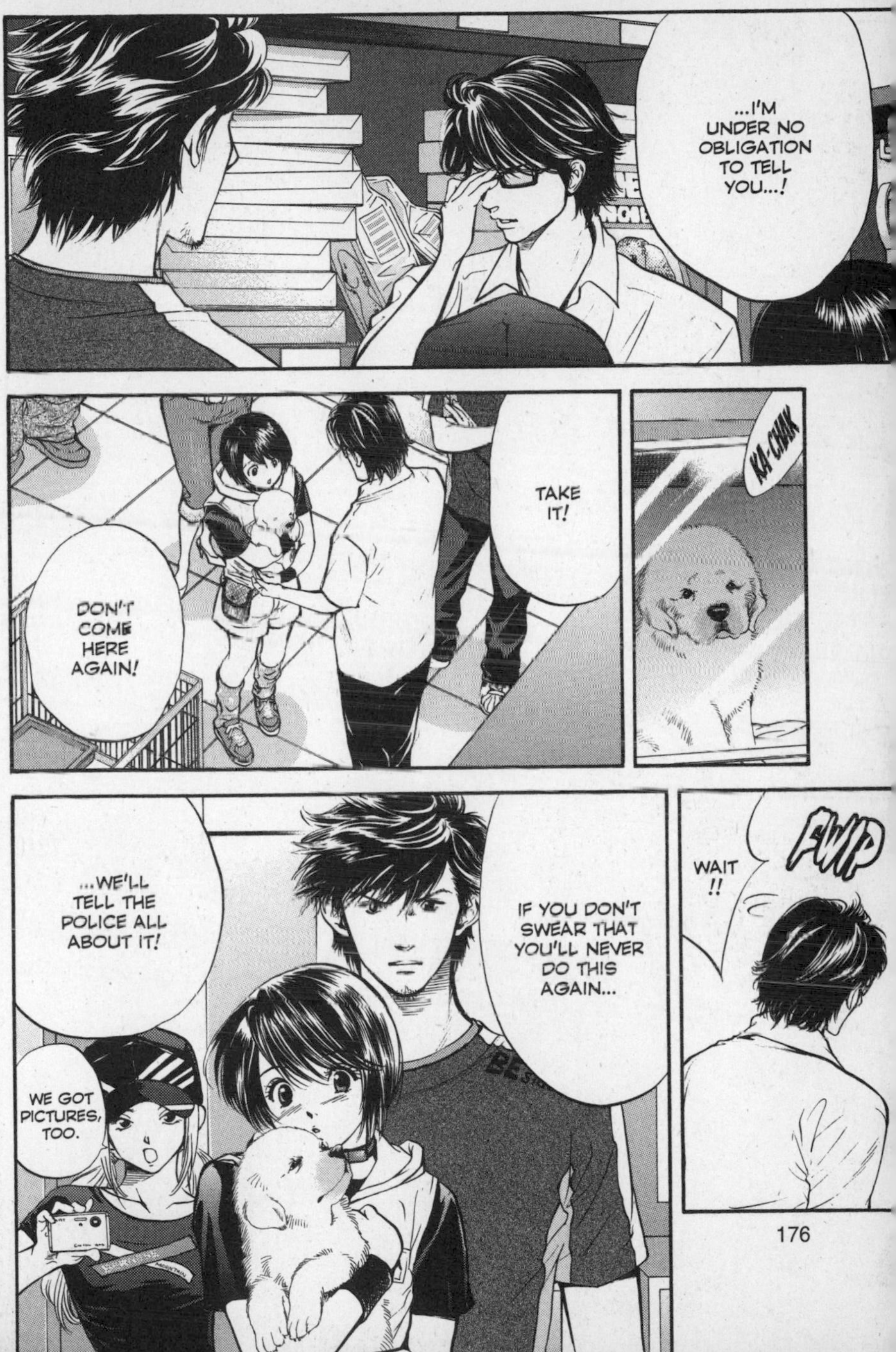

...I'M UNDER NO OBLIGATION TO TELL YOU...!
KA-CHAK
TAKE IT!
DON'T COME HERE AGAIN!
FWIP
WAIT!!
IF YOU DON'T SWEAR THAT YOU'LL NEVER DO THIS AGAIN...
...WE'LL TELL THE POLICE ALL ABOUT IT!
WE GOT PICTURES, TOO.

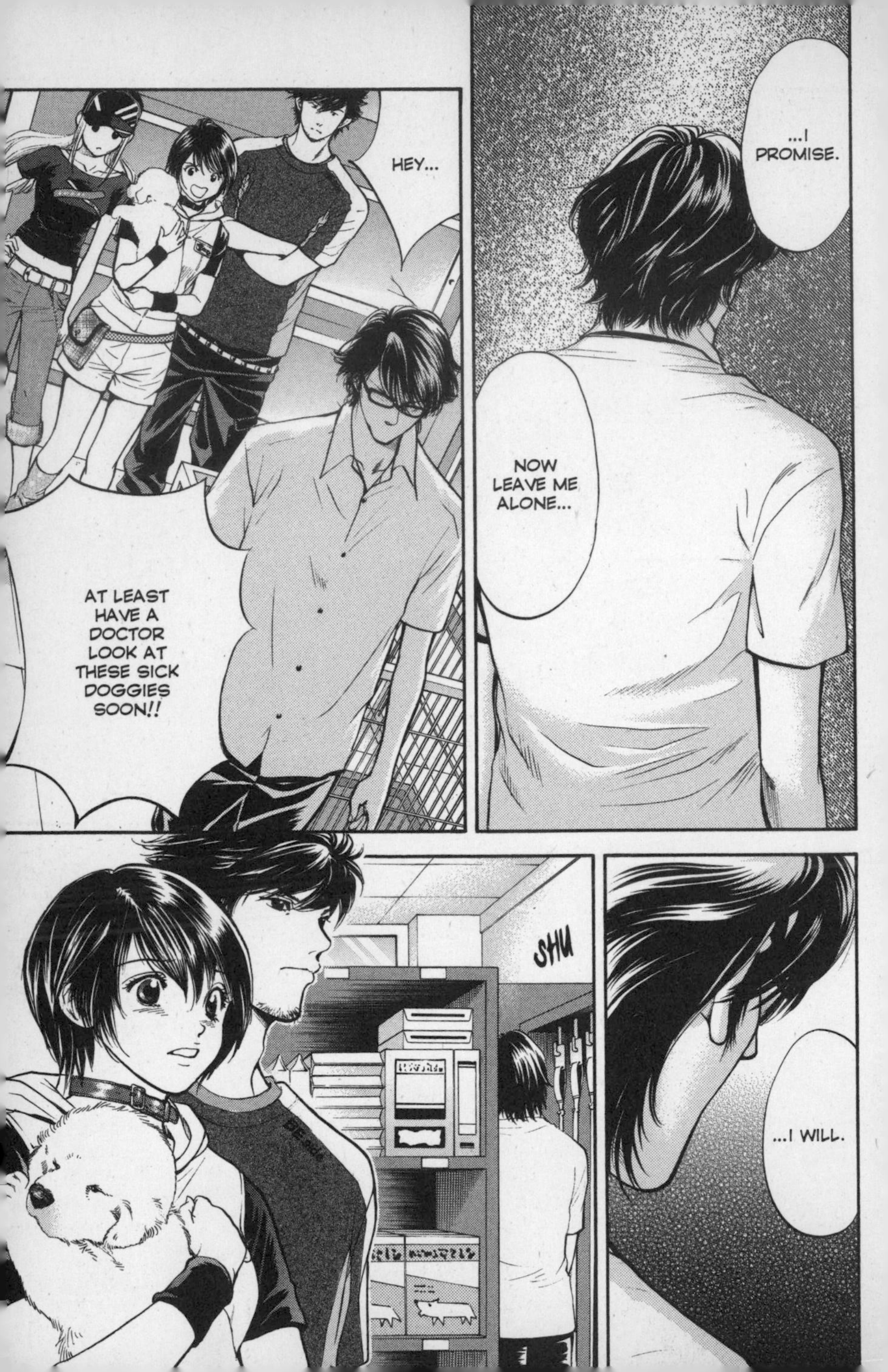
...I PROMISE.
NOW LEAVE ME ALONE...
HEY...
AT LEAST HAVE A DOCTOR LOOK AT THESE SICK DOGGIES SOON!!
...I WILL.
SHU

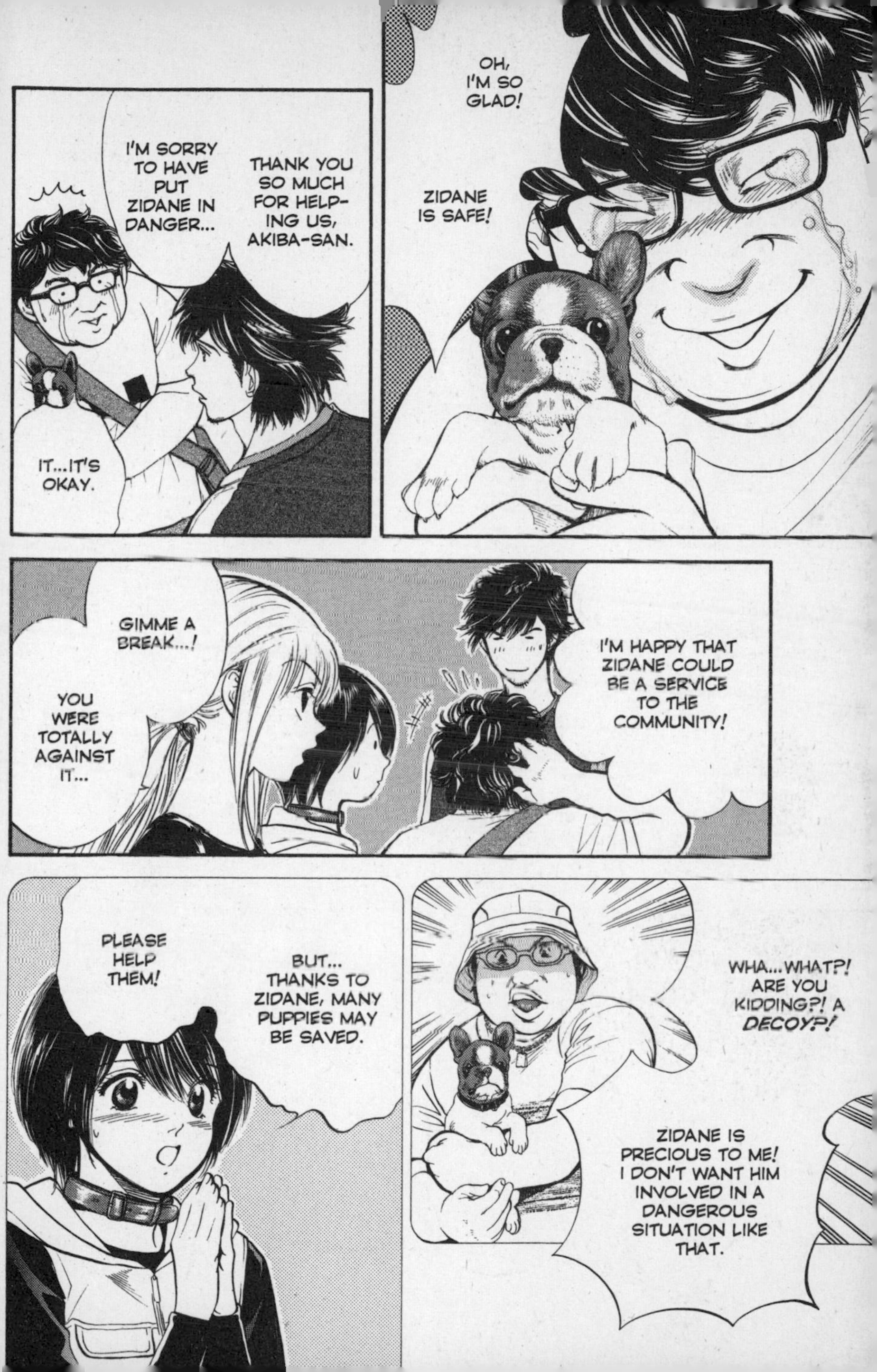
OH, I'M SO GLAD!
ZIDANE IS SAFE!
THANK YOU SO MUCH FOR HELP-ING US, AKIBA-SAN.
I'M SORRY TO HAVE PUT ZIDANE IN DANGER...
IT...IT'S OKAY.
I'M HAPPY THAT ZIDANE COULD BE A SERVICE TO THE COMMUNITY!
GIMME A BREAK...!
YOU WERE TOTALLY AGAINST IT...
WHA...WHAT?! ARE YOU KIDDING?! A *DECOY*?!
ZIDANE IS PRECIOUS TO ME! I DON'T WANT HIM INVOLVED IN A DANGEROUS SITUATION LIKE THAT.
BUT... THANKS TO ZIDANE, MANY PUPPIES MAY BE SAVED.
PLEASE HELP THEM!

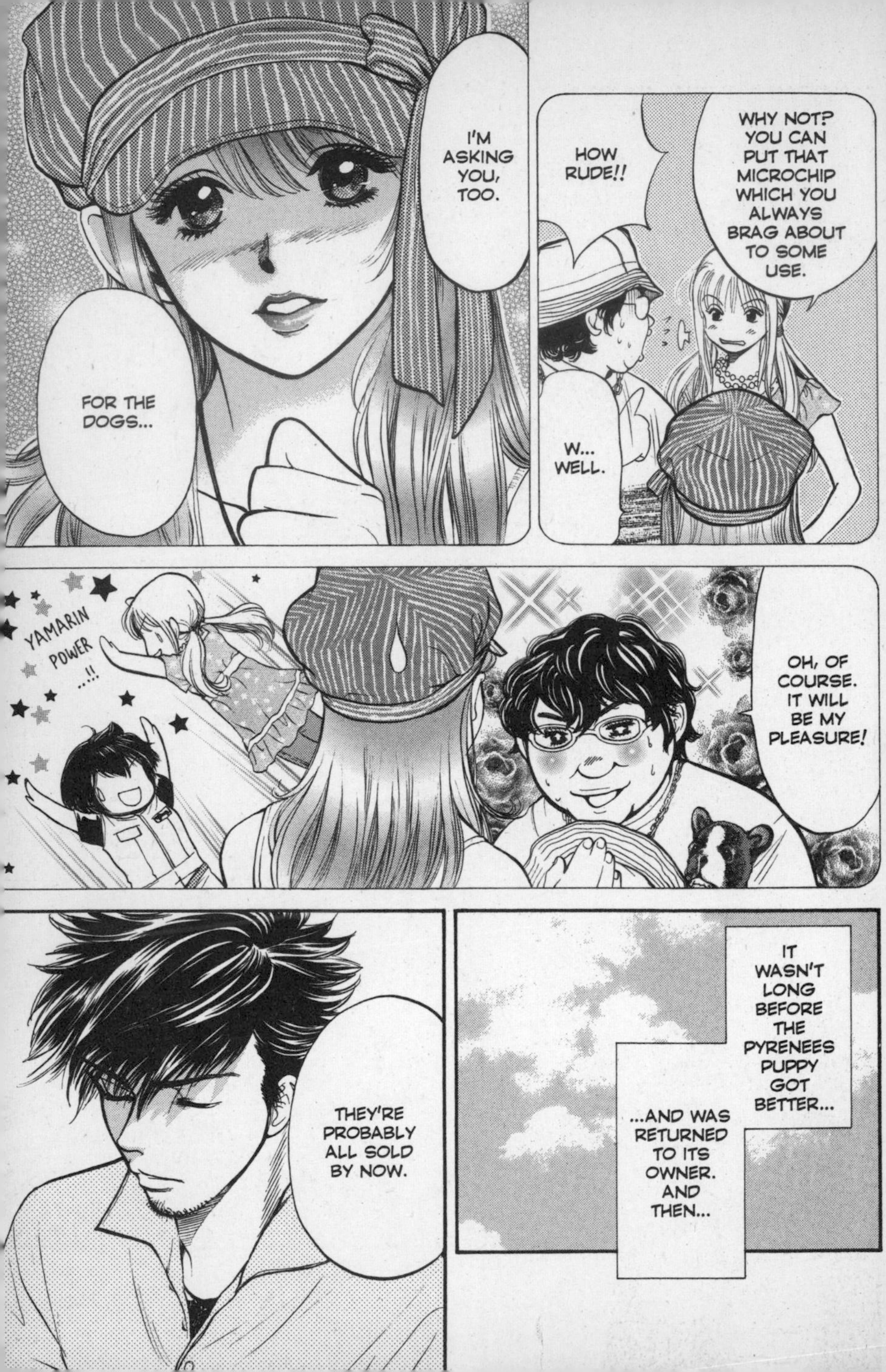
WHY NOT? YOU CAN PUT THAT MICROCHIP WHICH YOU ALWAYS BRAG ABOUT TO SOME USE.
HOW RUDE!!
W... WELL.
I'M ASKING YOU, TOO.
FOR THE DOGS...
OH, OF COURSE. IT WILL BE MY PLEASURE!
YAMARIN POWER ..!!
IT WASN'T LONG BEFORE THE PYRENEES PUPPY GOT BETTER...
...AND WAS RETURNED TO ITS OWNER. AND THEN...
THEY'RE PROBABLY ALL SOLD BY NOW.

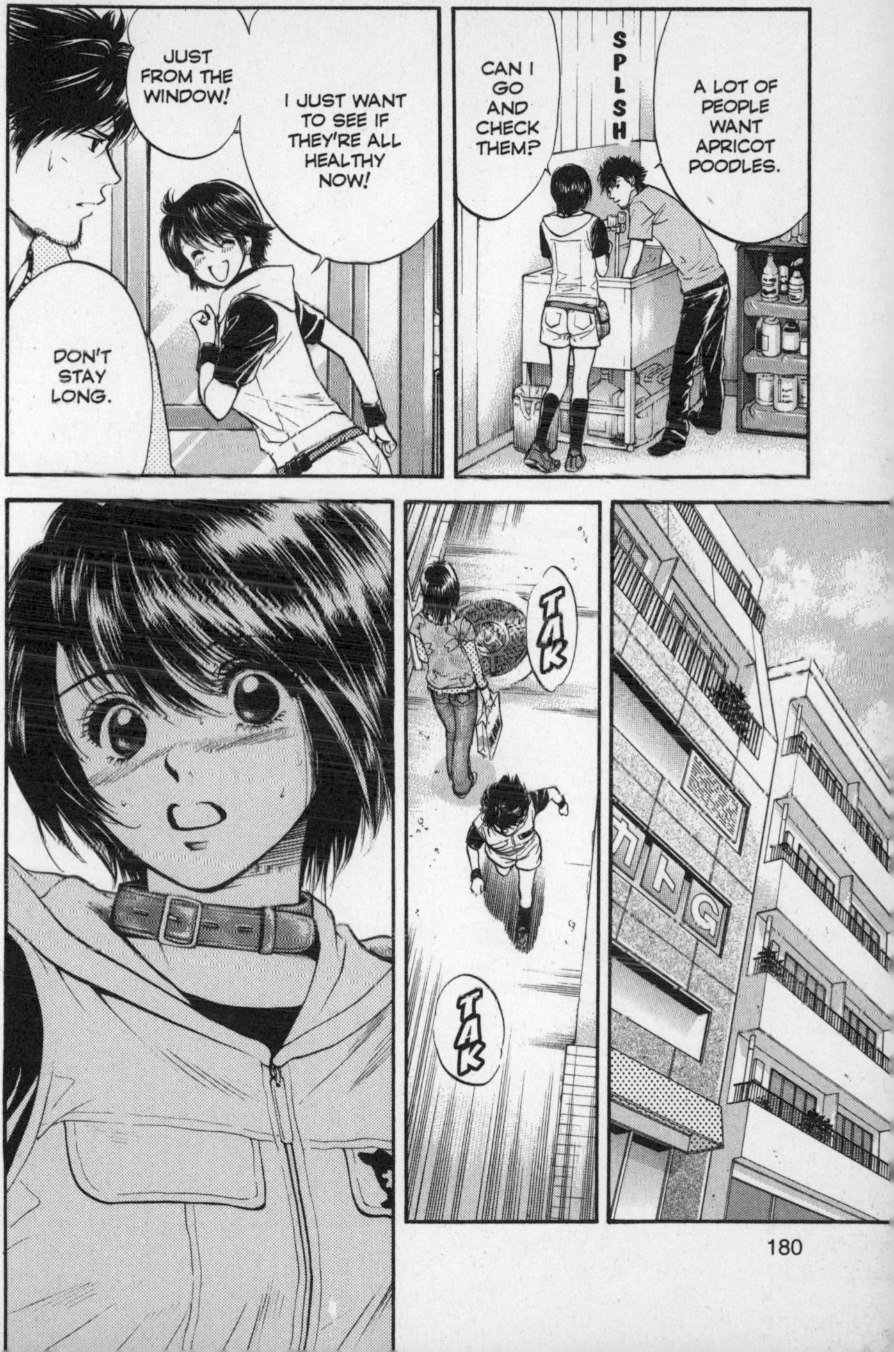
A LOT OF PEOPLE WANT APRICOT POODLES.
SPLSH
CAN I GO AND CHECK THEM?
I JUST WANT TO SEE IF THEY'RE ALL HEALTHY NOW!
JUST FROM THE WINDOW!
DON'T STAY LONG.
TAK
TAK

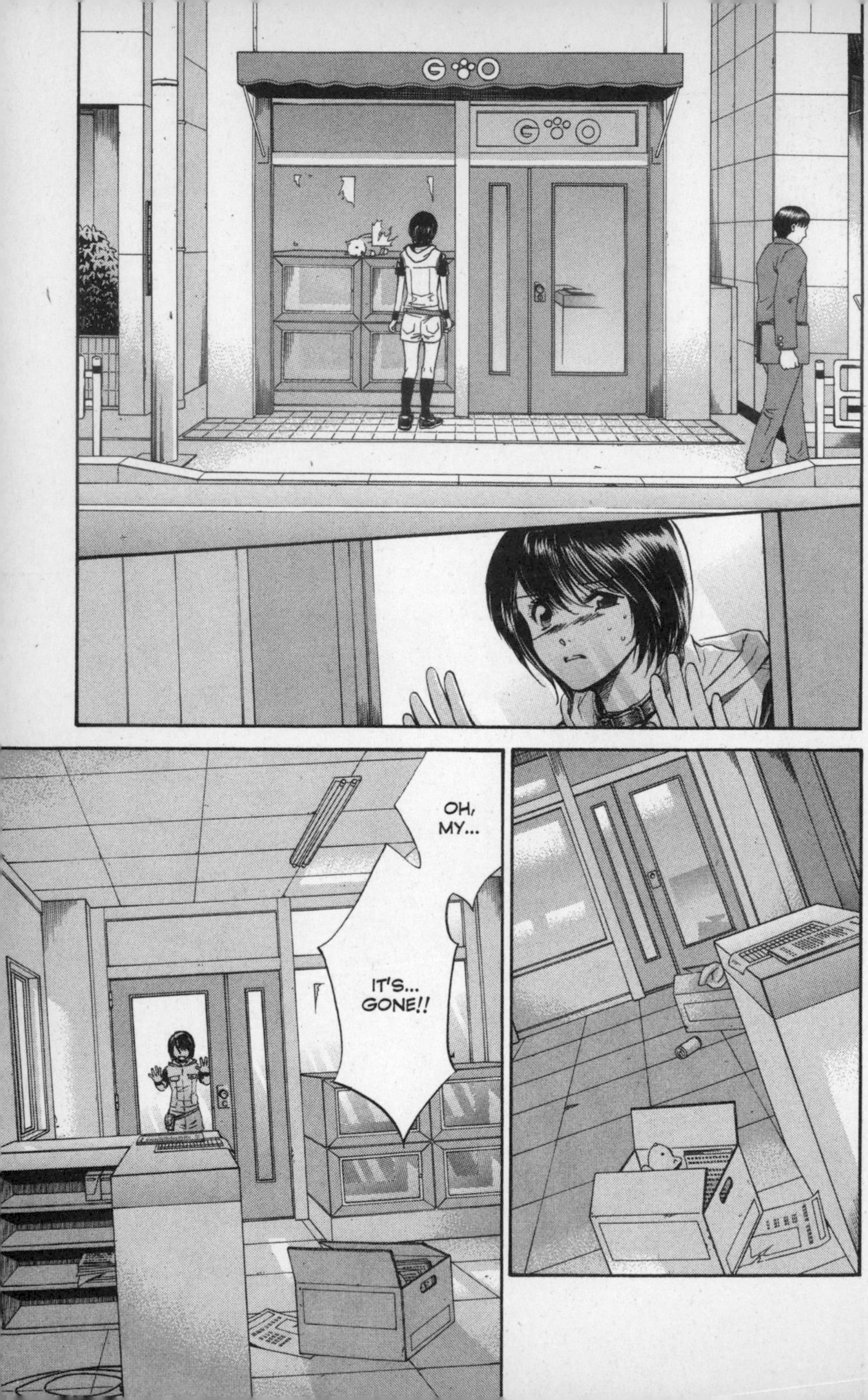
OH, MY...
IT'S... GONE!!

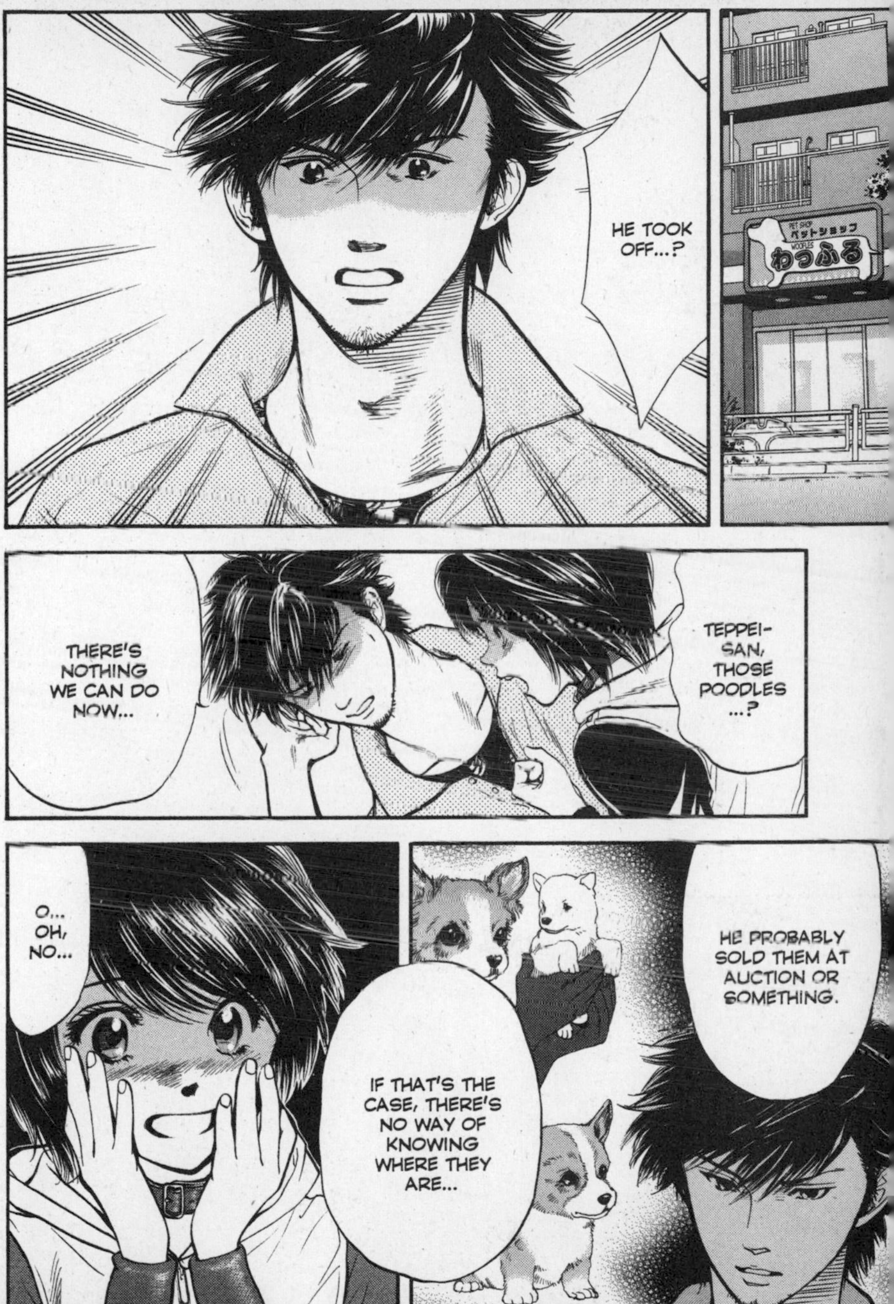
PET SHOP
ペットショップ
WOOFLES
わっふる
HE TOOK OFF...?
TEPPEI-SAN, THOSE POODLES ...?
THERE'S NOTHING WE CAN DO NOW...
HE PROBABLY SOLD THEM AT AUCTION OR SOMETHING.
IF THAT'S THE CASE, THERE'S NO WAY OF KNOWING WHERE THEY ARE...
O... OH, NO...

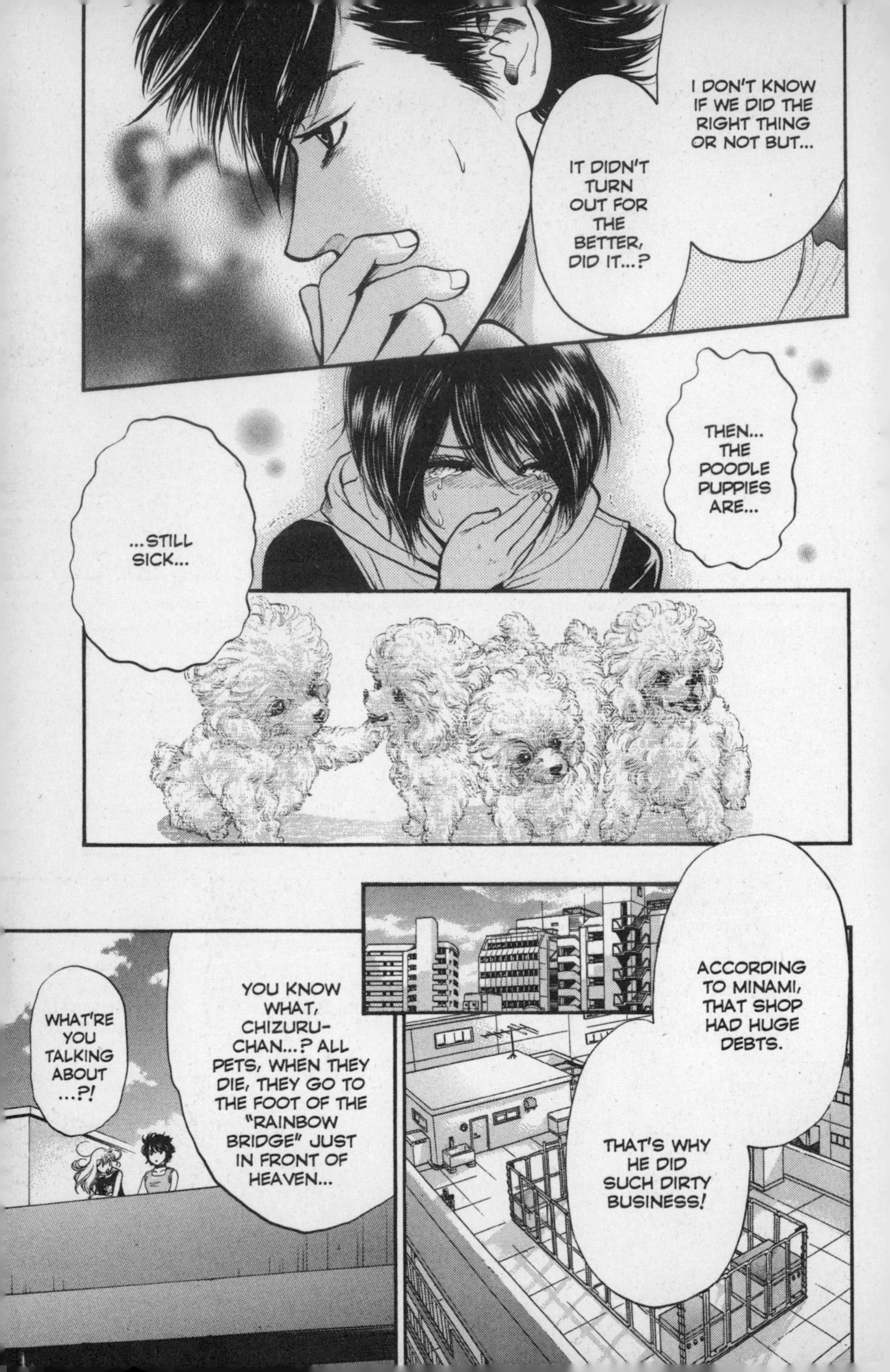
I DON'T KNOW IF WE DID THE RIGHT THING OR NOT BUT...
IT DIDN'T TURN OUT FOR THE BETTER, DID IT...?
THEN... THE POODLE PUPPIES ARE...
...STILL SICK...
ACCORDING TO MINAMI, THAT SHOP HAD HUGE DEBTS.
THAT'S WHY HE DID SUCH DIRTY BUSINESS!
YOU KNOW WHAT, CHIZURU-CHAN...? ALL PETS, WHEN THEY DIE, THEY GO TO THE FOOT OF THE "RAINBOW BRIDGE" JUST IN FRONT OF HEAVEN...
WHAT'RE YOU TALKING ABOUT...?!

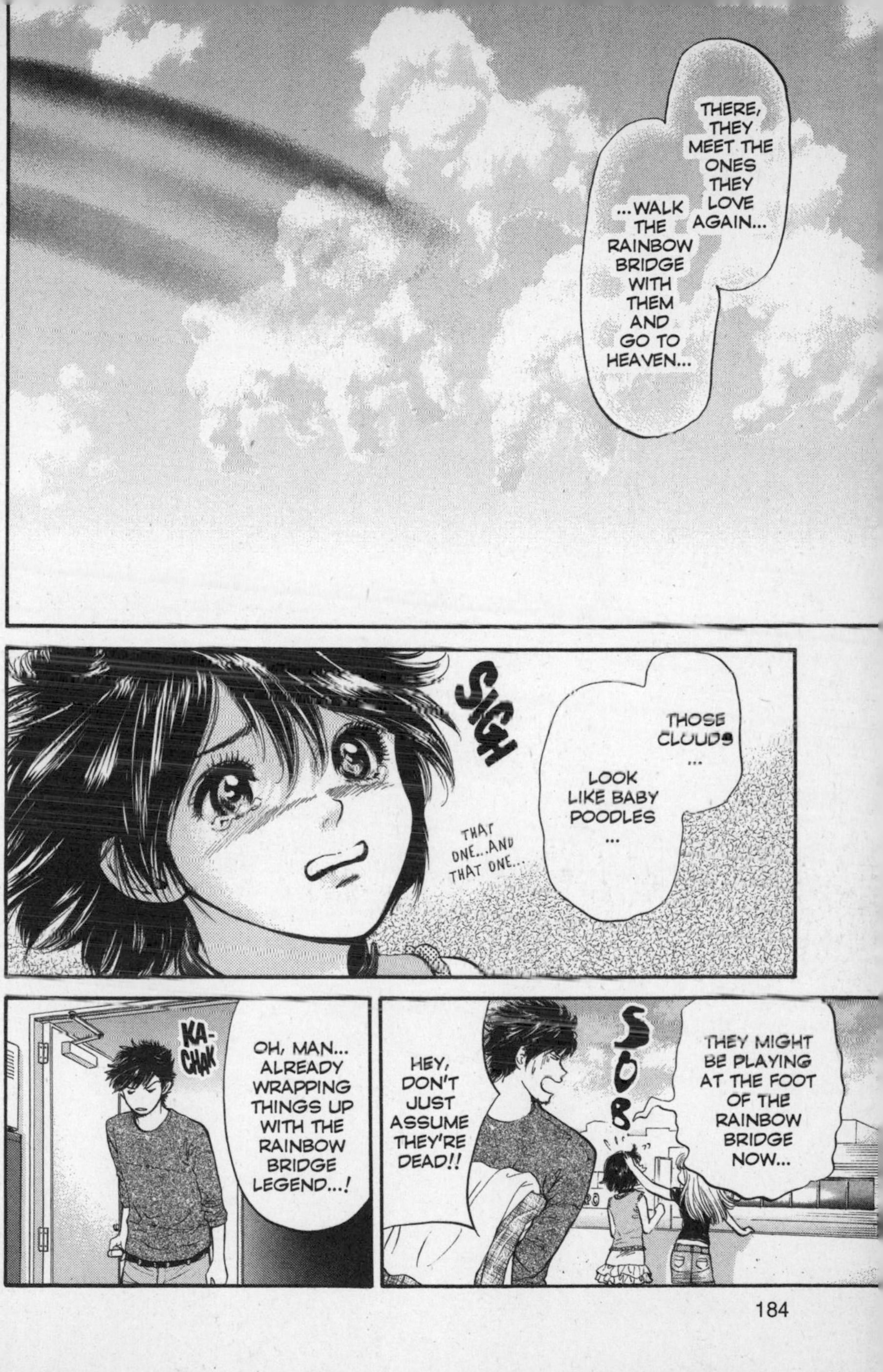
THERE, THEY MEET THE ONES THEY LOVE AGAIN...
...WALK THE RAINBOW BRIDGE WITH THEM AND GO TO HEAVEN...
SIGH
THOSE CLOUDS...
LOOK LIKE BABY POODLES...
THAT ONE...AND THAT ONE...
SOB
THEY MIGHT BE PLAYING AT THE FOOT OF THE RAINBOW BRIDGE NOW...
HEY, DON'T JUST ASSUME THEY'RE DEAD!!
KA-CHAK
OH, MAN... ALREADY WRAPPING THINGS UP WITH THE RAINBOW BRIDGE LEGEND...!

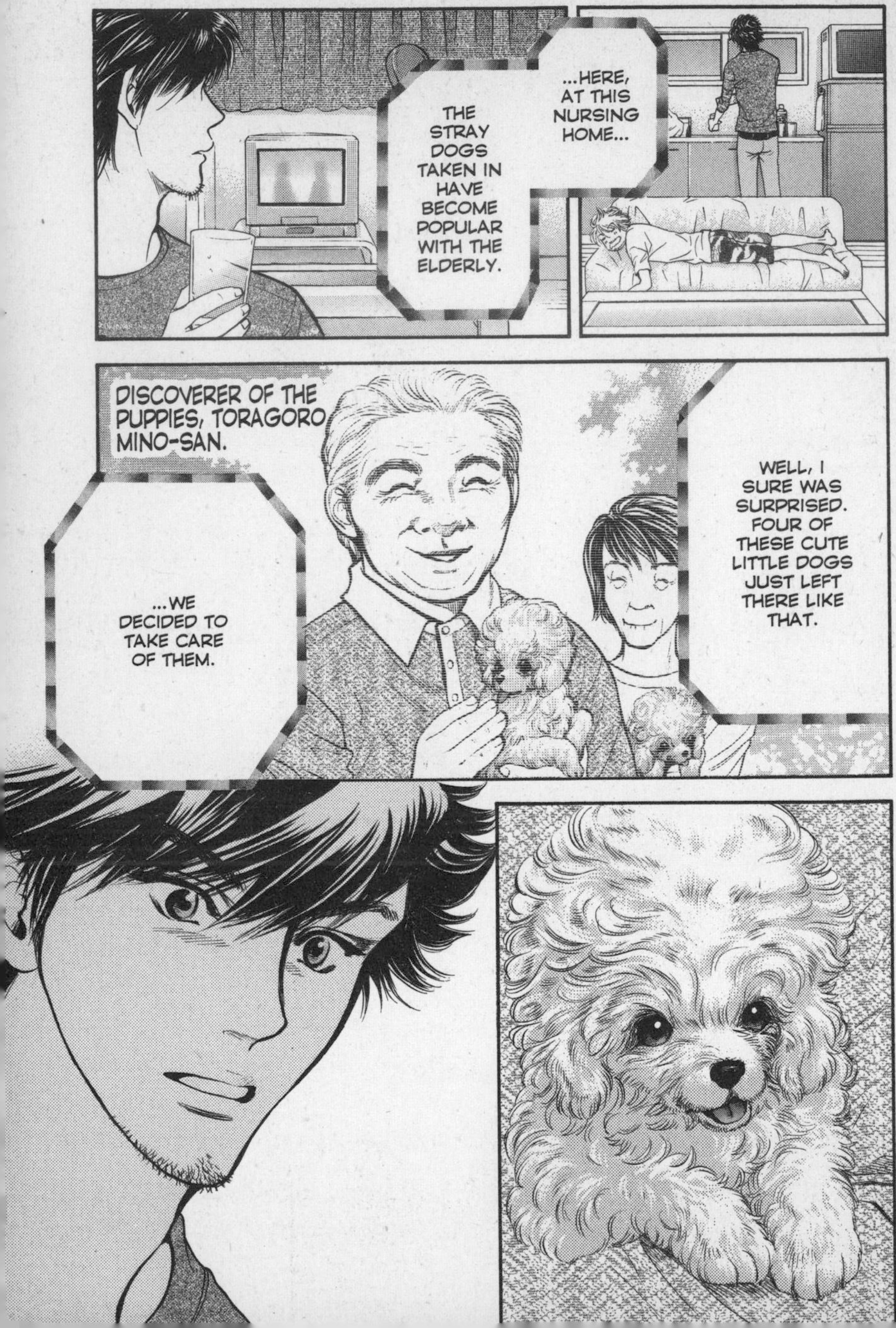
...HERE, AT THIS NURSING HOME...
THE STRAY DOGS TAKEN IN HAVE BECOME POPULAR WITH THE ELDERLY.
DISCOVERER OF THE PUPPIES, TORAGORO MINO-SAN.
WELL, I SURE WAS SURPRISED. FOUR OF THESE CUTE LITTLE DOGS JUST LEFT THERE LIKE THAT.
...WE DECIDED TO TAKE CARE OF THEM.

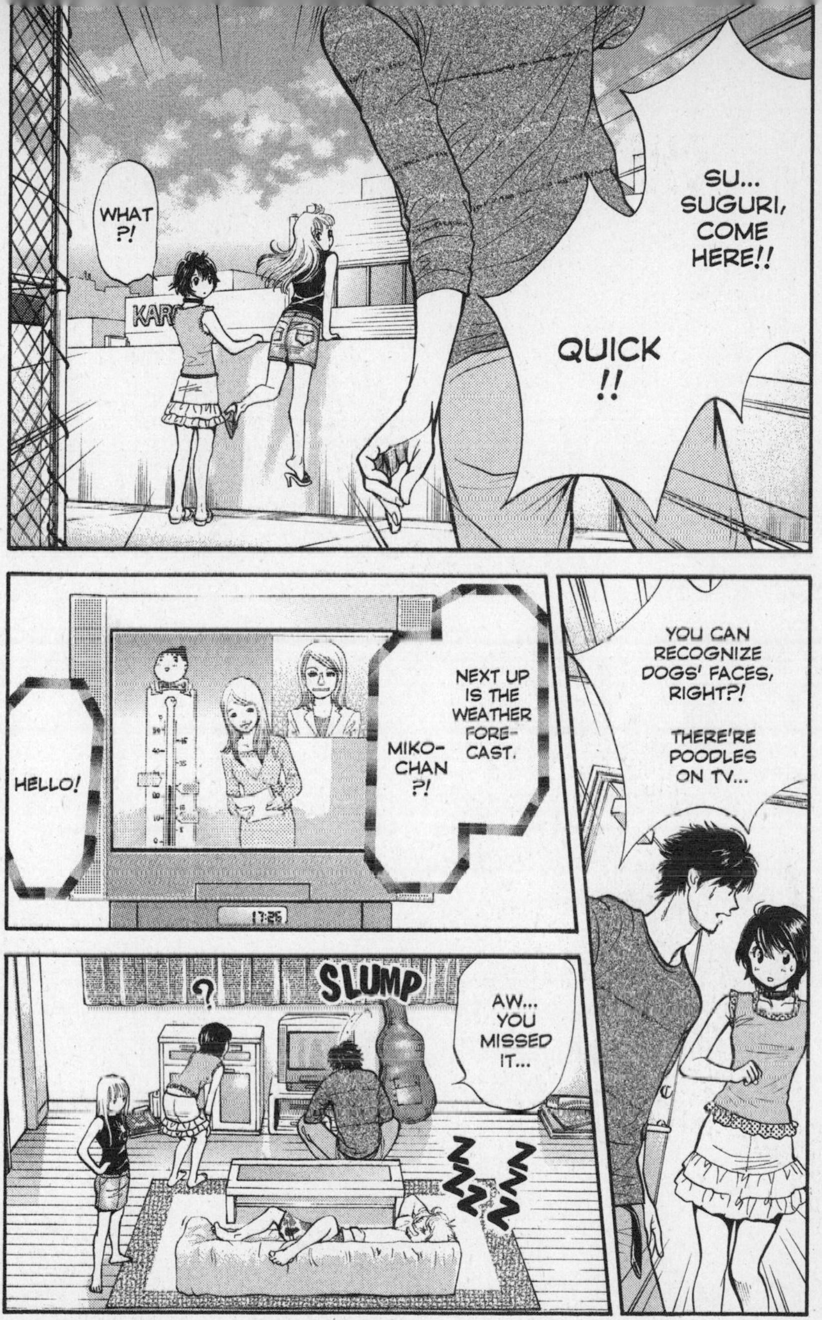
SU... SUGURI, COME HERE!!
QUICK!!
WHAT?!
YOU CAN RECOGNIZE DOGS' FACES, RIGHT?!
THERE'RE POODLES ON TV...
NEXT UP IS THE WEATHER FORE-CAST.
MIKO-CHAN?!
HELLO!
SLUMP
AW... YOU MISSED IT...
?
ZZZ

CHAPTER 30: REAL FAMILY

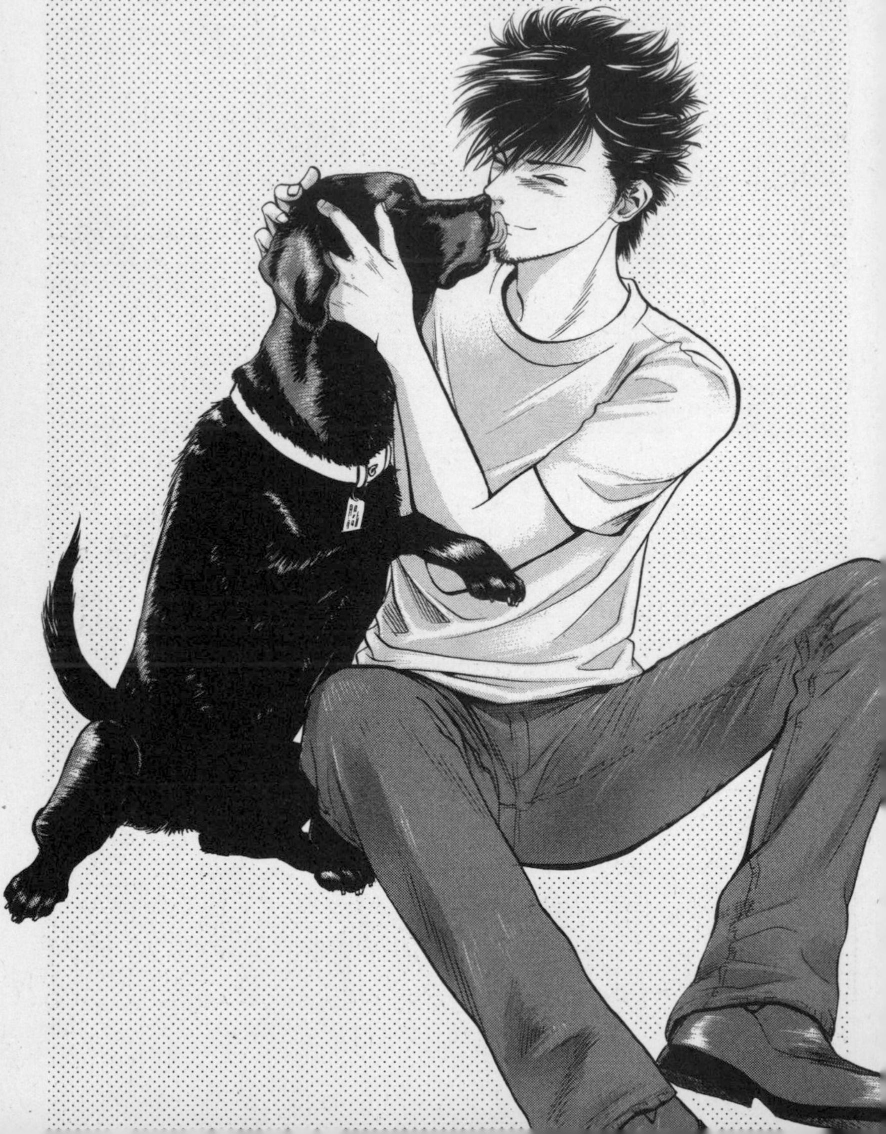

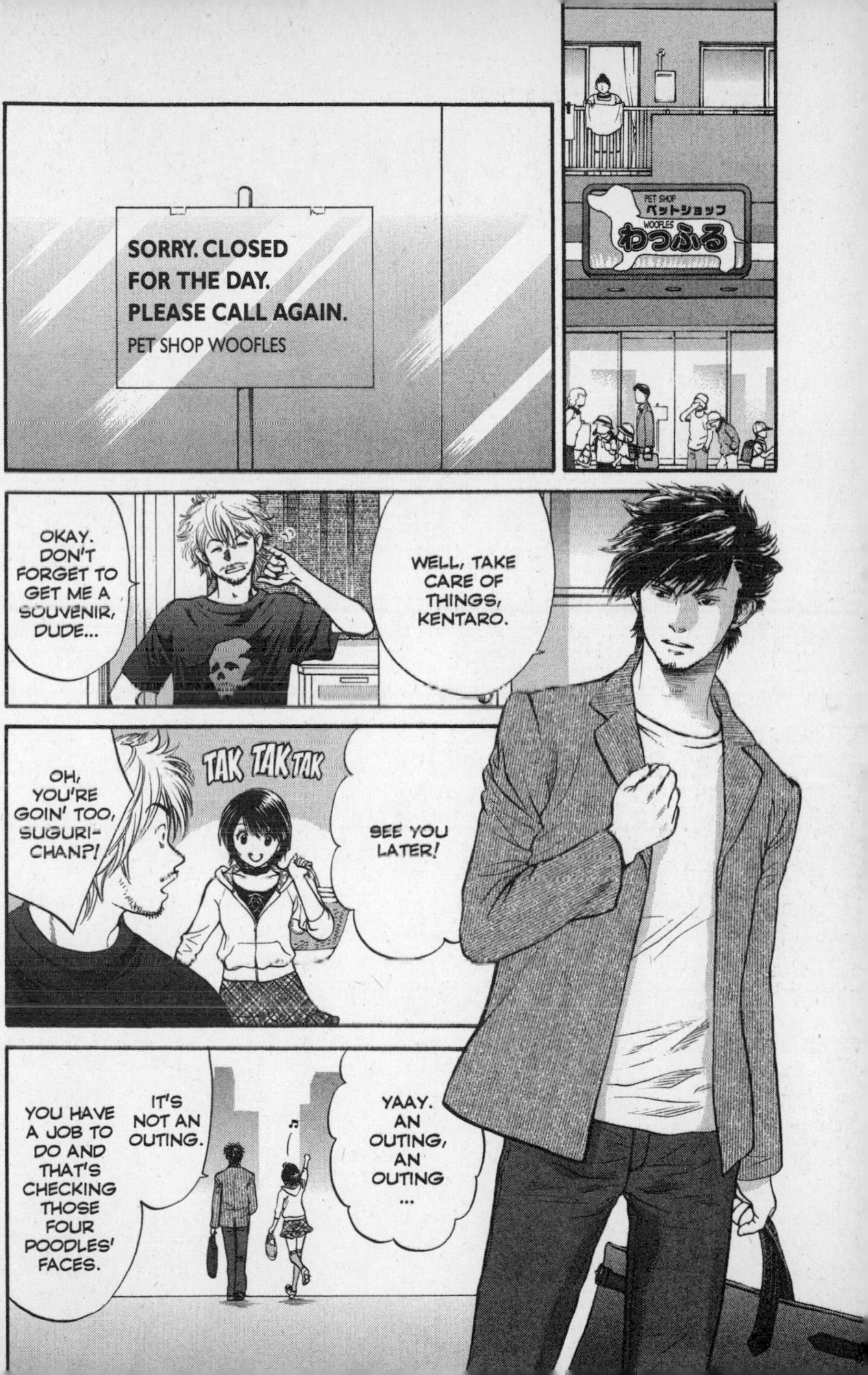
PET SHOP
ペットショップ
WOOFLES
わつふる
SORRY. CLOSED FOR THE DAY. PLEASE CALL AGAIN.
PET SHOP WOOFLES
WELL, TAKE CARE OF THINGS, KENTARO.
OKAY. DON'T FORGET TO GET ME A SOUVENIR, DUDE...
SEE YOU LATER!
TAK TAK TAK
OH, YOU'RE GOIN' TOO, SUGURI-CHAN?!
YAAY. AN OUTING, AN OUTING ...
IT'S NOT AN OUTING.
YOU HAVE A JOB TO DO AND THAT'S CHECKING THOSE FOUR POODLES' FACES.

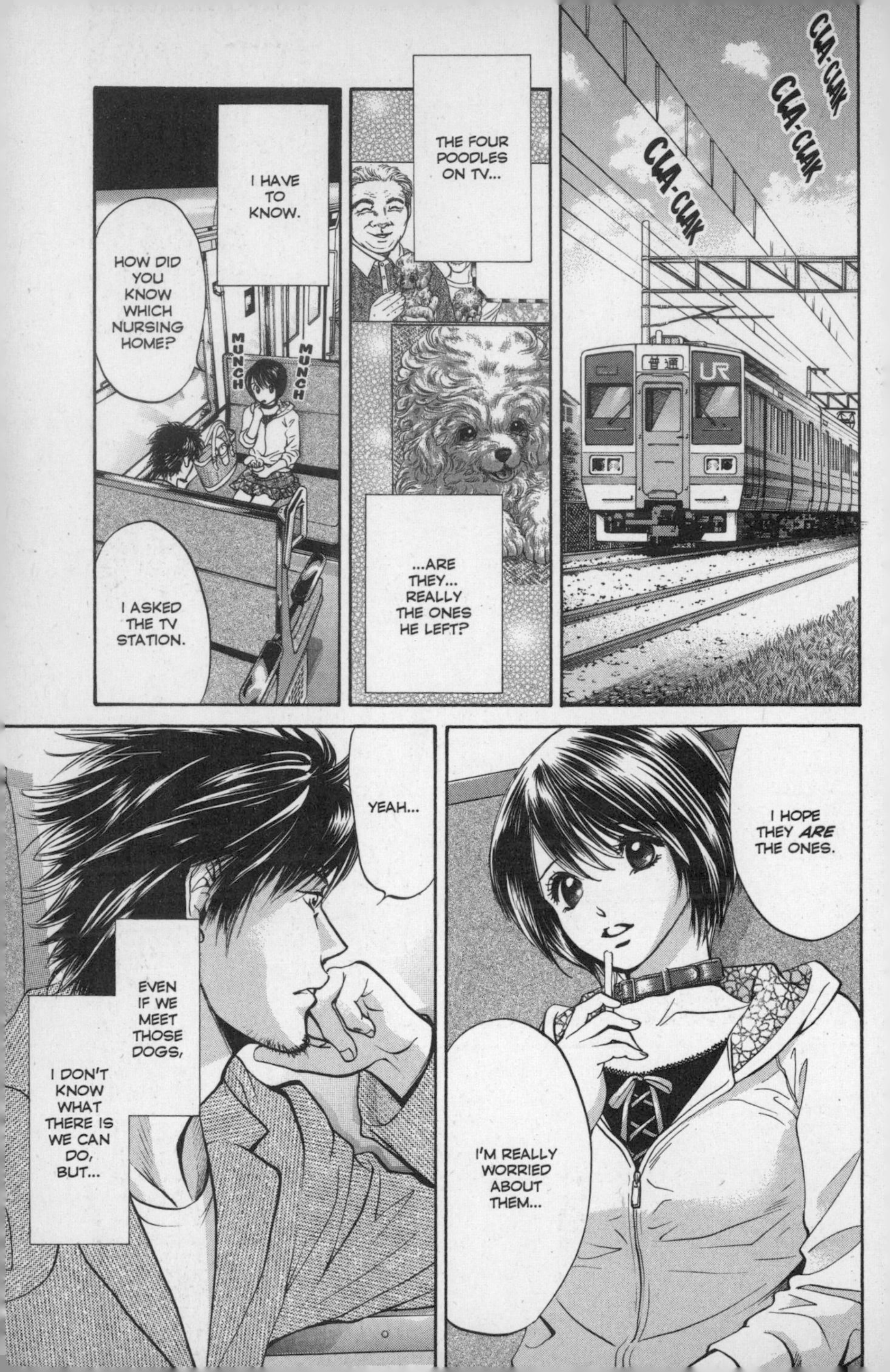
CLA-CLAK
CLA-CLAK
CLA-CLAK
普通
THE FOUR POODLES ON TV...
...ARE THEY... REALLY THE ONES HE LEFT?
I HAVE TO KNOW.
HOW DID YOU KNOW WHICH NURSING HOME?
MUNCH
MUNCH
I ASKED THE TV STATION.
I HOPE THEY *ARE* THE ONES.
I'M REALLY WORRIED ABOUT THEM...
YEAH...
EVEN IF WE MEET THOSE DOGS,
I DON'T KNOW WHAT THERE IS WE CAN DO, BUT...

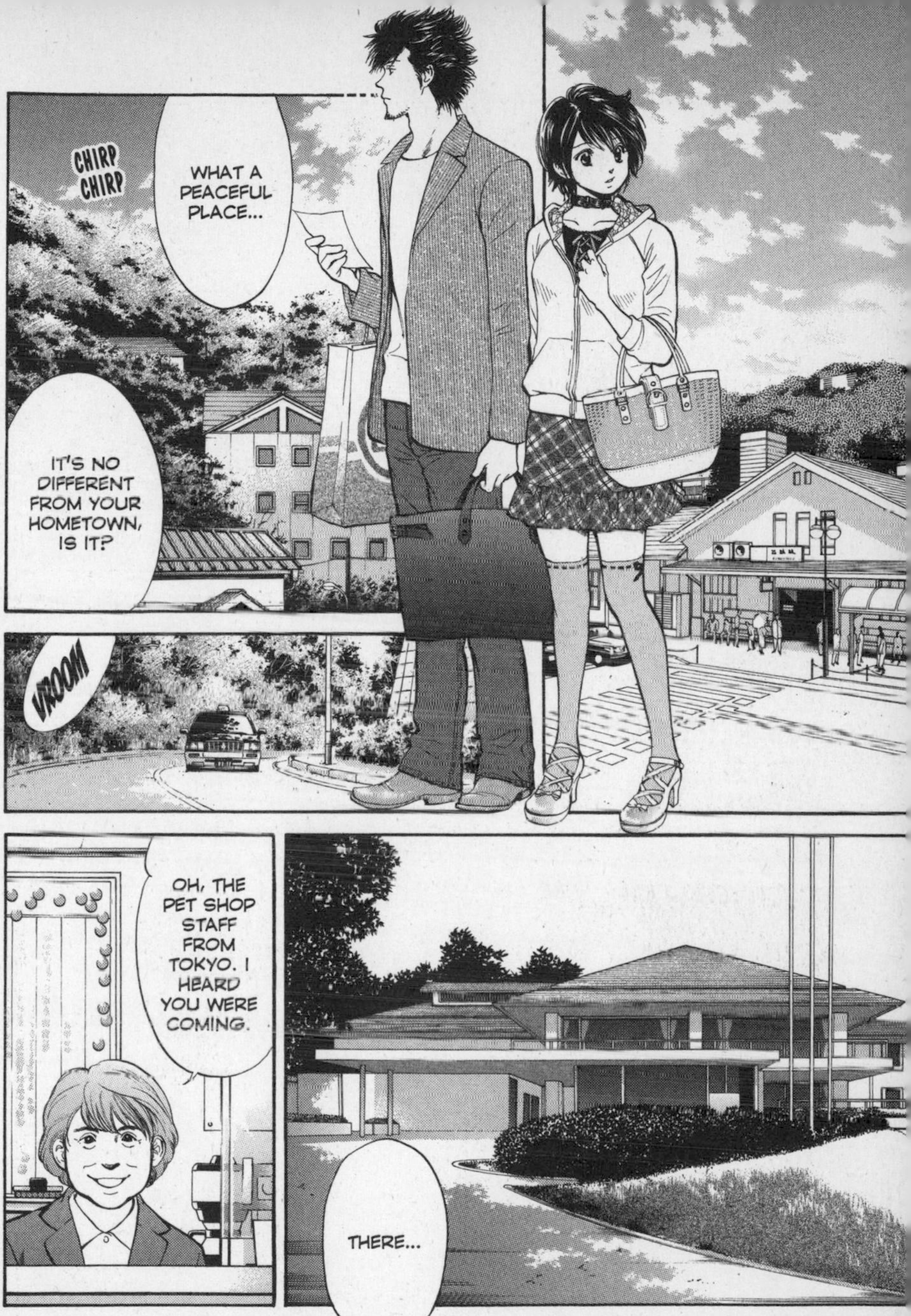
CHIRP CHIRP
WHAT A PEACEFUL PLACE...
IT'S NO DIFFERENT FROM YOUR HOMETOWN, IS IT?
VROOM
THERE...
OH, THE PET SHOP STAFF FROM TOKYO. I HEARD YOU WERE COMING.

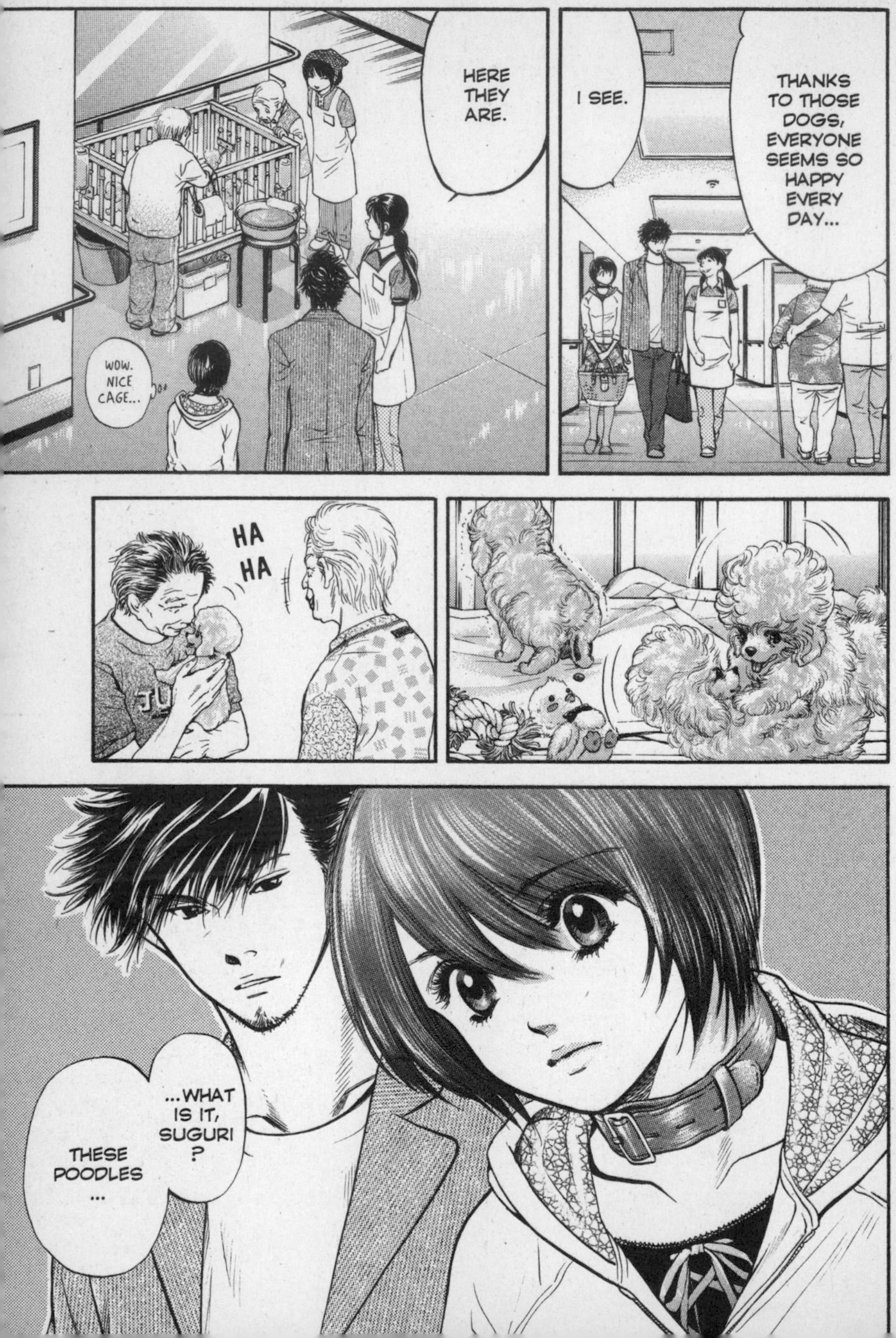
THANKS TO THOSE DOGS, EVERYONE SEEMS SO HAPPY EVERY DAY...
I SEE.
HERE THEY ARE.
WOW. NICE CAGE...
HA HA
...WHAT IS IT, SUGURI?
THESE POODLES ...

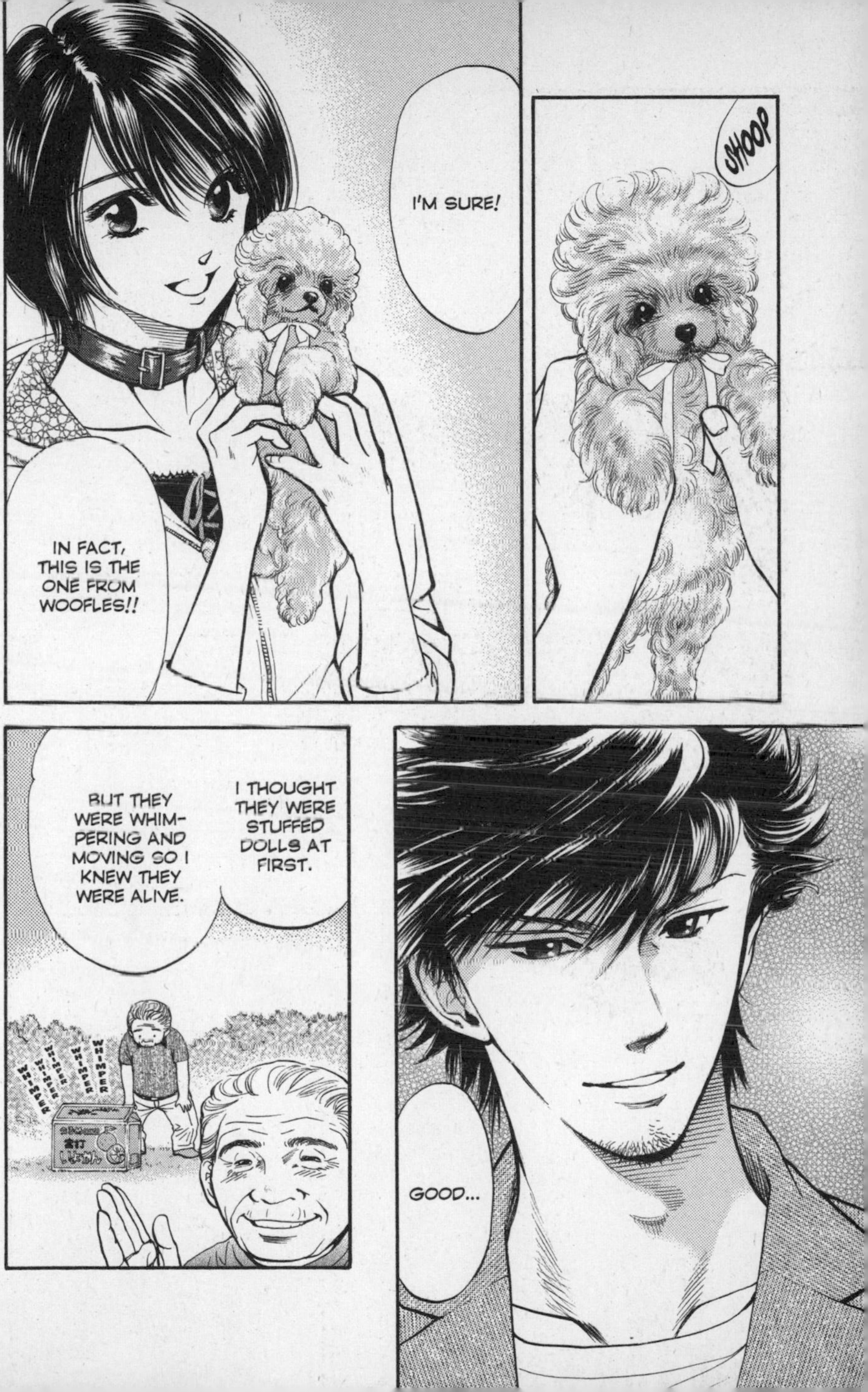
SHOOP
I'M SURE!
IN FACT, THIS IS THE ONE FROM WOOFLES!!
GOOD...
I THOUGHT THEY WERE STUFFED DOLLS AT FIRST.
BUT THEY WERE WHIM-PERING AND MOVING SO I KNEW THEY WERE ALIVE.
WHIMPER
WHIMPER
WHIMPER
WHIMPER

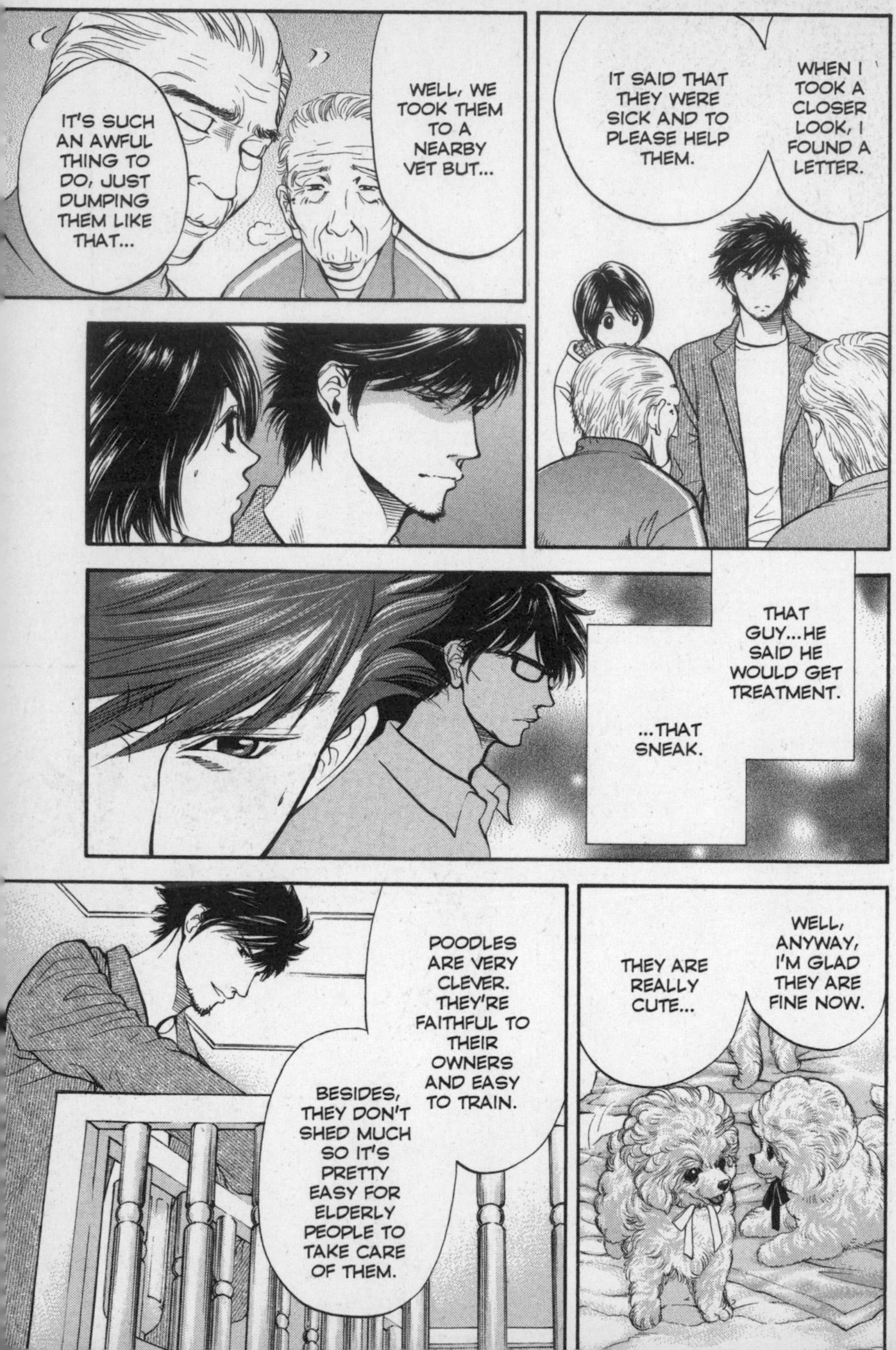
WHEN I TOOK A CLOSER LOOK, I FOUND A LETTER.
IT SAID THAT THEY WERE SICK AND TO PLEASE HELP THEM.
WELL, WE TOOK THEM TO A NEARBY VET BUT...
IT'S SUCH AN AWFUL THING TO DO, JUST DUMPING THEM LIKE THAT...
THAT GUY...HE SAID HE WOULD GET TREATMENT.
...THAT SNEAK.
WELL, ANYWAY, I'M GLAD THEY ARE FINE NOW.
THEY ARE REALLY CUTE...
POODLES ARE VERY CLEVER. THEY'RE FAITHFUL TO THEIR OWNERS AND EASY TO TRAIN.
BESIDES, THEY DON'T SHED MUCH SO IT'S PRETTY EASY FOR ELDERLY PEOPLE TO TAKE CARE OF THEM.

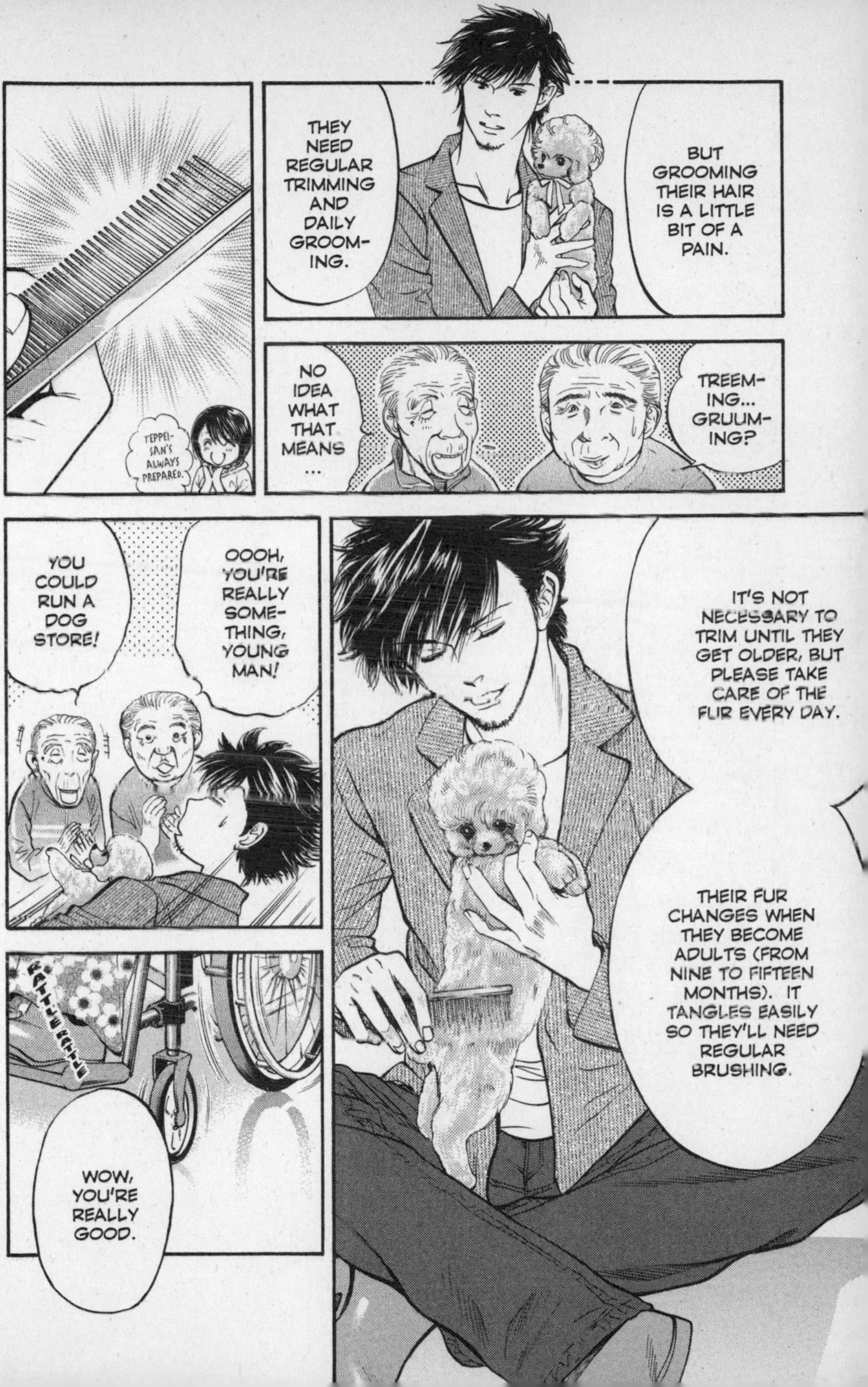
BUT GROOMING THEIR HAIR IS A LITTLE BIT OF A PAIN.
THEY NEED REGULAR TRIMMING AND DAILY GROOMING.
TREEMING... GRUUMING?
NO IDEA WHAT THAT MEANS...
TEPPEI-SAN'S ALWAYS PREPARED.
IT'S NOT NECESSARY TO TRIM UNTIL THEY GET OLDER, BUT PLEASE TAKE CARE OF THE FUR EVERY DAY.
THEIR FUR CHANGES WHEN THEY BECOME ADULTS (FROM NINE TO FIFTEEN MONTHS). IT TANGLES EASILY SO THEY'LL NEED REGULAR BRUSHING.
OOOH, YOU'RE REALLY SOMETHING, YOUNG MAN!
YOU COULD RUN A DOG STORE!
RATTLE RATTLE
WOW, YOU'RE REALLY GOOD.

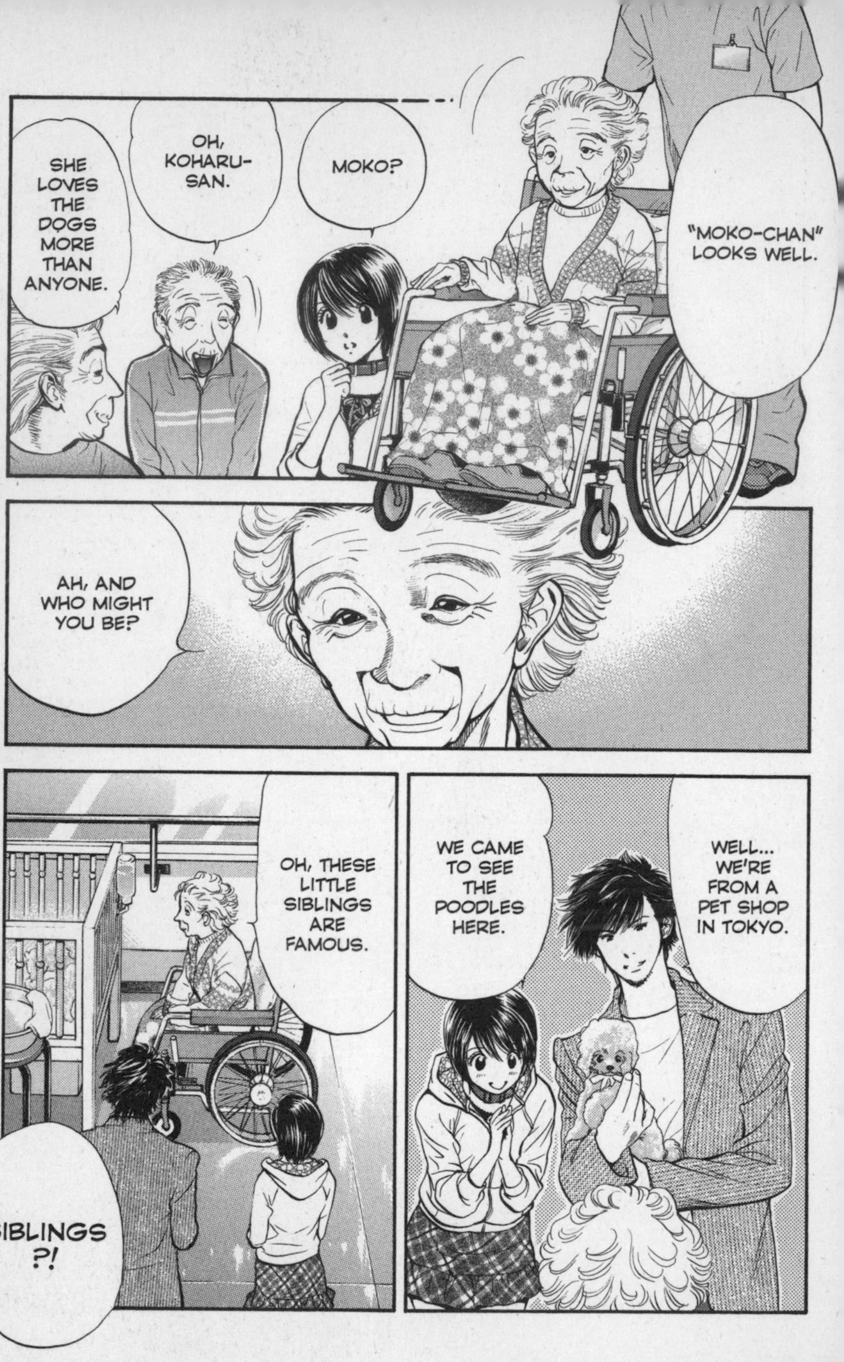
"MOKO-CHAN" LOOKS WELL.
MOKO?
OH, KOHARU-SAN.
SHE LOVES THE DOGS MORE THAN ANYONE.
AH, AND WHO MIGHT YOU BE?
WELL... WE'RE FROM A PET SHOP IN TOKYO.
WE CAME TO SEE THE POODLES HERE.
OH, THESE LITTLE SIBLINGS ARE FAMOUS.
SIBLINGS ?!

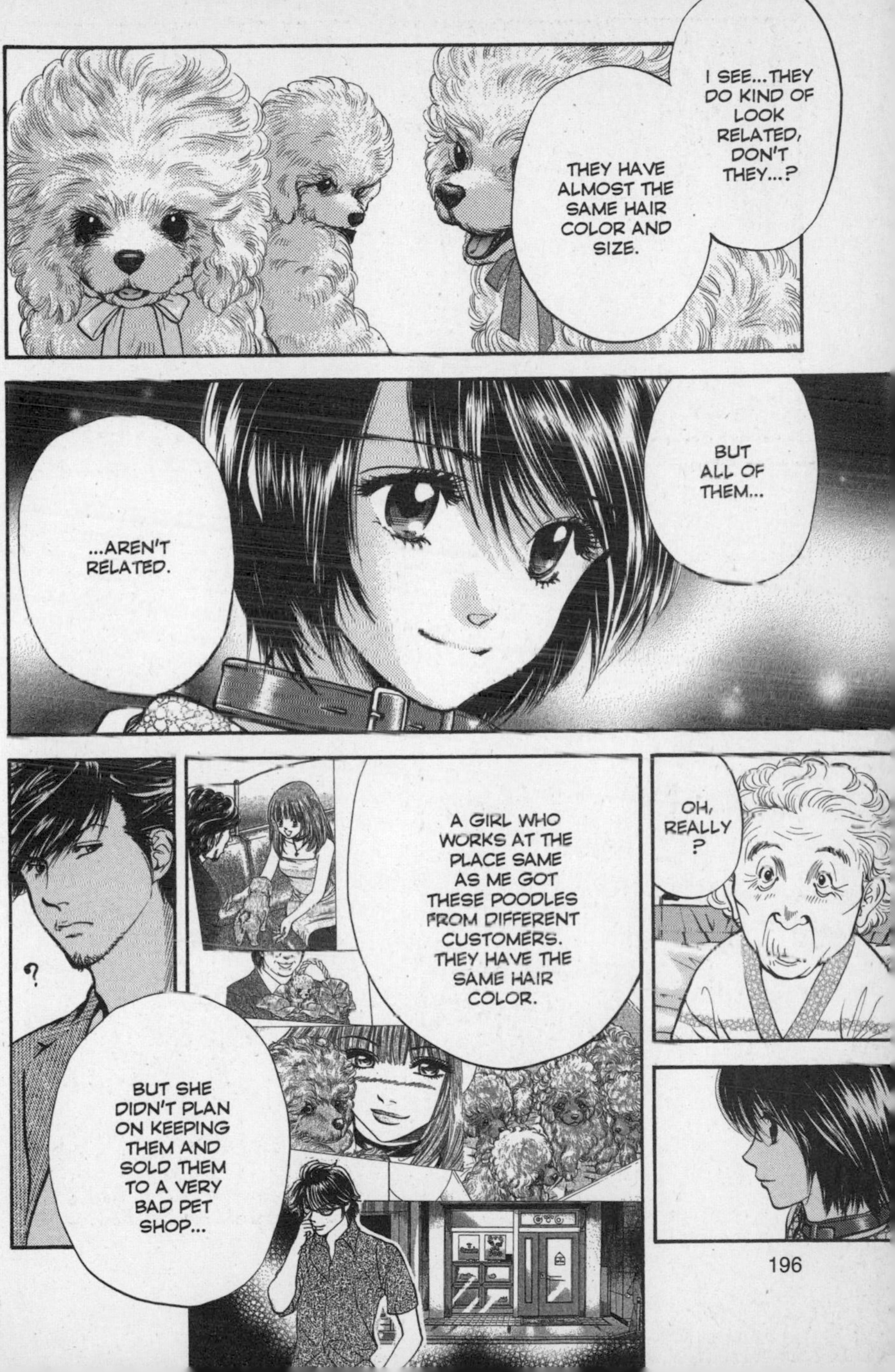
I SEE...THEY DO KIND OF LOOK RELATED, DON'T THEY...?
THEY HAVE ALMOST THE SAME HAIR COLOR AND SIZE.
BUT ALL OF THEM...
...AREN'T RELATED.
OH, REALLY ?
A GIRL WHO WORKS AT THE PLACE SAME AS ME GOT THESE POODLES FROM DIFFERENT CUSTOMERS. THEY HAVE THE SAME HAIR COLOR.
BUT SHE DIDN'T PLAN ON KEEPING THEM AND SOLD THEM TO A VERY BAD PET SHOP...
?

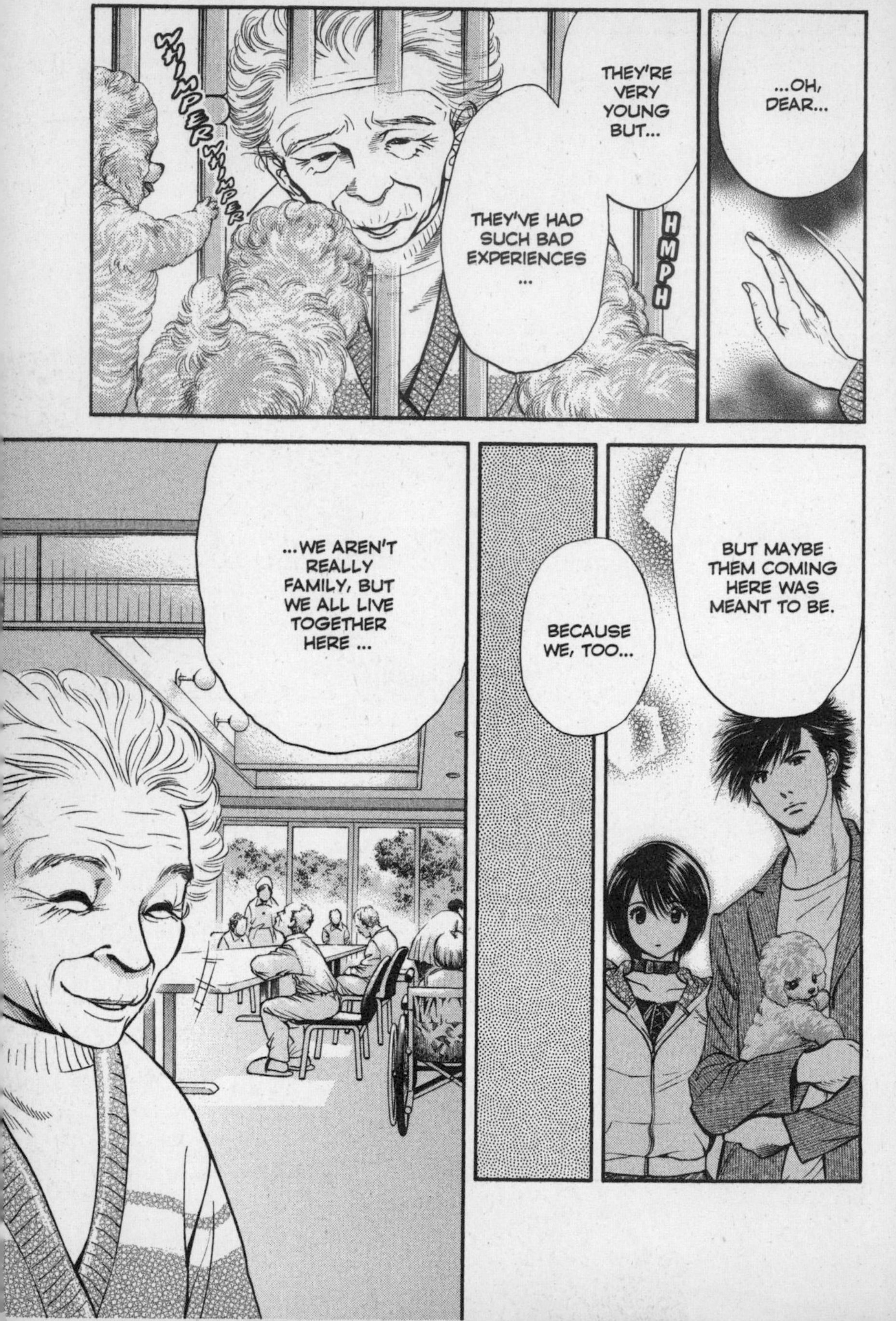
...OH, DEAR...
THEY'RE VERY YOUNG BUT...
HMPH
THEY'VE HAD SUCH BAD EXPERIENCES ...
WHIMPER WHIMPER
BUT MAYBE THEM COMING HERE WAS MEANT TO BE.
BECAUSE WE, TOO...
...WE AREN'T REALLY FAMILY, BUT WE ALL LIVE TOGETHER HERE ...

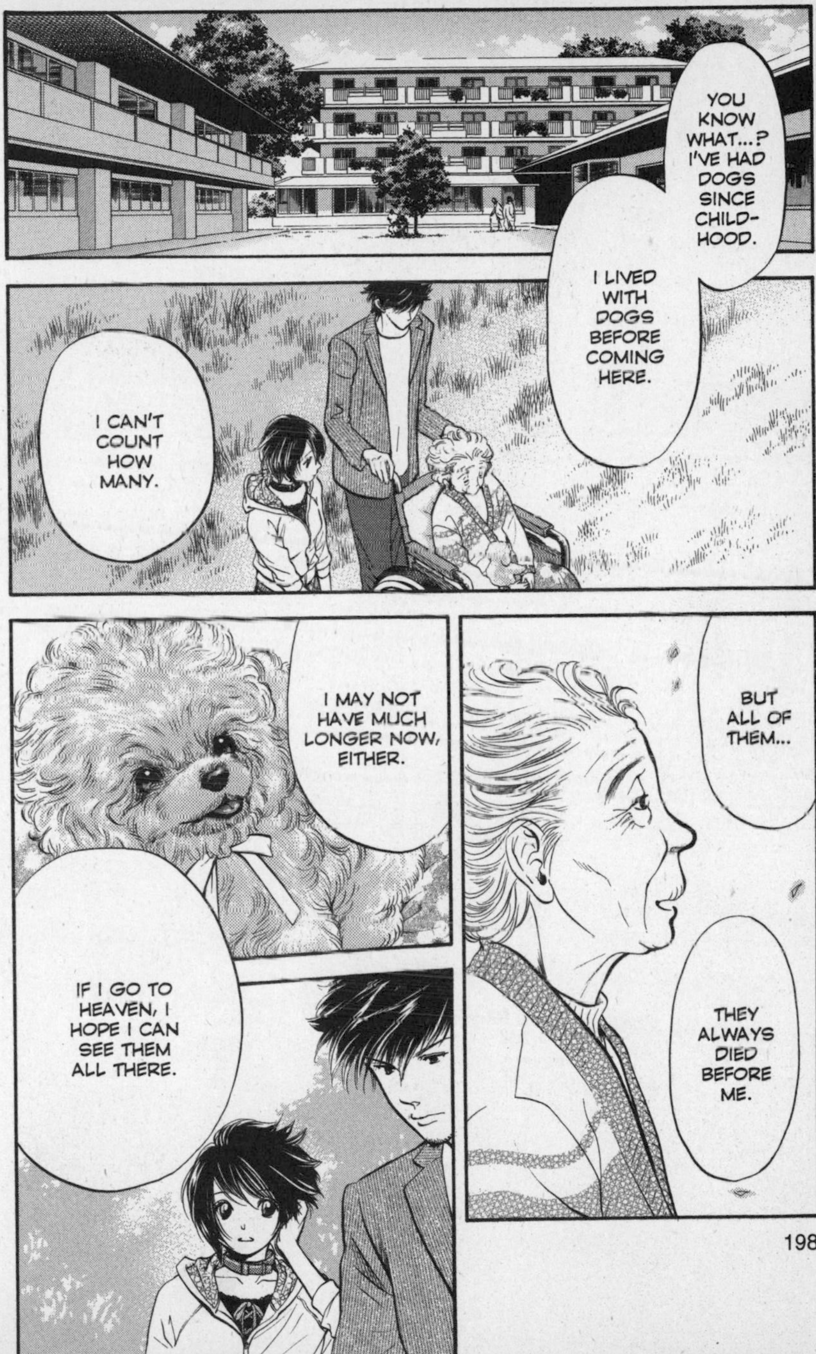
YOU KNOW WHAT...? I'VE HAD DOGS SINCE CHILD-HOOD.
I LIVED WITH DOGS BEFORE COMING HERE.
I CAN'T COUNT HOW MANY.
BUT ALL OF THEM...
THEY ALWAYS DIED BEFORE ME.
I MAY NOT HAVE MUCH LONGER NOW, EITHER.
IF I GO TO HEAVEN, I HOPE I CAN SEE THEM ALL THERE.

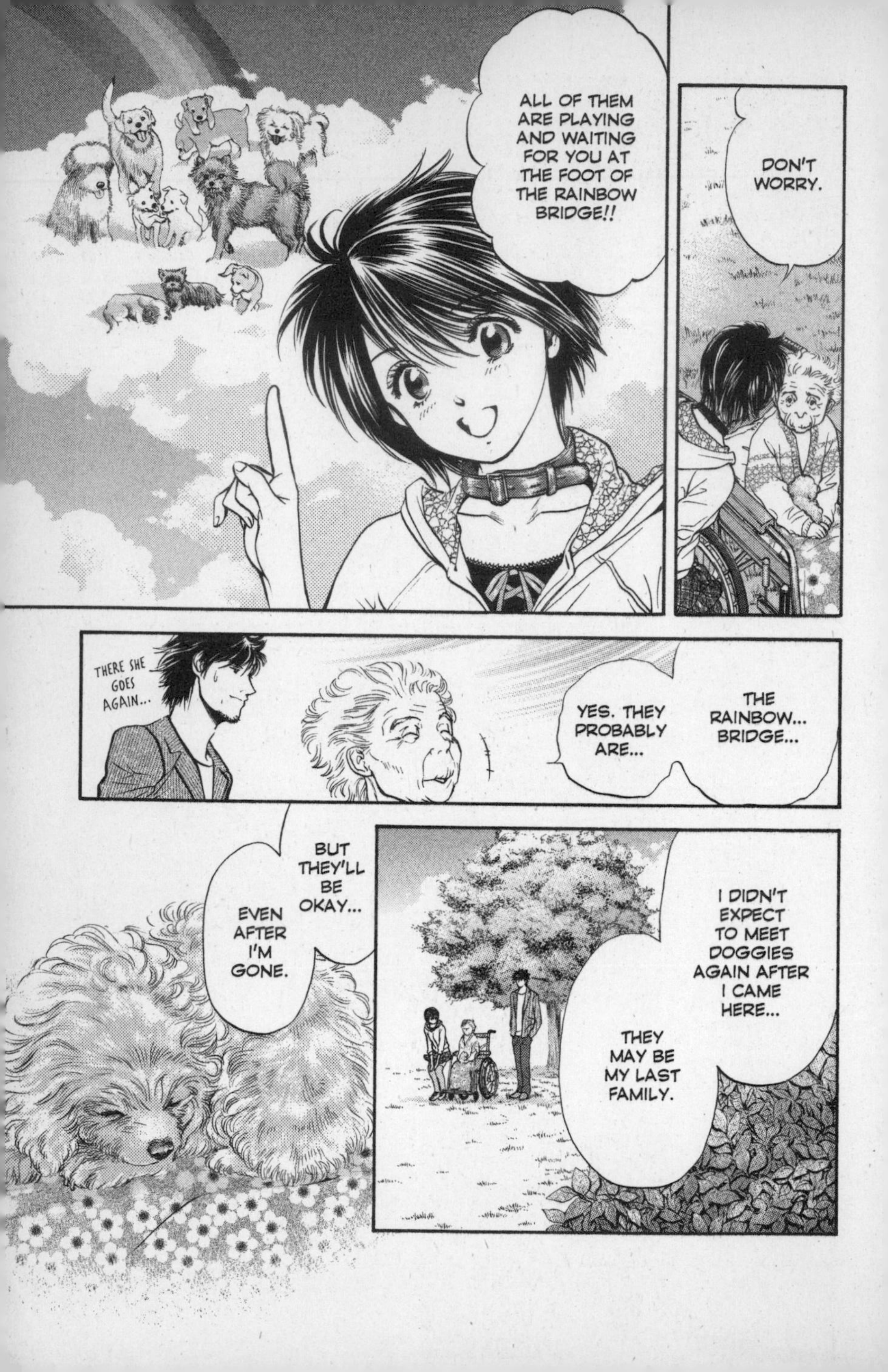
DON'T WORRY.
ALL OF THEM ARE PLAYING AND WAITING FOR YOU AT THE FOOT OF THE RAINBOW BRIDGE!!
THE RAINBOW... BRIDGE...
YES. THEY PROBABLY ARE...
THERE SHE GOES AGAIN...
I DIDN'T EXPECT TO MEET DOGGIES AGAIN AFTER I CAME HERE...
THEY MAY BE MY LAST FAMILY.
BUT THEY'LL BE OKAY...
EVEN AFTER I'M GONE.

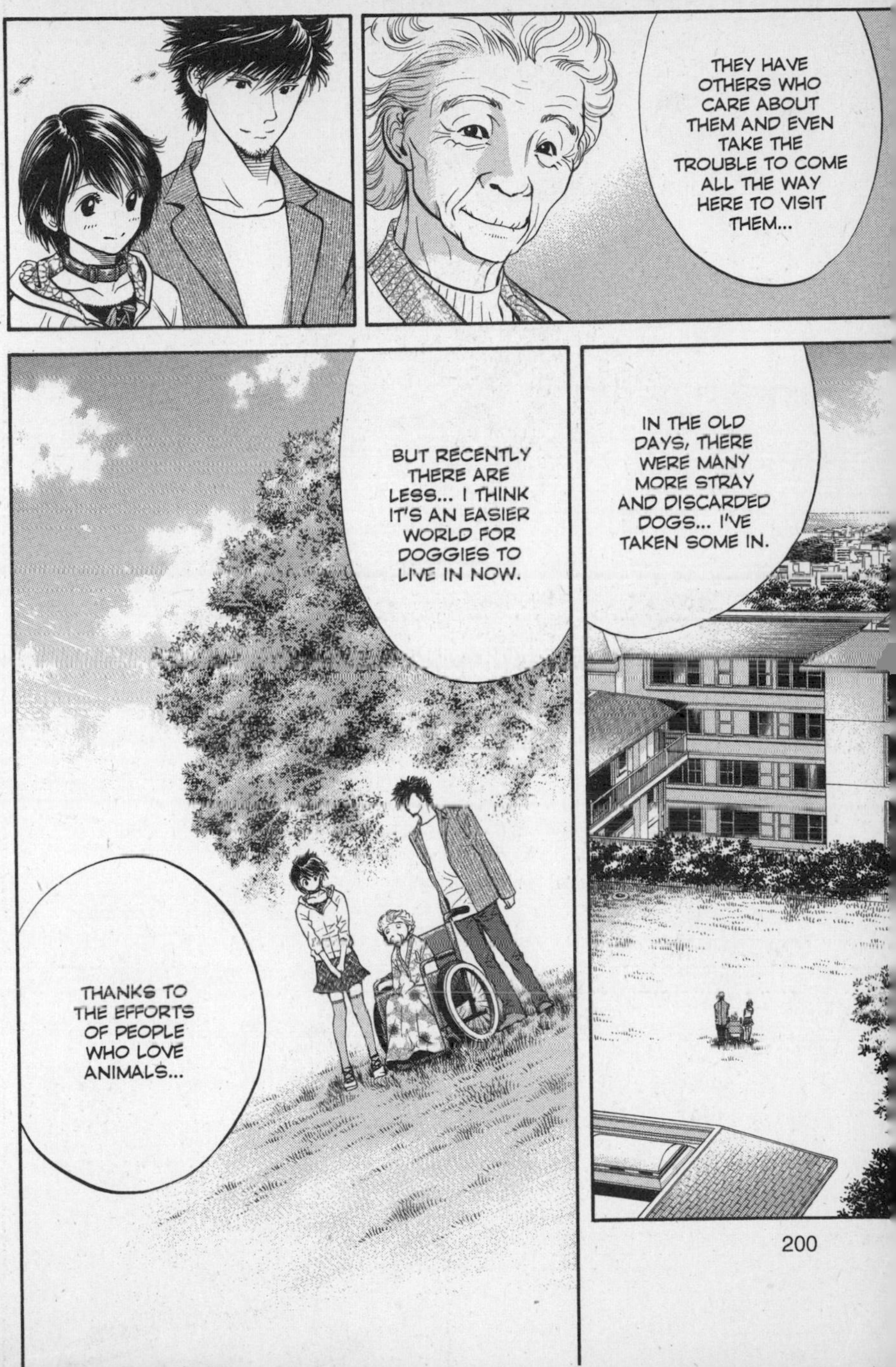
THEY HAVE OTHERS WHO CARE ABOUT THEM AND EVEN TAKE THE TROUBLE TO COME ALL THE WAY HERE TO VISIT THEM...
IN THE OLD DAYS, THERE WERE MANY MORE STRAY AND DISCARDED DOGS... I'VE TAKEN SOME IN.
BUT RECENTLY THERE ARE LESS... I THINK IT'S AN EASIER WORLD FOR DOGGIES TO LIVE IN NOW.
THANKS TO THE EFFORTS OF PEOPLE WHO LOVE ANIMALS...

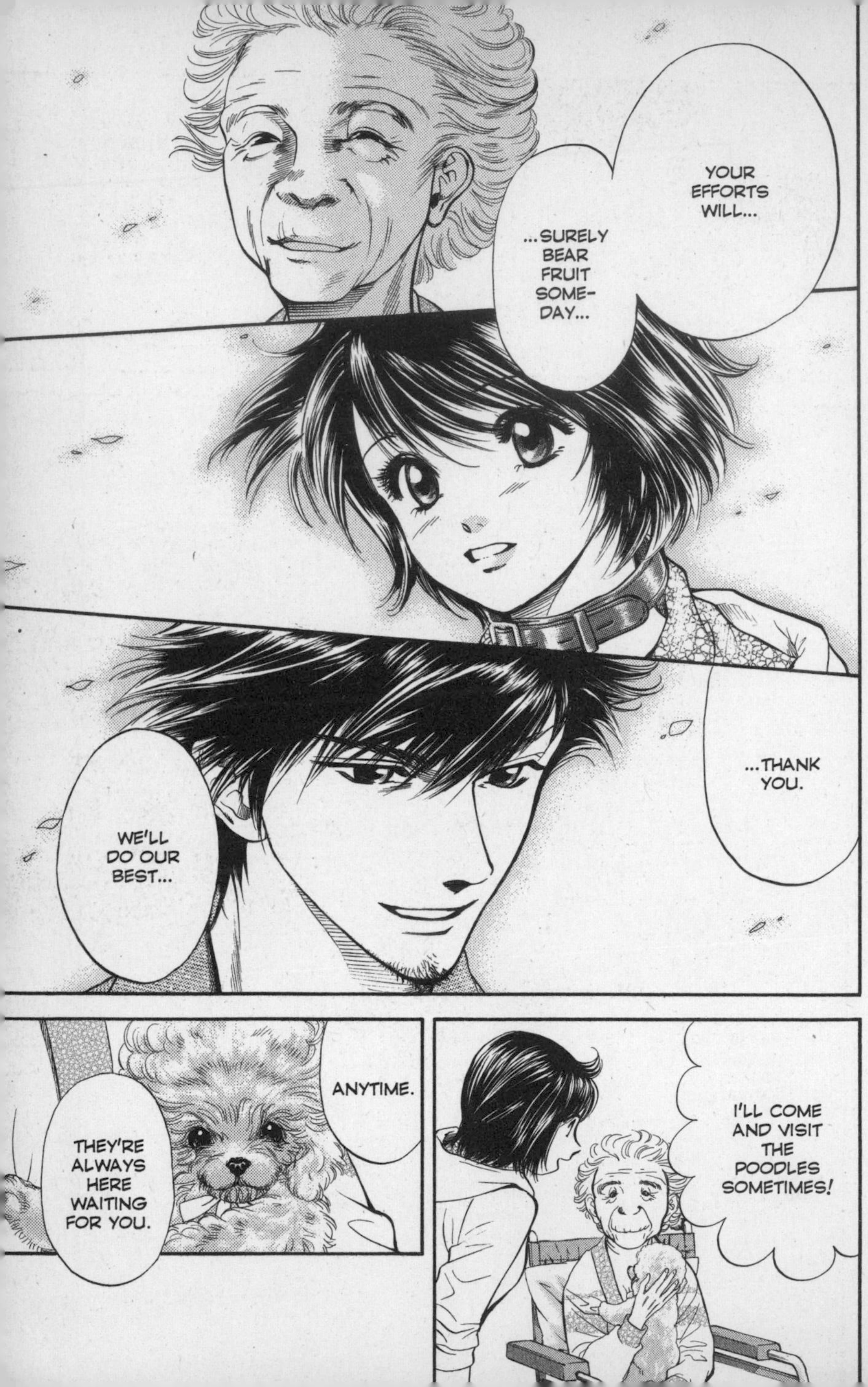
YOUR EFFORTS WILL...
...SURELY BEAR FRUIT SOME-DAY...
...THANK YOU.
WE'LL DO OUR BEST...
I'LL COME AND VISIT THE POODLES SOMETIMES!
ANYTIME.
THEY'RE ALWAYS HERE WAITING FOR YOU.

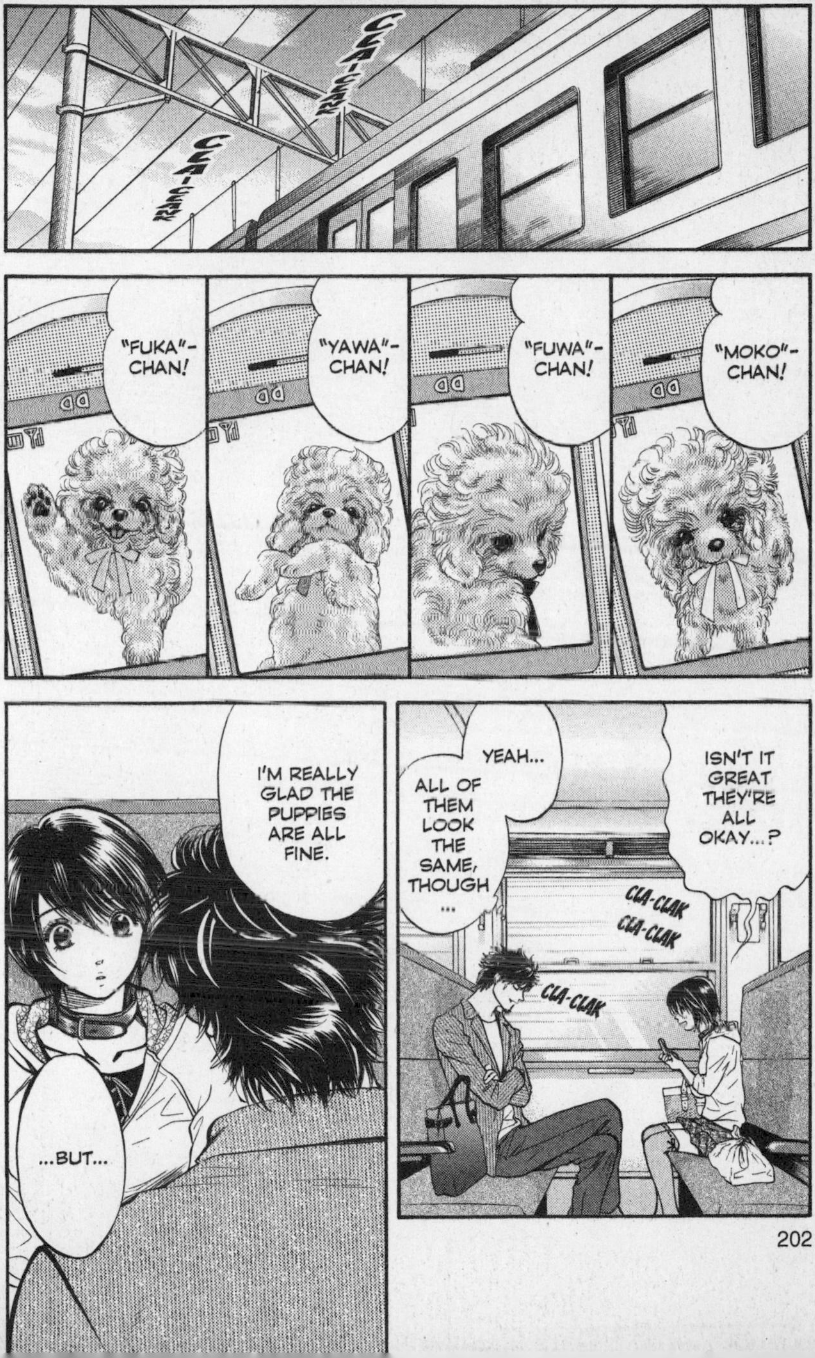
CLA-CLANK
CLA-CLANK
"MOKO"-CHAN!
"FUWA"-CHAN!
"YAWA"-CHAN!
"FUKA"-CHAN!
ISN'T IT GREAT THEY'RE ALL OKAY...?
YEAH...
ALL OF THEM LOOK THE SAME, THOUGH ...
CLA-CLAK
CLA-CLAK
CLA-CLAK
I'M REALLY GLAD THE PUPPIES ARE ALL FINE.
...BUT...

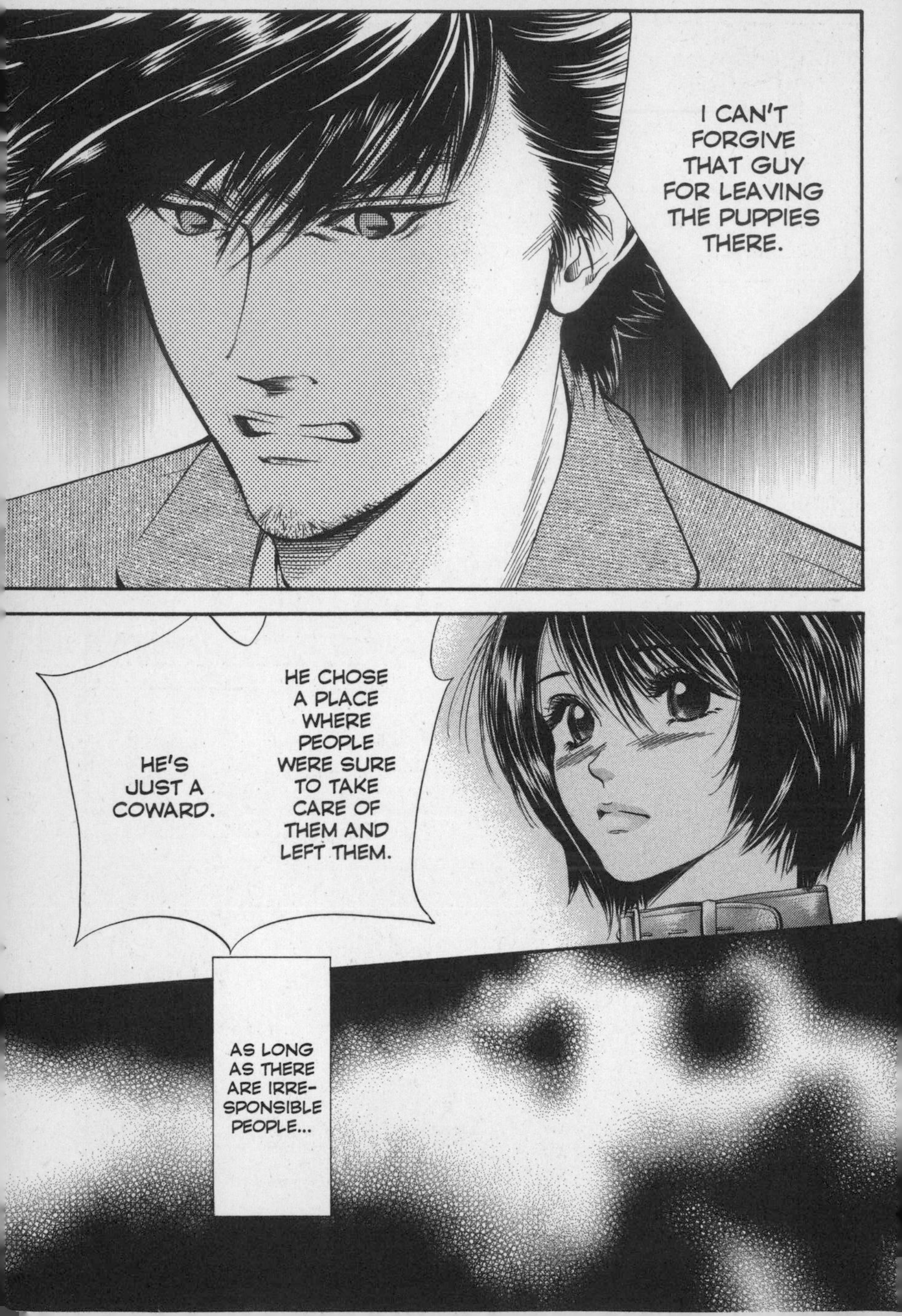
I CAN'T FORGIVE THAT GUY FOR LEAVING THE PUPPIES THERE.
HE CHOSE A PLACE WHERE PEOPLE WERE SURE TO TAKE CARE OF THEM AND LEFT THEM.
HE'S JUST A COWARD.
AS LONG AS THERE ARE IRRE-SPONSIBLE PEOPLE...

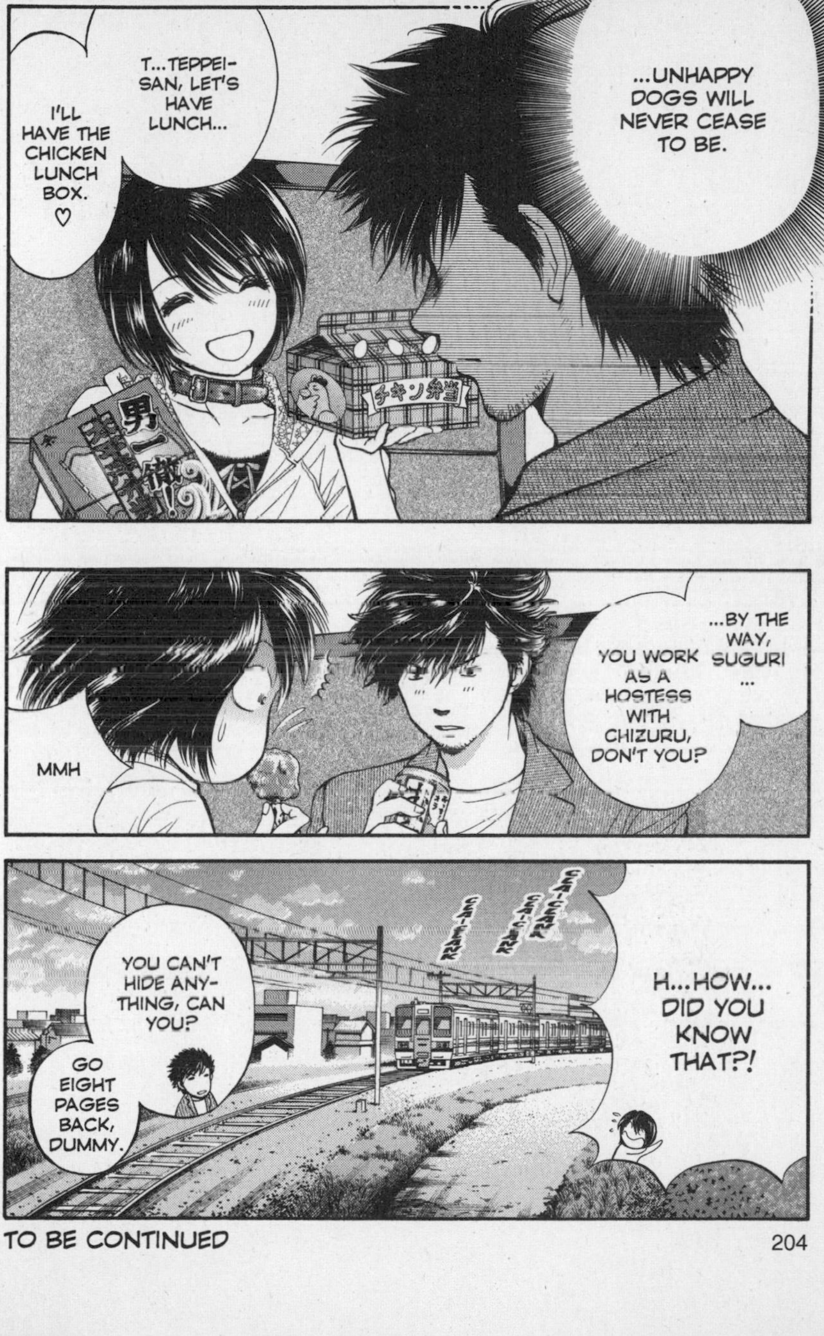
...UNHAPPY DOGS WILL NEVER CEASE TO BE.
T...TEPPEI-SAN, LET'S HAVE LUNCH...
I'LL HAVE THE CHICKEN LUNCH BOX. ♡
チキン弁当
...BY THE WAY, SUGURI ...
YOU WORK AS A HOSTESS WITH CHIZURU, DON'T YOU?
MMH
H...HOW... DID YOU KNOW THAT?!
CLA-CLANK
CLA-CLANK
CLA-CLANK
YOU CAN'T HIDE ANY-THING, CAN YOU?
GO EIGHT PAGES BACK, DUMMY.

TO BE CONTINUED

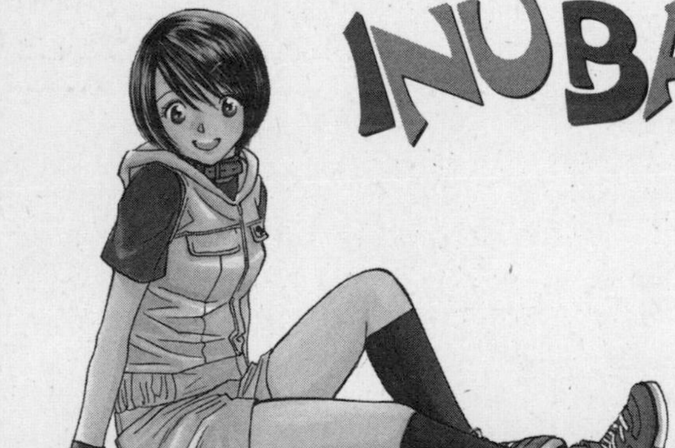

INUBAKA

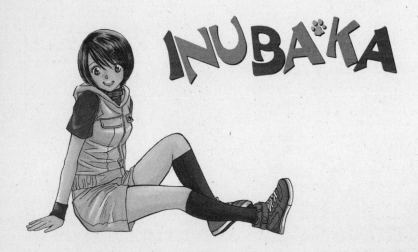

INUBAKA

Everybody's Crazy for Dogs!

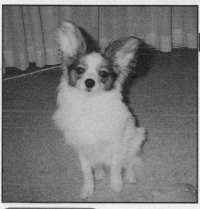

**From Yoshida-san
in the Hyogo prefecture:**

🐾 Komugi-kun (Papillon)

When Komugi-kun walks on the streets he's afraid of meeting other dogs. He's not toilet-trained properly yet...but he is a star in the family because of his natural cuteness. He's just 7 months old. Please take a long-term view and love him!

Yukiya Sakuragi It will be fun to see when his ears become like butterflies. My dog also had trouble toilet training. He will learn how to do it soon so don't worry!

**From DAI-san
in the Akita prefecture:**

🐾 Chame-kun (Shiba mix)

Chame-kun is gallant and intelligent. He sometimes says "meals" or "Mom." He can even sing! [He can?!] He has a biting habit, though. He's sad because his girlfriend, Lucky, died. Please live long—for her sake too!

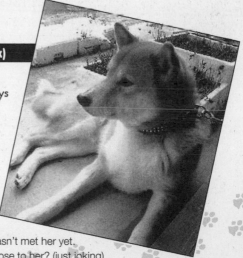

Yukiya Sakuragi

My dog has a fiancée, but he hasn't met her yet. Should I teach him how to propose to her? (just joking)

From Tanaka-san in the Hyogo prefecture:

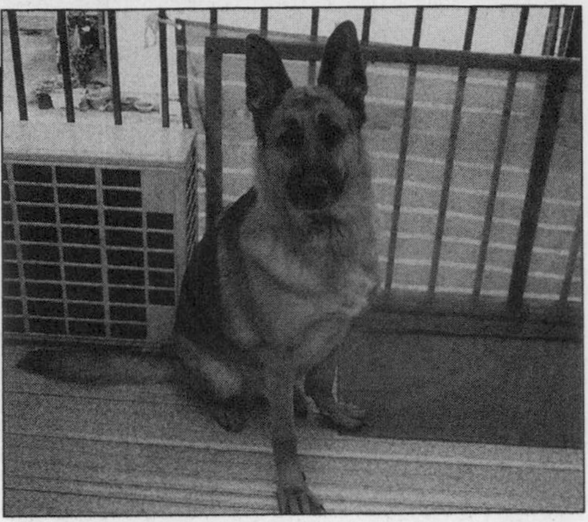

Ginga-kun (Shepherd)

Ginga-kun is kind of a big baby, but he is very intelligent. He obeys his owner, doesn't follow strangers and won't eat food from them without permission. Good boy! He has a brave face and his character is very gentle. He loves balls and he's collected a whole bunch of 'em!

Yukiya Sakuragi Cool! I like big dogs. Shepherds are on my list of dogs to get. I'd love to have such a reliable partner.

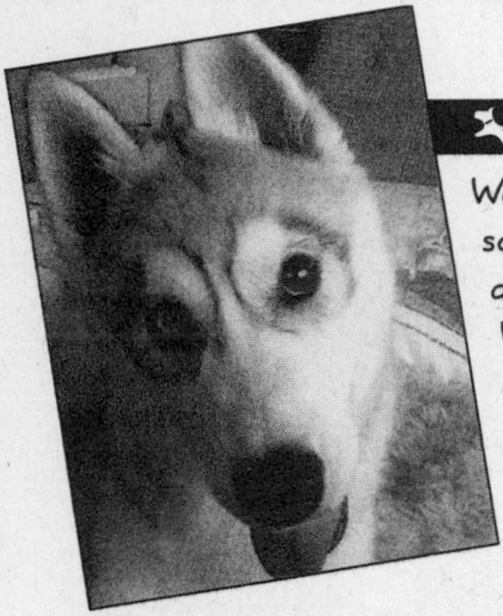

From Aachan-san in the Kanagawa prefecture:

Kotone-chan (Siberian Husky)

We used to have a husky called Blanc (the same name as Sakuragi-san's dog). After it died peacefully we looked hard for another. We then found Kotone-chan. Her left and right eyes are different colors! And she has patterns around her eyes that make it look like she's wearing glasses! (It's a shame they are disappearing.) It is good to see Mom and the others smile again!

Yukiya Sakuragi At my house the family follows Blanc's pace. But thanks to that we talk much more than before. (lol). Kotone-chan's glasses are cute! I want to see her again when she grows up.

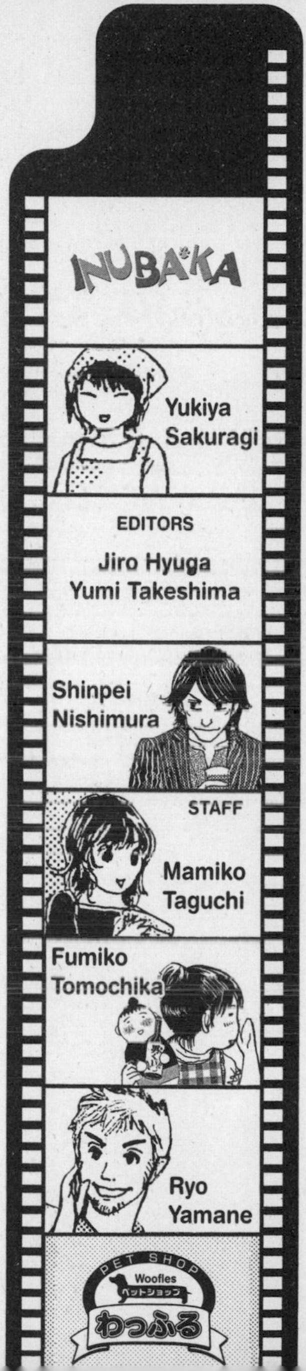
INUBAKA
Yukiya Sakuragi
EDITORS
Jiro Hyuga
Yumi Takeshima
Shinpei Nishimura
STAFF
Mamiko Taguchi
Fumiko Tomochika
Ryo Yamane
PET SHOP
Woofles
ペットショップ
わっふる

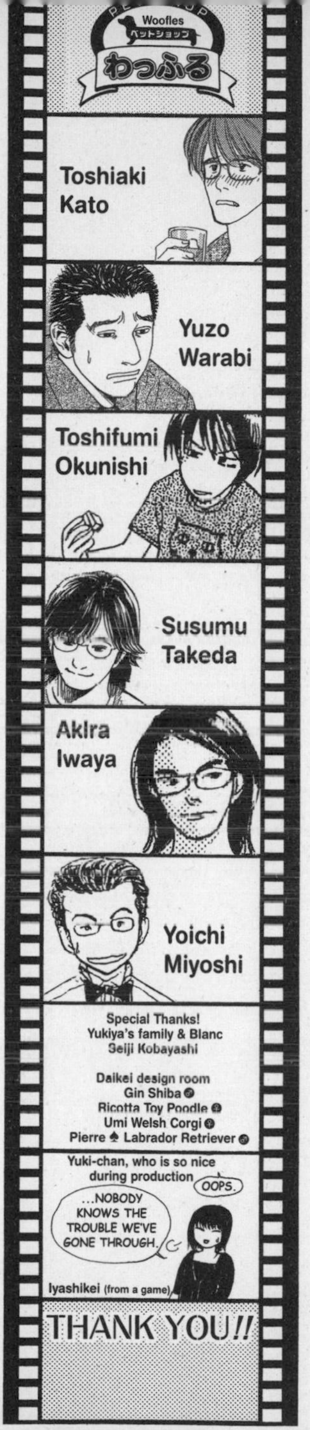
PET SHOP
Woofles
ペットショップ
わっふる
Toshiaki Kato
Yuzo Warabi
Toshifumi Okunishi
Susumu Takeda
Akira Iwaya
Yoichi Miyoshi
Special Thanks!
Yukiya's family & Blanc
Seiji Kobayashi
Daikei design room
Gin Shiba
Ricotta Toy Poodle
Umi Welsh Corgi
Pierre ♠ Labrador Retriever
Yuki-chan, who is so nice during production
OOPS.
...NOBODY KNOWS THE TROUBLE WE'VE GONE THROUGH.
Iyashikei (from a game)
THANK YOU!!

Inubaka
Crazy for Dogs
Vol. #3
VIZ Media Edition

Story and Art by
Yukiya Sakuragi

Translation/Hidemi Hachitori, Honyaku Center Inc.
English Adaptation/Ian Reid and John Werry, Honyaku Center Inc.
Touch-up Art & Lettering/Kelle Han
Cover and Interior Design/Hidemi Sahara
Editor/Ian Robertson

Editor in Chief, Books/Alvin Lu
Editor in Chief, Magazines/Marc Weidenbaum
VP of Publishing Licensing/Rika Inouye
VP of Sales/Gonzalo Ferreyra
Sr. VP of Marketing/Liza Coppola
Publisher/Hyoe Narita

Printed in the U.S.A.

Published by VIZ Media, LLC
P.O. Box 77010
San Francisco, CA 94107

10 9 8 7 6 5 4 3 2 1
First printing, June 2007

www.viz.com
store.viz.com

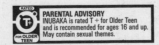

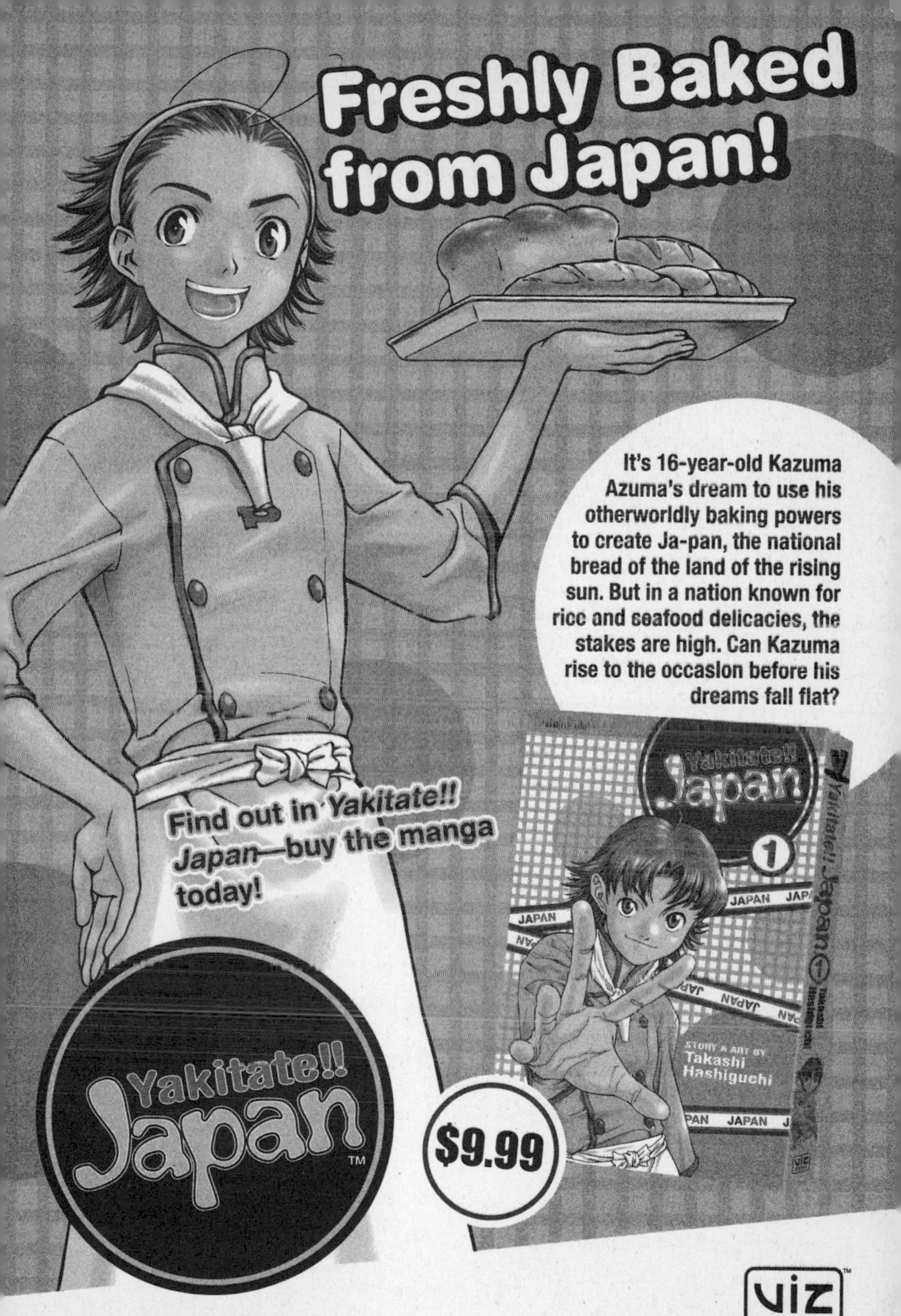
Freshly Baked from Japan!
It's 16-year-old Kazuma Azuma's dream to use his otherworldly baking powers to create Ja-pan, the national bread of the land of the rising sun. But in a nation known for rice and seafood delicacies, the stakes are high. Can Kazuma rise to the occasion before his dreams fall flat?
Find out in Yakitate!! Japan—buy the manga today!
Yakitate!! Japan 1
STORY & ART BY Takashi Hashiguchi
Yakitate!! Japan TM
$9.99
VIZ MEDIA
www.viz.com

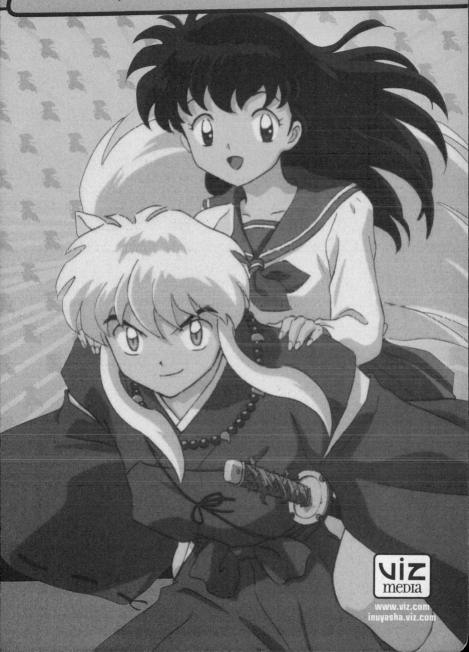

INUYASHA

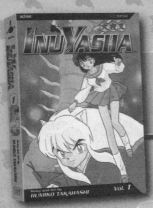

Read the action from the start with the original manga series

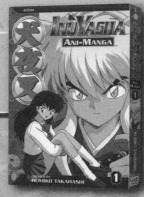

Full color adaptation of the popular TV series

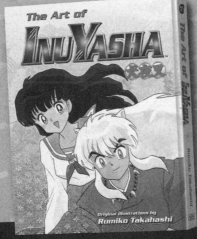

Art book with cel art, paintings, character profiles and more

TV SERIES & MOVIES ON DVD!

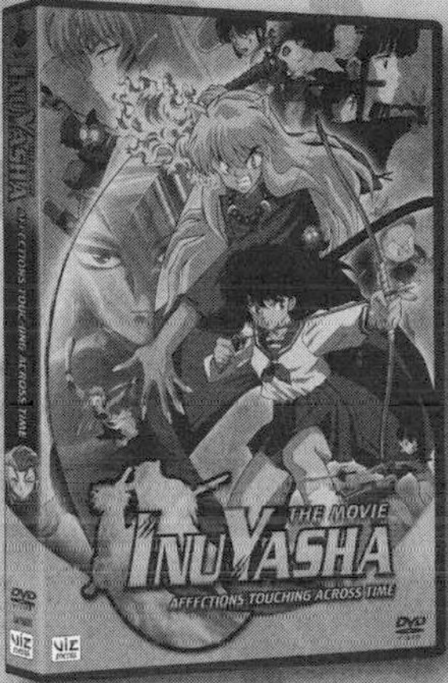
THE MOVIE
INUYASHA
AFFECTIONS TOUCHING ACROSS TIME

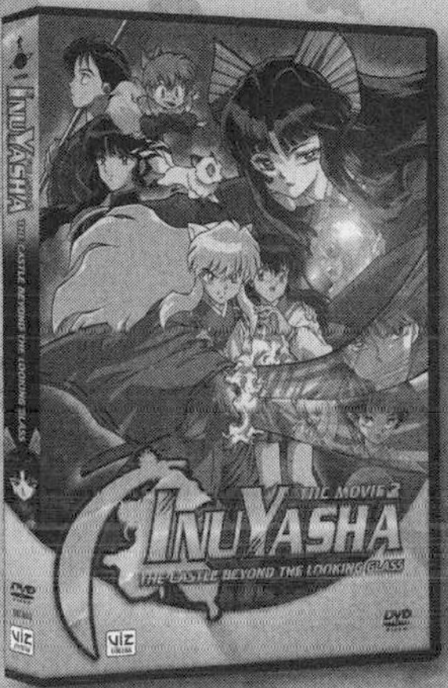
THE MOVIE 2
INUYASHA
THE CASTLE BEYOND THE LOOKING GLASS

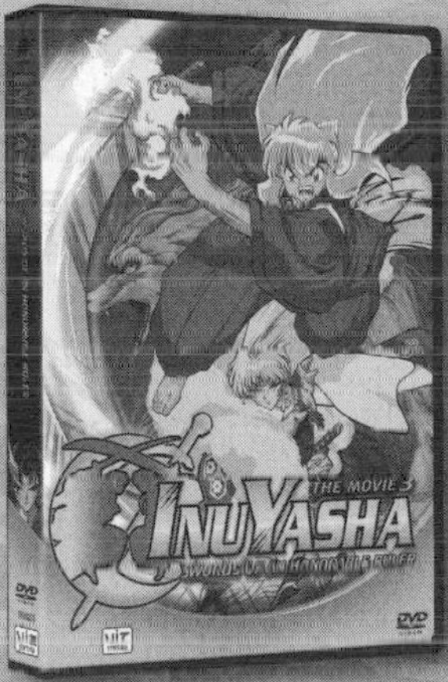
THE MOVIE 3
INUYASHA

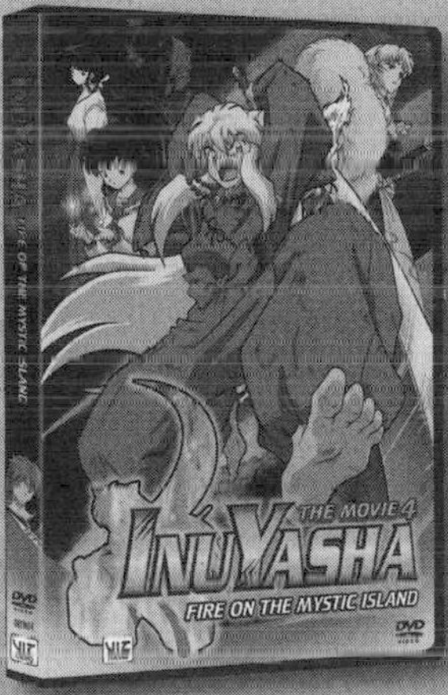
THE MOVIE 4
INUYASHA
FIRE ON THE MYSTIC ISLAND

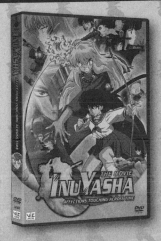

See more of the action in Inuyasha full-length movies

www.viz.com
inuyasha.viz.com

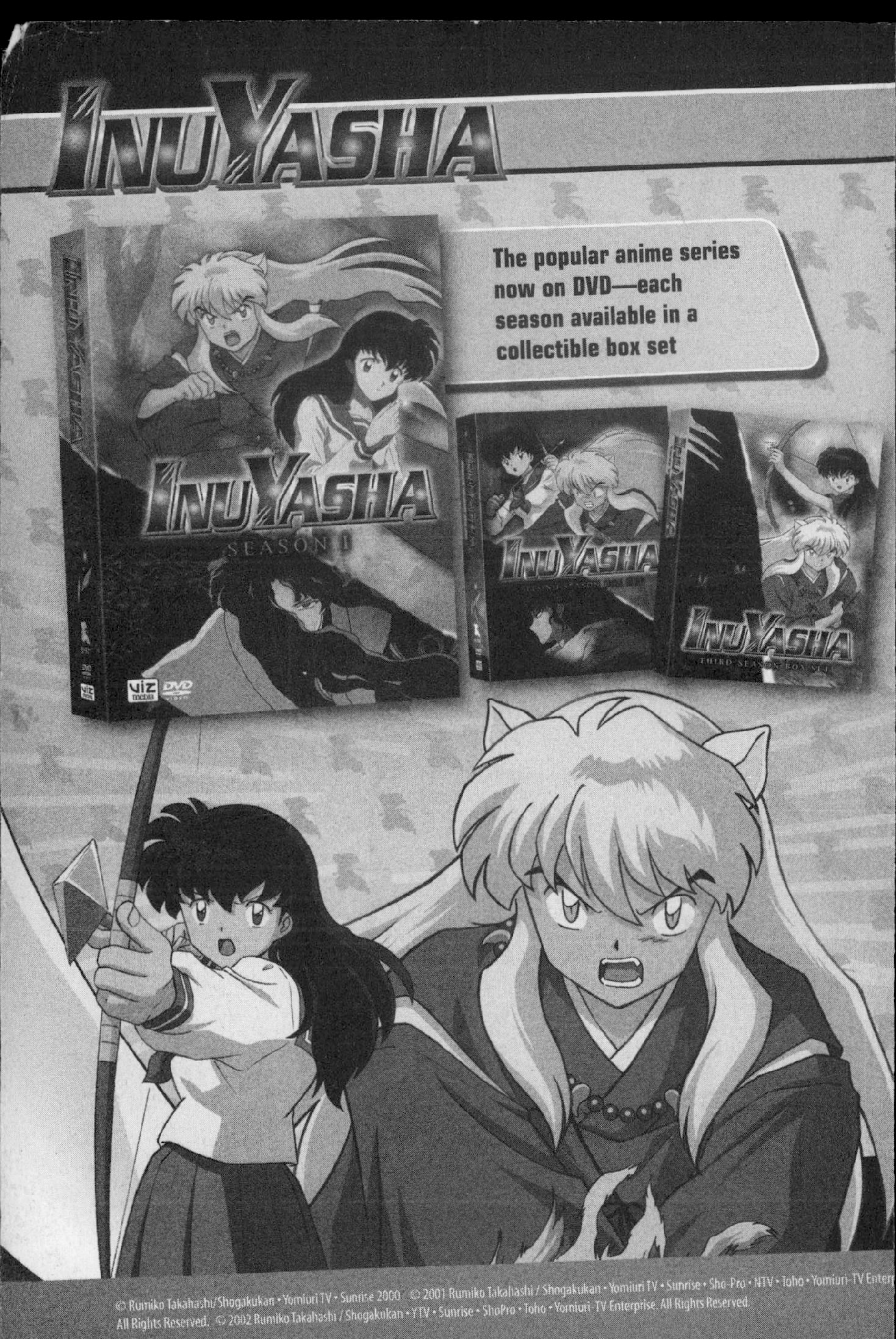

LOVE MAN

LET US KNOW WHAT YOU THINK!

AVAILABLE ONLINE. PLEASE VISIT:
VIZ.COM/MANGASURVEY

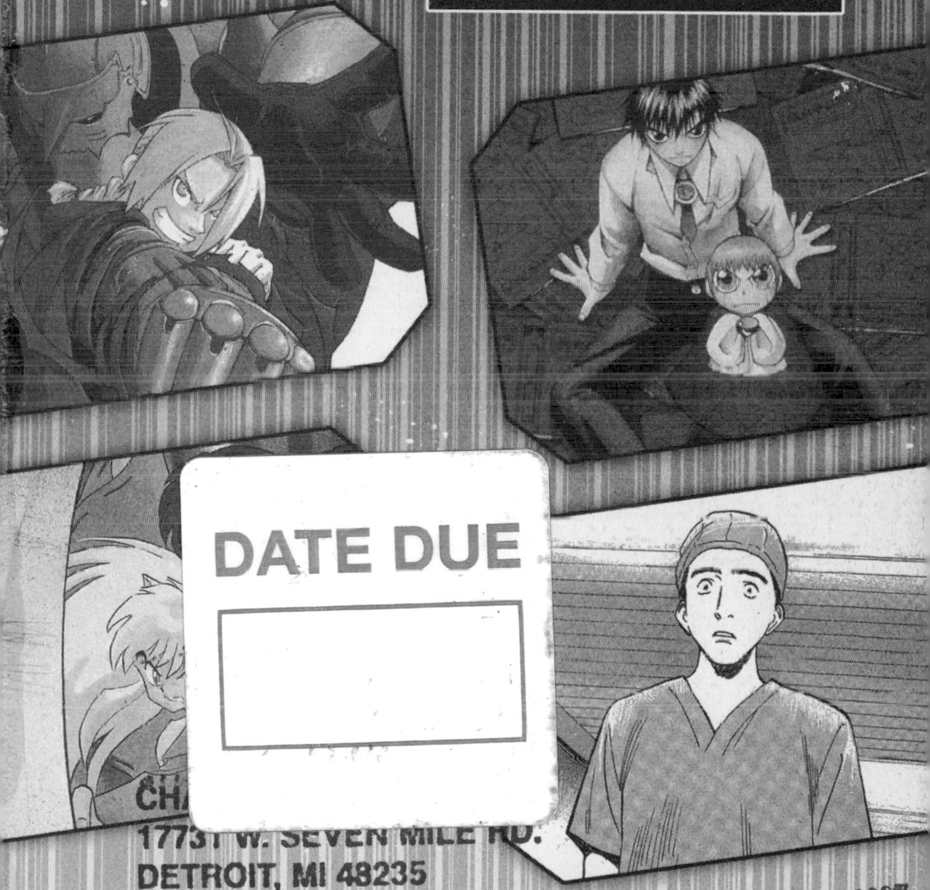

HELP US MAKE THE MANGA YOU LOVE BETTER!

viz media